D0899140

studies in jazz

Institute of Jazz Studies
Rutgers—The State University of New Jersey
General Editors: Dan Morgenstern and Edward Berger

Jazz in New Orleans

The Postwar Years through 1970

Charles Suhor

Studies in Jazz, No. 38

The Scarecrow Press, Inc.
Lanham, Md., & London
and
Institute of Jazz Studies
Rutgers—The State University of New Jersey
2001

SCARECROW PRESS, INC.

Published in the United States of America
by Scarecrow Press, Inc.
4720 Boston Way,
Lanham, Maryland 20706
www.scarecrowpress.com

4 Pleydell Gardens, Folkestone
Kent CT20 2DN, England

British Cataloging in Publication Information Available

Library of Congress Cataloging-in-Publication Data

Suhor, Charles.
   Jazz in New Orleans : the postwar years through 1970 / Charles Suhor.
     p. cm.— (Studies in jazz series : #38.)
   Includes bibliographical references and index.
   ISBN 0-8108-3907-5 (alk. paper)
    1. Jazz—Louisiana—New Orleans—History and criticism. I. Title. II. Studies in jazz;
   no. 38.

ML3508.8.N48 S85 2001
781.65'09763'35—dc21

                                             00-059545

for Don Suhor and Bill Huntington
and the most inspiring drummers: Baby Dodds, George Wettling,
Max Roach, Ed Blackwell

CREDITS

Permission was granted by *Down Beat* magazine to reprint the following articles by Charles Suhor: "New Jazz in the Cradle," Part I, August 17, 1961; Part II, August 31, 1961; "Pete Fountain," November 23, 1961; "The Jazz Museum," March 15, 1962; "New Orleans Rebirth—Preservation Hall," January 17, 1963; "Caught in the Act—Buddy Prima, Playboy Club," October 22, 1964; "Caught in the Act—Art Hodes and Raymond Burke," Your Father's Moustache, September 9, 1965; "The Jazz Archives at Tulane," June 30, 1966; "Review: Jazzfest '68," July 11, 1968; "Jazz and the New Orleans Press," June 12, 1969; "Farewell to Louis," *Music '72*, February 1972 (*Down Beat* Annual).

Permission was granted by *New Orleans* magazine to reprint the following articles by Charles Suhor: "Problems of Modern Jazz in New Orleans," August 1967; "Jazz—A Festival for a Funeral?" January 1968; "Hello, Central, Give Me Doctor Jazz—Edmond Souchon," November 1968; "The Stage Band Movement in New Orleans," January 1969; "George Lewis—The Last Rites of a Jazzman," February 1969; "Al Hirt in Perspective," April 1969; "Jazzfest 1969," April 1969; "Jazz Off Bourbon Street," June 1969; "The Dukes of Dixieland," March 1970; "The New Orleans Jazz Club," November 1970; "New Orleans Jazz—with a Foreign Accent," November 1972.

Permission was granted by *Jazz Journal*, Ltd., London, to reprint the article by Charles Suhor entitled "New Orleans Today," February 1965.

Permission was granted by the Midlo International Center for New Orleans Studies to print transcriptions from the videotape of the 1998 New Orleans Music Colloquium program "Modern Jazz In Post-WWII New Orleans—The First Generation," April 22, 1998.

Permission was granted by Conde-Nast Publications, Inc., to reprint the article by Charles Suhor entitled "The Unique, Non-Jet Set Rhythm of New Orleans," *Gentlemen's Quarterly*, April 1970.

Photographs as follows are published through the courtesy of the Hogan Jazz Archive at Tulane University: Orin Blackstone; group picture of Raymond Burke, Doc Souchon, and others; Louis Armstrong's birthplace; Bunk Johnson, Baby Dodds, Bill Robinson; Sharkey's Kings of Dixieland; Oscar (Papa) Celestin's Band; sketch of Bill Russell by Al Rose; Dukes of Dixieland; Basin Street Six; George Lewis Band at Preservation Hall; Al Hirt; Dooky Chase Band.

Photos of early jazzmen at Bill Huntington's house, Joe Burton Quartet, and Buddy Prima Trio are published through the courtesy of Bill Huntington; Al Belletto Sextet and Fred Crane courtesy of Al Belletto; Nat Perrilliat with Ed Blackwell and Alvin Batiste courtesy of Alvin Batiste; AFO Records musicians/executives courtesy of Harold Battiste; Don Reitan band courtesy of Lee Charlton; Laverne Smith recording for Vik courtesy of Phil Darois; Modern Jazz Pioneers at symposium courtesy of Al Kennedy; Charles Suhor with Loyola big band courtesy of Loyola University; Joseph (Mouse) Bonati courtesy of Diane J. Bonati Meswarb; Earl Williams Band courtesy of Earl Palmer; Irving Fazola with Bob Haggart courtesy of Duncan Schiedt and the Hogan Jazz Archive at Tulane University; Chink Martin, Charles Suhor, and Don Suhor; Loyola big band bas; and Joe (Cheeks) Mandry with Don Suhor courtesy of Don Suhor; Don Suhor at Goodman contest courtesy of New Orleans *Times-Picayune*; Charles Suhor dust jacket photo courtesy of Terry M. Bush.

Contents

Timeline Charts

Editor's Foreword to Charles Suhor's
Jazz in New Orleans

In one of my earlier incarnations, when I was editor of *Down Beat* magazine, I had the great pleasure of the services of Charles Suhor as our New Orleans correspondent. I knew I could depend on him for accurate, timely, and well-written reporting from a city which, while no longer at the creative center of the music to which (deconstructionsists to the contrary notwithstanding) it had given birth, still occupied an important position in jazz.

The book at hand indeed makes just that point, and very well indeed. From his unique vantage point as a musician, scholar, and journalist, Suhor has given us an objective and authoritative overview of jazz in New Orleans during a period when much more was going on than the standard histories have told us. "Objective" is a key term here. Anyone who has had even the slightest involvement with the jazz scene in that remarkable city will have learned that there are at least three sides to every story when you're way down yonder, but Suhor always gets it right. And just as he is not beholden to any clique or party line, he is also free from musical preconceptions and able to deal with equal insight and empathy with the traditionalists and the modernists.

There is a lot of important information here, and it is, thankfully, presented in a manner that makes it a joy to absorb. It is a pleasure to add this distinguished title to our series.

DAN MORGENSTERN
Director, Institute of Jazz Studies, Rutgers University

Preface

This book is an attempt to provide accurate information about, and a credible interpretation of, jazz in New Orleans from the end of World War II (in August 1945) through 1970. It was written specifically to counter what I believe are misconceptions about the jazz scene during those years, errors that have hardened into orthodoxies in a surprisingly short time.

The areas of misunderstanding are set out in three key topics: the local Establishment's views of jazz, from outright shame to belated pride; the profusion of "New Orleans revivals," including a local revival that has been basically ignored; and modern jazz and its many pioneers in postwar New Orleans. The introductory chapter explains the genesis of this book in terms of my experiences as a listener, musician, and writer in New Orleans during the postwar years. The text is then divided into three sections, each exploring one of the main topics at length. An overview essay begins each section and is followed by pertinent articles I wrote for national and local journals, mainly *Down Beat* and *New Orleans* magazines.

I might well have grouped some of the articles in different sections, or even constructed some of the main topics differently. In the real world everything is wonderfully, complexly contextual to everything else, so choices must be made about ways of configuring and presenting ideas. My groupings are a convenience, then, a useful handle for imposing narrative coherence on topics that are distinguishable yet highly interrelated. Indeed, the topics are interwoven into the autobiographical chapter, and they appear frequently throughout the book, brought into specific focus in the overviews that begin each section. This results in occasional repetition, but in each case the information or event recounted is integral to the text in which it appears.

One extremely important topic—racial politics and relations among black and white musicians, jazz fans, and the general public—is not the focus of a separate section. The fact is that the topic enters into innumerable events described in this text. Abstracting racial themes from the numerous contexts would not have been illuminating. In the autobiographical chapter, the overviews, and the articles, I have commented often and candidly on matters of race in connection with the settings and events under discussion.

The inclusion of actual articles and documents published during the postwar years, modified only to correct misspellings or other minor errors, ensures accountability to the viewpoints and information presented when those materials were written. The overviews provide broader perspectives on each topic, adding new materials as well as tracing relationships among the articles and across the three topics. An overview typically cites examples of current misconceptions about the topic; brings in diverse opinions, including those counter to my own; shows intrasection and intersection relationships; and provides further commentary to fill in gaps or raise new questions about a topic. The overviews rather than the articles take precedence when there are factual or interpretive disparities that I did not specifically address. I have avoided a citation format that clutters the text with bibliographic detail. However, the text always includes information easily referenced alphabetically in the bibliography.

Fidelity to the texts of the vintage articles will no doubt bring a little discomfort with outmoded usages, terminologies, and slang. But it is important to remember the times. In the early 1960s, "Negro" was the accepted term, long since replaced by "black" or "African American." Sexist pronouns (the universal "he") were coin of the realm. And terms like "groovy" were . . . well, hip.

Section I, "Jazz and the Establishment: From Flouting to Flaunting," focuses on some cultural and institutional settings in which jazz was first battered and then nurtured. It deals with the remarkable reluctance of power brokers and custodians of culture in New Orleans to accept jazz as art—until the music proved itself elsewhere and was easily recognizable as a marketable commodity. The press and the education community, which might have shown vision in advancing our rich native art, were among the chief denigrators of jazz. A few mavericks with social and political connections did agitate through groups like the National Jazz Foundation and the New Orleans Jazz Club, and they scored partial victories for preswing jazz styles. But ironically, many of the most visible changes were not for jazz as a living art but for what might be called significant mummifications—the Jazz Archive at Tulane, the Jazz Museum, and belated tributes to individual artists, mainly funeral obsequies. Not until Jazzfest '68 did the Establishment follow through wholeheartedly with major civic and financial support for jazz. But numerous social and political problems had to be worked out before a major festival could be mounted. There were three false starts and a bevy of intrigues—concern about racism in the city, the dabblings of eccentric amateurs, earnest protests from New Orleans jazz purists. I covered some of the early misfires during the 1960s in *Down Beat*, but the snippets are tied together here, hopefully laying to rest the oft-stated suggestion that the festival began, sans precedent or gestation, in 1970.

Section II, "'Revivals' Beaucoup: Traditional, Dixieland, and Revivalist Jazz," moves specifically to the music and the musicians. It highlights the artists who were central in a significant but often-ignored popular revival of traditional and Dixieland jazz in New Orleans between 1947 and 1953. For reasons related in part to the early 1940s rediscovery and recording of trumpeter Bunk Johnson and others, the hot little late 1940s revival that produced young second-liners like the Dukes of Dixieland and Pete Fountain has been given short shrift or no shrift at all. This section describes the growth and decline of the revival and highlights its leading bands and promoters. In contrast, the Preservation Hall revival that began in the early 1960s generated almost immediate nationwide interest, spawning imitators both worthy and bizarre. The record cries for some sorting out, and this section attempts that. The perennial question of whether young players can or will carry on the traditional New Orleans and Dixieland styles is also discussed.

Section III, "An Invisible Generation: Early Modern Jazz Artists," should help dispel the stubborn myth that almost no one was playing be-bop or other modern jazz styles in New Orleans before the current generation of young artists, beginning with the gifted Wynton Marsalis, appeared in the 1980s. In the postwar years a formidable cadre of creative modern jazz players was performing, mainly in underground venues. Tragically, many died young. The surviving pioneers—many of them no longer active—are at least in their sixties. Their music was even less acceptable than traditional and Dixieland jazz to local leaders and average citizens, and recognition of their art and their struggle is past due. A symposium of early modern jazz artists gathered in 1988 to shed light on the early pioneers, and a transcript of their discussion is part of this section.

Appendix 1, "Four Cross Sections," consists of survey articles done in 1965, 1966, 1968, and 1970 for different publications. As New Orleans became widely reestablished as a jazz mecca, articles that provided cross sections of the local scene, tinged with boosterism and interspersed with critical comments, were in demand. Read sequentially, they give a sense of how things were evolving during a six-year span.

Appendix 2, "Early Modern Jazz Musicians in New Orleans, 1945–1960," is a very long footnote to section 3. It puts on record some 120-plus modern jazz musicians who were known to be active in New Orleans in the postwar years.

I believe that this book provides the most comprehensive picture to date of jazz in New Orleans from 1945 to 1970. I do not claim to be a professional historian, but I hope that this book reflects my respect for accuracy and my training as a researcher. I hope also that I have made fair use of my life experiences as a jazz watcher, musician, and writer. I have tried to account responsibly for the viewpoints of others, using the overviews in particular to extend the topics and critique certain aspects of my earlier writings. I stand ready for response and criticism. As Orleanian Dorothy Dix, the mother of all advice columnists, once said, "Writing is like firing in the dark. You never know whether you hit anything or not. And so it is good to hear the bell ring every now and then."

Acknowledgments

Special thanks to the National Endowment for the Humanities for providing a grant in support of this book. The New Orleans International Music Colloquiam (NOIMC), led by Connie Atkinson and Joseph Logsdon of the University of New Orleans in 1988, generously videotaped and transcribed the NOIMC session at Loyola University that is the basis for chapter 26 in section 3.

A major research resource was the William Ransom Hogan Jazz Archive at Tulane University. Bruce Boyd Raeburn, Alma Freeman, and Charles Chamberlain were ever patient and helpful during numerous visits there. Bruce also encouraged two projects that led to the development of this book—a 700-page collection of my writings, correspondence, and related materials for the archive and an article for the May–December 1995 issue of *Jazz Archivist*. Bob Heister, a jazz fan of encyclopedic knowledge and a tolerant and reflective reader, was exceptionally helpful in responding to early drafts of the manuscript. Parts of the text were also critiqued by Elaine Hughes, Bill Huntington, and Don Suhor. Preview readers Gilbert Erskine, Sybil Kein, Doug Ramsey, Tom Sancton Jr., and Tex Stephens kindly read the entire text. I am grateful to all these people for their frank and useful comments.

Many interviewees graciously responded to my questions about times past and offered fascinating interpretations and anecdotes. Between September 1997 and April 2000 I spoke with Richard Allen, Helen Arlt, Alvin Batiste, Harold Battiste, Germaine Bazzle, Warren Bell, Al Belletto, Louis Berndt, Jerry Boquet, Bert Braud, Eluard Burt, Sam Butera, Lee Charlton, Dooky Chase, Ed Lewis Clements, Shirley Trusty Corey, Richard (Bing) Crosby, Phil Darois, Wallace Davenport, Quint Davis, Joe Delaney, Gilbert Erskine, Oliver (Stick) Felix, Dennis Formento, Nick Gagliano, Al Hermann, Phil Hermann, Bill Huntington, Monifa Johnson, Connie Jones, Edward (Kidd) Jordan, Sybil Kein, Al Kennedy, Ronnie Kole, Steve Lord (Loyacano), Mundell Lowe, Frank Mannino, Ellis Marsalis, Charlie Miller, Tony Mitchell, Ron Nethercutt, Jimmy Nolan, Earl Palmer, Richard Payne, Don Perry, Ralph Pottle, Doug Ramsey, Dick Russell, Clinton Scott, Art Scully, Mike Serpas, Rhodes Spedale, Gus Statiris, Frank Strazerri, Tex Stephens, Don Suhor, Louis Timken, Barry Ulanov, Reed Vaughan, and

George Wein. My apologies to any whom I have inadvertently omitted from this list.

The vintage articles in this book were the result of much earlier interviews with numerous musicians, writers, jazz fans, and others. I gratefully recall conversations with Frank Assunto, James Black, Ed Blackwell, Joe Burton, Lars Edergan, Pete Fountain, Ed Frank, Johnny Fernandez, Al Hirt, Armand Hug, Allan Jaffe, Henry Kmen, George Lewis, Pete Monteleone, Grayson (Ken) Mills, Nat Perrilliat, Buddy Prima, Bill Russell, Gerry St. Amand, Edmond (Doc) Souchon, Harry Souchon, Earl Turbinton, Willie Turbinton, Clay Watson, Johnny Wiggs, and others too numerous to list here. Of course, none of the articles that became part of this book would have been possible without the openness and encouragement of editors and others at three publications—Gilbert Erskine, Don DeMichael, and Dan Morgenstern at *Down Beat*, Jim Autry and George Bacon at *New Orleans,* and Bill Bryant at the *Vieux Carre Courier*. *Down Beat* had faith in a maverick writer and in the continuing vitality of the New Orleans musical culture. The three local editors had the vision to go beyond the bland daily papers, deepening and expanding coverage of and commentary on life in New Orleans.

I have special affection and gratitude for individuals who helped me over the years to break out of ruts I did not even know I was in as a listener, musician, and writer. My brother Don introduced me to the visceral joy of jazz and to its marvelous subtleties. Lou Dillon was a teacher who articulated various conceptions of drumming and clarified complex techniques. Earl Palmer and Ed Blackwell's live performances in New Orleans showed how it's all done. Bill Huntington has been a valued friend and constant teacher about the art of jazz, through music and conversation, for over four decades. My sister Mary Lou, a career journalist, helped me to move from academic writing to a wider range of styles.

Finally, Katie Regen at Scarecrow Press was quick and able in responding to my questions and making the pathway to publication smooth and understandable. In making these acknowledgments, I implicate others in the positive contributions of this book. Responsibility for errors and vagrant opinions is my own.

1

Discovering Myths, Reclaiming the Past

Sometime in the mid-1940s I became a jazz fan, musician, evangelist, and chronicler, led by chance and hubris to write about jazz for *Down Beat*, *New Orleans*, the *Vieux Carre Courier*, and other publications. The years between 1945 and 1970 were an exciting time in New Orleans, and I counted myself incredibly lucky to be listening to, playing, and writing about jazz in my hometown. As I took stock in the late 1960s, I thought that I had written some useful things for the record, tracing the paths of the city's many jazz styles and reporting the activities of innumerable musicians. Over the years I had also helped to persuade the local guardians of culture that jazz was not a tuneless embarrassment but an art and an asset.

So I started to look toward writing more extensively in my main career area, English education. There was plenty to write about. The neoprogressive movement was growing rapidly in public education in the late 1960s. I plunged in with gusto, not expecting to return to reportage or commentary on jazz.

But around the mid-1980s, some strange things started to happen. First, I was meeting people from all parts of the country who, having recently attended a Jazz and Heritage Festival and dined at K-Paul's, were drawing wildly incorrect inferences. Surely, they said, I must have had a supportive social climate for my interest in jazz as I grew up. And what did I think of the newest wrinkle—youngsters like Wynton and Branford Marsalis who were *from New Orleans* but playing *modern* jazz, no less? And I must have known innumerable Cajuns and enjoyed a big gang of blackened catfish, cher.

Straightening out the question of Cajun geography was easy enough: Cajuns = Southwest Louisiana; Charlie the Yat = Ninth Ward, New Orleans. Still, they could not quite believe that New Orleans had been a hostile environment for jazz in my lifetime or that the city was home to a large number of postwar modern jazz artists. This was a pyrrhic victory of sorts. The tourist commission and chamber of commerce were finally embracing jazz wholeheartedly, just as the aficionados had hoped for years. But Image New Orleans had been slapped like a cheap handbill over the complex grain of the city's postwar history.

The second oddity was that numerous writers, from established critics like Whitney Balliett to journalists and generalists like Jason Berry and Grace Lichtenstein, were saying things about jazz in postwar New Orleans that were poorly researched or downright incorrect. The pattern seemed to work like this: start with the popular impression about a topic like New Orleans jazz revivals or early modern jazz artists, and use that as a lens for writing about the matter. Worse than clueless, these writers were following unreliable clues. Popular misconceptions were hardening into unchallenged mythologies.

My first reaction was astonishment. The events that I and others from the postwar years had lived, day by day, were being called "history" by strangers bearing manuscripts. I could handle being half a century old, but the drift toward popular and scholarly misunderstanding of some extremely distinctive times, key years of musical and cultural change in New Orleans, was disturbing.

Discovering the new mythologies, I felt a need to recover the past, the postwar years in New Orleans that I knew from the inside out. As a kid in the Ninth Ward, I had wandered without roadmap or guile into experiences that later became the stories I told to myself and others about jazz—the stories in this book about the Establishment's antipathy toward jazz, about a brisk local revival in the late 1940s, about the early development of modern jazz, and about how racial politics in some measure affected all of these experiences.

In the beginning, of course, I was aware only of the fact that I loved the music I was hearing. I was ten years old in 1945 when I asked Memere and Nainainne to play my favorite record again, the one Nainainne called zippy, "High Society," by the guys with the funny names—Monk Hazel and Sharkey Bonano. Later I plunked innumerable nickels into the wonderfully blasting Wurlitzer at Savoie's Ice Cream Parlor on St. Claude and Pauline to hear Bunk Johnson's band play "Tishomingo Blues." I started spending my allowance on records by Bunk, Bob Crosby's Bobcats, and George Hartman at Vallon's Music Maison, two blocks down from Savoie's on St. Claude.

When Rudi Blesh's *This is Jazz* Mutual Network broadcasts began in 1947, I sat ritually by the radio, outright proud of the fact that players like Baby Dodds, Edmond Hall, and Pops Foster were from New Orleans. Another high point that year was the release of the United Artists movie *New Orleans*. Despite a soppy love story, Louis Armstrong and several other native Orleanians looked and sounded great on the big screen.

By 1947 I was a regular at Harvey and Orin Blackstone's New Orleans Record Shop on Baronne Street, a dingy meeting place for moldy figs (i.e., lovers of early jazz) since fall of 1945. The backroom jam sessions at the record shop introduced me to artists like clarinetist Raymond Burke, a very young George Girard on trumpet, the unsung drumming wizard Freddie King, jazz fans Dick Allen and Gilbert Erskine, and others.

My 78 rpm record collection grew rapidly. Although I favored the great Commodore sessions with Wild Bill Davision and George Brunis and the bright Dixieland releases on the Jump label, I also had Louis, Bunk, Bix, Bechet, Ory, the Bobcats, Muggsy, Art Hodes, Pete Daily, and some revivalist sides by Turk Murphy and the Castle Jazz Band. Most of these were available locally only at the Blackstone brothers' shop. My brother Don had taken up clarinet and gathered a fine record collection composed mainly of Shaw and Goodman. But he also had most of Irving Fazola's 1940s records, plus Jimmy Noone, Hank D'Amico, and others. He and our oldest sister, Mary Lou, had accumulated a miscellany of big band singles from Erskine Hawkins to Stan Kenton. Don's collection expanded in the late 1940s to include combo records by modernists like Buddy DeFranco, Charlie Parker, Miles Davis, and Lee Konitz, and I was soon tuned into new musical worlds.

Always, I was guided and tutored by Don. His reputation as a teenage wonder blossomed in June 1947, when at age fourteen he won the Benny Goodman contest, ostensibly a search for the city's best young clarinetist. Don's first influence, ironically, had been Artie Shaw. Not yet secure as an improviser, he had memorized several of Shaw's finely sculpted solos, mastering nuances, accents, and highly technical runs, and he played them for the contest. (Pete Fountain, lacking swing-based material, didn't make the finals.) To an awed kid brother, Don was an able and authoritative mentor. He would explain with enthusiasm and skill the stylistic differences among jazz artists and the development of the music. Before long I was drumming on cardboard boxes behind him and our record collection in our living room on Bartholomew Street.

I lurked around Don's gigs and went to Sharkey Bonano concerts and New Orleans Jazz Club meetings/jam sessions. I listened to live jazz radio shows of the late 1940s, when Bonano, Papa Celestin, the Parisian Room All-Stars, and others were on the air regularly. Phil Napoleon's Dixieland group was broadcast from Nick's in New York, with Orleanian Tony Spargo (Sbarbaro)—formerly a member of the Original Dixieland Jazz Band—on drums and kazoo.

Jazz artists like Armstrong, Bonano, Dodds, and Hazel were my heroes. In our liberal Catholic household no one thought it remarkable that some were black and some were white. By my simple reckoning, everyone who heard them should admire them and love their music. But the kids I knew at Washington Elementary School were mainly interested in the dreamy ballads, novelty songs, and, surprisingly, country music hits of the postwar years. A few scornfully called jazz "nigger music." As odd as it may seem today, jazz was widely regarded as lowbrow or even shameful by local leaders and many citizens in the 1940s. While it was acceptable to hire a jazz band for dances or other social events, quality folks simply did not take the music seriously or respect the musicians as artists.

Of course, an adolescent who is called an outlander is likely to be energized. Outlandish was fine with me—I now had a cause. I became an initiate, part of a hip cognoscenti with liberated attitudes about race and special insight into our music and culture. That was when the proselytizing and the chronicling began, with no special plan but in dead earnest.

Harvey Blackstone of the New Orleans Record Shop pointed me to an item in the April 1949 issue of Orin's *Playback* magazine—a request for a

New Orleans pen pal from an English fan named Alan Wheatley. I was thirteen and Wheatley was nineteen, but we hit it off well and exchanged information and ideas about jazz. He sent me negative comments about jazz in New Orleans published in the British tabloid *Melody Maker*, based on transcriptions of the flatfooted Tony Almerico band at the Parisian Room. *MM* printed my letter stating that a lot of excellent jazz was being performed in New Orleans, better even than Humphrey Lyttelton, the British trad favorite. I went on Roger Wolfe's popular Saturday night *Dixieland Jazz* radio show on WDSU, telling about the teenage musicians I knew who were playing jazz around town.

I bought a mix-and-match drum set from Phil Zito (a true eccentric, I later learned) and in 1949 started playing weekend gigs with Dixieland/dance combos and dance bands that played stock arrangements. The next year I sat in at a New Orleans Jazz Club meeting/jam session with Don, trumpeter Stuart ("Red Hott") Bergen, bassist Chink Martin, and others. I joined the Nicholls High School band in my junior year after a few ill-understood lessons with onetime percussion great George Peterson. In his younger years Peterson had taught Ray Bauduc and Leo Adde, played in numerous dance and show band settings, and gained a national reputation as an innovative timpanist. But he was nearly blind in 1950 and could not tell how badly I was misreading the exercises.

Charlie Wagner, the band director at Nicholls, was a cornetist, a true-blue jazz lover, and a great storyteller who had once played across the street from his idol, Bix Beiderbecke. He was not a jazz activist but a truly gentle man who gave quiet support and a great deal of latitude to young players. During the dance band's intermissions at school events he would comp on piano behind the students who could play melodies by ear or take jazz choruses. He encouraged players like clarinetist Paul Vicari and trumpeter Jack Barratini (Jay Barry), who had a teenage quartet that played Dixieland and dance music at the Harmony Inn on North Claiborne Avenue in the late 1940s.

Don formed a similar group with trumpeter Paul Emenes and others from Nicholls. Emenes's conception was relentlessly corny but he faked melodies well, so the band had a good repertoire for teen dances at places like the Woodmen of the World Hall. Besides popular and Dixieland standards, Don introduced the band to lesser known material like Art Hodes' intensely blue "Clark and Randolph" and the Bobcats' "Don't Call Me Boy" and "You're Bound to Look Like a Monkey When You Grow Old," both sung engagingly by Emenes in Don's group.

During marching band practice, Vicari or Don would occasionally jam their way through the trio section of the march with contrapuntal jazz lines, and Wagner did not say a word. Wagner also winked, or maybe it was a smile, when Charlie Little and I did a snare drum stunt during a marching cadence in 6/8 time. We turned two bars of straight eighth-note triplets into a sixlet crescendo in which I accented 1, 3, and 5, and Little stressed 2, 4, and 6. The effect of the simple interplay—quarter-note triplets with accented response beats—woke up the kids who had two left feet and stimulated the others along an interminable parade route.

Wagner encouraged me to start a student Dixieland band in my senior year. We were a very limited group. Only trumpeter Lawrence (Frosty) Francingues, pianist Theresa Kelly (Peterson's granddaughter), and I had a sense of the liberating energy of jazz, and the band had a repertoire of just six or seven tunes. But we rehearsed earnestly and played in a no-nonsense Dixieland style. Buoyed by a revival of local interest in jazz that had begun in the 1940s (the revival that is virtually invisible in writings about the post-war years), the young band was wildly popular with students in 1951–1952. We won a high school competition against a straw-hat band from Fortier High School and a freewheeling combo from Warren Easton that included trombonist Larry Muhoberac, clarinetist Eddie Winston, and drummer Paul Ferrara. We thought that the Easton group had overpowered and outplayed us. But traditional cornetist Johnny (Hyman) Wiggs of the increasingly active New Orleans Jazz Club was one of the judges, and we were speaking his language.

Wagner's permissiveness backfired on one occasion. On a schmaltzy concert band arrangement of "Look for the Silver Lining," I improvised a woodblock and rimshot sequence à la Ray Bauduc during the written "stop chorus" (i.e., the band punching out the melody in crisp, staccato phrases). Wagner like it and kept it in. So when Rene Louapre, supervisor of music for the school system, called up the song while conducting during a school visit, I had to decide whether or not to run the unauthorized ad libs.

When Louapre dropped in, band directors and students alike felt the stab of his baton. A balding and rotund elf in wolf's clothing, he affected a superior mien that was the dread of the district. His image as the ultimate Establishmentarian was enhanced by his society band, which played for the New Orleans elite. Louapre's group—all good musicians, to be sure— played the choice Mardi Gras balls, debutante parties, and dances that called for his Lombardo-style book. In later years I came to know Louapre as a colleague and friend. But as a kid I was put off by his pompous manner, so I relished throwing a jazz pie in his face. *Look* clicketa *for* clicketa-WHOP, *the-sil-ver-li* clicketa-*ning* ta-da-clicketa-WHOP . . . When Louapre harrumphed and asked what was going on, Wagner sheepishly said he was trying to "allow a little creativity in the percussion section." A truly gentle man.

I also waved the jazz banner in my eleventh grade English class. I asked Edwin Friedrich, a marvelous English teacher and lifelong maverick, to let me write my term paper on the Dixieland versus be-bop debate that had been fueled in the national jazz press. He knew that I was a child of popular culture with no interest in literary study. I did not cultivate traditional scholarly interests until I went to college. After outgrowing comic books, my readings were *Band Leaders*, *Metronome*, *Down Beat*, *Record Changer*, *Jazz Record*, the afternoon newspaper, and *Time*. By neighborhood standards, I should add, this made me an intellectual. Being a good Deweyian, Friedrich let me run with my passion for jazz instead of doing a library paper that we both knew would draw heavily on *Classic Comics*. I proceeded to write my first-ever extended essay, researching and writing with enjoyment.

Early in my high school years, my love of jazz overtook my childhood love of cartooning. My father, an accountant, was a frustrated artist who spent Sunday afternoons copying existing works, mainly calendar art, in oils, water color, and pencil. He could not do original drawings, though, so he was pleased by my knack for inventing comic strip characters. But I had no direction or formal training, and during four years of undemanding art courses at Nicholls, I drew an inordinate number of pictures of jazz artists and jam sessions.

Playing drums and championing jazz rescued me from the social stigma of being the son of an accountant and a schoolteacher in a working-class environment. Like my four older siblings, I got good grades in elementary school and was a favorite of the teachers. I was in my mother's class in fifth grade, I had skipped a grade, and I was a head shorter than many of my classmates—a sure formula for peer harassment. In high school I managed to deflect attention from my grades by highlighting my music activity and cussing occasionally. This worked well. When it was announced on the p.a. system that I was class valedictorian, one student looked around incredulously and said, "Suhor? Da drummer?"

My weekend engagements were branching out. An early memorable gig was at Jefferson Buzzards Hall on Annunciation Street. I was sixteen years old, playing the Saturday night dances with a five-piece combo led by alto saxist Joe Helwick. The band included a truly swinging Dixieland electric guitarist named Angelo Palmisano. Tom Brown, then over sixty, was on bass and trombone. I knew that Brown was the first to take a jazz group out of town, going to Lamb's Cafe in Chicago in 1915, but he was not much of a talker during breaks so I did not get stories from him.

Although I never stopped working with Dixie and dance combos, other styles fascinated and challenged me. Thanks to Don's continued mentorship and three years of study with the versatile drummer Lou Dillon, I moved into work with big bands and modern jazz groups. I had ample opportunity to work out new ideas in the perpetual living room sessions with Don, who added a dimension with choruses on piano. He was self-taught but knew the chords to innumerable songs and had surprisingly good technique as a soloist. He played good ideas in a boppish, Bud Powell style and comped so well that his piano playing was welcomed at jam sessions.

Lou Dillon was an excellent all-around musician, a fast reader who played and understood swing, modern jazz, Latin rhythms, and show drumming, the last being his specialty. I had heard about Dillon from Reed Vaughan in 1951, when we were both in high school. Reed was at Holy Cross, also in the Ninth Ward, and playing weekends with youngsters like trumpeter Murphy Campo, clarinetist Pee Wee Spitelera, and tenor saxist

Charlie (Chicken) May. Reed was improving at quantum speed because of Dillon's work on solid reading skills, left-hand and bass drum independence (using the then-revolutionary Jim Chapin book), and various other jazz techniques. My later years of moonlighting as a percussion teacher (1960–1966) at Campo's Music Store were in a large part adaptations of Dillon's intelligent and big-hearted teaching.

In 1952 I entered Loyola University to study English education, getting a partial music scholarship for playing in the concert band and dance/show band. Admirers of today's jazz program at Loyola would be amazed by the postwar administration's tireless but fruitless efforts at suppressing jazz, described in chapter 7 of this volume. Students kept the big band going and held impromptu modern jazz jam sessions in the basement practice rooms in the School of Music on St. Charles Avenue.

By then I had become imbued not only with big band jazz but also with the rich invention of the city's modern jazz artists (discussed in detail in section III). A far-flung aggregate of gifted musicians, they were even more invisible to the local Establishment than the neglected traditional and Dixieland artists. I jammed and spot-gigged with Don's Loyola and French Quarter coterie of modernists—Joseph (Mouse) Bonati, Fred Crane, Mike Serpas, and others—and with newcomers like trombonist Al Hermann, pianist/vocalist Theresa Kelly, pianist Buddy Prima, and Bill Huntington, then a brilliant guitarist. Also part of the scene was a contingent of Orleanians at LSU—Reed Vaughan, trombonist Larry Muhoberac, and others who continued the modern jazz tradition initiated there by Mose Allison, Al Belletto, Carl Fontana, and others.

I was lucky to work weekends in the mid-1950s with two beautiful and gifted pianists/vocalists, Lee Burton and Theresa Kelly. Neither played soaring jazz piano, but both were marvelous singers. Lee's husband, a superb all-around trumpeter named Bill Pruyn, was in from Baton Rouge to study at Tulane. He sometimes sat in with the Loyola big band and worked regularly with various combos and dance bands. A keen if often arrogant intellectual, Bill would hang out at Lee's gig at Ched's Lounge on Mirabeau. Bonded by interests in music, philosophy, and social activism, we argued endlessly and enjoyably about religion and philosophy—he, the village agnostic, and I, the neo-Scholastic. Lee, Bill, and I became great friends during their New Orleans years.

Theresa Kelly had come a long way since playing with my Dixieland group at Nicholls High School. She formed a trio with bassist Louis Pendarvis and myself in 1954. We were all at Loyola at the time, so we played several radio shows on Loyola-owned WWL. During our weekend gig at the Swamp Room, Theresa was intent on developing her jazz piano style, going beyond the skilled popular/cocktail approaches that were a guarantee of regular work for players like Lee Burton, Laverne Smith, and herself. We did a few simple unison vocals that came off well because Theresa's thin upper register contrasted well with our throaty baritones. The biggest attraction, always, was Theresa's ever moving vocals on standards and her stunning, diminutive beauty.

As passionate as she was about cultivating her jazz piano, Theresa's style remained amorphous. She played well-accented lines, always within the chord, but the effect was nondescript. In retrospect, I believe that if Bill Evans had been an available model at the time, she might well have seized his ethereal grace as an entree into a well-formed and more intense jazz expression. About a year later, Theresa married a young lawyer named Harvey Couch. They spent several years in Germany, where she turned to intensive voice study and became a serious student of opera. She moved to New York, divorced Harvey, and years later tried to break through both in opera and as a popular singer. But fame eluded her in the hypercompetitive environment.

The personal subtext here is that I had fallen hopelessly in love with Theresa in high school in 1950, just when she became addictively enamored of an incredibly talented teenager, pianist/vocalist/trombonist/arranger Larry Muhoberac. These were your basic futile, star-crossed, irrevocable adolescent attachments. Our best break was that Theresa embraced me wholeheartedly as a lifelong friend and confidante. We kept warm contact over the years until she ended her life in 1989 after a debilitating illness.

Don, Bill, Theresa, and I, with other young white players of the 1950s, frequently went to hear amazing black musicians like Ed Blackwell, Ed Frank, and Earl Palmer, who played at both white and black clubs. We were welcome at their sites (e.g., modern jazz at Hayes' Chicken Shack, a concert at Booker T. Washington High School Auditorium by Jazz at the Philharmonic) but sadly, the white clubs were at best drafty places for black customers in the postwar years. Further, Louisiana laws prohibiting racially mixed performers from appearing onstage together discouraged varied and sustained musical interaction. Trumpeter Mike Serpas tells of an incident in the 1950s when he was beaten by police as he left a gig at an Algiers club with vocalist Blanche Thomas. In the section III symposium (chapter 26), Earl Palmer and Al Belletto describe how they were jailed for jamming together at Benny Clement's house in French Quarter.

Ever zealous, in my junior year I organized a Loyola/Xavier bop combo to play during the judging of an interracial high school talent show. The program was sponsored by SERINCO (Southeast Regional Interracial Conference), a blatantly subversive Catholic coalition from Loyola University, Xavier University, and Dominican College. Trumpeter Johnny Fernandez, then playing crisply in a Clifford Brown style, was one of the Xavier students in the combo. The whole event was highly illegal but it went unchallenged. In the laissez-faire climate of New Orleans in the mid-1950s, there was no political capital to be gained from a raid on Jesuit High School auditorium.

Although there were some notable crackdowns on integrated musical performances, it cannot be said that the New Orleans police had a coherent policy on the matter. In the early 1950s, clarinetist Sid Davilla was coproprietor of the Mardi Gras Lounge on Bourbon Street, and he sat in regularly with

Freddie Kohlman's Dixieland house band. In the same period, the New Orleans Jazz Club integrated its monthly meeting/jam sessions at major downtown hotels. Photographs of Davilla with black artists and of other integrated groups—including a wide shot of several white and black bands on stage at the finale of a 1951 New Orleans Jazz Club concert in Beaugerard (Congo) Square—can be found in the pages of the NOJC's *Second Line*. A January 1956 modern jazz concert at the black YWCA included Mouse Bonati and Benny Clement along with Ellis Marsalis, Earl Palmer, Red Tyler, and others—all openly announced in a story headlined "Big Jazz Concert Set Sunday" in the January 21 *Louisiana Weekly*. In a policy-driven environment, raids, arrests, and prosecutions would have been routine. In retrospect, we might infer that police policy went something like this: lean only on those who lack a semblance of public support, and only if it's politically useful to do so.

After Loyola I went directly for a master's degree in the 1956–1957 session at Catholic University in Washington, D.C. At that time the education M.A. at Catholic U. was a research degree. My adviser, a warm and open-minded septuagenarian named Eugenia Leonard, let me do a comparative study of jazz-oriented and nonjazz-oriented college music students. Grades, performance experience, knowledge of prominent artists in both classical music and jazz, and other factors were points of comparison. By stating the problem as genuine inquiry and always wearing a tie, I got cooperation from Catholic U. and nearby University of Maryland, and in Louisiana from Loyola, LSU, Southern, and Tulane. The results, published in a *Down Beat* article six years later, showed jazz-oriented students to be superior in every category—a very big deal in those days, since jazz education was in its infancy, and an incubator baby at that.

Back in New Orleans, I spent the 1957–1958 school session as a first-year English teacher at my alma mater, Nicholls High School. It was rough going, but I loved it and had a wonderful weekend gig for almost nine months with pianist-vocalist-trumpeter Buddy Prima, Bill Huntington on guitar, and Clinton Montz on bass at Prima's Fountain Lounge on Harrison Avenue.

I had played with Buddy and Bill on and off since 1954. My introduction to Bill was memorable. Buddy had a trio gig at a West End club and invited Bill to sit in. We had a good, romping trio pulse going, and guitarists I had worked with were mainly heavy four-to-the-bar strummers, so I was not anxious to see this kid plugging in his amp. He comped lightly and then played a short phrase to begin his solo. There is no name for what I felt, but if I had to verbalize it, the words would be something like "jazz essence." He was digging far deeper than the rest of us, and I found myself searching for a way to get calmly into his groove.

At the Fountain Lounge, Buddy and Bill and I formed a deep friendship. Bill, who had played banjo as a preteenager with George Lewis and other first generation jazzman (see chapter 22), was the most mature musician in the combo. His intense musical conception and his reflections on jazz were marvelous. Unfortunately, after a few months the quartet was cut to a trio. Bill was out. Buddy's father, Leon, who owned the club and paid the freight, wanted to economize. The group taped several fifteen-minute radio shows for Loyola on WWL and gained a small following among jazz fans and musicians.

In May 1958 I worked weekends with traditional jazz trumpeter Dutch Andrus on the Steamer *President*. Historian Hank Kmen, who was doing the doctoral work at Tulane that led to his landmark *Music in New Orleans* book, was playing tenor sax and clarinet. Hank was a generous and amiable teacher during breaks and postgig discussions. He would begin a conversation on Friday night with, "You know, Charlie . . ." just where we left off the previous Saturday, as if we had paused momentarily to sip a drink. We were on the gig the night of Saturday, May 31, when Mayor deLessepps ("Chep") Morrison integrated the streetcars and buses by executive action, without fanfare or previous announcement. When we left the *President* at midnight the deed was done, the segregation signs down. Hank cited Morrison's dictum: If you talk to Orleanians about integration, they see red. If you integrate, they see black.

I was drafted the next month. After boot camp at Fort Chaffee, Arkansas, I was assigned to the band training unit. This was good duty. The base was about to be closed down, so no one had an interest in following a strict military regimen. There was work on base and in Fort Smith with a jazz quartet headed by Charlie Brown, an excellent Rollins-like tenorman from Brooklyn. A none-too-swift local drummer named Pudgy Perez was unhappy to be losing the jazz gigs to a hotshot soldier, so he brought his beautiful next-door neighbor, Jessie Miller, to distract me while he sat in. It worked out well for me. I still got the good gigs, and six months later Jessie and I were married.

At my next assignment in Fort Jackson, South Carolina, a surplus of drummers sent me to the band supply office as a clerk-typist. I played a few times with musicians like pianist Peter Duchin and trombonist Roger Delillo. Peter, Eddy Duchin's son, later led a highly successful eclectic society band described by one critic as "the worst of every era," but at the time he was deeply into jazz. The king of the hill at Fort Jackson, though, was drummer Al Beldiny. Like Delillo, he was just off the Woody Herman band, and there were several other good jazz drummers on base.

I was humbled by this but I was also enjoying married life and had great reading time in the supply office, thanks to a sergeant who covered for his staff as long as we did the job. This was the peacetime army, after all, and there were only three hours a day of actual clerical work to be done. But unlike Fort Chaffee, most of the permanent cadre had a spit-and-polish mentality. The poor bandsmen were harassed on principle, picking up pine cones in blistering heat, only to have the NCOs toss them out again and call for another Sisyphean round of grounds maintenance.

I decided at Fort Jackson that public school teaching would be my main career. I would keep music as an inspiriting sideline by playing casuals, teaching privately, and championing jazz in whatever ways I could. Accordingly, I applied for an early release from the army due to the teacher shortage in New Orleans. No one expected the request to be granted. But I was frowning my way through Joyce's *Ulysses* one morning when the orders came through. In October 1959 I was back in the classroom, this time at Rabouin Vocational High School in downtown New Orleans. I finished my military duty with the National Guard band at Jackson Barracks, where Charlie Blancq was a fellow percussionist.

For quite a while I got varied and classy music gigs based on my previous reputation—a summer with the New Orleans Pops, spot jobs or subbing for drummers with Lloyd Alexander, Joe Burton, Leon Kelner, Rusty Mayne, Vaughn Monroe—but my skills were clearly down, good enough for weekend combos but not for scorching jazz tempos or rapid sight-reading.

I looked toward spreading the word about jazz through speaking, writing, and teaching. In my senior year at Loyola I had done a lecture and demonstration on the history of jazz drumming for the annual Phi Mu Alpha music fraternity program. I was invited back for talks on jazz at Loyola Music School, and my Catholic connections led to presentations, typically with recorded examples, at St. Joseph Seminary near Covington, as well as the Collegium Series in Shreveport in 1961 and 1962.

I taught drums twice a week from 1960 to 1966 at Campo's Music Store, where Johnny Vidacovich, now a premier jazz and studio drummer, was among my students for several years. Like Lou Dillon, I emphasized reading and stick control before going on to teach jazz, Latin, and other rhythms. I added cross-drum exercises and practice with records from my library and the students' collections. Lloyd Campo, always generous, put a second-hand drum set in the studio where I taught, allowing close attention to coordinated independence and other sophisticated jazz techniques.

I recall that Johnny was not initially the ace reader that he became, but his first formal lesson on the set was remarkable. The set consisted of a lame sock cymbal, a ride cymbal with an indecently meandering sound, and an unmatched snare, bass drum, side tom, and floor tom. To me it was a foregone conclusion that we were to make do with the traps during lesson time, getting acceptable sounds from our drums at home. Johnny, about thirteen years old at the time, leaned tentatively into the ride cymbal, adjusting his wrist and his stroke instinctively until it got a resonance and a consistency of sound I had not heard before. He approached the snare, bass, sock, and other drums with the same relaxed inquiry into their sonic potential. His ear and his reflexes made it clear that he was a natural, and I never looked scornfully at the old set again.

In the 1960–1961 school session, the New Orleans integration crisis almost ended my teaching career. Federal district judge Skelly Wright had ordered the public schools to integrate. The two schools selected—Frantz and McDonogh 19—were Ninth Ward elementary schools not far from my alma mater, Nicholls High School, where I was teaching again. With plenty of time to rouse rabble, state officials engaged in outrageous grandstanding gestures. Governor Jimmy Davis, a former country/gospel singer (he wrote "You Are My Sunshine"), called the legislature into special session. There were some fierce speeches on states' rights, along with concrete actions to close New Orleans schools and withhold teachers' salaries.

Judge Wright ordered the schools to stay open, giving teachers a principled and prudential choice—to show up and risk being fired by the legislature or to stay home on the assumption that racism would triumph in the end. I showed up, of course, and did not get my November paycheck (about $400) until later. But neither did the teachers who cast their lot with the legislature. The schools were finally integrated, as the schools in Little Rock had been integrated three years before. The New Orleans crisis has been chronicled by observers such as John Steinbeck and psychologist Robert Coles. I wrote about it for local journals later in the decade, when I was indestructibly tenured. In 1997 I met and exchanged war stories with Coles when he spoke at a National Council of Teachers of English luncheon.

Several of my attempts at getting local jazz projects off the ground failed in the 1960s. I submitted two unsuccessful proposals for an educational TV series on modern jazz, using the best local modern jazz artists, to the city's public television station, WYES-TV. I was informally offered a chance to script a radio program on the history of jazz for the New Orleans Public Schools station. Astonishingly, I was told I would have to emphasize white artists like the Original Dixieland Jazz Band and downplay the likes of Oliver and Armstrong. Impossible, I said, and that was that. As for the *Times-Picayune* and other local newspapers, they had a long record of ignoring or debasing jazz. It seemed that my best bet for a writing outlet would the national jazz press.

I had a connection of sorts at *Down Beat*, so I gave it a try. Gilbert Erskine, a good friend of Don's at Loyola and a founder of the New Orleans Jazz Club, was living in Chicago and doing reviews of traditional and Dixieland jazz records for *DB*. I wrote to him in 1960 reminding him of our meeting years ago at the New Orleans Record Shop and inquiring about a possible article on modern jazz in New Orleans. That did not fly at first, but a few months later I almost levitated when he wrote that incoming editor Don DeMichael wanted to give me a try as New Orleans correspondent.

DeMichael wanted to add New Orleans to the six or so cities included in the twice monthly "Where & When" listings of jazz clubs and artists—an opportunity to put New Orleans back on the national jazz map, and the *Picayune* be damned! (Author Walker Percy once called the *Picayune* "a house organ for its advertisers.") As correspondent I would also do frequent entries in the "Strictly Ad Lib" column, reporting briefly on various developments in the city, and there were further possibilities for occasional news stories and articles.

I started out with two goals for my work with *Down Beat*. First, in the absence of local coverage, the *DB* listings and other materials would be a comprehensive record of clubs, artists, and developments in the jazz community, embracing all jazz styles. In fact, *DB* was essentially the only game around. Its competitor, *Metronome*, ceased publication in 1961. The feisty journal called *Jazz* was in publication, but editor Pauline Rivelli bent it toward features, reviews, and social criticism, with no attempt at city-based news coverage. My second goal was to continue pressing *DB* for a full-length article on the least known aspect of jazz in the city—modern jazz.

The first goal was a matter of networking and endurance. Working mainly by phone, I contacted musicians, club owners, and promoters, and submitted copy faithfully twice a month for most of the 1960s. My first "Where & When" list of clubs and artists in the May 25, 1961, issue included Joe Burton, Murphy Campo, Octave Crosby, Ditymus, Pete Fountain, Albert French, Al Hirt, Armand Hug, Mike Lala, the Last Straws, Ellis Marsalis, Santo Pecora, Buddy Prima, Leon Prima, and Alvin (Red) Tyler. As the decade unfolded, I was able to report regularly in *DB* and sporadically in other journals on the growth of Preservation Hall, the Jazz Museum, the city's increasingly visible modern jazz constituency, and the first two jazz and heritage festivals. Embedded in much of this reportage was information on the decline of segregation and on changes in local civic leaders' attitudes toward jazz.

Because of state anti-integration laws, I was at risk for appearing on the masthead of a magazine that openly espoused integration and splashed the cover of the March 1962 issue with the phrase "racism and prejudice in jazz." But the chances of any member of the Louisiana legislature reading *Down Beat* were slim, so I shrugged it off.

My second goal for *DB* was no struggle at all. In June 1961 editor DeMicheal wrote that he liked the New Orleans coverage and invited me to convince him about the modern jazz idea. Within two weeks I sketched out the concept and got the okay. The article, called "New Jazz in the Cradle," appeared in two parts in the August 17 and 31, 1961, issues. (See chapters 21–22.) DeMichael avidly supported news and articles from New Orleans until his resignation in 1967.

As it turned out, the structure of the modern jazz article—looking briefly at historical and cultural contexts in preparation for the exposition—was a model for many later articles on traditional and Dixieland jazz and other topics. A historical backdrop and other contextual materials typically set up new perspectives, set forth in interviews and commentary. Because the developments of the 1960s were situated in then recent history, descriptions of the early postwar scene were part of most of the articles in *Down Beat* and *New Orleans* magazine that are reprinted in the following chapters.

Back in my classroom, I was integrating jazz into my English and history programs when it seemed natural to do so. It often did, and synchronicities, New Orleans style, abounded. Once I asked my sophomores at Franklin High School to critique alternative endings to my *DB* Preservation Hall article. On another occasion I taped percussion background for some poems my tenth graders were studying. Poet James Nolan, then a witty, intense student, recalls that the nontraditional approaches and creative writing assignments were a strong influence on his growth as a writer. Nolan is a widely published poet and translator (Neruda, Gil de Biedma) who has given readings, sometimes with musicians, in New Orleans, San Francisco, and in Madrid, Spain, and elsewhere. I had little idea in the Franklin years that he and others were gathering extraordinary life experiences by hanging out with French Quarter bohemians at places like the Dream Palace, La Casa, and the Quorum Club (discussed in section III).

In response to an open-ended writing assignment at Franklin in 1965, an excellent eleventh grader named Tom Sancton Jr. wrote about his afternoons at Preservation Hall learning to play traditional jazz clarinet under the tutelage of veteran trumpeter Punch Miller. I had long known about Tom's father, Thomas Sancton Sr., the local writer whose 1956 novel *Count Roller Skates* prompted *Time* magazine to call him "the New Thomas Wolfe." A former managing editor for *New Republic* and Washington correspondent for *The Nation*, he was a rabid jazz fan and regular contributor to the New Orleans Jazz Club's *Second Line* in the 1950s.

The young Sancton was clearly a gifted writer. His Punch Miller narrative, "Portrait of a Jazzman," was touching and brilliant. We submitted it to the annual Achievement Awards in Writing Program sponsored by the National Council of Teachers of English, the organization that would later be my employer. It was a winner. I sent the piece on Don DeMichael at *Down Beat*, and it was published in February 1967. Sancton went on to Harvard and started a revivalist band that was recorded on George H. Buck's New Orleans label. His ninth album, a 1999 Fleur-De-Lys CD called *Riviera Reunion*, features a rhythm section only, demonstrating his evolution to an eclectic, swing-based style. But Sancton's main career was in writing, not music, and he remembered his roots. As senior editor and Paris bureau chief for *Time* magazine, he put aside his assignments on national affairs to do the cover story on Wynton Marsalis for the October 22, 1990, issue.

I started writing for *New Orleans* magazine in 1967, the year of its inception. As described in chapter 2, on jazz and the local press, negative attitudes toward jazz had softened by then. The first two editors, Jim Autry and George Bacon, gave me considerable freedom to write about jazz and education, my two assignments as contributing editor. As with *Down Beat*, my first article (August 1967) was on modern jazz in New Orleans. Shortly after, Bill Bryan contacted me about writing for his feisty weekly tabloid, the Vieux Carre *Courier*. During the decade, I also did one-shot articles on jazz for *Delta Review*, *Gentlemen's Quarterly*, *Jazz*, and *Jazz Journal* (London).

New Orleans magazine and the *Courier* (the latter, especially) introduced many new writers and sought out inactive veterans to provide provocative commentary on architecture, education, media, music, preservationism, and other aspects of local culture. Among their writers were Tom Bethell, Don Brady, Betty Cole, Bruce Eggler, Bob Krieger, Bill Rushton, and Tom Sancton Sr. They modeled contemporary journalism in ways that ultimately edged the staid dailies toward broader and brighter reportage and criticism.

The changes in climate in the New Orleans public schools in the late 1960s were revolutionary. A national neoprogressive education movement was on the upswing when I was appointed English supervisor for the district in 1967. I had taken a sabbatical during the previous session for graduate study at the University of Illinois (tenor saxist Rene Coman did *Down Beat* reportage during that year), and I was ready to press for innovation in a new job in my beloved district. My boss and mentor at the central office was a fearless and flamboyant liberal, Edwin Friedrich (yes, the English teacher who had permitted me to write the Dixie vs. bop term paper in high school a dozen years earlier).

Gone were the days when the administration favored dead white guys to the neglect of contemporary and ethnically diverse writers and musicians. Almost immediately, I was able to work with teachers to introduce contemporary literature, black literature, young adult literature, thematic literary study, media study, and new approaches to teaching composition, all supported by abundant state and federal funding for paperback books and media equipment.

As noted earlier, by the late 1960s my writings about jazz seemed to have made some points and run their course. The first large-scale jazz festival, Jazzfest '68, was a culmination of sorts. I worked behind the scenes with Willis Conover and Durel Black during the planning, got extensive advance publicity in *Down Beat* and *New Orleans*, wrote a piece on local jazz for the printed program, did a lengthy review for *DB* . . . and exhaled. (See chapters 8–10 and appendix 1, "The New Orleans Jazz Scene Today.") It occurred to me that the surprises and breakthroughs I had seen since my first Ad Libs column in 1961 would never be new again.

On the other hand, writing about education provided fresh stimulation. I was finding local and national audiences for writings related to my main career track and getting involved with exciting academic and sociopolitical projects in New Orleans (e.g., the Innovative Education Coalition, New Orleans Media Institute) and with the National Council of Teachers of English. Publishers were involving me in cutting-edge textbook projects.

I kept the jazz machine running, though, in school-related projects. In 1969 I got federal funds to develop an audiotape of black poetry for the district. I arranged for several poems to be backed by a jazz group consisting of Earl Turbinton on alto sax, Willie (Tee) Turbinton on piano, Richard Payne on bass, and David Lee on drums. One of the readers was poet Sybil Kein, then a splendidly rebellious teacher at Clark High School. As president of the New Orleans Affiliate of NCTE, I organized a performance of original readings by Kein, accompanied by her brother on guitar and other instruments.

During the same period of ferment, my colleague Shirley Trusty (Corey), supervisor of cultural resources, was developing programs of school-site visits with artists from various fields. One of her first victories was a three-year artist-in-residence program for modern jazz clarinetist Alvin Batiste, effected despite a bit of grumbling from supervisor of music Rene Louapre. (Yes, the same Louapre who choked on my unauthorized solo on "Look for the Silver Lining" years earlier.) She went on to bring pianist Armand Hug and drummer Dave Oxley in for play-and-talk sessions with students.

The epitome of Trusty's work came in 1975 with the establishment of the New Orleans Center for the Creative Arts (NOCCA). Ellis Marsalis was the first teacher in the NOCCA jazz program that produced celebrated young artists like Terence Blanchard, Harry Connick Jr., Donald Harrison, the Jordan brothers, the Marsalis brothers, Nicholas Payton, and others. The school was her conception, the result of two years of writing position papers, beating the bushes for funding, and wearing down reluctant administrators.

I helped institute the writing program at NOCCA, but that was my parting shot with New Orleans Public Schools. Conservatism was dominating education nationally. Not coincidentally, a district-wide administrative reorganization in 1974 removed the consultants from the offices of the subject matter supervisors, crippling our outreach into the schools. Although it was clear that many of the program gains in English would not be reversed by the growing back-to-basics movement, the climate for productive change had evaporated. It was time to move on.

In autumn of 1977 I began twenty years of work as deputy executive director at the National Council of Teachers of English, the association for English teachers that had been inspirational during my teaching and supervisory years. As already noted, in the 1990s I returned to writing about jazz history because of myths and misconceptions that have evolved about New Orleans jazz in the postwar years.

SECTION I

JAZZ AND THE ESTABLISHMENT: FROM FLOUTING TO FLAUNTING

In a real sense, just about everything in this book could be placed in the category of jazz and the Establishment. I am not just invoking the Marxist bromide about politics permeating all of life. The story of jazz in New Orleans is composed of incidents that are replete with political skirmishes in a lumbering cultural war. The music was born of many cultures, and it became part of life in New Orleans in complex ways and without the express consent of anyone. Clearly, the Establishment in New Orleans—its political, business, religious, and social leaders, its press, educational institutions, and other guardians of culture—had no idea of how to react to jazz and its power to move the feet, booty, and soul of the populace.

The introductory chapter described my ongoing dance with, and often around, the Establishment between the end of World War II and 1970. This section will provide some cultural contexts for my experiences and those of the musicians who were devoted to jazz in the postwar years. The first article focuses mainly on jazz and the New Orleans press during those years. But long before the war (1941–1945), jazz was the subject of scornful reportage and commentary, and it is illuminating to look at this backdrop to the postwar scene.

Historians of the earliest jazz years have uncovered a long tradition of negative depictions of jazz in local newspapers. Donald Winston infers credibly that local papers were referring to early jazz disparagingly even before the music had a name. In reports on crime in black night clubs after the turn of the century, the papers used phrases like "discordant music" . . . "disgusting" . . . "with an indecent ring."

In *Storyville, New Orleans* Al Rose speculates that a cartoon in the sensationalistic weekly *Mascot* of November 15, 1890, was "the earliest known illustration of a jazz band." And perhaps the earliest known condemnation. Both the drawing and the description are racist and contemptuous of the music. Four buffoonish black musicians, playing instruments resembling a trumpet, trombone, clarinet, and bass drum, are on the balcony of Robinson's Dime Museum on Basin Street, ostensibly playing to attract customers. Well-dressed whites are moaning and fainting in the street, pelted by the notes from the horns. The text states, "We have been visited by a sad affliction . . . several 'coons' armed with pieces of brass have banded together. . . . If their object was to inflict torture upon this suffering community . . . they are doing right well. . . . This man Robinson came here with a monkey and a blue parrot. . . . The town knew him not, but a nigger brass band betrayed him. . . . Robinson's balcony serenade is enough to make the dead rise."

The now-classic "Jass and Jassism" editorial diatribe against jazz in the June 20, 1918, *Picayune* (mistakenly cited by Rose as June 17, 1917) is reprinted in its entirety in chapter 2. Bruce Raeburn notes that some letters to the editor favorable to "jass" appeared around that time. But in terms of the papers' editorial commentary, Donald Marquis is essentially right in stating that the "first nonderogatory statement about jazz in the New Orleans press" appeared in April 1933, in *Louisiana Weekly.* The black newspaper, which is still published, ran two articles called "Excavating Local Jazz" by E. Belfield Spriggins. The articles contained an interview with Willie Cornish, who had played trombone with the legendary Buddy Bolden.

In fairness, newspapers in other cities were also unkind to jazz in the early years. Luther Williams's study of references to jazz in the New York *Times* in the 1920s showed dominant patterns of condemnation, racism, simple ignorance, and a total exclusion of jazz musicians from the debate. In news reports, editorials, and feature stories, jazz was blamed for, among other things, the heart attack of an elderly classical cornetist, an unfavorable trade balance between the United States and Hungary, the waning quality of Italian tenors, the frightening of bears in Siberia, and the decline of modern civilization.

Incredibly, Donald Winston takes the opposite view, claiming that the New York *Times* "came close to good coverage, meaningful coverage," of jazz. But his study attends mainly to *Times* reports that focused not on jazz and its practitioners but on Paul Whiteman, Irving Berlin, George Gershwin, Jerome Kern, and other popularizers and songwriters. Also, numerous derogatory citations discovered by Luther Williams apparently eluded Winston. He does mention some antijazz copy, though, such a March 13, 1925, editorial in which the *Times* encouraged the quick exodus of American jazz musicians to Europe. He also cites a report of January 3, 1922, in which an Episcopal minister lambasted jazz as the "savage crash and bang" of "African jungle music."

In his conclusion Winston acknowledges the *Times*'s "failure to report on the activities of Negro jazzmen." Stating the crucial flaw as if it were a point of mitigation, he observes that the music of black jazzmen must have "seemed especially crude to the *Times* reporters and music critics." Confusing cause with effect, he states that "this failure to cover Negro activity and music . . . resulted in a poor understanding of the whole jazz environment and its musical sense."

Even so, the New York *Times* published an article sympathetic to jazz in 1926, seven years before the Spriggins series in *Louisiana Weekly.* A black writer named Nicholas Ballanta stood the "savage jungle music" cliché on its head. He took a stand that was thoroughly radical at the time, claiming that jazz was derived from many cultures, with distinctive African elements *enriching* American music by *developing* the "American sense of rhythm."

By 1929, Williams reports, the immense popularity of jazz both domestically and abroad trumped the New York *Times* debate about the merits of jazz. In contrast with the New Orleans press, *Times* reportage had begun to reflect glimmers of pride in the music and recognition of its value as a cultural export. He writes,

> In April, 1929 the death knell was sounded not for jazz but for the controversy surrounding it in an article in the *Times* recounting the European travels of Sandhor Harmati, Director of the Omaha Symphony. He said that jazz . . . was the only American music known by the European generation of that day. It appeared that jazz had arrived to stay.

Winston's rationalizations of the New York *Times* jazz coverage are in contrast to his straightforward analysis of the Chicago *Defender*. He sees the black newspaper's coverage of jazz between 1918 and 1926 as a reflection of its general editorial mission: to counter antiblack discrimination by praising the products of African-American culture. This made the *Defender* a rare, if not evenhandedly critical, champion of jazz in its early years. For example, a March 9, 1918, item on the entertainment page praised a New Orleans band led by cornetist Emanuel Perez. "Have you heard Emanuel Perez's Creole Band? . . . that wonderful . . . music that the people of Chicago are going wild about? It's gripping the dancers of the Windy City, and causing people to come to the Peking dance pavilion . . . and hear the music that's all the rage in the East and in the West."

The *Defender*'s tendency to report about jazz in superlatives was not accompanied by coverage of the musicians themselves, Winston notes. And worse, it was not a policy that was consistently carried out when other purposes related to the paper's mission could be served. In connection with a high school essay contest for Music Week, for example, the *Defender* ran these student comments about jazz on June 10, 1922: "Nothing is bad enough to say about this pestilence. . . . Jazz indicates a tendency toward insanity."

When did things loosen up in New Orleans? In the early post–World War II years, civic leaders were inheritors of the long tradition of jazz bashing at the local and national levels, a tradition that identified jazz with booze, prostitution, crime, and other vices. And in fact, the settings in which jazz was nurtured after the turn of the century in New Orleans did include bars, brothels, and brawls in Storyville and elsewhere. By and large, there was no political risk in perpetuating the stereotype of jazz as lewd and immoral music.

But local leaders had some reason to consider softening their attitudes toward jazz. They knew from their experiences in the community that jazz could not be equated with vice. For decades jazz had been the music of choice at innumerable dances, debutante parties, picnics at Milneberg and Lincoln Park, social club events, and other sites. And ever since the repeal of Prohibition in 1933, the national spotlight had turned away from early jazz

styles associated with flappers and speakeasies. The focus was on big bands
and swing between the mid-1930s and the end of World War II. Despite the
quick rise and fall of National Jazz Foundation in 1944–1946, described in
this volume, local fandom had increased during the popular revival of interest in jazz in the late 1940s, bolstered by the New Orleans Jazz Club.

Jazz had become less an outrage than an embarrassment to class-
conscious leaders by the postwar years. Absent the kind of chaotic sociopolitical context that resulted in the closing of Storyville in 1917, there was no
urgent reason to drag jazz to the foreground for public pillorying. This fading stigma is not to be confused with endorsement, of course. At best, the
Establishment maintained an attitude of malign neglect until the rest of the
world made it totally clear that jazz—at least, *some* jazz—was okay.

Local validation came gradually. The efforts of the New Orleans Jazz
Club, the work of Roger Wolfe on WDSU radio, and the resonance of the
national revival of interest in jazz were factors in the postwar popular revival in New Orleans. But the Establishment did not take powerful notice of
jazz until it gained national and international fame, first by several white
artists—the Dukes of Dixieland, Pete Fountain, and Al Hirt—then by
Preservation Hall, which featured predominantly, though not exclusively,
black artists. The stories of the ascent of local artists to worldwide fame are
fleshed out in section II of this book. But their key role in giving jazz the
stamp of respectability for image-anxious leaders warrants a brief description below and inclusion on timeline chart 1, "Commercial and Cultural Victories for Traditional and Dixieland Jazz," at the end of this overview.

The Dukes of Dixieland gained modest national attention in 1949. Using
the name Junior Dixieland Band, they were teenagers when they won the
Horace Heidt talent competition on network radio. In 1956 the Dukes gained
genuine celebrity status as the first jazz band to be recorded in high-fidelity
sound. They did an unabashedly commercial session that was a national
best-seller for Sid Frey's groundbreaking Audio-Fidelity label.

Pete Fountain, one of the original Junior Dixielanders/Dukes, became an
overnight national sensation in 1957, when Lawrence Welk featured him on
Dixieland tunes on Welk's weekly ABC-TV show. The exposure ran for two
years, making Fountain a national star. Equally important, Fountain did not
stay on the road, as the Dukes did after their breakthrough. In 1959 he opened
his own club on Bourbon Street. It did not escape the notice of the business
community that Pete's place was soon the most sought-out club in town.

Al Hirt, who won the Heidt competition in 1950 with dazzling speed and
range on a "Night and Day" solo, was next. He was playing virtuoso trumpet in a Dixieland combo format at Dan's Pier 600 on Bourbon Street in
1959 when he was discovered by Monique Van Voohren, whose husband
was promoter Gerald Purcell. Bookings in Las Vegas, recording sessions,
and national TV followed until Hirt was virtually a household name. As with
Fountain, when Hirt's celebrity grew, his presence on Bourbon Street became a decided boon. He bought the Pier 600 around 1963, remodeled it,

and reopened in summer of 1964 as Al Hirt's Club. His talent director and house band leader, pianist Ronnie Kole, started importing big-name artists (e.g., Cannonball Adderley, Dizzy Gillespie) to maintain the club's "star" image during Hirt's frequent out-of-town activities.

In summer of 1961 Preservation Hall was established on St. Peter Street in the French Quarter by genuine moldy figs (rabid traditional jazz fans) and their friends. The idea of first-generation New Orleans jazz musicians becoming active again, this time at a "kitty hall"—a room with a few chairs, no drinks, financed by donations at the door, a "requests" basket, and record sales on site—was not only authentic but quintessentially quaint. The national media could not resist it. By 1963 the Hall had become a national phenomenon. Its focus on traditional New Orleans jazz gave a whole new dimension to the argument that jazz was a major asset to the city. Equally, it helped revive pride in early jazz, including marching bands and related institutions such as black social clubs.

It was obvious by the late 1960s that the city's Dixieland and traditional New Orleans jazz heritage was a major tourist attraction, right up there with gumbo, wrought iron railings, and charming but apocryphal legends. Even the tinniest ear could hear the peal of local cash registers in the crescendo of commercial successes for New Orleans artists. Better yet, there might be some money in flaunting the music that the *Picayune* in 1918 called "a low streak in man's taste" and the *Louisiana Weekly* in 1928 assigned to "immediate oblivion."

The financial backing, cooperation of local agencies, and social climate were right for a major jazz festival. So in 1968 the first Jazzfest was held—a week-long, multisite festival of music, food, and related activities. True, this was more than a decade after Newport, Rhode Island, a site of no previous jazz relevance, turned its elegant turf over to an annual celebration of the jazz art. But late was better than never by a mile and a bundle of money.

In fairness, there had been three earlier attempts at mounting a festival in the 1960s, with results that were, in turn, unproductive, disastrous, and ludicrous. The untold stories of the would-be festivals and the 1968 triumph are discussed later in this overview. The articles that follow include contemporaneous materials on the first two festivals, including the only comprehensive review, to my knowledge, of the first event.

As the success stories of local jazz artists were building in the postwar years, then, a mischievous idea had grown among the cultural gatekeepers: jazz, besides being a marketable tourist attraction, might have cultural value and artistic legitimacy. But the acknowledgment of jazz as an important part of our culture and as an art form advanced obliquely and with caution. Several articles in this section deal with the first high-culture breakthroughs—the Jazz Archive at Tulane University (1958) and the Jazz Museum (1961), the latter being essentially a project of the New Orleans Jazz Club (NOJC). The relationships of the NOJC (and its failed predecessor, the National Jazz Foundation), the archive, and the museum to a recalcitrant local Establishment are discussed in this volume.

THE SHORT, HAPPY LIFE
OF THE NATIONAL JAZZ FOUNDATION

The genesis of the New Orleans Jazz Club in 1948 and its growth in the postwar years are described in chapter 3. This overview will provide a fuller discussion of the club's complex relationships to the local Establishment. Those relationships were shaped in interesting ways by the NOJC's predecessor, the short-lived (1944–1946) National Jazz Foundation (NJF). For reasons that will become clear, many of the NOJC's goals and methods represented a clean break, conceptually, from the NJF.

Unlike the NOJC, the NJF died before it got to write its own history, so its odd story is worth telling here. The information on NJF was gathered mainly from the group's *Basin Street* newsletter and minutes of their meetings (housed at the Tulane Jazz Archive), several interviews, the *Louisiana Weekly*, and Bruce Raeburn's invaluable study.

When I was interviewing Johnny Wiggs, Don Perry, and others for the 1970 *New Orleans* magazine NOJC article below, the common consensus was that the National Jazz Foundation could be dismissed as a flop. This is true, but it was not a *mere* flop. On one hand, it was more well-connected than the NOJC from the start, more enterprising in its goals, and more catholic in the music it embraced and promoted. On the other, its failure set back the acceptance of jazz by the Establishment by as much as fifteen years, almost guaranteeing that any organization of jazz boosters that followed would be have to start from scratch as a grassroots crusade of tenacious advocates.

The NJF started out in 1944 far more ambitiously than the NOJC. Its agenda included involving sympathetic Establishment leaders in the initial planning as a wedge for future active support; sponsoring concerts that combined nationally known jazz artists with locals; getting major national publicity at the outset; and raising money to buy Mahogany Hall and convert the famed Basin Street bordello and music spot into a National Museum of Jazz.

The group hit the ground sprinting. The organizational meeting, significantly at the plush Arnaud's Restaurant, was attended by reporter and jazz enthusiast Scoop Kennedy, who would become the NJF's first president; Belgian critic and writer Robert Goffin; Dr. Edmond (Doc) Souchon; and five simpatico Orleanians with contacts in the media or the business or social communities—Wilson Arnold, John Lester, Frank Mace, Ted Liuzza, and John Sonfield Jr.

The group's publicity brochure announces, fortissimo, "YOU OWN PART OF A *NEW* ORLEANS GOLD MINE." It lists the city's already celebrated treasures as the Vieux Carre, the Sugar Bowl, Mardi Gras, and the Spring Fiesta, and announces that jazz is the "new gold mine." The National Jazz Foundation is described as "an organization of people who *recognize jazz as a musically and historically significant art form*—and people who recognize New Orleans' historic connection with *jazz as a potentially price-*

less civic asset." The pamphlet boasts that the NJF leadership is composed of "*a group of New Orleans' most prominent business and civic leaders. . . .* They are *interested in the welfare of New Orleans*" (italics added).

The italicized phrases point to the extraordinary boldness of the NJF project. Rather than accept the role of humble petitioners for jazz arriving with hat in hand at the door of the business community, the group began with the assumption that the NJF was a coalition of leaders bearing gifts of gold for New Orleans. At the same time, they acknowledged that there was plenty of work to be done. Jazz is the *new* gold mine, as yet only a "*potentially* priceless civic asset." Surely this was a brilliant conceptualization—but could they could pull it off programmatically?

It seemed so. Consider this rapid-fire series of events, reported in *Basin Street*, the NJF's mimeographed bulletin that was edited by a full-time executive secretary, Pat Spiess.

- In October 1944 the NJF sponsored a successful Benny Goodman concert at Municipal Auditorium. True to the group's goals, two local bands were on the program—a white band that included Dixieland stalwarts Irving Fazola and Monk Hazel and a black group headed by cornetist Sidney Desvigne, a Storyville veteran who had also played with the Excelsior Brass Band and on riverboats with Fate Marable.

- In January 1945 a three-city celebration of jazz (New York, Chicago, and New Orleans) was broadcast nationally under the sponsorship of *Esquire* magazine. The NJF presented a New Orleans segment composed of Louis Armstrong, Bunk Johnson, and Sidney Bechet. NJF paid the union dues for the entire Johnson band so they could appear on the program. Local dignitaries were cannily given brief talking slots as an ego sop. Trumpeter Leon Prima (Louis' brother) led a Dixieland band that was among the lesser-known local groups receiving national exposure on the hookup.

- Ever mindful of publicity and events with a unique twist, in February 1945 the NJF presented a private concert by Bunk Johnson's band for seven French journalists. Among them was Jean-Paul Sartre, whose now classic existentialist works *Being and Nothingness* and *No Exit* had been published two years earlier. Sartre's reaction, reported in the March *Basin Street* newsletter, can be read either as throwaway comment or, with a stretch, as a philosophical bon mot: "There is nothing quite like this."

- In December 1945 the NJF sponsored a high school jazz band contest that was attended by over 1,000 at Municipal Auditorium. Groups from Easton, Fortier, Maumus, Nicholls, and Peters entered. Bassist Oliver (Stick) Felix, then playing trombone with the winning Dixieland band from Peters, recalls that the band included future be-boppers Benny Clement on trumpet and Frank (Chick) Power on clarinet and tenor sax.

- Consistent with its announced intention "to promote not just Dixieland Jazz, but all good jazz as part of the American way of life," in 1946 the NJF was southern regional sponsor of a national amateur big band/small combo competition conducted by *Look* magazine. State finalists from Alabama, Florida, Louisiana, and Georgia were in New Orleans for the event. The winning big band was from Louisiana—an all-city group from New Orleans led by Al Belletto, then an eighteen-year-old student at Loyola University. Belletto adds that under the sponsorship of Werlein's Music Store on Canal Street, the group went on to win the national competition at Carnegie Hall in New York.
- The NJF gave its official endorsement to the Bunk Johnson Band's excellent 1946 Victor album. In return, the liner notes included the NJF address along with an invitation to join. The NJF also helped to finance Johnson's 1945 trip to New York for what became a disagreeable gig reuniting the trumpeter with Sidney Bechet.
- In May 1946 the NJF brought Eddie Condon to town. Condon was not a household name like Goodman and Armstrong, but the concert featured a cadre of jazzmen well known to Dixieland fans—Max Kaminsky, Wild Bill Davison, Vernon Brown, Dick Carey, Gene Schroeder, and Jack Lesberg; ex-Orleanians George Brunis and Tony Parenti; and others. Because Condon's clarinetist, Joe Dixon, canceled out, local reedman Gene Meyers filled in. Unlike the previous NJF galas, no local group was featured on the program. But in general, the NJF looked after its own. For example, it gave a members-only concert featuring players like Irving Fazola and Monk Hazel. Prefiguring music therapy, the group sponsored record-listening sessions and a live concert with Hazel, Larry Shields, and others at LaGarde Army Hospital.

Through the energy of Scoop Kennedy, and perhaps through the NJF's early connections with internationally known figures like Robert Goffin and John Hammond, the NJF received an absolutely remarkable amount of national publicity. *Esquire, Look, Newsweek, Down Beat,* and *Metronome* were among those providing enthusiastic reportage, reviews, and support. Yet the phenomenal success that began in mid-1944 was dying at the end of 1946.

How did this happen, given national visibility, the powerful support of local leaders, and several apparently successful concerts?

Considerable mystery surrounds the rapid decline of the NJF. To be sure, negative factors had been lurking from the beginning. Local musicians like Johnny Wiggs were unhappy about the top billing and good money that went to headliners at NJF concerts—even though it was clear that figures like Goodman and Condon were needed to draw large local audiences and national attention. Also, NJF held limited appeal to the purists, locally and elsewhere. The moldy figs no doubt endorsed the attention given to Bunk Johnson and his sidemen but could feel no kinship with NJF's stated catholicity of taste that encouraged high school swing bands and embraced "schools of thought from Bolden to Ellington." The purists were aware that NJF was, after all, the National Jazz Foundation, not the New Orleans Jazz Foundation. The group's *Basin Street* newsletter even boasted international membership and proposed chapters in every state and in foreign countries as a future project.

Also, one of the NJF's greatest initial strengths—the presence of esteemed local leaders on its board—might well have been a spoiler and an intimidation. Tight little groups of collectors and jazz fans no long "owned" the music as cultists if the likes of Arnold and Sonfield were at the helm. And the unanticipated prospect of future national fame opened up by go-getters like Scoop Kennedy was probably daunting to musicians who had resigned themselves to the limited status of prophets without honor in their own land. More practically, the NJF must have felt the loss of high-energy hustle and press connections when Kennedy left town to work with the Red Cross in the war effort in March 1945.

But such problems might have been solved if prosperity had reigned. The bottom line seems to be that the NJF ran out of money rather suddenly in late 1946. As reported in my NOJC article, it was rumored back in 1970 that someone ran away with the treasury and a stripper, leaving the group flat broke—a story still in circulation today.

The minutes of the NJF's meetings suggest a less dramatic scenario without making the conclusion of the matter clear. The February 1946 minutes report than John Reilly had withdrawn his previous financial assistance—most likely, free office space—and that the group now had to subsist solely on its dues and other revenues, which were slim. The concerts had not been budgeted for a surplus, and the NJF's generosity to Bunk Johnson and others had taken a toll.

Concern was at a higher pitch at the September 1946 meeting. Acting president Henry Alcus said he would resign if the board "continued on its present scale despite the uncertain financial conditions." With red ink threatening to rain on their jazzy cruise, these pragmatic businessmen were inclined to jump ship. Donald Baird, a sales promoter recently arrived from New York, offered to help put NJF on a self-sustaining basis if he could realize one-third of the receipts and "have full charge of all operations" under the jurisdiction of a small committee. At the group's last known meeting in October, Alcus read a letter from Baird proposing terms for his work, which the board accepted. Alcus stated that he would close down the NJF and "operate on a scale best suited under the present circumstances" if there was no indication of financial stability by November 1. This was a highly ambiguous statement and a strange deadline, if Baird was to be given a chance to set up a promotional plan.

I found no further records from the National Jazz Foundation. Raeburn writes that the group disbanded in April 1947, a likely outcome based on the October minutes. But the NJF name resurfaced curiously a year later as sponsor of two concerts at the Municipal Auditorium. An April 30, 1948, program headlined Louis Armstrong's All-Stars, along with Stormy's jazz band. (Yes, Stormy, the wildly popular stripper from the Casino Royal on Bourbon Street, billed in a New Orleans *Item* ad as "America's Most Beautiful Band Leader.") A June 2 concert featured Stan Kenton, identified in *Louisiana Weekly* as "The Most Photographed White Bandleader in the World by the Negro Press." *Item* columnist John Lester, a charter member of the NJF, was cited in *LW* as emcee, promoter of the concerts, and current president of the NJF.

"Scoop" Jones's review of the Armstrong concert in the May 8 *LW* noted that Stella Oliver, widow of King Oliver, and Captain Joseph Jones, director of the Colored Waifs' Home, where Armstrong played as a youth, were given lifetime memberships in NJF. Jones's June 12 write-up of the Kenton concert noted that traditional jazz artists Papa Celestin and Alphonse Picou (who would soon be prominent in the local jazz revival) were honored with plaques. A picture of Lester and Celestin accompanied a story titled "NJF's Epic Program Rates Raves." Lester was described as "alert, energetic," and a "militant man about town," and a plug was given to NJF: dues $3.00, offices at 311 Carondelet Street. The address suggests lack of continuity; it is different from previous NJF sites (610 Hibernia Building until early 1945; thereafter, 407 Cotton Exchange Building).

The *Louisiana Weekly* gave far more coverage to these concerts than the dailies, thanks to its policy of championing black causes and culture. Within the black community, the paper continuously, even repetitively, reviewed with effusive praise the early rhythm and blues bands and other entertainment in the LaSalle Street area. At the NJF concerts, white audiences witnessed the art and the honoring of black figures, making the programs highly newsworthy to *LW*. Lester, undoubtedly a risk-taking liberal, came in for special praise.

But Lester's latter-day leadership of the apparently resuscitated National Jazz Foundation is a mystery. Possibly, he connected somehow with other past leaders of a dormant NJF and got permission to use its name and remaining funds for an attempt at reorganization. Possibly, he acted unilaterally, audaciously promoting the concerts himself under the banner of a defunct group and setting up shop on Carondelet Street.

To this horseload of uncertainties, add the fact that the longstanding rumor about an NJF treasury rip-off and escape with a stripper attributes the mischief to none other than John Lester and Stormy. If this is so, it seems odd that the adventuresome theft took place over a year after the group died, or perhaps hibernated. On the other hand, the story is plausible on several counts. Lester's column in the *Item* halted abruptly in June 1948, just after the Kenton concert. The profits must have been formidable, if the *Item's* June 3 report of 5,000 attendees is anywhere near accurate. Further, Lester was known as a self-styled bon vivant who might well have hit the road with a celebrated stripper. Reed player Frankie Mann (Frank Mannino), who worked with Stormy's band, recalls that she and Lester were romantically involved and that Lester took her to New York sometime in the late 1940s. Stormy was back in town without him in the 1950s, practicing the stripper's art and finding outrageous ways to generate publicity.

I cannot help thinking that the Lester and Stormy caper, whether true or not, is a great New Orleans story. It lends comedy, irony, titillation, and absurdity to the sad biography of the NJF. As a researcher, I acknowledge a lack of data on the matter, but as an Orleanian, I find the fly-by-night scenario irresistible.

What, in summary, was the legacy of the National Jazz Foundation? Bruce Raeburn has suggested that the NJF paved the way for the formation of the New Orleans Jazz Club. It would be truer to say that the NJF set land mines for any projazz organization that was unlucky enough to follow it. The NJF was conceived with enthusiasm, born into power, and nurtured through two years of glitzy success. It dropped out of sight, returned for a ghostly visit, and then disappeared entirely. Civic leaders and high-powered businessmen who lent their names and support to the project would not readily take another chance on jazz. If a successor was to appear, it would not be likely to start at the top.

THE NEW ORLEANS JAZZ CLUB:
A SABRE-TOOTHED GADFLY

Enter the New Orleans Jazz Club, established on Mardi Gras Day, 1948, at a gathering of true believers in traditional New Orleans and Dixieland jazz. Although the club had some early links to the Establishment that were cultivated sporadically over the years, its founders initially hoped to attract bona fide jazz fans rather than trot out dubious supporters from the business community.

As the original goals enumerated in the NOJC article (chapter 2) show, the specific intention was advocacy of local music and musicians. They hoped also that their bottom-up effort would "awaken the people of N.O. to the debt of gratitude they owe to N.O. Music"—a grandiose enough vision after the NJF's failed plans for local/national/international influence. The one goal that the NOJC held in common with the NJF was the establishment of a jazz museum, a dream that was not realized until thirteen years later.

The NOJC article celebrates many of the club's achievements between 1948 and 1970 while acknowledging that the price of its eventual success was a larger membership that brought less knowledge of, let alone passion for, New Orleans jazz. (The article differs slightly from the original as published in *New Orleans* magazine, in which a typesetting error placed the paragraphs in incorrect order, with strange effect.) I will focus here on two aspects of the NOJC's relationship with the Establishment—its ambivalence in alternately courting and cussing the press, even as it protected its own fragile status; and its approach to handling race relations within the organization and its publication, *The Second Line*.

Two of the club's gritty and tenacious workers—Dr. Edmond ("Doc") Souchon and his brother, attorney Harry Souchon—should be mentioned at the outset. They were among the NOJC's most prestigious members—each well-connected and each, in his own way, highly vocal. Doc's way was, putting it mildly, bumptious. A noted surgeon and a guitarist who had heard many of the earliest jazz artists in his youth, he collaborated with Al Rose on the indispensable *New Orleans Jazz: A Family Album.* Souchon spoke and wrote openly and often on his beliefs about jazz, its players, and the social and political climate in which jazz was embedded. He is quoted at length in the discussion below about attitudes toward race in the NOJC. My eulogy to Doc, written for *New Orleans* magazine after his death in 1968, is reprinted in chapter 4.

Harry Souchon's manner was gently charming, well suited to his effective behind-the-scenes work. I interviewed him in the *Down Beat* article on the jazz museum (chapter 5), which opened in November 1961. Not quite accidentally, I engaged Harry and museum director Clay Watson in a low-key tête-à-tête about whether the museum would accept artifacts from prominent New Orleans artists from the swing and modern jazz eras. I am sure that Harry recognized the trap. But typically, he responded with grace and commented only after the article was published that he was "a little embarrassed to be quoted so much."

Returning to the New Orleans Jazz Club's relationship with the local power structure, it is important to note that even as the NOJC alternately courted and cussed the local media, the group itself became a miniestablishment. The club received a limited and wavering respect that it monitored closely. The pages of the NOJC's periodical, the *Second Line*, abundantly reflect the club's tenuous outsider/insider status. For example, the second issue reported a March 1950 lecture on jazz by Doc Souchon at the hallowed Delgado Art Museum (now the New Orleans Museum of Art). In connection with a traveling art exhibit, Souchon had been invited to talk about parallels between jazz and modern art. The event was described hyperbolically as "epochal," but it did lead to annual joint NOJC/New Orleans Art Association meetings, with live music, that continued until the mid-1950s.

The next issue of *Second Line* expressed gratitude for jazz coverage in the New Orleans *Item,* the most flexible of the local dailies. But in 1952 the *Line* complained, accurately, "rarely does the dignified *Times-Picayune* use the word jazz." The March-April 1954 issue carried this lightly sarcastic comment:

> It might be amusing . . . to know that . . . *The Record Changer* was under the impression that *The Second Line* was paid for by the New Orleans Chamber of Commerce! Actually, so little attention has been given to local contemporary musicians by the trade publications that *The Second Line* was originated mainly for that reason.

Later that year the club boasted of positive "reviews"—for the most part, simple reportage with praiseful adjectives—of its concert in the three local dailies. In 1958 the club thanked reporter Bob Morris for his support of jazz in the *Item*.

Unlike the National Jazz Foundation, the NOJC's advocacy for jazz extended only to Dixieland and traditional New Orleans jazz. Swing was a nonentity, and be-bop an obscene mutant. A 1949 article by Peggy Mengis in the *Times-Picayune-States-Item* Sunday magazine trashed modern jazz while boosting the Parisian Room sessions on Royal Street that were initiated by the New Orleans Jazz Club. (The Mengis antibop article reflected the destructive national debate in the mid-1940s between the fig-purists and advocates of modern jazz, which is discussed in the overview to section II.)

Needless to say, the *Second Line* did not acknowledge, let alone celebrate, the national recognition accorded to Al Belletto's modern jazz sextet in 1954. The slick and swinging jazz/vocal group was recorded by Capitol on the *Stan Kenton Presents* series. The struggle that Belletto and other modernists waged to gain acceptance with the Establishment is integral to the story of the growth of modern jazz in New Orleans, described in section III. Within the New Orleans Jazz Club's defined range of Dixieland/traditional New Orleans styles, then, the NOJC received modest local publicity for its concerts and occasional reviews by sympathetic, if inexpert, writers in the New Orleans press.

The NOJC came close to nudging the Establishment toward a major endorsement of jazz in 1955. The city's central railroad station at the corner of Canal and Basin Streets—the gateway to old Storyville—was torn down, and NOJC president George Blanchin spoke at a civic ceremony dedicated to the "beautification" of Basin Street (i.e., razing historic Storyville structures), which had been going on for years. For example, Lulu White's Mahogany Hall (where the National Jazz Foundation once hoped to house a jazz museum) was flattened to make room for a parking garage for the Krauss Department Store in 1949. The neglect and ultimate destruction of other Storyville landmarks is chronicled in the pages of Al Rose's invaluable volume, *Storyville, New Orleans: Being an Authentic, Illustrated Account of the Notorious Red Light District.*

Blanchin wisely used the ceremony as a platform to urge construction of "several monuments to great musicians who'd played in this vicinity." The *Second Line* and local dailies reported Mayor Chep Morrison's statement that several statues of jazz greats would indeed be placed along the new "parkway."

The statue became a hot issue in the press. Protests, some tinged with racism, others merely reflections of bourgeois contempt for jazz, were published in subsequent weeks in letters to the editor. The outcome of the dispute is still visible on the corner of Canal and Basin—a statue of the Venezuelan liberator, Simón Bolívar. The motive for honoring Bolívar was transparently commercial. For years Morrison and business leaders had been cultivating relationships with Latin American countries in the interest of port traffic and other trade benefits.

The NOJC also stood in an ambiguous relationship to oppressive state segregation laws and racist attitudes among some of its members. The club's approach to advancing race relations was gradualism—a belief that small, incremental changes would result in peaceful integration without the polarizing confrontations that come with aggressive action. And in fact the club did urge the acceptance of white and black artists, both within the club and with civic leaders. Early on, the group conformed outwardly to state laws while providing under-the-table support for black artists—perhaps a necessary strategy in the early years, Raeburn argues.

In *I Remember Jazz*, Al Rose claims credit for the first integrated NOJC public performance at a meeting/jam session in 1954. Stating that he had "failed to notice" (!) the absence of blacks on the club's bandstand until NOJC-founder Don Perry called it to his attention after six years, Rose tells how he brought trumpeter Lee Collins to a session at the Roosevelt Hotel to play alongside the young George Girard. There were no criticisms, Rose says, and the precedent of integrated meetings was established and followed without incident thereafter.

But Bill Huntington remembers an earlier occasion, probably in 1953, when he bootlegged an integrated group into an NOJC meeting/jam session at the Roosevelt. Only sixteen years old at the time, he showed up with a traditional New Orleans jazz group composed of himself on banjo (he had long been studying with Bunk Johnson's banjoist, Lawrence Marrero) and black artists Percy Humphrey, trumpet; Emile Barnes, clarinet; and Cie Frazier, drums. Jack Delaney quickly joined them on trombone, as did Doc Souchon on guitar, and George Girard picked up the bass. Huntington recalls that a few people left, but his efforts were encouraged by regulars like Dick Allen and Nick Gagliano.

The NOJC has been stung by direct charges of racism over the years. The first black NOJC board member, Charlotte McCullom Boutney, was seated in 1972. One wonders if the club's leadership "failed to notice" this lack of black participation, similar to Rose's comment about the NOJC jam sessions. Raeburn states that the situation might well have resulted from lack of interest in jazz by blacks in New Orleans. To be sure, middle-class blacks were not prone to identify with jazz in those days. The story of the local revival that began in the late 1940s, told in section II, is a matter of white and black bands playing for almost exclusively white audiences, with young white musicians like Huntington, Pete Fountain, and Warren Luening as apprentices. Among black youth, rhythm and blues was rapidly becoming the popular music of choice. Even so, numerous black jazz musicians were available to serve as NOJC leaders. At the vary least, the late date of Boutney's appearance is a clear sign that nothing resembling affirmative action was going on.

A particularly harsh attack on the club by Berta Wood appeared in the May 1957 issue of *Ebony* magazine. Doc Souchon responded with typical pique in the in the autumn issue of the *Second Line*. He said that Miss Wood does not know that during our Festivals they [black artists] are always included; she has no idea of the innumerable jobs (spot and otherwise) they have obtained through the NOJC; of the great number of recording dates that have been thrown their way; of the efforts of *The Second Line* to call the general public's attention to these records and to the Negro musicians on the dates. Nor has she taken the trouble to look over the past files of our little magazine—and actually *count* the articles and pictures of Negro musicians. It would come as a surprise to her, I am sure, to find that the totals add up to almost 50-50 of the two races. For this particular effort in behalf of colored musicians, we are bitterly attacked by a large number of white musicians (and also a large number of NOJC members). So . . . here we are, between a cross-rough *[sic]* . . . Miss Wood, belittling our efforts, and local men condemning our "Crow Jim" attitude!

The points made by Souchon about the NOJC's journal and activities are accurate. It is also true, though, that to that date no black writer had been published in *The Second Line,* ostensibly, for lack of manuscript submissions. The "cross-rough" (ruff) referred to is quite credible; but a socially conscious leadership would have been programmatic in seeking manuscripts by black writers and meeting "Crow Jim" complaints more energetically and publicly.

Sad to say, it is not necessary to search deeply into Doc Souchon's prose or editorial policy for evidence of paternalism or insensitivity. Phrases like "thrown their way" are tossed about with curmudgeonly aplomb. And in the issue of *Second Line* after his impassioned response to Berta Wood, he thanked a reader profusely for sending in "De Fust Banjo," several stanzas of doggerel in ersatz plantation dialect, with lines like "she soun' like forty-leben bands a-playin' all togedder" and "for whar you finds dem ragtime guys, dar's de banjo an' de 'possum." As the article on Souchon in this volume testifies, with Doc it was always what-you-see-is-what-you-get, and you always got a bundle of things to set you on edge, along with fierce long-range dedication to good causes.

The NOJC was both well-intentioned and important. Indeed, chapter 3 focuses mainly on its numerous positive contributions. But with regard to social action, the club was at best a sabre-toothed gadfly during the postwar years. The NOJC made its presence known, sometimes vexingly, but it seldom demonstrated the strength to buck, intimidate, or lead the Establishment in matters of racial politics. It simply was not regarded as a power to be reckoned with. The club could not muster sufficient support for a statue dedicated to jazz in 1955. Worse, it did not have the strength to stop a local construction company from bulldozing the Armstrong birthplace in 1964 (described below). Pleading an ineffectual gradualism, it missed opportunities to integrate its all-too-insular cadre of leaders. Further, an imaginative, high-powered NOJC might have found support in the business community to turn the club's annual jazz concerts, held from 1949 to 1955, into an event of national importance, tourists and all, gaining experience that could have accelerated the development of the Jazz and Heritage Festival. Instead, the

NOJC concert series petered out, and its leaders played a slim role in conceptualization of the first Jazzfest program in 1968.

VICTORY THROUGH ENSHRINEMENT

The founding of the Jazz Archive in 1958 at Tulane University was a huge boost for jazz, a scholarly imprimatur not easily pooh-poohed by old-line culture vultures. While the players in this significant victory overlapped somewhat with NOJC leaders and members, a much broader context made the establishment of the archive possible.

It happened, after all, in the halls of Academe—at the Department of History at Tulane, the city's most esteemed institution of higher education. Not an accident. Research by the current jazz archive curator, Bruce Boyd Raeburn, makes the larger cultural and historical settings clear. Jazz was first taken seriously by rabid record collectors in the 1930s and 1940s. These purists searched for rare early jazz releases and were passionately interested in details of band personnel, musicians who knew and were influenced by each other, chronologies of recording sessions, and similar minutiae that are normally associated with meticulous scholarship. Clearly, the collectors were historians by inclination, if not by vocation.

Equally important, jazz had captured the imagination of young intellectuals. A roll call of jazz collectors and writers of the 1930s and 1940s shows that many who later became highly influential figures had credentials from major universities. As listed in *The New Grove Dictionary of Jazz* (edited by Barry Kernfeld), George Avakian, John Hammond, and Wilder Hobson were from Yale; Frederic Ramsey, Princeton; Ralph Gleason, Columbia; Rudi Blesh, Dartmouth; Marshall Stearns, Harvard. Their writings—jazz reportage, criticism, biography, discography, and history—and their work as promoters and agents had wide-ranging impact. Gleason, for example, was a founder of an early jazz periodical, *Jazz Information*, in 1939, and also of *Rolling Stone* in 1967. Hammond helped organize the Benny Goodman band in 1934 and brought Count Basie's band to national attention in 1936. Stearns, author of the seminal *Story of Jazz* in 1956, founded the Institute of Jazz Studies (a research and archival center now at Rutgers University) in 1952, six years before the establishment of the Tulane Jazz Archive.

The context for the establishment of a jazz archive in New Orleans, then, was a broad and deep subcultural movement in America and abroad. The nature of that movement made the Tulane University History Department an acceptable site for honoring jazz—albeit early jazz only—in New Orleans in 1958. Moreover, the selection of William (Bill) Russell—composer, author, historian, collector, violinist, and all-around maverick—as the first curator was absolutely brilliant. Russell's admirers had long ago elevated him to the status of cult figure (to his dismay), creating confusion about the New Orleans "revivals" that will be discussed in section II. But his unique background, commitment to early jazz, and personal warmth made him the perfect choice for the job.

The Jazz Museum opened in November of 1961, three years after the archive. Both had immense substantive and symbolic value. "Jazz Has Made It," a *Picayune* editorial declared when the museum opened in 1961. But the bitter counter-symbolism was also unavoidable. Say "archive," and non-academics think of a musty preserve, dewey-decimalled and isolated from the present. What is a museum, if not a repository of esteemed objects from the past? Jazz, the music of life, energy, invention, relevance, and surprise, was now in places of quiet study and reverential observation.

In short, acceptance at the level of artifact did not equate with acceptance of jazz as living art. I rarely find myself agreeing with Al Rose and Tom Bethell, but Rose was right on the mark when he wrote in the 1984 edition of *New Orleans Jazz: A Family Album* that the earliest forms of jazz had moved from the bandstand to accept an "institutionalized role in our libraries and museums . . . the province of scholars and researchers rather than the live object of enthusiasm of a variety of audiences." Tom Bethell, George Lewis's biographer, commented similarly about "musical museums," complaining that "such recognition was often self-congratulatory, and the opinion was expressed that enlightenment had finally won out. Now that it was dying out, New Orleans jazz was admitted to the cultural centers."

The acceptance of jazz in higher education settings looks quite different, in fact, when we move from historical enshrinement to active advocacy of performance. Jazz could be safely regarded as fair game for historical scholarship, but the postwar academic community had little intention of formally encouraging students to play the music. And in fact, few college students cared about playing traditional New Orleans or Dixieland jazz. Dance bands that played well-worn swing fare were the glamour ticket after World War II; and the more serious and adventurous young musicians were typically experimenting with modern jazz.

The article below on the tumultuous evolution of jazz performance at Loyola University after World War II (chapter 7) illustrates the resistance of most local educators to the students' desire to cultivate their abilities as jazz artists. (The title of the Loyola piece differs from that of the originally published version, which was misnamed "The Stage Band Movement in New Orleans." As I recall, the manuscript read ". . . at Loyola" but a change was made before publication.)

The struggle for acceptance of jazz as a performing art in institutions of higher education in postwar New Orleans is closely linked to the larger story of the growth of modern jazz. As will be seen in section III, situations somewhat parallel to Loyola's existed at Dillard, Xavier, and other universities in the area. Students who played the new music were more like canny cell leaders and guerrilla fighters than romantic, in-your-face rebels. They won a few quiet victories in their time, but they often set the scene for future generations of students. Equally important, they went on to work as jazz-oriented teachers in the public schools and *agents provocateurs* in the community. As with the press and other institutions, though, the changes in education in New Orleans came only after the national climate was teeming with testimony that jazz was, in its own way, culturally swanky.

THE STRANGE CASE OF
THE JAZZ AND HERITAGE FESTIVAL

The quirky events that led up to the now-famous annual Jazz and Heritage Festival have never to my knowledge been traced systematically, so I will give considerable attention here to key social and political contexts, fleshing the picture out further in the reviews and commentaries in chapters 8–10.

Unfortunately, a tenacious mythology has grown to the effect that the city's first large-scale jazz festival was the excellent 1970 New Orleans Jazz and Heritage Festival that involved George Wein, Quint Davis, Allison Miner, and others. Putting aside for the moment two aborted attempts much earlier in the decade and a sad, ragtag nonfestival staged by a local eccentric, the 1970 designation ignores the seminal jazz festivals of 1968 and 1969.

Jazzfest '68 and the 1969 New Orleans Jazz and Food Festival represented a major breakthrough in support from the local Establishment. The local business community, finally awakened by the worldwide fame achieved by the Dukes of Dixieland, Pete Fountain, Al Hirt, and Preservation Hall, engaged in 1968 in a genuine risk-taking venture. The concrete and ambitious venture went beyond symbolic affirmations such as the politically safe, belated, and inexpensive homage to Louis Armstrong in 1965, discussed below.

The 1970 date of origin is cited routinely in the local press, working no doubt from releases submitted by the current festival administration. In the winter 1999 issue of *Tulanian* (the university's alumni magazine), Nick Marinello touts the party line, Jazzfest in the Year of Our Lord 1970, all the way. In Michael P. Smith's *New Orleans Jazz Fest—A Pictorial History*, Davis (who was my drum student for a brief time in the early 1960s) acknowledges vaguely that "another organization, headed up by Durel Black, . . . put on several festivals in the late 60s" but claims it was Wein's unique vision to produce a wide-ranging, multi-area event—which precisely describes the programs of 1968 and 1969.

Smith's spare text (the book is essentially an attractive coffee table volume with striking photographs) brazenly calls the 1970 festival the first and snips off memory of the previous foundational work with statements like "the first [1970] Jazz Fest is generally remembered by those who attended as one of the greatest events in the history of the city . . . word spread rapidly." Jason Berry, et al., also cite the 1970 event as the launching of the festival. Lichtenstein and Danker refer to "various concerts" in the 1960s but note that the 1970 effort was a "multidimensional festival at Congo Square." For reasons that will be made clear, the 1970 festival was actually a scaled-down version of the previous events. The program grew smaller before it went through the changes that made it the mammoth success of recent years.

If administrative continuity (i.e., the work of the Wein/Davis/Miner collaboration and the New Orleans Jazz and Heritage Foundation) were the only criterion for tracing the origins of the festival, then the 1970 event might be called the first. But by any other reasonable standard, the 1970 festival was a direct and immediate descendant of Jazzfest '68 and the 1969 New Orleans Jazz and Food Festival. The concept of an expansive cultural festival in the historical home of jazz, the model of multiple indoor and outdoor events, and the publicity momentum of the two previous festivals were key to the 1970 Jazzfest. In many respects the 1970 festival would have started from Square One rather than from Congo Square without the experience of the two preceding years. Indeed, in April 1970 the Vieux Carre *Courier* called it "the 1970 edition" of the festival and reviewed it in May as "Jazz Fest."

At best, a lack of graciousness and a poor sense of history underlie the claims of origination in 1970. The printed programs for the 1968 and 1969 festivals and the contemporaneous descriptions and reviews in chapters 8 and 10 of this volume demonstrate the range and scale of those programs. They were week-long, multisite, ethnically diverse events that featured dozens of major and lesser-known jazz figures—local, national, and international—at the Municipal Auditorium. Numerous other presentations included open-air concerts in the French Quarter, parades with various marching bands, a concert on the Steamer *President*, a youth concert, a jazz Mass, food festival, folklore lecture, and blues, gospel, and Cajun groups.

I will return to the story of that seminal event, Jazzfest '68, but it is important to note that earlier attempts at large-scale jazz festivals were made in the 1960s. Their failure to get off the ground was bound up with larger sociopolitical issues such as Jim Crow laws and racial discrimination.

George Wein's first link with a potential festival, accurately noted by Lichtenstein and Danker, was in 1962. In a 1998 telephone interview Wein generously clarified several points, one being that he was approached in 1962 about developing a large-scale event but felt that the Louisiana segregation laws would make it impossible to mount a program in New Orleans.

This nibble was followed by a near catch in 1965. Thanks to the 1964 Civil Rights Act, a jazz festival was possible. In a February 11, 1965, *Down Beat* news story titled "Congressional Act Helps Launch a Southern Festival," I reported plans for a May 27–30 program, with George Wein as producer. City Park Stadium was to be the site of three afternoon and four night concerts, with tentative plans for events such as parades, workshops, and lectures.

Olaf Lambert, general manager of the plush Royal Orleans Hotel, was the festival president. Other leaders included Mayor Victor Schiro, Dr. Alvin Ochsner, Harry Souchon of the New Orleans Jazz Club, Roosevelt Hotel manager Seymour Weiss, architect Arthur Q. Davis (Quint's father), Louis Read of WDSU-TV, and tourist commission head Harry England. Talent advisers included Edmond (Doc) Souchon, Dick Allen of the Tulane Jazz Archive, writer Thomas Sancton Sr., Pete Fountain, Al Hirt, and George Lewis, Lewis being the sole black member of the leadership group.

Disaster struck almost immediately. I reported it with chagrin in the February 25 issue of *DB* in a story headed "New Orleans Jazz Festival 'Postponed' — Till Further Notice."

The first major jazz festival in the South (DB, Feb. 11) had been "postponed," a spokesman for the event announced. To have been held in New Orleans in May, it would have been the first integrated festival in the southern states.

(According to a spokesman for George Wein, who was to produce the festival, there was no postponement, only a cancellation.)

Among the official reasons given by the New Orleans spokesman for postponing the festival till next year or 1967 was that the additional time would allow for better planning.

Unofficially, there was speculation that last month's walkout of 21 Negro football players scheduled to participate in the American Football League's All-Star game was the major contributing cause. The players refused to play in New Orleans because they were allegedly discriminated against in the city. The game was later played in Houston, Texas.

There was no doubt locally that the "speculation" was accurate. Whereas discriminatory laws had prevented a jazz festival in 1962, discriminatory behavior was a stopper in 1965. With the onus and odor of the failed All-Star game still in the air, local leaders decided that following through with plans for the festival would highlight the negative image of the city. "Postponed" was a euphemism, since none could guess when the atmosphere would be cleared of the scent of racism.

Enter Dean Andrews, a cigar-chomping attorney who claimed to be taking up the festival idea dropped by the elite leadership group. Compared to Andrews, Louis Prima had the demeanor of a Trappist. Andrews spoke loudly and in superlatives with a great New Orleans dialect, exuding overconfidence while inspiring no confidence whatever. He later played a mysterious role as an insider-informant in New Orleans district attorney Jim Garrison's investigation of the assassination of President Kennedy. John Candy portrayed Andrews as a compulsive braggart in Oliver Stone's film *JFK*. I can honestly say that Candy's wacky performance was, if anything, underplayed.

In any case, it was not my job to marvel at Andrews's colorful audacity but to report an immanent festival. In the July 1, 1965, *DB* "Ad Lib" column I wrote,

A jazz festival in miniature will be presented at Luthjen's Lounge June 27–30 by a new group called the International Jazz Festival of New Orleans, Inc. According to attorney **Dean Andrews,** the president of the group, this year's presentation will be open only to sponsors and the press, while plans for next year include a mammoth international festival at Municipal Auditorium. This year's festival will include mostly local artists.

Plans had changed by the August 12 issue. I dropped in on the concert and sent an unenthusiastic report that was in the "Potpourri" section that preceded the city-based segments of *DB*'s "Ad Lib" feature.

The first New Orleans International Jazz Festival, held late last month and originally set up as a "pilot" festival for sponsors and the press at a small Crescent City club, was moved to the Roosevelt Hotel's Grand Ballroom because of requests from the general public for tickets. The festival's scope was still limited, however, since the bands included were almost all local. And a youthful rock-and-roll band billed as modern jazz raised eyebrows from the press and tepid response from the audience. . . . Next year's program will be a larger event at the Municipal Auditorium, according to festival manager **Dean Andrews.**

I never heard from Andrews again but followed the local media coverage of his self-proclaimed knowledge about the Kennedy assassination. Coincidentally, Nick Tadin, who was the Musicians Union's "business representative" (a euphemism in those days for the troubleshooter who, among other duties, looked for union musicians playing nonunion gigs), was also linked to the JFK investigation. He claimed to witness a meeting of defendant Clay Shaw and the shadowy, if not weird, David Ferry. Tadin was the opposite of Andrews in that he was utterly guileless, a man with no interest in self-promotion. I trusted his straightforwardness. At first I had liked District Attorney Jim Garrison, who frequently went dancing with his wife at the Golliwog on Canal Street, where I was playing weekends for most of the 1960s. But I lost patience as Garrison became increasingly obsessed with finding patterns of conspiracy in the flung confetti of evidence in the case.

The jazz festival idea was revived by New Orleans leaders in earnest in 1967—a wonderful choice, since the program could be planned for 1968 as part of the city's 250th anniversary celebration.

A group of business leaders led by Durel Black of the International Trade Mart was spearheading the movement. Al Belletto recalls that he and WDSU-TV journalist Doug Ramsey, a first-rate writer and jazzophile, were among those called in as advisers at an early meeting. They found that the powerhouse business leaders had slim knowledge either of jazz or the nature of large-scale music festivals. It was the efforts of Belletto, Ramsey, Danny Barker, Tex Stephens, and a few others that identified a credible range of national and local attractions and later brought in the noted Willis Conover as emcee.

In the August 24 *DB* "Ad Libs" column, Rene Coman reported that a festival was in the planning stages. Coman, a fellow public school teacher and tenor saxist who led the group at the Golliwog, had been subbing as *DB* correspondent during my 1966–1967 sabbatical year for graduate study at the University of Illinois. I returned to New Orleans in the summer of 1967 and got great cooperation on advance publicity from Jim Autry, editor of the then-new *New Orleans* magazine, and Dan Morgenstern, recently appointed to replace Don DeMichael as *DB* editor.

The festival was the lead news story in the November 30, 1997, issue of *Down Beat*. Morgenstern used my six-paragraph description of the range of events, program sites, and anticipated local and national artists. In months that followed, items about the festival appeared sporadically in "Ad Libs" and "Potpourri" entries, and the April 18 issue carried another news story. The 1968 festival was the cover story in the May 2 issue. Pete Fountain was on the cover, and a three-page layout of fine black-and-white shots by local photographer Jim Whitmore was accompanied by my brief text called "New Orleans: A Do-It-Yourself Jazz Festival." The festival was touted, along with the claim that one could fashion a jazz festival at any time by making the rounds of local clubs. The shots included Al Belletto at the Playboy, Ronnie Kole at Kole's Corner, Pete Fountain at his club, Papa French at Dixieland Hall, and others.

The local dailies treated the festival as a bright commercial event, mainly providing information from press releases. During the late 1960s, *New Orleans* magazine and the feisty weekly Vieux Carre *Courier* were looking to bring some life into the journalistic flatland. *New Orleans* had embraced jazz coverage the year before by publishing my piece on modern jazz in August 1967 (chapter 23). A January 1968 article, which I unfortunately titled "A Festival for a Funeral?" (chapter 19), was intended as a rumination on whether early jazz styles would be carried on by younger players. It was mistakenly interpreted by a Carolyn Kolb of the New Orleans Jazz Club as a put-down of early jazz and a criticism of the festival, which I had been busily promoting all along. I tried to smooth things out in a letter to Kolb, with copies to Harry Souchon and Gilbert Erskine, and I wrote a booster article on local happenings called "The New Orleans Scene Today" for the Jazzfest '68 printed program (appendix 1).

I hasten to add that my involvement with festival planning was minimal. For reasons of reportage and personal interest, though, I was in frequent contact with general chairman Durel Black, who was a leader in the business community and the New Orleans Jazz Club, and with Willis Conover. I admired Black's let's-get-it-done attitude, probably essential to the success of such a huge undertaking, but his affection for jazz seemed lost in the shuffle of administrative demands. It was hard to imagine him sitting with his ear to a Victrola or guffawing at a well-turned lick at a jam session. Even so, the city had an abundance of jazz fans and too few sleeves-up administrators, so I valued his work immensely.

Willis Conover (now deceased) was internationally known as the expert spokesman for jazz on Voice of America, the radio service that penetrated the Iron Curtain. I remembered him also as director of THE Orchestra, a fine big band in Washington, D.C. He appeared relaxed and unassuming throughout the turbulent 1968 and 1969 preparations, always putting the musicians up front. Although he emceed the major concerts both years—being hired too late in the 1968 to help significantly in shaping the events—the printed program in 1968 did not mention him, and in 1979 his picture appeared on the last page, with the caption "Musical Director" and no further biographical information.

Conover's desire to keep a shadowy profile might or might not be explained by the sad politics behind his initial hiring, which I learned about only recently. I confirmed in a conversation with George Wein that he had been contacted originally by local business leaders to serve as talent director. Researcher Monifa Johnson reports that the minutes of the jazz festival planners' meeting state that Wein was not hired because they could not come to terms in a contract. But according to Wein, the situation behind the scenes had an ugly twist. When Mayor Victor Schiro learned that Wein was married to a black woman, plans to employ him were scrapped and Conover was brought in later as luminary-emcee. If Conover was aware of this lamentable situation, his reluctance to be highlighted would be understandable.

Actually, Mayor Schiro's reputation was less as a racist than a frightened opportunist. During the gutsy, fifteen-year administration of de Lesseps ("Chep") Morrison, Schiro was known mainly as a dependable gofer, showing up with smiles and clichés at ribbon cuttings and cornerstone-laying ceremonies. He came to power during a leadership gap after Morrison took major hits from racist leaders in Louisiana during the 1960–1961 school integration crisis. Morrison's national stock had risen, though, so he resigned to accept the post of U.S. ambassador to the Organization of American States. The city council appointed Schiro to succeed him. Suddenly, the cheerful hack was mayor of New Orleans. Playing it safe remained Schiro's strongest suit. It is likely that if he had thought that miscegenation would play well when Jazzfest was being planned, he would have flaunted it and welcomed Wein.

Wein did not need the Jazzfest role on his vita, of course, and he expressed no bitterness in discussing the 1967 events. He even dismissed an apocryphal story that had been circulating in New Orleans to the effect that he had backed out after his wife was refused admission to a planning meeting at the high-toned Boston Club. As the local story goes, the rejection was based solely on the fact that the Boston Club was exclusively male, and the Weins interpreted it as a racial issue, resulting in his resignation. Wein insists that no such intrigue occurred and that his wife was at no time shown disrespect in New Orleans. It was Schiro who made the call about his participation, based on the Mayor's dubious notions of political prudence.

A more visible but less consequential obstacle was created in early 1968 by Al Rose. I reported in the March 21 "Ad Libs" that Rose "has been waging a one-man war on the festival. Rose, a jazz purist who maintains that the modernists on the program are not jazz musicians, tried unsuccessfully to elect several anti-festival candidates to the board of directors of the New Orleans Jazz Club last month." Rose went too far in his campaign for purism when he personally insulted Al Belletto, then the city's best-known modern jazz artist and musical director of the local Playboy Club. Belletto tells of Rose's statement to the effect that the only way Belletto could get close to jazz would be by buying a ticket to a concert. Belletto's lawyers from Playboy served papers on Rose, who subsequently made a public apology.

Like the National Jazz Foundation of 1945–1947, then, the Jazzfest '68 planners were open to many kinds of jazz. Unlike the NJF, the festival leaders were not in the position of a small confederation of visionaries trying to convince everyone that jazz was a "potential gold mine." By 1968 everyone smelled the money. Even Rose must have known that a many-faceted jazz festival would get the kind of sustained international attention that the NOJC's long series of concerts by traditional and Dixieland artists did not command. And surely, the NOJC would not, indeed could not, stop a festival that had the backing of the business community and most local musicians of every jazz style.

The final lineup for Jazzfest '68 was wonderfully varied. The Municipal Auditorium concerts included high-powered imports such as Cannonball Adderley, Dave Brubeck, Gary Burton, Ray Bryant, Duke Ellington, Woody Herman, Gerry Mulligan, Ramsey Lewis, and Carmen McRae. Among the local bands at the same concerts were Danny Barker, Al Belletto, Louis Cottrell, Papa French, Armand Hug, Ronnie Kole, Thomas Jefferson, Santo Pecora, and Willie Tee (Turbinton). As the July 11 *DB* review shows (chapter 8), numerous local and out-of-town groups performed at other events during the festival week. Surely the locals received a fraction of the fees that went to big names like Ellington and Mulligan, but I heard no echoes of Rose's complaints. Everyone knew that the festival was a quantum leap for jazz events in New Orleans. If it could be sustained, huge benefits would accrue to musicians, club owners, hotels, other businesses, and the city coffers.

To give Rose his due, it must be admitted that as years went by, the New Orleans Jazz and Heritage Festival went from emphasis on jazz to emphasis on New Orleans' excellent blues, funk, and rock 'n' roll artists. In the 1990s the program unraveled conceptually to the extent of including music by Trout Fishing in America, Joan Baez, Jimmy Buffett, the Allman Brothers, a pipe and drum troupe with Scottish dancers, and other, er, remote offshoots of New Orleans music traditions.

The first Jazzfest was a success, despite the early organizational hassles and some logistical snafus that were an embarrassment at the major concerts. The 1969 event was retitled the New Orleans Jazz and Food Festival—although most people simply called it Jazzfest. Once again, the events ran for a week at several sites. Durel Black oversaw the operation and Willis Conover was hired early this time to serve not only as emcee but as musical director. The board of directors list in the 1969 printed program showed familiar names like Scoop Kennedy, Al Belletto, and Doug Ramsey. A host of business and media figures appeared again among the twenty-five directors. Two black musicians, Danny Barker and Louis Cottrell, were listed as directors, and journalist/promoter Tex Stephens was also very active. There were no black members on the more powerful groups, namely, the officers and the executive committee.

The lack of significant black participation and leadership was a point of increasing tension during the Wein/Davis/Miner years, culminating in a near revolt in the mid-1970s. Michael Smith reports that a boycott was threatened by the African-American coalition that was formed to deal with the problem. The group called for more black staff, board members, and vendors. Smith notes that George Wein was immediately sympathetic and responded rapidly, averting a crisis.

Returning to the 1969 program, the festival repeated many features of Jazzfest '68: the star-studded Municipal Auditorium concerts, the steamer *President* concert, outdoor events, inclusion of Gospel singers and international bands. But thanks to Conover's earlier and more active input, it was far better planned. Among other things, the program achieved some continuity through the recurring appearance of the all-star Festival House Band led by trumpeter Clark Terry. A Sunday afternoon concert focused on religious roots of jazz. Saturday night was an all–New Orleans concert. In a preview article for *New Orleans* in April (chapter 9 in this volume), I stressed the coherence of Conover's program conception and used the introductory paragraphs to discuss some of the culture wars that had to be won before the initiation of the festival the previous year.

The *Down Beat* connection in 1969 repeated the previous year's publicity but included a new, major coup. I once again sent in numerous advance items, and Dan Morgenstern again made the festival the cover story for a key issue (June 12). Additionally, though, Conover wrote a short article for the issue and I did an angry "Jazz and the New Orleans Press" article (chapter 2 in this volume). Morgenstern wrote a brief, absolutely beautiful editorial called "The Meaning of New Orleans." Best of all, Morgenstern arranged to have the entire issue bound into the printed program for the festival.

When I wrote the article about the tragicomic ineptness of the local press, I did not know it would be put in the face of the perpetrators and seen by the local jazz-loving audience that attended the festival. I was ecstatic when I heard about Morgenstern's coup. The same was true of Conover, who declined to do a booster piece for the festival but wrote a personal statement, a fine blending of equanimity and rage called "New Orleans, New Orleans Jazz, the New Orleans Jazz Festival, and Me."

Conover's piece must have seemed very strange indeed to *Down Beat* readers accustomed to seeing routine previews of festival events. The theme of his essay was hypocrisy. Conover began by citing general examples of hypocritical types, apparently drawn from his wide-ranging career ("radio and television executives with their public interest plaques on the wall—and their cold directives to the sales department"). Then he brought things chillingly close to home.

People who couldn't tap a foot to Basie, parroting "Jazz is America's only art form" out of one side of their mouth and saying "nigger" out of the other.

People who say they're in it "only for the love of those people who have been exploited for years" but don't mind making a few bucks out of it too. . . .

How does this apply to New Orleans?

I don't know.

I know how to find out, though: Watch and see who gets angry. Hypocrites are everywhere, including New Orleans. The straight people of New Orleans will get a warm smile from what I've written here, even if they don't show it. The hypocrites will tremble, turn pale, and grind their teeth.

Among the straight people working for the good of New Orleans jazz . . . are these cosmopolitans: Chuck Suhor, Mike Carubba, Doug Ramsey, Joe Gemelli, Danny Barker, Ronnie Kole, Jim Nassikas, Louis Cottrell, Dave Winstein, Al Belletto, Father Jarreau, Joe Simon, Bill Manschot, Dan Mikalak, DeAlton Neher, Mel Leavitt, Steve Loyacano, Joe Mares, George Sanchez, and others too numerous to name.

I was glad to be on Conover's list and to see that the final phrase gave unnamed participants a chance to count themselves among the "others too numerous to name." But Conover's strategy made it obvious to close readers of his text—a small set, admittedly—that omission of the most highly visible leader, Durel Black, was intentional. Unfortunately, the strategy also cast suspicion on high-level leaders who might have been omitted because they did not participate much or because their Jazzfest positions were titular to begin with. For example, executive committee member Scoop Kennedy was known as a true-blue jazz booster whose work dated back to the 1944 National Jazz Foundation. In my limited contact with Black and others during the planning, I was insulated from direct revelations of racism or cupidity, and I had neither the time nor the inclination to ask Conover for an account of who were the objects of his conscious omissions.

Morgenstern flew to New Orleans to cover the main 1969 Jazzfest events for *Down Beat*. I did a critical review in two parts for the Vieux Carre *Courier* (chapter 10 in this volume). The program was undoubtedly an artistic success. Doug Ramsey recalls that the big-name musicians who played on the program called it one of the best jazz festivals ever held, a testimony to the hip and reflective planning.

But the financial picture was bleak. Researcher Monifa Johnson reports that the second festival ended up some $20,000 in the red, and the sponsoring group declared bankruptcy. Subsequently, George Wein called Dick Allen of the Tulane Jazz Archive (where Allison Minor was working) to inquire about the festival, and Wein worked with Durel Black—who was an administrative link with the two initial festivals—to keep the festival alive. Miner was dating eighteen-year-old Quint Davis, who says that his father helped underwrite the 1970 festival. Quint Davis's special interest was local rhythm and blues artists, and he was instrumental in putting together an R&B segment of the program that would become increasingly dominant.

A new corporate entity, the New Orleans Jazz and Heritage Festival, launched the 1970 event. The group made use of many board of directors members and advisers from the previous year, but neither Belletto nor Ramsey played strong roles in planning. Ramsey recalls that he met with Wein early on but backed off when it became clear that the local Establishment, understandably concerned about the financial nosedive in 1969, wanted a moneymaking "commercial party." Judy Kolb of the Vieux Carre *Courier* quoted Wein as saying that the added features were aimed at attracting not jazz fans but a tourist audience.

Ironically, the result was another financially unsuccessful program, far less commercial than in previous years insofar as it lacked a roster of expensive national stars. The emphasis was decidedly local, with the main exception of Duke Ellington, who had been one of numerous name bands in 1968. The Ellington band played a sacred music concert on Sunday and played for a sparse Saturday night crowded on a bill with Germaine Bazzle, Al Belletto, Al Hirt, the Onward Brass Band, and James Rivers. Saturday afternoon programs called "Roots of Soul" and "Soul Now" featured Gospel singers, the Meters, Oliver and the Rockettes, and the Joe Fox Trio.

Only the Wednesday jazz cruise on the Steamer *President* and afternoon open-air events were well attended, according to Bill Bryan's May 1 *Courier* wrap-up report. Over all, the performers were fine local and state artists who played many musics: Cajun, brass band, Gospel, blues and soul and R&B, ragtime, and traditional, Dixieland, and modern jazz. Music stages, food booths, folklore exhibits, and art were arrayed in Congo Square; but these were not new to Orleanians, and the tourists did not turn out as had been hoped.

In retrospect, the 1970 program was far "purer" than the previous two. Even though many of the same local artists and styles had been heard in 1968 and 1969, in the first two years the musicians played shorter sets and were juxtaposed with the big names. Lacking a cluttered marquee of stars, the profile of the 1970 festival as a cultural celebration was clearer, albeit lacking in drawing power. It is beyond the scope of this book to explore the further evolution of the Jazz and Heritage Festival (which is still called "Jazzfest" in common parlance and in the local press) into the highly lucrative, everything-plus-the-kitchen-sink lineups of recent years. The goal here has been to place the development of the festival in the context of the postwar years, when social and political barriers gradually fell, making a major festival in New Orleans possible.

HONORING LOUIS ARMSTRONG

Section 1 concludes with the Louis Armstrong Memorial Ceremony story from *Down Beat's Music '72* (chapter 11). The piece more or less wrote itself in my consciousness as the memorial program unfolded. I had resigned from my *DB* role as New Orleans correspondent and went to the ceremony with no intention of writing about it. But the events seemed to illustrate, both sadly and hilariously, how slim an understanding the civic-minded planners had of a New Orleans audience, and how incapable they were of extemporizing when things did not appear to be going their way. Although the idea of a ceremony was in itself an appropriate official gesture of respect for Louis, the Establishment instinctively grasped for and tenaciously stuck with a properly imaged event and could not move with the spirit of the thing.

The fact that Armstrong has deservedly become a major cultural icon disguises the fact that throughout his career he was regarded with ambivalence by numerous Establishments, from jazz critics to the black middle class and militants to civic and government leaders. This issue comes to play in the text below, which focuses on two aspects of Armstrong and the postwar years in New Orleans. First, two of his visits to the city—in 1949 and 1965—received considerable attention. Second, a not quite parallel world of Armstrong lore evolved as a result of local, and later national, attempts to memorialize and honor him in New Orleans.

In 1949 Armstrong came to town to fulfill a lifelong dream of reigning as the King of Zulu at the Mardi Gras. The parade had begun in 1907 as a spoof of Rex by the Zulu Social Aid and Pleasure Club, a black fraternal organization. Major national coverage in 1949 included Armstrong's picture on the cover of the February 21 issue of *Time*. Mayor Chep Morrison gave him the key to the city. The down side of the celebration, Marc Miller notes, was long-standing criticism of the pseudo-savage, minstrel-like image that the parade projected. Armstrong, like Zulu kings before him, threw coconuts to the crowd and wore a straw skirt and exaggerated blackface makeup.

Concern about the image projected by Armstrong was deep-rooted. He had often been called an Uncle Tom because of his on-stage gesticulations and his willingness to play the darky on film and in cartoon voices. As will be seen, the personae he assumed would even be a part of the controversy over his statue a quarter of a century later. Armstrong's mannerisms have since been reconsidered more thoughtfully as survival techniques, showmanship, and satirical "signifyin' ." But they were anathema to the struggling black middle class of the 1940s and 1950s, militants of the 1960s, white liberals, and jazz fans who just wanted more music and fewer shenanigans.

In contrast, Armstrong's 1965 appearance in New Orleans was virtually unnoticed outside the city. But it was a crucial checkpoint in the evolution of the local Establishment's jazz consciousness. Armstrong had often been quoted as saying that he would not return to New Orleans because of segregation laws. Indeed, Miller describes a scene of cruel irony during Armstrong's 1931 three-month visit to the city for an engagement at the Suburban Garden.

> Armstrong enjoyed a hero's welcome in the black community with a parade, honorary banquet, and special "Armstrong" souvenir cigar. Still the city's Jim Crow laws prevented blacks from attending his performance. On opening night,

as 5,000 whites crowded into Suburban Garden, 10,000 blacks sat on the levee hoping to catch the music through the open windows.

But in 1965 those laws were gone. Numerous gains for jazz described above and noted on timeline chart 1 had awakened local leaders. Armstrong was brought to town by the New Orleans Jazz Club to play a benefit concert for the Jazz Museum—his first visit since an unheralded one-nighter at the Municipal Auditorium in 1952—and the big question was, Is the Establishment really awake or just stumbling toward the coffee pot?

I was happily stunned when virtually all of officialdom turned out. In a *Down Beat* news story of December 16, 1965, titled "New Orleans Hails Conquering Hero Pops," I reported that New Orleans "went all out to welcome Louis Armstrong back to his home town." He was greeted at the airport by the Onward Brass Band and his old friend and former sideman, drummer Paul Barbarin. He received the key to the city, and Mayor Victor Schiro declared October 31 Louis Armstrong Day. The Louisiana Tourist Development Commission presented Armstrong with a plaque of appreciation from Governor John McKeithen, and a delegation of business leaders presented a special memento. The Zulu Carnival Club was on hand with an award, as was the International House of New Orleans. Armstrong was also cited by Dillard, Loyola, and Xavier Universities for his contributions to music.

Yes, the visit was a triumph. But once again, a broader perspective reveals the pathetic tardiness of many of the 1965 tributes in New Orleans. The 1931 honors were overwhelmingly from the black community. The international celebration of Louis's return in 1949 seemed to catch the leadership by surprise. (He had come to town the year before for a cancer-fund benefit concert at Municipal Auditorium without fanfare.) Since the mid-1950s, Armstrong had become a living legend, touring the world for the U.S. State Department as "Ambassador Satch." It is not cynical to say that some of the praiseful words lavished on Armstrong in 1965 were tinged with hypocritical self-interest, revealing more about the recently converted representatives of social institutions than about the genius of Louis, who had endured much at their hands over the years.

The New Orleans Jazz Club was, of course, among those who had long revered Louis Armstrong, and they deserve credit for orchestrating the 1965 return and for other efforts at honoring him. For example, in 1962 a valued NOJC acquisition at the Jazz Museum was the cornet that Armstrong played on at the Waifs' Home in 1914. *Down Beat,* ever receptive to copy about the city, ran my news story on the event and a photo of Manuella Jones, widow of Waifs' Home superintendent Captain Joseph Jones, presenting the horn to Harry Souchon.

Two years later Harry Souchon and other NOJC leaders tried gamely but failed to save Armstrong's birthplace from destruction. The two-bedroom cottage on Jane Alley was in an area scheduled for razing in order to build a new police complex. I reported the Kafkaesque situation in a story headed "Armstrong's Birthplace Center of Confusion" in the July 16, 1964, *DB.*

An Associated Press news story erroneously reported that the club had already purchased the house. The owner denied the story, and an avalanche of rumors followed concerning to whom, if anyone, the house would be sold, given, or loaned. A reliable source reports that a wealthy Negro leader is trying to acquire the house and set it up as a tribute to Armstrong as a major Negro artist. There are also rumblings to the effect that protests are imminent from anti-Negro politicians in neighboring parishes (counties) who look askance at preserving the Armstrong house as an artistic shrine. Another rumor is that the cottage might be sold to an interest that would exploit it commercially rather than set it up as a museum piece.

Confusion gave way to chaos, and possibly subterfuge, in the days that followed. My July 30, 1964, story was sadly headed "Deadline Passes: Armstrong Birthplace Torn Down." Who dropped the ball? This too was wholly unclear.

Attempts to shift the blame for the loss of the house were rampant, but the essential reason seems to lie in the fact that several interests were wooing the Bal Construction Co. for the house, while the city fathers and Mike Battalmente, owner of the Company, were interested mainly in clearing the lot.

The New Orleans Jazz Club, working on a tip that the house would be destroyed unless some group offered to move it, confronted the Bal company. . . . Then the company's lawyer began consulting with World's Fair officials about the possibility of having the house sent to the Louisiana pavilion, where Armstrong's band might make an appearance—after which the house would be given to the jazz club. . . .

When it became evident days later that Louisiana would withdraw its pavilion altogether from the fair, the way should have been clear for the Jazz Club to acquire the house.

Several sources report that complications introduced by a representative of the city hindered the club from proceeding at that time. However, according to an official statement released by Helen Arlt, the club's president, the club was not informed of the availability of the house, and its persistent efforts at obtaining final permission to move the house "were thwarted . . . by the construction company and its attorney."

Armstrong was back in New Orleans in 1968 for the first Jazzfest. In the cluttered, star-laden, week-long festival, neither the Armstrong tributes nor the band's performance was remarkable. I reported in *DB*'s July 11 "Ad Libs" column that Armstrong received awards from the Zulu Club and Governor McKeithen—at a party given in honor of pianist Armand Hug. My Jazzfest review (chapter 8) notes that the Armstrong band played a short set that was a rerun of the songs and routines they had been doing for years.

In 1970 another Armstrong controversy arose, this time over the movement to erect a statue in New Orleans. As described above, the New Orleans Jazz Club had argued in 1955 for placement of statues of jazz greats at the corner of Basin and Canal streets. The idea would not sell before its time, being protested by citizens who still thought of jazz and Storyville as disgraceful. Surprisingly, the protest in 1970 came not from local conservatives but from a respected British jazz critic, Valerie Wilmer.

In the January 8, 1970, issue of *Down Beat*, the news story headed "Satchmo Statue Fund-Raising Drive Is On" announced that veteran saxophonist Benny Carter and Floyd Levin, a longtime California jazz fan, had begun a Louis Armstrong statue fund. They got the idea from a remark by New Orleans guitarist Danny Barker during a sight-seeing tour connected with the 1969 Jazzfest.

Editor Dan Morgenstern must have gotten that information from a California source, since I am sure I did not know about the Carter effort. I do believe, though, that I submitted copy describing a New Orleans statue committee headed by business leaders Durel Black and James Nassikas through the chamber of commerce. Apparently, the Los Angeles–based fund-raisers were working in tandem with the New Orleans committee.

To everyone's surprise, Valerie Wilmer's "Open Letter to Benny Carter, Leonard Feather, Floyd Levin, and Clark Terry" in the May 28, 1970, *DB* opposed the statue. Her point was that a Louis Armstrong Adventure Playground would be far more useful, significant, and appropriate than a statue. This is plausible if one is forced into either/or thinking. The problem was that her letter was downright snotty, assuming a high moral ground and taking cheap shots at the city and the fund organizers.

I was angry enough to answer in kind. My letter in the July 23 issue quoted her barbs and defended the idea of statues as cultural statements.

> I usually enjoy Valerie Wilmer's writings, but in her open letter . . . I feel that she cut up my hometown unfairly in the interest of getting off a good line.
>
> Miss Wilmer admits that she has never been to New Orleans but states that if an Armstrong statue is erected, "future Orleanians will be able to bask in its shade, to let their dogs pee against it, and to marvel that a man who rose from such humble beginnings should have merited a lump of stone in what *db* described as 'a proper site for the statue.'" This statement has considerable rhetorical swagger, but it is presumptuous, arrogant, and insulting. . . .
>
> Ms. Wilmer's letter, besides being unfair, is short-sighted. We could use a Louis Armstrong Adventure Playground. Very practical, very helpful. But a society's choice of symbols is important, too, because its values are reflected in the individuals who are singled out for the special reverence of a monument.
>
> Miss Wilmer says, "You sure as hell can't learn much from looking at a statue." Well, the statue of General Lee which has towered over a major traffic circle for decades has taught a lot—too much, in fact—to generations of black children about who carries the stick in New Orleans. Suppose Lee Circle were Armstrong Circle. Suppose Beauregard Square were officially re-named Congo Square, and a statue of Louis were placed there.

The next month I received a scathing personal letter from Wilmer, blasting not only my opinions but also statues, Southerners, and Americans in general. I figured that it was time for détente, so I sent a temporizing note and got a pleasant response. Wilmer later visited New Orleans and I took her on a windshield tour of the city. With no need to appear clever and righteous in print, we had a fine time talking about the city and its music.

There were no objections to the statue from the city fathers and mothers in 1970. On the contrary, Durel Black and James Nasikkas were esteemed voices in the business community, fully capable of negotiating with the city administration about a site for the statue. Mayor Moon Landrieu, a Loyola alumnus, wrote to me endorsing the idea of the Armstrong statue after I sent him a copy of the exchange with Wilmer.

Louis Armstrong died on July 6, 1971. The planning for the statue moved ahead, affected neither by Wilmer's protest nor rumors of unhappiness among racists who were appalled by the prospect of a tribute to a black artist. But Marc Miller tells of new controversies over the style of sculpture and the posture and visage that the statue displays. The monument committee had asked sculptor Elizabeth Catlett to avoid abstract approaches in favor of a realistic depiction. She agreed to that but declined their request for a broadly smiling facial expression. Catlett believed that even a carefully crafted smile would invoke the old image of Armstrong as an Uncle Tom. Miller reports the sculptor's statement that "as a black person living at that time, I understand the reasons behind Louie's clowning, but I don't want to perpetuate it and it shouldn't be part of a monument."

A final barrier arose unexpectedly late in the game. Catlett had executed the particular pose recommended by the committee—Armstrong with his arm raised, as if waving to an audience. Some locals noticed a devastating coincidence: this posture was similar to that of *The Happy Darky,* a statue located in Baton Rouge. The juxtaposition of photographs of the two statues would sooner or later be inevitable, turning a major victory into a setup for continuous ridicule. Although the arm was already cast, the sculptor changed its position so that it was congenially bent at the elbow. Finally, on July 4, 1976, the statue was unveiled in Jackson Square. In 1980 it was placed in Armstrong Park at the Congo Square site.

The articles in this section, all presented essentially as written for *Down Beat, New Orleans* magazine, and the Vieux Carre *Courier* in the 1960s and early 1970s, deal with then-current developments and look back at many events of the late 1940s and 1950s in New Orleans. A common thread is the theme of the struggle for acceptance of jazz and its practitioners by the city's social and political elites. The articles, based on innumerable interviews and considerable research at the time they were written, have been contextualized, expanded upon, and sometimes corrected in the overview above. Timeline chart 1 (page 49) gives a bird's-eye view of key historical events described in both the overview and the articles in this section.

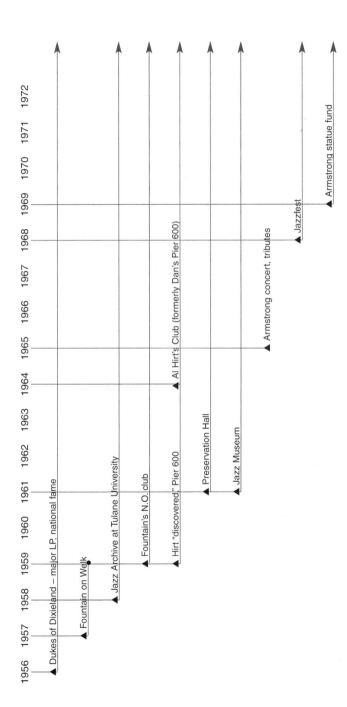

Timeline Chart 1 – Commercial and Cultural Victories for Traditional and Dixieland Jazz
(Underlines indicate continuation/duration)

2

Jazz and the New Orleans Press

Down Beat, June 12, 1969

The popular press has typically been more interested in profits than in prophets. It is easier—and safer—to report the news that the Establishment considers to be news, to adopt its policies and its attitudes, than it is to establish contact with the really creative forces in a community.

The underground press is another thing altogether. Underground writers find a genius in every garret, a prophet under every rock. And while the underground press collectively can be closer to what is happening in the United States today than the popular press is, any particular underground paper is likely to be a motley mixture of perceptive reporting, propaganda, pornography, and hysteria.

Of course, the popular press has been around long enough to know better. In the last century or so, big-city papers should have learned a few things about prophets without honor in their own country, if only because prophet-seeking can be profitable in a society in which speculation pays off. In America, the man who prognosticates successfully about anything from ouija boards to silly putty is likely to wind up with a million dollars, and his picture in the Business section of *Time.*

The popular press has specialized in the most facile and insidious kind of crystal-ball-gazing—the self-fulfilling prophecy. An influential newspaper often can predict the success of a local theater group, foretell the outcome of a state election, or even (as in the scandalous role of the Hearst papers in bringing about the Spanish-American War) forecast an international conflict. The trick, of course, is to use your medium to promote what you predict, using editorial policy, selective news coverage, and slanted reporting to keep destiny running along the lines of prophecy.

A perceptive press corps in New Orleans might have borne witness to the growth of a vital new art form in the city at the turn of the century. However, it is clear from Henry Kmen's *Music in New Orleans* that the city's best newspaper, the *Picayune,* was hipper in the late 1830s that at any time since. At that time the *Picayune* followed the fortunes of a street singer and vendor named Corn Meal and praised his programs at the famed St. Charles Theater, where operatic troupes like Italy's Montressor Company had appeared.

The *Picayune's* interest in local color, however, proved to be an ephemeral fascination. Toward the end of the 19th century the paper was complaining about the license taken by certain marching bands that were vulgarizing Sousa with unseemly syncopations. And a classic editorial from 1918, reprinted here, shows how the paper's distaste for jazz had developed.

In the days when even a little press support would have meant a lot for jazz, the *Picayune* didn't know the difference, except for the obvious ones, between Louis Armstrong and Lulu White. Frederic Ramsey, Bill Russell, Rudi Blesh, Orrin Keepnews, Hugues Panassié, and just about everybody scooped the *Picayune* when it came to knowing what was going on—aside from hanky-panky—in Storyville in the early 1900s.

Substituting hindsight for insight, the *Picayune* celebrated the opening of the Jazz Museum on November 11, 1961, with an editorial announcing "Jazz Has Made It." The editorial confessed earnestly that "jazz and jazzmen have had their ups and downs" but concluded that "the museum represents a significant addition to the cultural heritage of the city."

Of course, jazz fans knew better. Jazz had made it as an exciting, uniquely American art more than half a century before. When the *Picayune* praised the public display of a handful of jazz relics, it was the *Picayune* that had made it—at least in a tentative, limited, and anachronistic sort of way.

At its worst, the New Orleans press still looks on jazz as speakeasy music. For example, a carefully planned jazz history course at Tulane University in 1966 prompted columnist Maud O'Bryan to comment in the *Picayune and States & Item* that the course would be "good for laughs" and that the inclusion of such a course in a university was tantamount to college instruction in drum majoretting. The late Dr. Edmond Souchon took issue with Miss O'Bryan's simile in a gentlemanly letter of protest, which she subsequently pooh-poohed in her column.

The local papers' clumsy, piecemeal attempts at covering the jazz scene have produced some masterpieces of camp. In 1963 someone named Jack Kneece (his name did not appear in the phone book or city directory for that year) reviewed a concert at Municipal Auditorium by British jazz trumpeter Kenny Ball and his band.

The write-up began: "Imagine a jazz band with dream talents—like Gene Krupa on drums, George Lewis on clarinet, a hopped-up Tommy Dorsey on trombone, the best Negro banjo player in old New Orleans, Al Hirt surpassing himself on trumpet, and a magician for a piano player." The pianist-magician is later described in terms intended, one suspects, as complimentary. "If you can imagine how Van Cliburn could play if he were to completely change his character, taking Dexedrine and drinking gin for five days in a row, then you've got an inkling of how good Weatherburn is."

A story on the Dukes of Dixieland in the *Times-Picayune and States & Item* early last year combines multiple error with outlandish prose. Although my favorite sentence is the one saying, "From the very beginning the Dukes were meticulous, even arbitrary, about technical and stylistic perfection," there are howlers generously distributed throughout. According to the story, "About 10 years ago the Horace Heidt troupe visited New Orleans for the

purpose of discovering new talent; for this challenge the Assuntos got together a seven-piece unit . . . the Junior Dixie Band. . . . Realizing they could
not be 'Juniors' forever, the unit underwent another change of name—to the
Dukes of Dixieland—and this is what they are known by today.

"The Dukes of Dixieland have a style basically from that of the original
Dixieland band, which enjoyed its peak popularity during the early 20th
century. Actually the Dukes are a perfect illustration of a kind of feed-back
in jazz whereby contemporary musicians perform in the humble tradition of
Negro song and dance bands of yesteryear—slow, easygoing, and even
lazy—the Dukes have a more virile style that imparts considerably more
character to whatever they play."

Even with allowances for a typographical error or two, the story is a briar
patch of misinformation and tangled syntax. The Heidt show referred to
came to town in January 1949—about 20 years ago. The Dukes got the inspiration for their name from the band they admired and imitated most,
Sharkey Bonano's Kings of Dixieland. They are no more indebted to the
Original Dixieland Jazz Band than they are to Boyd Senter's Senterpedes.
The 51-word nonsentence about feedback, Negro bands of yesterday, and
virility is irrefutable because it is unintelligible.

Many significant happenings in the jazz community are ignored in the
local press while others are printed as received without critical editing.
The *States & Item* story on the death of traditional jazzman Joe Robichaux in 1965, a newsworthy item in itself, was marred by this bit of
trivia: "The pianist is remembered for his rendition of *Tiger Rag.* At the
break in the middle of the song, he would fill in by sitting on the piano
keys, a move that brought howls from the audience." (The *Picayune* had
the good taste to delete this point.) When pianist Sweet Emma Barrett recently returned to the music scene after a long illness, the papers faithfully reported someone's nonsense statement that this would be "a great
moment in the history of jazz."

There seems to be a strong relationship between the newspaper coverage
of the New Orleans jazz scene and the amount of power and money represented by the organization sponsoring the program. (Author Walker Percy
recently wrote that the *Picayune* might as well be the house organ for its advertisers.) The annual Jazzfest is potentially a major tourist attraction for the
city. It received the best coverage—in quantity—of any jazz event in years,
although one writer for an important eastern newspaper was shocked by the
poor quality of the festival copy.

The *Jazz on a Sunday Afternoon* concert series sponsored by the prestigious New Orleans Jazz Club is at best a solid but unimaginative presentation of well-known local Dixieland bands. A separate series of modern jazz
concerts last summer, sponsored by a group called the Sunday Afternoon
Jazz Society, was contrastingly innovative in its organization and format and
adventurous in its policy of importing artists such as Roland Kirk, Sonny
Stitt, and Freddie Hubbard.

The New Orleans Jazz Club received extensive publicity for its series, while the modern jazz group had to beg for a few inches of space here and there.

The new jazz society folded by the end of the year.

Reviews of jazz acts in local night clubs were as rare as Freddie Keppard records in the days when jazz was not considered a hot commercial item, and even today such reviews are limited to name groups in swank clubs and lounges owned by people who are close to the Establishment. Dizzy Gillespie and Ramsey Lewis can get a review when they appear at Al Hirt's club, and Mel Torme is written up when he is at the Blue Room of the Roosevelt Hotel. But James Moody went unnoticed by the press during an engagement at Mason's VIP lounge, even as John Coltrane failed to get a review when he appeared at an uptown restaurant and lounge several years ago.

Moreover, feature stories and reviews in an alert press might have saved or at least increased the longevity of outstanding local modern groups like the Ellis Marsalis quartet at Marsalis' Mansion, Fred Crane's trio at the Black Knight, and Willie Tee and the Souls at the Ivanhoe. Musicians in these combos can testify that it is easier to get national and international recognition of their talents than it is to get the attention of the *Times-Picayune* and the *States & Item.*

The Souls are an excellent avant garde group currently in residence at the Jazz Workshop and Listening Eye Gallery on Decatur St. The Workshop/Gallery is an artistic and educational venture led by the group's alto saxophonist, Earl Turbinton. Nightly jazz concerts and rotating photography shows are augmented by clinics for aspiring young musicians and photographers in the daytime. Newspaper coverage of this unique project was limited to a few lines in James Perry's amusements column and scattered news items that were the approximate size of a Friends of the Library monthly meeting announcement.

When Marshall McLuhan said, "We look at the present through a rearview mirror," he could have been talking about the coverage of jazz in New Orleans' popular newspapers. Today the New Orleans press, with its eye fixed squarely (very squarely) on that mirror, is tardily supporting musicians it rejected or ignored in the days when their music was a challenge to their generation and a prophecy to the world.

Meanwhile, the brilliant younger musicians are reliving the frustrations of their musical forebears—working with commercial groups, getting day jobs, and leaving town to get better exposure.

Orleanians who haven't heard of Ed Blackwell, Bill Huntington, James Rivers, or Nat Perrilliat in the local papers must bide their time. Local musicians have a way of turning up in the national media. And when their talents are adequately fossilized, their instruments museum pieces, and the musical forms they are creating safely a part of jazz history, they probably will show up on the cover of the *Picayune* Sunday supplement.

Jass and Jassism
New Orleans *Picayune,* June 20, 1918

Why is the jass music, and, therefore, the jass band? As well ask why is the dime novel or the grease-dripping doughnut? All are manifestations of a low streak in man's tastes that has not yet come out in civilization's wash. Indeed, one might go farther, and say that jass music is the indecent story syncopated and counterpointed. Like the improper anecdote, also, in its youth, it was listened to blushingly behind closed doors and drawn curtains, but, like all vice, it grew bolder until it dared decent surroundings, and there it was tolerated because of its oddity.

We usually think of people as musical or nonmusical, as if there were a simple line separating two great classes. The fact is, however, that there are many mansions in the house of muses. There is first the great assembly hall of melody—where most of us take our seats at some time in our lives—but a lesser number pass on to inner sanctuaries of harmony, where the melodic sequence, the "tune," as it most frequently is called, has infinitely less interest than the blending of notes into chords so that the combining wave-lengths will give new aesthetic sensations. This inner court of harmony is where nearly all the truly great music is enjoyed.

In the house there is, however, another apartment, properly speaking, down in the basement, a kind of servants' hall of rhythm. It is there we hear the hum of the Indian dance, the throb of the Oriental tambourines and kettledrums, the clatter of the clogs, the click of Slavic heels, the thumpty-tumpty of the negro banjo, and, in fact, the native dances of the world. Although commonly associated with melody, and less often with harmony also, rhythm is not necessarily music, and he who loves to keep time to the pulse of the orchestral performance by patting his foot upon the theater floor is not necessarily a music lover. The ultra-modernists in composition go so far as to pronounce taboo upon rhythm, and even omit the perpendicular lines on their bars of written music, so that the risk of a monotonous pulsation is done away with.

Prominently, in the basement hall of rhythm, is found rag-time, and of those most devoted to the cult of the displaced accent there has developed a brotherhood of those who, devoid of harmonic and even of melodic instinct, love to fairly wallow in noise. On certain natures sound loud and meaningless has an exciting, almost an intoxicating effect, like crude colors and strong perfumes, the sight of flesh or the sadic pleasure in blood. To such as these the jass music is a delight, and a dance to the unstable bray of the sackbut gives a sensual delight more intense and quite different from the languor of a Viennese waltz or the refined sentiment and respectful emotion of an eighteenth century minuet.

In the matter of jass, New Orleans is particularly interested, since it has been widely suggested that this particular form of musical vice had its birth in this city—that it came, in fact, from doubtful surroundings in our slums. We do not recognize the honor of parenthood, but with such a story in circulation, it behooves us to be last to accept the atrocity in polite society, and where it has crept in we should make it a point of civic honor to suppress it. Its musical value is nil, and its possibilities of harm are great.

3

The New Orleans Jazz Club: From Ragtime to Riches

New Orleans magazine, November 1970

***Moul-die Fygge** or **Moldy Fig** mol-de fig, n. [origin uncertain]: a jazz purist; one who has inordinate love of traditional New Orleans jazz, devoting excessive time to listening to early jazz music, collecting and trading recordings, and memorizing details about the careers of practitioners of early jazz.*

There is no one more resolute, or more impractical, than a New Orleans jazz fan. A jazz fan will drive hundreds of miles on the chance of catching a jam session, rummage through thousands of old records in search of recordings that probably were never made, risk asphyxiation in dank little back rooms listening to unknown musicians, and spend thousands of dollars recording or otherwise employing his favorite musicians with little hope of a return on his investment.

In the 1940's—the classic decade of the moldy fig—a cult of Orleanians followed the old jazz worshipfully, hovering over phonographs to hear collectors' items, reading esoteric magazines like *The Record Changer* and Art Hodes' splendid *Jazz Record,* meeting at the New Orleans Record Shop on Baronne Street for Saturday afternoon jam sessions, and hunting down old musicians who still might carry within their breasts the essence of the True Jazz.

The fig underground was a loose confederation of people who had little in common beyond their *idee fixe:* Save your King Oliver records, boys, jazz will rise again. Among them were worthies like Orin and Harvey Blackstone, Bill Russell, Myra Menville, Dick Allen, Edmond and Harry Souchon, John Walls, Roger Wolfe, and Bob Matthews.

From the quaint, cockeyed evangelism of such jazz fans the New Orleans Jazz Club was born. Five of them—Al Diket, a clerk for the federal government; his wife, Babette; Gilbert Erskine, a Loyola University music student; Johnny (Wiggs) Hyman, a mechanical drawing teacher at Easton High School and part-time cornetist and music teacher; and Don Perry, an audiovisual specialist with New Orleans Public Schools—stopped off for lunch after second-lining behind a brass band in the Zulu Parade on Mardi Gras day of 1948 when they decided that they would form a jazz club, by heaven, one that would wake up New Orleans and make people realize that this music was their native art and their gift to the world.

That night Wiggs prepared a set of goals for the New Orleans Jazz Club; the frayed, yellowing paper is still preserved at his Metairie home. The list is reproduced in its entirety below, although a line is drawn through the second item on Wiggs' original draft.

1. To nurture and advance N.O. Music.
2. To encourage the use of the term N.O. Music rather than Jazz.
3. To encourage N.O. musicians and make it possible for them to earn a living here at their profession.
4. To acquaint the local public with their own music. (They are now being fed, almost 24 hours a day by radio, music created in N.Y., Hollywood, etc.)
5. To give N.O. Music a chance to live in its birthplace.
6. To clear up the fallacy that N.O. Music was born in the bawdy house. (It is obvious that this music is a creation of the Negro and he takes it with him wherever he goes—to bawdy house, church, etc.)
7. To establish an information bureau of N.O. Music.
8. To establish a Museum of N.O. Music.
10. To awaken N.O. people to the debt of gratitude they owe to N.O. Music. (It is a known fact that this music has had a great part in making N.O. the fabulous city that it is. And it has carried the name of N.O. to all parts of the world.)

The probability of survival of the club, much less success in carrying out such grandiose goals, was small. Jazz fans are notorious quibblers, and their penchant for dreaming impossible dreams is not matched by a gift for large-scale organization. An earlier local jazz club, the National Jazz Foundation, had failed (after a few memorable concerts) when an officer reportedly copped the money in the treasury and headed north with a stripper.

Yet the New Orleans Jazz Club's first activities were modest enough: Monday night record sessions at members' houses, informal jam sessions, lectures by musicians and fans. Diket broke into the local media in 1948 with a WTPS radio show featuring jazz records, and shortly after the club began its WWL recording-documentary program, which is still running. The club's meeting-jam sessions grew in popularity and were soon moved to hotel ballrooms. In 1950 WNOE carried portions of the monthly sessions live from the St. Charles Hotel.

The club had ventured into the concert business early in its career. In its first year the membership dared to rent the Parisian Room on Royal Street for $50.00 for a Sunday afternoon concert featuring Johnny Wiggs. After expenses, a profit of $1.75 was chalked up, and by the next month attendance had doubled for a Sharkey Bonano concert, convincing the owners of the room that this was too good a thing to be left in the hands of amateurs. They promptly hired Sharkey's band for weekly concerts, which were aired on WWL to the delight of jazz fans in the area. Regrettably, the quality of the

Parisian Room sessions dropped sharply as inferior jazzmen replaced the artists that the jazz clubbers had selected. Finally, Tony Almerico's raucous, ear-splitting band became the regular feature, and the moldy figs bequeathed the Parisian Room to the tourists and the money-changers.

The Jazz Club pushed on relentlessly. In summer of 1949 the club sponsored eight outdoor pops concerts in Beauregard Square, netting exactly $3.41 and an immeasurable moral victory at the end of the series. *Newsweek* and ABC radio had covered the sessions, and even the local press was warming up to the jazz thing as more and more establishment types showed up in the club. By October of 1950, membership had grown to 440 — 265 active local members and 175 corresponding members.

One of the club's most significant and least discussed achievements was its success in winning the support of the business community, the newspapers, and the social elite in New Orleans, all of which had previously preferred the music of the salon to what they thought was the music of the saloon. This was accomplished largely through a nucleus of jazz fans who were socially prominent or at least well known to business, political, and social leaders. The late Dr. Edmond Souchon was a tireless champion of jazz in polite society, as is his brother, attorney Harry Souchon (now president of the Jazz Club). Mrs. John (Myra) Menville was another standard bearer in the battle to make jazz respectable. Scoop Kennedy was a link between the Jazz Club and the press. More recently, retired businessman Durel Black has been consolidating the gains made by the early jazz clubbers and winning friends for jazz in the business community. It is not an accident that the jazz club has grown to be a socially prestigious organization, gaining membership in the Cultural Attractions Fund and getting coverage on the Society page as well as the Amusements section of the *Picayune,* which once called jazz "brothel music."

Many of the old guard jazz fans feel that the Jazz Club has lost sight of its original goals as it has won wider support. Commercial and political considerations, they say, have taken precedence over the integrity of the music and the artists.

The early jazz club meetings/jam sessions, for example, were informal gatherings where everybody sat in with everybody else, one set blending into the next without the staginess of a concert or the strained sophistication of a night club. The sessions became increasingly structured and stilted as the club grew larger. Musicians who seldom showed up for the old musical free-for-alls began to breeze in with over-rehearsed bands to plug a new record or publicize the opening of a new club. Teen-age bands with electric guitars would labor through memorized stock arrangements of *Tin Roof Blues.* Non-jazz and near-jazz performances by barber shop quartets and the Trombones Beaucoup have been programmed, resulting in less interest by the genuine jazz artists and aficionados.

When the first annual *Jazzfest* was being planned by the club in 1968, a crucial Jazz Club meeting was invaded by Al Rose and a group of fig stalwarts who tried, unsuccessfully, to make the festival primarily a showcase for local artists. There was considerable protest against the high prices paid for nationally-known performers who, they contended, had contributed little to the creation and development of their art. A *sub rosa* protest had circulated among musicians for some time over the flat union scale often paid for *Jazz on a Sunday Afternoon* concerts, the profits of which went to the preservation of dead musicians' instruments in the Jazz Museum while living musicians tried to eke out an existence in the birthplace of jazz.

Don Perry and Johnny Wiggs, the two Jazz Club Founders who still live in the New Orleans area, were asked to comment on the evolution of the club. Perry, now working in WDSU-TV's film department, still has a serious interest in jazz, filming jazz landmarks and events for his own pleasure and perhaps for future publication. Wiggs, long retired from teaching, still plays cornet occasionally around town and on tour. Gilbert Erskine is a busy executive with American Industrial Leasing Company in Chicago, but he is still a frequent contributor to *Down Beat* magazine. The Dikets are living in Thibodeaux, La., where Al teaches history but has generally lost contact with jazz.

Perry, soft-spoken and bespectacled, talked about the club as a scientist might speak of a laboratory experiment—emotionally detached, but intensely interested in its progress. "I go through periods when I say to myself, 'Gee, I wish I didn't have anything to do with them.' And then I go through periods when I'm very proud of it."

Perry commented on the shift in character of the club's membership. "I was at the meeting Monday night. I don't think most people there care one way or another. This is a place to go every two months to hear some music. . . . I think they *like* the music, but I don't think they care, really, where it comes from or how."

In the halcyon days, the club's members were a kind of gutbucket aristocracy. According to Perry, "In the very beginning, we played records, we took films, pictures . . . everybody was enthusiastic about everyone else's thing—things they were going to show or listen to" at the meetings.

Perry is concerned over a disturbing trend towards elevation of the jazz fan to a position of prominence at the expense of the artist. "To me, in jazz the musician is god. . . . And when I see people who are trying to make a name in jazz because they're listeners, I don't think they deserve it. The musician is the thing."

Of the Jazz Club's founders, Johnny Wiggs is the only one who has won recognition as a musician. In Edmond Souchon and Al Rose's *New Orleans Jazz: A Family Album,* Wiggs is described as "the idol of 'purists' around the world." Wiggs was critical of the Jazz Club, but not bitter as he spoke of its development. He compared the current state of the New Orleans Jazz Club to that of the old National Jazz Foundation in the mid-forties. "The main reason I wanted to get something going for New Orleans Jazz was that the National Jazz Foundation . . . overlooked the local jazzmen, and the same identical thing is happening now with the New Orleans Jazz Club. They push the local men in the corner and they pay fabulous prices for this *nothing* music."

Wiggs pointed to John S. Wilson's New York *Times* review of the 1969 jazz festival to underscore his point. "After listening to a whole week of the New Orleans *Jazzfest,* there was *one group* that he picked out—er . . . modesty forbids . . . [*It was Wiggs' band*] that he said played what he had come to hear." Wiggs added that Preservation Hall had adhered to a traditional jazz policy and was financially successful with real New Orleans music. He candidly summed up his feelings: "New Orleans jazz is known better than anything which America has created. So why in the name of heaven do they have to put all the phony business in?"

Has success really spoiled the New Orleans Jazz Club? Undoubtedly the club's leadership and membership are on the whole less passionate about jazz and less sensitive to the needs of the jazz musician than the first jazz clubbers were. But it is undeniable that the New Orleans Jazz Club and its members have initiated or supported every major advancement for traditional jazz in New Orleans since the club's beginning in 1948. It is also clear that an organization of 1,000 members—the club's present enrollment—cannot be conducted like a tree-house brotherhood. The moldy figs were too free-wheeling and idealistic a group to tackle the political and economic intrigues involved in establishing something as big as the Jazz Museum. And despite the obvious commercial elements in the programming of the annual jazz festivals, the planners (who, incidentally, were not exclusively jazz clubbers) have generally been earnest in trying to juggle artistic, financial, and political considerations.

The Jazz Club's latest project is erecting a statue of Louis Armstrong in New Orleans. A similar project failed due to lack of both grass roots and high level support in 1955, when the club was just beginning to become a power-oriented organization. This time, the drive for a jazz monument began with a press conference called by Durel Black. George Wein of Newport fame was there to play piano and present a check. Cameras rolled and flashed, reporters took notes. This time, there will be an Armstrong monument. The *New* Orleans Jazz Club might be low on soul, but it is high on moxy.

4

Hello, Central, Give Me
Doctor Jazz: Edmond Souchon

New Orleans magazine, November 1968

I cannot say that I knew Edmond Souchon well; but when he died on August 24th of 1968 I had a deep feeling of personal loss. When I reflected on this feeling, I could not build a logical case for it. Doc Souchon had been for me both a symbol and a series of loosely related, though highly vivid experiences. Yet these experiences were strung sporadically, even capriciously, on the thread of my life, and they did not account for the sharp sense of loss I felt when Helen Arlt called me and said, "Doc Souchon is dead."

I first knew Doc Souchon as the Gentle Healer, a magic name uttered by my grandmother for the first eighteen years of my life and the last eighteen of hers. She loved far more to praise Dr. Souchon in her broken English-and-French than to complain about her ailments—a fact which spoke superbly for both *Memere* and the doctor. No other doctor knew what he was doing or was competent to take the measure of her maladies, and that was that.

I met Dr. Souchon personally for the first time in the maternity ward at Mercy Hospital in January, 1963, when my wife gave birth to the fourth of our nine children. By then I had learned from his writings and his reputation that he was far more dynamic than the wise doctor stereotype I held as a child. In fact, Doc's bedside manner was 100% off that day. He was busily chiding a patient, a girl whose tardiness in bearing had made him postpone his vacation since before Thanksgiving. Worse yet, she had decided to whelp right in the middle of a convention at which the doctor was to speak.

With this the image of the friendly medic that I inherited from my grandmother faded away forever and merged with a hundred other lovable doctor types of fiction and fancy. This doctor, Edmond Souchon, who scolded a woman for extended gestation, edited the New Orleans Jazz Club's *Second Line* and wrote for medical journals, lectured on jazz and surgery, and played guitar with Dixieland combos around town, was undoubtedly an original.

My later associations with Doc Souchon provided a series of anecdotes that further testify to the uniqueness and complexity of the man. He was a combination of jocularity and aggressiveness, quick wit and curtness, dogmatism and granite honesty. This should add up to a neurotic personality, but in Doc Souchon the sum total was an oddly pleasing and clumsy charisma.

Doc was what is known in the jazz world as a moldy fig—that is, a jazz purist. He loved New Orleans jazz, thought that most other so-called "jazz" was non-jazz, and didn't care a damn whether *Down Beat, Metronome,* Stan Kenton, or Dizzy Gillespie agreed with him or not. He grew up with the music, hanging around outside of Tom Anderson's Cafe and other Storyville bars to hear it before he was a teenager, and he guarded jealously his vision of the truth about jazz.

Yet the doctor was curiously immune from charges of bigotry and wrong-headedness. His friends accepted him, brusque and opinionated as he was. To those who did not know him well, he was something of a sacred cow. I remember attending a special preview of NET's *New Orleans Jazz* series at WYES-TV in 1964. During the first reel Dr. Souchon took exception, volubly, to something on the screen. If I had offered such a comment, I am sure that everyone in the room would have stared me to a cinder. But Doc Souchon pulled it off with no sterner rebuke than a few sidewise glances and a little uncomfortable chair-shuffling.

Doc had a scorn for the national jazz press that probably grew from the shabby treatment New Orleans jazz received during the Dixie-versus-bop controversy of the 1940s. The small Dixie-oriented magazines like *Jazz Record* and *The Record Changer* had by and large kept their dignity during the senseless reader-baiting dispute while widely circulated *Down Beat* and *Metronome* seemed to delight in teasing anti-bebop statements from Louis Armstrong and anti-Dixieland statements from Dizzy Gillespie. (I recall having drawn heavily from the latter journals—and also from a few more scholarly sources like the *Saturday Review*—for a term paper on the jazz war that I wrote in high school in 1951.)

Whatever the reason, Doc deeply mistrusted the national jazz press. When I was covering the story of the destruction of Louis Armstrong's birthplace for *Down Beat* in the summer of 1964, I called Doc Souchon about his photographs of the Armstrong house, which were supposedly the only ones extant. "Hell, no," he grumbled. "Why should I give my valuable pictures to these commercial magazines? They don't even have the courtesy to return them half the time, anyway. Someday I'm going to put them together in my own book where I'm sure they'll be well used."

I argued perfunctorily about the importance of making the jazz community aware of the tragic loss of an American landmark, but secretly I found myself cheering for Doc. The bit about the unreturned photographs was true, of course. But more important, I was proud of this man's fierce loyalty to New Orleans and of the deep respect for Armstrong that was evident in his testy arguments. A few months before he died, the LSU Press published *New Orleans Jazz: A Family Album,* a collection of Doctor Souchon's and Al Rose's photographs, including a picture of the Armstrong house.

Doc's last skirmish with the national press came in 1967 when he took on Pauline Rivelli's *Jazz* magazine for what he felt was a growing racist-black supremacy line. Doc had written articles for the magazine and served for several years on its International Advisory Board. He was upset by a series called "Jazz and Revolutionary Black Nationalism," and with typical Souchonian gusto he wrote this letter to the editor: ". . . All I can say is HO! HUM! After doing our best to read the features, we retreat into our own mouldy little chapel and pray that someday there will be an end to . . . your features. We further ask our southern deity to help all of us musicians, critics, and writers—white, black, Yankee, or deep-southerner—to speed us along the road that is not strung with vitriol, petty jealousies, and personal feuds.

"Me, I'm fast running out of years. I find time much too valuable to read page after page of pseudo-jazz and phony intellectualism, none of which resolve one iota of the sociological problems of the minorities or the cultists' attitude of jazz. I have long ago come to the conclusion that JAZZ finds it much cheaper to start a good running battle than to pay cash for good articles."

Doc had been around long enough to know that in letters to the editor, the editor always has the last word. The harsher the tone of your letter, the more of a setup you are for the editor's sniping. But as usual, Doc would have his say, and the editor could (and did) do as she pleased in her response. But it was a sound instinct that led him to break away from the magazine. Within a year *Jazz* changed its name to *Jazz and Pop* and continued to move away from the music that Doc considered to be the *real* jazz.

The Jazz Club's *Second Line* is after all the only magazine in the country that has spoken consistently and solely for the jazz purist. It has always been unashamedly an amateur product. For years the publication information has included the statement that the magazine is published "if and when the men and women engaged in this Civic, Non-Profit enterprise have time to devote to it." With the addition—"Attempt will be made to publish this magazine at least once every other month."

Since it admitted no obligation to slick professional standards, *The Second Line* developed something that many professional publications lack—a personality. And that personality was a ghost of Edmond Souchon, who wrote articles, editorials, reviews, and news stories for the magazine anonymously or under the not altogether cryptic name of R. A. Tiug.

Perhaps a casual acquaintance could feel Doc Souchon's death deeply because it was impossible for any acquaintance with him to be truly casual. With Doc, conversation was confrontation; interaction always meant action. In a time when mollification and euphemism were the laws of social life, he projected the image of a man of sharp, clear, well-formulated ideas which he offered generously for your consideration, take it or leave it.

Few men live a more active life than Edmond Souchon did. But with him, one felt that the private man was constantly brought forth in the public man, just as a jazz musician's personality emerges candidly in his improvisations. Perhaps it is this candor, this bent toward self-revelation, that generated the poetry of his personality.

Like many men who lead singular lives, Doc Souchon was granted a death that has the force of legend. He was having a party and jam session at his home with a few old friends—among them clarinetist Raymond Burke and bassist Sherwood Mangiapane—when he died of heart failure. He had just finished playing *Bill Bailey, Won't You Please Come Home.*

5

The Jazz Museum

Down Beat, March 15, 1962

The reactions of the jazz fan on visiting the New Orleans Jazz Museum are confused ones. Seeing Minor Hall's brushes, Sidney Bechet's soprano saxophone, and Johnny Bayersdorfer's cornet on unpretentious display, presenting themselves as genuine artifacts of U.S. culture, is an alternately gratifying and disconcerting experience.

The esoteric is no longer esoteric. The mostly forgotten, long-mourned-for greats are now remembered, and their names appear on charts and identification cards for the laity to peruse at will:

> *New Orleans . . . Bolden and Papa Jack Laine . . .*
> *Chicago . . . Teschemacher . . . Rod Cless . . .*
> *Kansas City . . . Benny Moten . . . Walter Page.*

You don't have to be a member of the "insiders" anymore or read the *Record Changer* or hang around Orin Blackstone's record shop, to see those secret names and joke about Slow Drag Pavageau's homemade bass. The bass is there, and so is a picture of Drag, and you wonder if the guy standing next to you really knows the meaning of the names and the instruments and the museum itself.

Nevertheless, there are compensations for this intrusion on your hot little world of jazz insights. The unmistakable air of victory pervades the museum's 16 by 33 feet of floor space and it is reflected in the confident, well measured words of the New Orleans Jazz Club's Harry Souchon and the contagiously ebullient manner of museum director Clay Watson.

Souchon, a prominent local attorney and brother of the noted surgeon-guitarist Edmond Souchon, is generally conceded to be the main force in bringing the museum into existence. He wisely employed the full-time services of Watson to design, build, and operate the museum for the club.

The cottage that houses the museum was originally one of several located in another part of the French Quarter and owned by an adjoining department store. When the store announced plans to demolish the cottages and construct a service building, the city's Vieux Carre Commission objected strenuously. After several unsuccessful attempts to compromise, a plan finally evolved at Souchon's suggestion to relocate the cottages elsewhere in the quarter, with one being donated for the establishment of a New Orleans jazz museum.

Souchon and Watson were still beaming with opening-night enthusiasm though almost two months had passed since its formal dedication.

The resourcefulness exercised by Watson in designing the museum was immediately apparent, for the room presented an uncluttered appearance despite an abundance of items. There were separate displays for the Original Dixieland Jazz Band, Tom Brown's band, and the New Orleans Rhythm Kings, as well as numerous memorabilia of such individual jazzmen as George Lewis, Irving Fazola, Sharkey Bonano, and Oscar (Papa) Celestin.

"We hope to have the use of the entire cottage within a few years," Souchon commented. "In the meantime, we have more items than we have room for, so we'll have to rotate our displays periodically."

Asked if the museum's activities would compete with the New Orleans Jazz Archive being compiled by Bill Russell and Dick Allen at Tulane University, Souchon declared, "Decidedly not. We're in cooperation with them, and they're in cooperation with us. In fact, if we receive something that's of interest to them, we let them have copies. Besides, their main interest isn't in things like musical instruments but in getting tapes, documents, and photographs of early musicians."

He pointed to a large stone sitting in the patio just outside the back door and asked, "What, for instance, could they do with that?"

An inscription on the stone read "Lulu White." It had once been the stepping stone for visitors as they stepped from their carriages in front of Mahogany Hall.

On a large pillar in the center of the room there were several telephones. "We call this the museumophone," Watson said. "For each number on the dial you hear a different phase of traditional jazz."

Only five of the tracks have been completed—blues singers, trumpeters, early string bands, early jazz bands, and marching bands. "We're planning to fill in the others soon," Souchon explained, "probably with Jelly Roll Morton, ragtime pianos and bands, foreign jazz bands, and a tape telling about the museum."

At the Tom Brown Band exhibit, the instruments of the front-line men are encased and near them is a contract dated March 1, 1915, for an engagement at Lamb's Cafe in Chicago, upholding the late trombonist's contention that his group preceded the ODJB up the river.

"You wouldn't believe how anxious the guys in that band were to get together again, even if it was in a museum," Souchon said with a smile.

It was good to hear this, for rumors had circulated earlier that some of the white and Negro musicians had been wary about donating to the museum, not knowing how much importance would be attached to their respective race's role in the beginnings of jazz.

"We had no trouble with this museum-wise," Souchon said. "In fact, most of the musicians wanted to get their instruments in. But there are some white musicians who are bitterly jealous of the colored. I don't know why—maybe it's the publicity and recognition some of the colored musicians have gotten. As for the museum itself, it isn't segregated."

The exhibits bear out Souchon's words. The clarinets of Leon Rappolo and George Lewis appear, and a tiny bust of Papa Celestin stands near Sharkey Bonano's famed derby hat. Even the charts tracing the history of jazz and significant jazz musicians are taken from Marshall Stearn's *Story of Jazz* and the French magazine *Jazz,* respectively, and reflect the views of no one member of the jazz club.

Does this liberalness extend to the acceptance of later forms of jazz? The only reference in the museum now to modern artists is in a casual pen-and-ink drawing called *Newport Doodlings* by the artist Freniere. In the same frame with Louis Armstrong and Mahalia Jackson are Thelonious Monk and Tony Scott.

Souchon and Watson simultaneously gave contradictory answers when asked if the museum would attempt to preserve artifacts of swing-era and modern artists.

Watson answered affirmatively: "If this is a jazz museum, surely these things will have some future value."

"But it's the *New Orleans* Jazz Museum," Souchon asserted. "We're interested in anything connected with New Orleans or New Orleans-influenced musicians, but as for progressive jazz, I don't know.

"For instance, we could use Muggsy Spanier's cornet because although Muggsy was from Chicago, he was influenced by early New Orleans musicians and developed from the New Orleans style. Or someone like Bix Beiderbecke. We could use anything of Bix Beiderbecke's."

"But you can't limit yourself," Watson objected. "If you put yourself into a slot of one particular era, you'll run into a brick wall. Isn't it possible that we'll branch out later and have exhibits for all that jazz?"

"Yes, it's possible, but at present we have no such plans," Souchon said.

It was apparent that the question of other-than-traditional jazz in the museum had not been explicitly dealt with before. Who ultimately would be responsible for a decision in the matter?

"The officers of the club," Souchon responded. "We're thinking now of having a special museum board besides the officers to deal with the museum. If we do that, the board will decide on museum policies."

The Christmas issue of the jazz club's publication, *The Second Line,* contained a page that gave perhaps the most concise illustration of the meaning of the jazz museum.

It was a reprint without comment of two editorials in the New Orleans *Times-Picayune,* separated by 44 years. The first, dated June 17, 1917, was entitled *Jass and Jassism.* It condemned jazz outspokenly as a vice, urging its suppression as "a point of civic honor." The other, *Jazz Has Made It,* was dated Nov. 11, 1961. It praised jazz freely and called the museum "a significant addition to the cultural heritage of the city."

Jazz has outlived the woolly protests of its detractors. It has climbed from the status of brothel music to recognition as our country's only truly indigenous art.

The jazz museum, whatever its problems with regard to space and schools of jazz, is a triumph for jazz. It is the incarnation of the social acceptance achieved over half a century by an art that is the most immediate expression of this country's experience.

6

The Jazz Archive at Tulane

Down Beat, June 30, 1966

In 1957 a jazz fan named Richard Allen consulted Dr. William Hogan, chairman of the history department at Tulane University, about a program for a master's degree in history. The conference resulted, indirectly, in the establishment of the Archive of New Orleans Jazz, which now boasts almost 500 taped interviews, 11,500 jazz records, 3,900 photographs, 8,700 pieces of sheet music, and innumerable magazines, posters, clippings, and other materials related to New Orleans jazz.

Hogan was impressed with Allen's idea of taping interviews with early traditional jazzmen who were still in the city, and with the help of Allen and writer Bill Russell he formulated the idea of a collection of tapes, magazines, books, and records to be gathered at the university, cataloged, and preserved for researchers.

Hogan applied for a Ford Foundation grant to finance the project, and in March, 1958, $75,000 was granted for establishment of the archive. Russell was named curator of the archive and Allen associate curator.

Russell and Allen had been best friends of jazz and each other for years. Allen had corresponded with Russell in the early 1950s when Allen was part owner, with Orin and Harvey Blackstone, of the New Orleans Record Shop. When Russell latter settled in New Orleans and opened his own record store, he and Allen worked together closely. In addition to his own interests, Allen cooperated with Russell in producing albums and writing liner notes for Russell's American Music label.

Russell, of course, is well known in the jazz field as an authority on traditional jazz, having published widely and recorded New Orleans musicians at a time when serious jazz criticism was practically nonexistent and the major record labels had little interest in recording early jazzmen.

Russell was a close personal friend of many of those whom he interviewed, and their confidence in him is reflected in the easy, spontaneous interchange of ideas and reminiscences between interviewer and subject on the tapes.

Russell's skill and unpatronizing gentleness in drawing meaningful responses from the late Alice Zeno (clarinetist George Lewis' mother), for example, is more than a display of good interviewing technique—it is an unwitting revelation of human warmth and an absorbing listening experience.

In 1959 Betty B. Rankin and Paul Crawford were added to the archive staff. Now associate curator, Mrs. Rankin is in charge of various administrative details. Crawford, an Alabama-born trombonist, prepares digests of the taped interviews. (He is co-leader of a local revivalist group, and Crawford-Ferguson Night Owls and was also co-leader, with trumpeter Mike Lala Jr., of the excellent but short-lived Michael Paul Band, a swing band that featured Crawford's strongly conceived Ellingtonian arrangements.)

The Ford Foundation gave a supplemental grant of $25,000 to the archive in June, 1960. A final grant of $56,000 was made in September, 1962. In accordance with the original agreement between Tulane and the foundation, the university assumed operation of the archive as a division of the university library on July 1, 1965. Allen was then appointed curator to replace Russell, who returned to personal projects, although he maintains an active interest in the archive and frequently brings in new materials.

Allen is pleased with the progress of the archive in its first eight years and optimistic about its future. Admittedly, only the groundwork has been laid, but it is solid groundwork. He points out that the 1,500 tape recordings, representing about 500 interviews with 400 musicians, are only useful if some codification of the storehouse of information can be achieved.

"We originally planned to make word-for-word transcriptions," Allen explained, "but this proved to be very tedious and rather cumbersome to use. So in the interest of time, we make digests, or summaries, of the interviews." After this, the names of the person interviewed and the musicians and topics discussed during the interview are indexed and cross-referenced in the master file.

The archive's main focus is on New Orleans jazz, but the taped interviews —which Allen calls "the heart of the collection"—are not limited to traditional jazzmen. Blues and Gospel singers also have been interviewed, and even modern jazzmen such as Chris White (Dizzy Gillespie's former bassist) are included, usually in discussions of traditional jazz.

"We concentrate on New Orleans musicians—older ones—but these things are not so peripheral as they seem," Allen commented. "Musicians from other schools are interested in New Orleans. Often they've played together [with New Orleans musicians]."

Does the archive collect data on important nontraditional jazzmen who have lived in New Orleans—for example, Lester Young, who spent some time in New Orleans as a child, or Ornette Coleman, who played there when he was developing his current style? Allen replied, "We're not seeking out that particular phase. But if it came up in an interview, we'd get it. . . . If people make donations of modern records, we keep them. Maybe someday we'll trade these things off to some other institution."

Allen laments the fact that projects similar to the Archive of New Orleans Jazz have not appeared in other cities. "I personally had hoped that there would be more archives springing up all over the country," he said. "I thought maybe there would be one in San Francisco and St. Louis and Kansas City, but it doesn't look like that's going to happen."

He notes, though, that there is some activity on the part of individuals who are interested in preserving vital materials on jazz. "John Steiner, for example, is doing a lot on Chicago, and he'll send us copies of his tapes. . . . He worked on the Columbia album on the Chicago scene, and as he was doing this, he was cooperating with us. Then there's the Institute of Jazz Studies in New York. Marshall Stearns [the institute's curator] has a marvelous collection."

Allen speaks of the gaps in the archive's collection of old and out-of-print books, recordings, and magazines. "We'd welcome contributions from anyone. Old jazz magazines disappear very rapidly. Early issues of *Jazz Information, Jazz Record,* and *Down Beat* are particularly rare."

Who uses the archive, and who is permitted to examine the materials in it? Allen said he believes that scholars engaged in research will ultimately be the main visitors to the archive. The most frequent requests for appointments to see the archive now come from musicians who are researching old tunes in the record and sheet music library and from foreign visitors, especially musicians and writers.

The materials in the archive are kept in two buildings on the Tulane campus because of crowded conditions in the library, where the main office is located. However, when the new library is built (scheduled for completion in 1969), the archive will occupy a room with adequate facilities for its ever-growing materials.

Like its popular counterpart, the Jazz Museum, the Archive of New Orleans Jazz is viewed by New Orleans musicians and jazz lovers as a major triumph for jazz. Only two decades ago, recognition of the cultural importance of jazz by the academic community seemed nowhere in sight. Today not only scholars but civic and social leaders as well are lending strong support to jazz, calling on specialists like Russell and Allen and the jazz musicians themselves to reconstruct the city's jazz past, boost the city's jazz present, and assure the future of jazz in New Orleans.

7

The Stage Band Movement at Loyola—Or, How to Start a Revolution While Really Trying Not To

New Orleans magazine, January 1969

For decades jazz has been the hidden curriculum in music education. In recent years jazz has come out of hiding a little, showing up in college catalogues under the titles like Lab Band and Improvisation Workshop. The fight for academic recognition for jazz is probably the longest continuing student revolution in America, and it contains in miniature the basic elements of today's widely publicized student revolts: impatient young men pleading for a relevant curriculum, inflexible administrators holding out for Our Broader Cultural Heritage, and frequent hostile confrontations that somehow culminate in change.

Loyola University is a case in point. The University's music school has, through little fault of its own, provided the impetus for the current upswing of stage band activity in New Orleans. The Loyola Stage Band, which was recognized last year as one of the best in the nation, is the result of years of ludicrous jousting between the students and the administration. The students won the battle, but largely by default. The old administration simply passed away and was replaced by ex-students whose revolutionary inclinations no longer looked revolutionary by the time they infiltrated the Establishment.

Loyola had a chance to be a pioneer in music education just after World War II, when a bumper crop of veterans and young musicians with a deep interest in many phases of jazz entered the music school. Among the enrollees were Al Belletto, Fred Crane, Richard Crosby, Woody Guidry, Tony Liuzza, Steve (Lord) Loyacano, Frankie (Mann) Mannino, Stanley Mendelson, Gerry St. Amand, Kenny Schmidt, Don Suhor, and Larry Valentino. These and other Loyola alumni later went on to play with bands like Woody Herman, Stan Kenton, Hal McIntyre, Ralph Marterie, Ray Anthony, Charlie Barnett, Billy May, and Ray McKinley.

While in school the students formed a big band called the Loyola Moods, which until recently was a standard of comparison for college bands in the area. They also organized Campus Capers, a public relations show troupe that played a weekly radio show on WWL and toured the South. The Loyola Music School was rapidly building a reputation as a "jazz school."

But the conservative administration didn't take the cue. They saw the growing "jazz" tag as a threat to their dignity, reputation, and place in the cosmos. They were justifiably proud of the school's voice department, which was developing brilliant young operatic talents like Charles Anthony, Audrey Schuh, and Norman Treigle, and they would not extend their imprimatur to jazz.

John Whitlock, the band director who had nurtured the Capers troupe, resigned suddenly in 1952, and Loyola brought in New Orleans Symphony trumpeter George Jansen to revive the sadly ailing concert band. (Whitlock had, in fact, worked overtime with Campus Capers while the concert band dwindled down to an unbalanced, unlistenable ensemble). The Capers band was given to excellent guitarist-reed man Paul Guma for a year, then turned over to student directors for the next fourteen years—in the hopes, it was rumored, of effectively killing the group.

The students' instinct for relevancy would not be squelched. They continued to compose, arrange, and perform for the Capers group for meager scholarship aid. They held record-listening sessions in practice rooms and conducted what must have been the world's longest floating jam session in the music school basement.

The basement jazz was particularly offensive to the administration, and in the late '40's and early '50's a hilarious cat-and-mouse game that could have been the script for a dozen grade B movies developed. Dean Schuyten, a crusty old German professor type, would shuffle down the hazardous basement stairs, burst into a practice room where five students were playing *Pennies from Heaven,* and bellow, "I will not have in my school this—this *woogie boogie!*"

By the mid-1950's, Loyola's official de-emphasis on jazz was firmly established. At the same time, other universities and a number of national musical and educational organizations were warming up to jazz. In 1956 North Texas State initiated its now-famous degree program in jazz. In the same year the MENC (Music Educators National Conference) offered a panel discussion on jazz that included Dave Brubeck, George Wein, and George Avakian at its national convention. During the previous year the National Music Council granted membership to the Institute of Jazz in New York and presented a forum on jazz at its annual convention. The Institute of International Education announced its support of jazz courses in conservatories and colleges of music in 1957.

Another sign of the times was the 1956 publication of two important scholarly works on jazz, Andre Hodeir's *Jazz: Its Evolution and Essence* and Marshall Stearns' *The Story of Jazz.* Between 1951 and 1955 journals like *Educational Music Magazine, Music Educators' Journal,* and *Music Clubs* were printing numerous articles favorable to jazz.

Meanwhile, Loyola students and alumni had been proselytizing for jazz at various levels of community life, helping to loosen up institutions and create a more sympathetic climate for jazz. A student named Gilbert Erskine was one of the originators of the now-prestigious New Orleans Jazz Club in 1948. Pianist F. A. Cassanova produced a successful series of recorded jazz programs for radio station WNPS (then owned by New Orleans Public Schools) beginning in 1957. Most important of all, Loyola music education graduates teaching in local high schools were bringing the hidden curriculum to the surface by training young instrumentalists in stage band work as well as in concert and marching band. The old high school dance band churning out Glenn Miller arrangements was being replaced by the precise and well-rehearsed stage band that played special arrangements and often original compositions by the band director and other interested local musicians.

The St. Aloysius High School Stage Band, under the direction of Clem Toca (Loyola '50), was the first local stage band to win national acclaim. Toca, one of the original arrangers for the Loyola Moods, returned to New Orleans in 1960 with an impressive teaching record from Mobile, Alabama. He proved that our young musicians could be trained to do first-rate stage band work and could compete with the best bands in the country. The Aloysius band won first place at the *Down Beat* stage band festival at Enid, Oklahoma, in 1963 and 1964. Top honors at Enid in 1965 and second place in 1966 were taken by the Warren Easton High School Stage Band, directed by composer-arranger Bert Braud (Loyola '58). In 1967 Joe Hebert (Loyola '63) brought an Aloysius group back to regain the first place spot won by Toca three years earlier.

Last year a Loyola-sponsored high school stage band festival was held at Kennedy High School Auditorium, and four of the six bands on the program were led by ex-Loyolians. Joe Hebert conducted the Loyola and Easton High School stage bands, Bob Morgan (Loyola '57) led the Abramson band, and Frank Mannino (Loyola '51) brought in a band from Holy Cross. The non-Loyolians on the festival were Milton Bush and Joe Valenti, directing bands from Kennedy and St. Aloysius.

Since the festival, Bush has moved to LSUNO, where he leads the concert and stage bands, assisted in the latter by Ben Smalley (Loyola, Assoc.). Bush's replacement at Kennedy is Gerry St. Amand (Loyola '58). Trumpeter Smalley is also director of the new lab band at Tulane. Another institution adding a stage band program is Delgado Junior College. The recently organized Delgado Music Department, headed by Klaus Sadlier (Loyola '50—another Moods alumnus), employed the ubiquitous Joe Hebert to direct the Delgado Stage Band.

With the former Loyolians prominent in key teaching positions and active as private music tutors as well, it is not surprising that many excellent young New Orleans musicians have moved towards the old Loyola music building on St. Charles and Calhoun Streets. A walloping 18 of the present 20-piece Loyola Stage Band were students of Loyola alumni while in high school, and in the past decade the Loyola Music School has recruited an astonishing number of highly competent stage band performers trained by ex-Loyolians.

Under the leadership of Dean Mike Caruba (Loyola '48—once a Moods saxophonist), the music school administration has loosened up considerably from the *woogie boogie* days of Deans Schuyten and Baccich. Caruba approved the stage band directorship as a faculty position in 1965, and in 1967 he established Stage Band as an official course accruing one hour of credit towards a degree in music.

Of course, none of this qualifies Caruba for the title of Crusader Dean. Stage and lab bands have not been innovative for over a decade, and even the most traditional administrator would find the accomplishments of the present Loyola Stage Band difficult to flick off the end of his finger. Under Joe Hebert's baton, the band took first place at the Mobile Intercollegiate Jazz Festival and was one of six bands to compete in the national stage band finals. Local musicians were startled to find that the Loyola group (which is 100 percent union) outshined professional bands of long standing at Local 174's *Dance of the Year* last October. The band is currently preparing for a return to the Mobile competition and has accepted an invitation to perform at *Jazzfest '69* next summer.

Loyola's Stage Band is cast in a Woody Herman mold. The emphasis is on swinging hard, with the crisp and powerful brass section kicked artfully by drummer Johnny Vidacovich. The smooth, tightly knit sax section is paced by alto saxophonist Charles Brent, a junior whose compositions, arrangements, and solo work mark him as one of the most promising young college musicians in the area. The rhythm section, graced by an attractive blonde pianist-singer named Angelle Trosclair, gained a valuable addition this year in Ronnie Eschete, a twenty-one-year-old guitarist from Houma, Louisiana.

Director Hebert is a native Orleanean who started playing tuba at Colton Junior High School under Rudy Valentino (Loyola '49) and continued in the Nicholls High School band under Joe Lewis (Loyola '49). After graduating from Loyola, Hebert took his Master's degree at Eastman in New York, where his extracurricular activities embraced engagements with the New York Philharmonic and the Village Stompers. In addition to his teaching duties at Easton High School, Loyola, and Delgado, he is the bassist with Dave West's modern jazz trio on Sundays at the Bistro lounge.

Musicians of Hebert's breadth of experience and interest make an important point about the jazz revolution in education. The young jazzmen asking for change were not mindless radicals out to destroy the foundations of music education. Like most students, they simply wanted to have access to the present as well as to the past so they could have the tools they needed for shaping the future.

It is probably in the nature of things that students know the sniff and savor of the present while educators have considerable intellectual, emotional, and professional stock in the past. Neither the student nor the educator needs to sell out or deny the validity of his experience, but each must listen to the other. As the educator recognizes that the student body is equipped with a student mind, he might discover, as music educators are discovering today, that the student's apathy towards the treasures of the past is based on the suspicion— often well-founded—that someone is trying to rob him of the present.

8

Jazzfest 1968: Review

Down Beat, July 11, 1968

Jazzfest '68 was an eight-day musical celebration of the 250th anniversary of the founding of New Orleans. The four evening concerts (beginning Thursday, May 16) were preceded by a number of activities that stressed the intimate relationship of jazz to the total culture of New Orleans.

Although there were some of those rough moments inevitable with first-time ventures, the festival was obviously a musical and financial success — so much so that festival officials were already talking about the Second Annual New Orleans International Jazz Festival by Friday.

The celebration opened officially with a memorial Mass for deceased jazz musicians at St. Louis Cathedral, immediately followed by a jazz concert just outside the church in Jackson Square. Regrettably, the idea of a Jazz Mass was vetoed by the clergy in favor of a traditional Mass by Dutch composer Jan Vermulst. Nevertheless, the ceremony was impressive. The Mass was ably performed by the Concert Choir of New Orleans, conducted by Rev. Carl Davidson and augmented by brass and tympani. Archbishop Phillip M. Hannan celebrated the Mass, assisted by Bishop Harold R. Perry and a legion of monsignori. The only jarring element was occasional lapses of taste in Rev. Davidson's brass and tympani scoring, which had overtones of a Cecil B. deMille production.

The concert after the services began a little self-consciously, with newsmen and camera bugs sniffing around the corners of the square for local color. Soon, however, the second-liners planted for the shutterbugs' benefit were joined by the local citizenry, visitors, and passers-by, and everyone began to have some honest-to-God New Orleans–style fun. In one hilarious St. Ann Street scene, a drunk wandered into a group of street dancers and immediately became engaged in some unforgettable Chaplinesque dancing and horseplay.

The four bands (the Olympia Brass Band, the Young Tuxedo Brass Band, the Crawford-Ferguson Night Owls, and Frank Federico's Dixielanders) were well chosen for the event. The brass bands presented some interesting contrasts and deviations within the marching band tradition. The Olympia has a unique member in ironlipped trumpeter Milton Batiste, who blasted out above the band, using the jumble of syncopations as a background for his raggedly exciting phrases. The Young Tuxedos showed some interesting approaches to marching band drum styles. Bass drummer Emile Knox and snare drummer Lawrence Trotter often played softly or even dropped out during the ensembles, coming in only at the end of each 8-bar phrase with clever snare-bass combinations that strongly resembled modern jazz "bass bops." (Most marching band bass drummers, incidentally, have abandoned simple 2/4 rhythms for an irregularly accented 4/4 or other variations.)

The Night Owls and Federico's group attracted less attention than the colorful brass bands, but the former were well worth hearing. The Crawford-Ferguson group is the only band I've heard that can use a tuba and two banjos yet avoid the archaic, constipated sound that bedevils most revivalist groups. Cornetist Jack Bachman and clarinetist Hank Kmen, who have found their places in the band without referring to classical models, are responsible for this.

The fourth band started late because guitarist-leader Federico discovered that there was no outlet on St. Peter Street for his amplifier. Nevertheless, drummer Al Babin held the rhythm section together creditably, and trumpeter Tony Dalmado carried the front line solidly through a series of Dixieland standards.

Monday and Tuesday featured random daytime appearances by local bands on Canal Street and the usual kaleidoscope of jazz at night in the French Quarter. On Wednesday evening, a parade began at Congo (Beauregard) Square and weaved through the French Quarter, ending up at the Canal St. dock. Participants were the Young Tuxedo Marching Band, the Olympia Marching Band, the Roman New Orleans Marching Band, the Olympia Brass Band, Barry Martyn's Band from England, the Barrelhouse Band from Germany, the Police Department Band, the Red Garter Band, and the Father's Mustache Band.

The parade was followed by a riverboat cruise and jazz concert aboard the Steamer *President*, which supposedly was to feature Dixieland groups from New Orleans, Chicago, and New York in a battle of bands. Nobody took the three-city gimmick seriously, since the New York group included such varied stylists as trumpeter Max Kaminsky, clarinetist Pee Wee Russell, and bassist Bob Haggart, while Art Hodes' Chicago group included New Orleans-born trombonist George Brunies. The battle of bands was no real cutting contest either, since the bands played separate sets rather than sparring tune for tune. And the "concert" became a dance when the crowd moved the chairs aside during Kaminsky's set and began to dance in every style from two-step to boogaloo.

Trumpeter Sharkey Bonano's local group played a strong opening set. All the musicians were keyed up to the situation and played a little more thoughtfully than in recent routine appearances. By far the most interesting player was veteran clarinetist Harry Shields, brother of the late Larry Shields of the Original Dixieland Jazz Band. Shields has a way of slurring up to a high note that is absolutely chilling. His lower register is beautiful and his three-chorus solo on *Tin Roof Blues* was the most moving blues performance of the evening.

Hodes' band sounded a bit ragged. The musicians were obviously having trouble hearing each other because of microphone problems, crowd noises, and the generally poor acoustics on the boat. Brunies and trumpeter Whitey Myrick romped through the set with considerable aplomb, but the rhythm section took to chopping wood and lost its finesse.

The audience was wildly responsive, though, and soon after Kaminsky opened his set with *Dippermouth Blues*, dancing broke out. Kaminsky earnestly urged the crowd to quiet down, unaware of the fact that when a New Orleans audience shouts and dances and spills beer on the floor the band is winning, not losing. The *President* has for years been a floating dance hall for Orleanians, and jazz in this city has always been thought of as a catalyst for the lustier aspects of life.

Apparently regarding the boat as a very large night club, Kaminsky proceeded with what appeared to be a typical club date set: a Herb Gardner trombone solo on *Willow, Weep for Me*, some bass and drum interplay between Bob Haggart and Bob Haggart Jr. on *Big Noise from Winnetka*, and a Dick Hyman piano solo on *Maple Leaf Rag*. The results should have been disastrous, but the group's superlative jazzmanship held the allegiance of the already enthusiastic audience. Kaminsky's best break came during *A Closer Walk With Thee* when a local Gospel singer named Delilah stepped up on the bandstand and poured several thousand decibels of salvation into the microphone, bringing the entire audience to its feet. Delilah's sound would make most Gospel singers sound like Joni James. In the upper register, her voice sounds like a scream trumpet, and her rendition of *Saints* should have shattered every glass on deck.

In the two final sets, Sharkey's and Hodes' groups maintained the excitement generated in Kaminsky's set. Bonano, a natural showman, joined the dancers during his sidemen's choruses, executing some mock-serious bumps and grinds. Hodes' band ended the session with a rockish beat on *Bye and Bye* that left drummer Red Saunders sweating buckets.

All of the major evening concerts were too long. The festival officials realized this after the first night, but the only alternative to five-hour concerts would have been to drastically cut the groups' time on stage, which they wisely refused to do.

Each concert opened with a brass band marching into the Municipal Auditorium from the adjoining Congo Square. On Thursday it was the Onward Brass Band, with Danny Barker as Grand Marshall and such notables as Alvin Alcorn, Louis Cottrell, and Paul Barbarin in the lineup. Emcee Willis Conover introduced Kaminsky's group, covering for Pee Wee Russell in his usual suave and witty manner when the clarinetist was late in getting on stage.

Jazz buffs expected Russell to steal the show, but this was not a one-star band. Predictably, the front line showed more control than on the previous night's session, and the excellent rhythm section provided unshakable support. Hyman comped imaginatively throughout the set and played a lovely solo (sans bass or drums) on *What's New?* A surprise vocal by Delilah on

A Closer Walk drew warm applause, but failed to match the spontaneous excitement created on the *President*.

A local modern quartet led by former Lionel Hampton drummer June Gardner was up next. A month before the festival, the group's co-leader, tenor saxophonist Alvin Tyler, underwent surgery, and tenor saxophonist-flutist James Rivers joined the combo at that time. Gardner opened with an up-tempo blues that never did quite find a groove. Bassist Lawrence Gayton could not be heard. Only Rivers seemed unabashed by it all as he ripped off a dozen choruses clearly identifying him as a fluent and adventurous avant garde musician. Rivers' flute solo on *Red Fox* was a high point of the program. He hummed, gasped, grunted, and groaned along with and between phrases, holding the audience spellbound. The society ladies who had come to hear Pete Fountain were completely disoriented, and their confusion was compounded when Rivers did the Roland Kirk thing with tonette, harmonica, and vaudeville whistle.

Fountain appeared in a bright blue sportjacket and Tide-white trousers that left an after-image if you shifted your gaze from the stage. Fountain has molded his four-piece brass section (which looked and sounded utterly clumsy last year) into a smoothly functioning unit. The rhythm section, sparked by the recent addition of Nick Fatool on drums, is thoroughly pro, and tenorist Eddie Miller and vibist Godfrey Hirsch have adapted to the oversized combo well.

Fountain was in good form on Dixie nuggets like *Jazz Me Blues*, *Way Down Yonder in New Orleans*, *Saints*, *Tin Roof Blues*, and *High Society*. Fountain and trumpeter Connie Jones were outstanding on *Tin Roof*, and in a Fatool-Fountain duet on *High Society*, the drummer humorously combined syncopated snare drum march beats with intermittent bass drum bombs. The set ended with an unexpected appearance by comedian Phil Harris, who added to the festival spirit with some fastpaced humor and a vocal on *Cabaret*.

Hodes' set was not musically interesting. The leader's usually compelling piano did not bring the group to life, and even his solo spot on *Grandpa's Spells* lacked his customary drive. Whitey Myrick was again dependable on trumpet, but Brunies did not repeat his impressive performance of the previous evening. Instead, he busied himself upstaging the soloists, and on his own choruses he often put the bell of his horn directly up to the mike, nearly blasting the audience back into Congo Square. Jimmy Granato's flimsily structured clarinet lines seemed to lead nowhere. Red Saunders' extended solo on *Battle Hymn of the Republic* (*every* drummer on the Thursday program played an extended solo) was a bore.

The audience took a little time to warm up to vocalist Teddi King, whose supperclub manner did not communicate well in the festival atmosphere. Her third selection, *When the Sun Comes Out*, was a belter that finally brought the crowd around. However, Miss King came back with the supersophisticated *Tennessee Williams Southern Decadence Blues*, and the audience was just not in the mood for all that cerebration.

Duke Ellington did not go on until nearly midnight, but his set was superb. The opening *A-Train* found Cootie Williams in an odd mood, playing raw, uneven, strangely haunting phrases. On the shuffle blues that followed, Williams was also effective in a more conventional plunger mute solo. A back-to-back spotlighting of clarinet solos by Jimmy Hamilton on *The Girdle Hurdle* and Russell Procope on *Swamp Goo* offered interesting stylistic contrasts— Hamilton, with his near-legit sound, always clean and fleet; Procope with a richly coarse sound and a style that harks back to Noone and Dodds.

Tenorist Paul Gonsalves was featured on two numbers and astonished this reviewer with his stylistic range. His playing on *Mount Harissa* was free, passionate, mature, and brilliant. The daring cadenza concluding his second solo spot showed that the avant garde has not left him behind.

The most intriguing composition of the set was *La Plus Belle Africaine*. This hypnotically moody piece featured extended in- and out-of-tempo solos by Harry Carney, Hamilton, and the excellent young bassist Jeff Castleman. Cat Anderson's role was also interesting—he followed his usual ensemble screams with random, squealing darts of sound that created an exotic setting for Castleman's and Carney's solos.

The band ended the concert with several old favorites, including *I Got It Bad* and *Satin Doll*, and a young singer named Trish Turner gave a slick performance on *Misty*. But this was lagniappe after the dynamic and absorbing Ellington of the first part of the set.

On Friday, the Young Tuxedo Band did the entrance march, loosening up the audience for trumpeter Thomas Jefferson's quintet. There was no trace of the first-night jitters that seemed to prevail on Thursday. Jefferson's swing-based group relaxed immediately, and the crowd appeared to sense that a groove was going. Drummer Freddy Kohlman laid it down effortlessly on a rapid *Fidgety Feet* and a medium-bounce *Butter and Egg Man* while Jefferson and tenor saxophonist-clarinetist Sam Dutrey offered fluent, well-constructed solos. Jefferson's pleasant vocal and electric trumpet on *St. Louis Blues* prompted Willis Conover to characterize the set as "a capsule history of jazz."

Willie-Tee and the Souls, the New Orleans avant garde combo so highly touted by Cannonball Adderley, was excellent in its brief set. The group obviously seeks out fresh material and approaches, and like their musical forebears, the musicians have a gift for collective improvisation. One humorous tune (dedicated to Joe Zawinul) sounded like a combination of an ultra-hip chart and *Goosey Gander*. The solos started in a funky groove, then moved into some frantic triplet figures, drummer David Lee jabbing out varied accents while Willie-Tee produced Martian sounds from the organ. Alto saxophonist Earl Turbinton's *Ma Rainey*, a grabber of a chart that begins with a single bent note, found guitarist George Davis stretching out against a background of drum and organ explosions, echoes, and ripples. The Souls were well up to their appearance at a major jazz festival; they certainly deserve wider exposure.

Dapper pianist Ronnie Kole's mixture of jazzmanship and showmanship came through well on a long blues and an overblown version of *When Johnny Comes Marching Home*. The former was a reasonably straight jazz performance, except for the group's addiction to quoting from everything from *Mary Had a Little Lamb* to *Way Down Yonder in New Orleans*. The staginess of *Johnny* was redeemed by a surprisingly adept Bellson-like drum solo by Dickie Taylor. Bassist Everett Link was in excellent form throughout.

The set by the Louis Cottrell-Paul Barbarin traditional band with singer Blanche Thomas might have been fine but for the constant rushing of pianist Dave Williams. Drummer Barbarin's sure sense of time was continually thwarted by the pianist's odd, impulsive acceleration. Miss Thomas' vigorous vocals helped to draw attention away from the battle in the rhythm section, but it was guitarist Danny Barker's witty, compose-as-you-go vocal on *St. James Infirmary* that saved the set.

Dave Brubeck and Gerry Mulligan, assisted by bassist Jack Six and drummer Alan Dawson, started out sounding like a sax man with a rhythm section on *Basin Street Blues*. On *Cielito Lindo*, though, they were obviously stimulated by possibilities of superimposing 4/4 on the basic 6/8 rhythm, and the group's time firmed up considerably. A slow unidentified Latin number brought forth Mulligan's best solo of the set, while the entire group caught fire during Mulligan's choruses on *Out of Nowhere*. Dawson was the prime mover here, second-guessing Mulligan at every turn, supporting Brubeck's solo with some beautifully controlled bass drum work, and complementing the counterpoint choruses at the end with perfect taste. The audience clamored for more, but Gentleman Dave pointed out that there were many bands to be heard in the festival.

Barry (Kid) Martyn's British group was spurred on by Sammy Rimmington's persuasive traditional clarinet on standards like *Panama, High Society*, and the seldom-heard *Red Man Blues*. However, the group was hampered by a trumpeter who was working too hard at getting an "old" sound. His erratically romantic phrasing on *Tin Roof* destroyed the unity of the front line and his solos were marked by the kind of short phrases played by old men whose wind is failing. Drummer Martyn and the other sidemen performed adequately, but with neither the verve nor the conception of genuine early jazz stylists.

Pianist Armand Hug's set laid an enormous egg. Hug's formidable talent is heard to best advantage in a small group, but he brought with him five hornmen who were strung out across the stage like mannequins in a store window. Hug took a good seven minutes to introduce and eulogize them all. The one outstanding soloist in the front line, clarinetist Raymond Burke, could not be heard during his chorus on *Original Dixieland One-Step*. A mediocre vocal by bassist Sherwood Mangiapane on Hoagy Carmichael's *New Orleans* drew tepid applause. Hug and drummer Paul Edwards' shaky duets on *Maple Leaf Rag* and a bland original called *Royal Orleans Moods* intensified the gloom.

Just when things were going badly, trumpeter Wingy Manone showed up as a surprise guest and made them worse. He played three tunes and talked incessantly, mostly about himself. It was evident to everyone but Manone that the audience was nearing a state of revolt. By the time he had ended *Isle of Capri*, the lobbies were filled with smokers awaiting the appearance of Cannonball Adderley.

Cannonball rescued the audience with an Afro-rock tune by Joe Zawinul called *Rumpelstiltskin*. Happily, Nat Adderley was singing out in the crisp, extroverted style which I have always preferred to his cooler, Milesian moments. After *A Day in the Life of a Fool* the group moved into three short, soulful but solo-less numbers, including the popular *Mercy, Mercy, Mercy*. A blues closed out the set and the second evening concert, the most uneven of the week.

Saturday morning's Youth Concert for students in the federally-funded Project Genesis was handled mainly by guitarist Danny Barker. Barker communicated beautifully with the small audience. The Olympia Brass Band illustrated the points in Barker's talk, and the Barrelhouse Band from Frankfurt, Germany, was living testimony to the universality of jazz. A completely charming Cajun folk trio (violin, accordion, triangle) left the kids cold after three selections, but the few adults in the audience were enthralled by their innocent songs and lilting, pleasantly redundant rhythms.

The Saturday night concert was the most varied of the evening sessions. After the march-in opening by the Olympia Brass Band, the German Barrelhouse Band began the program with its interpretation of traditional jazz— a titillating combination of King Oliver, the ODJB, Boyd Senter, Freddie Schnikelfritz Fisher, and lesser-known sources. Some snappy head arrangements for alto sax and clarinet behind cornetist Horst Dubuque on the opener were followed by solos that for the most part hit dead center between jazz and corn. However, leader-clarinetist-arranger Reimer von Essen did have command over New Orleans–style clarinet in the Dodds tradition, and it would be interesting to hear him in a different context. On the final choruses of each tune, where the head arrangements gave way to free-wheeling group improvisation, the entire group had a decidedly more virile jazz sound. With the band was a voluptuous 19-year-old blonde vocalist, Angi Domdy, who rendered *Weeping Willow Blues* in Bessie Smith style with considerable credibility.

Singer Lurlean Hunter's set was delightful. She charmed the audience with a winsome manner, well-chosen material, and, it should be mentioned, some fine jazz singing. It must have been a long set, because Miss Hunter sang six songs, including a moody bossa nova treatment of *A Day in the Life of a Fool*, a musical monologue called *Guess Who I Saw Today*, and a slow, booting version of *You're Gonna Hear from Me*. But the set zoomed by, and she was obliged to return for two choruses of *Our Love is Here to Stay* before the audience would let her go.

Trombonist Santo Pecora's Tailgate Ramblers played one Dixie tune, *Bourbon Street Parade*, then moved on to other things. *Sorrento* and *Night*

Train featured tenor man Bill Theodore, who just about stole the set, despite the fact that he handled his material with far less assurance than on local club dates. Pecora moved smoothly, if a bit perfunctorily, through a solo on *I Had the Craziest Dream.* Trumpeter Armin Kay's firm lead was a boon throughout.

The Ramsey Lewis Trio, looking 100% hip in Nehru jackets of different hues and matching orange turtle-neck sweaters, was the biggest hit of the festival. Lewis and his sidemen (bassist Cleveland Eaton and drummer Maurice White) were as tight as a trio can be. They seemed to thoroughly enjoy everything they did, and their jazz conception was flawless. Among the goodies in Lewis' set were several of his best-sellers and two pretty Afro-rock numbers, *Maiden Voyage* and *Ode.*

I was one of the minority in the audience, however, who found Gary Burton's set the most exciting of the festival. Hearing Lewis' trio is always a pleasure, but seldom a challenge. Burton's quartet demonstrated in its brief set what the liberated imagination is capable of. Roy Haynes, at 43 still one of the youngest drummers in jazz, constantly urged the group forward with his free, asymmetrical patterns. Larry Coryell's guitar solos brilliantly assimilated jazz, folk, and rock elements. During Steve Swallow's probing bass solo on *General Mojo's Well-Laid Plan* Coryell eased into some straight strumming in 4/4 which, however unexpected, seemed inevitable once he had done it. Burton's consistently inventive playing justified Willis Conover's comment that he has created a new and viable approach to the jazz vibraharp.

A band led by veteran banjoist Papa French had the unenviable spot between Ramsey Lewis and Gary Burton. But the traditionalists were confident, able performers who engaged the audience so thoroughly that by the end of the set, French and clarinetist-vocalist Joe (Cornbread) Thomas were leading community singing on *You Tell Me Your Dream and I'll Tell You Mine.*

Thomas' warm clarinet and unassuming vocals were complemented by Jay Willis' excellent trumpet work. Willis is one of the few trumpeters under 40 who can play in traditional bands without losing his musical identity. He swung lightly in the ensemble on *Sensation Rag* and offered a fine muted solo on *Darktown Strutter's Ball.* Although I have heard French's band on several occasions at Dixieland Hall, their performance at the festival showed that their magnetism is by no means dependent on the quaint setting of the kitty hall.

The final Saturday set was Louis Armstrong's. It was a typical Armstrong set, which could never be bad. But it was also a routine Armstrong set, with the usual spotlighting of each sideman and predictable selection of tunes like *Indiana, Hello, Dolly,* and *Saints.* In light of the tremendous historical and sentimental value of Armstrong's appearance at the first New Orleans jazz festival, a more imaginative program might have been arranged—a reunion of Armstrong and Barbarin, perhaps, or a three-generation angle with Armstrong, Pete Fountain, and an outstanding teenage instrumentalist.

The Onward Brass Band was the march-in band for the last night of the festival. A welcome addition to the program was the Ebeneezer Baptist Radio Choir and a new Gospel quartet from Dillard University, called the Gospel Gems. The Ebeneezer Choir is well salted with Negro university graduates who have chosen not to deny their rich musical traditions. The choir was impressive on *I'll Wear a Golden Crown* and *I Thank the Lord*, and the four Dillard youngsters, though lacking in polish and power, captured the spirit of their material and could become a first-rate group as they gain experience.

Pianist Ray Bryant's trio was undistinguished except for *Li'l Darlin*, in which Bryant fought his way out of the soul bag and played some adventurous modern jazz piano. Bassist Jimmy Rowser and drummer Lenny Brown looked bored, although the former took an adequate solo on the funky *Shake a Lady*.

Roy Liberto's Bourbon Street Six quickly made friends with the audience with a high-speed version of *Hindustan* that was nevertheless too fast for the comfort of the rhythm section. Liberto's show-oriented band drew earnest applause after each number, but the excellent jazzmanship of some of his sidemen was lost among the vapid vocals, circus tempos, and gimmicks that cluttered the set. Harold Cooper's highly listenable clarinet was buried under layers of nonsense in his feature number, *Nola*. Newcomer Marcel Montecino sounded like a promising pianist, but he had little chance to show his wares. Liberto's brisk trumpet work did come through in the ensembles and in several brief solos. With a bit more respect for the jazz talent among his sidemen, Liberto could hit that happy medium between jazz and entertainment that Pete Fountain has achieved.

Carmen McRae, backed by the Woody Herman Band, emerged as the surprise hit of the festival. After two songs that met with thundering applause, Miss McRae announced that this was her first time in New Orleans. Someone shouted, "We love you!" and that summed it up.

Her performance was superlative, whether on rarities like *I Went and Fell in Love* or familiar material like *Alfie*. Her rendition of *Stardust* made me feel as if I had never heard the lyrics before. *I'm Always Drunk in San Francisco* was intoxicating, and *Day by Day*, revived by some ingenious rhythmic manipulation, was magnificent. Miss McRae brings you *into* a song, and you don't want to get out. If she doesn't return for frequent engagements at the city's major clubs, local clubowners are missing a good bet and jazz fans will miss a great singer.

There were no fire-eaters in alto saxist Al Belletto's quartet, but the group turned in a workmanlike set. The rhythm section (Bill Newkirk, piano; Richard Payne, bass; and Louis Timken, drums) had been heard in earlier concerts accompanying Teddi King and Lurlean Hunter. They were most effective during Belletto's set on the lengthy tribute to the late Monk Hazel, *We Remember You*. Belletto played feelingfully on the Hazel dedication, but his best moments came on a boppish *Stars Fell on Alabama*, when he doubled the time while the rhythm section moved at an easy walking tempo.

The Dukes of Dixieland were joined by Papa Jac Assunto, leader Frank Assunto's father. For many Orleanians, this reunion stirred memories of the late Fred Assunto, who had often stood beside his father doubling trombone parts with the Dukes. Frank's competent, many-faceted trumpet work was the whole show. He recalled Armstrong on *Down in Honky Tonk Town*, played a Howard McGhee–like boppish horn on *Sweet Georgia Brown*, and generally kept a mediocre band moving. A long drum solo by Paul Ferrara brought the usual hurrahs, but much more impressive was the growing maturity reflected in his tasteful ensemble work.

Woody Herman wrapped up *Jazzfest '68* with a memorable big band bash that left many wondering whether this was not his best band in a dozen years. It is a young band, yet it is true to the Herman tradition. The selection of tunes for the set might be criticized as safe festival fare *(Watermelon Man, Days of Wine and Roses, Boogaloo, Woodchopper's Ball)*, but even the oldies were transformed into a fresh experience by the band.

The rhythm section (John Hicks, piano; Carl Pruitt, bass; John Von Ohlen, drums) is surely one of the most powerful and cohesive on the big band scene. Von Ohlen's control is fantastic; he gets a maximum of sound and pulsation with no tension, no wasted motion, no theatrical body-English. The soloists were highly capable, although tenor man Sal Nistico did not soar to his usual heights. The band's major strengths are clearly its precise, fiery ensemble work and its non-stop rhythm section.

Jazzfest '68 was born despite problems of initial financing, in-fighting among critical cultists and musicians, and the inertia that normally operates against initiating such a mammoth project. Now that it has happened, it seems self-evident even to skeptics that New Orleans should have had a jazz festival years ago. Unlike other major festival sites, the city has more to offer than temporary picnic grounds for jazz lovers. It has its own living culture, and that culture is closely tied to the origins of jazz. It has a cadre of gifted musicians, and, as men like Willie-Tee and Thomas Jefferson demonstrated, they are not all candidates for Medicare.

The fact that the festival wound up solvent (all bills were paid by Monday noon) assures the support of the city fathers for next year. The artistic success and cultural relevance of the festival should help to close ranks among musicians and jazzophiles who had reservations about the musical values that would be perpetuated on the program. Granting a few weak musical moments and some minor failings in planning, it must be said that *Jazzfest '68* was a great first try at a major jazz festival.

9

Jazzfest 1969: Preview

New Orleans magazine, April, 1969

Jazzfest '68 looked like a shaky operation in the planning stages last year, but when the week's celebration got under way the whole thing seemed as natural as moss on oak. Why hadn't we done this years ago? everybody asked. New Orleans has much more to offer than Newport's vast picnic grounds and stately homes. It has the right cultural context, a living tradition that makes it the most natural place in the world to start a jazz festival.

The argument is very logical, but in the real world mammoth arts festivals do not depend on logicians but on investors who like to have the warm feeling that people who have money to spend are going to buy what they have to sell. And New Orleans has been slow to embrace jazz as its offspring, just as the patrons of the arts in America have been generally slow to surrender their contempt for native culture and their worship of imported culture.

Despite the fact that Americans have always been far better at innovation than imitation, the instinct of the connoisseur in this country has characteristically brought him back to European models of artistic excellence. Only the prophets in early America saw that the common man could be fundamentally creative, that he could blaze new trails in the arts as well as in the forests. The devotees of high art blushed at the criticism of Sidney Smith, who asked in the *Edinburgh Review* in 1820, "In the four quarters of the globe, who reads an American book? or goes to an American play? or looks at an American picture or statue?" They did not guess that the Golden Age of American literature was only decades away and that Poe, Melville, and others would become respected figures in world literature. They could not imagine that the masses, who caroused savagely at the inauguration of Andrew Jackson, would someday produce artists like Louis Armstrong, Thomas Wolfe, and Jackson Pollock and would someday be eulogized by poets from Whitman to Sandburg to Ginsberg.

Fortunately for jazz, the genuine culture vulture—the one who really believes that Milton is great bedtime reading and jazz is noise from the jungle—is just about extinct. For all his pretensions about good taste, he was basically following the party line of the highbrow community. He could not hold out for long after *The Saturday Review*, Leonard Bernstein, and Bergen Evans admitted that jazz can be good music.

It is no longer sufficient for the responsible patron of the arts to have a sniffing acquaintance with the artistic achievements of Western man in the European tradition. The complete humanist is under considerable pressure to learn about art that grew separately from, even in defiance of, that tradition. His LP collection must include Bach, Beethoven, and Bartok, but it must also extend to Beiderbecke, Basie, and Brubeck. He must have an interest in theater, but he must also know the new art of the film and its early development in America under directors like Griffith and Sennett. He must dig Andy Warhol and Grandma Moses as well as Rembrandt and Picasso.

Jazz festivals had to wait for jazz to gain general respectability, and *Jazzfest* had to overcome longstanding local prejudices against jazz. *Jazzfest* would have been unthinkable in the days when jazz was supported by a heterogeneous underground who huddled around phonographs, subscribed to *The Record Changer*, and hung around that memorable hole-in-the-wall on Baronne Street, the New Orleans Record Shop. It would have been impossible in 1957, when public sentiment vetoed the idea of a jazz monument at the head of Basin Street where a statue of Simón Bolívar now stands. (One irate citizen suggested that it would be equally appropriate to build a monument there to Lulu White.)

To put it bluntly, *Jazzfest* could not happen until the Establishment accepted jazz. The Establishment has a tin ear, of course, so it had to consult the local aesthetes. The highbrow community of New Orleans—a stuffy non-confederation of organizations composed of intellectual camp followers, genuinely sensitive individuals, and a few artists who usually look like they would rather be elsewhere—had made some progress towards acceptance of jazz. Tulane University exercised admirable leadership in 1958 by establishing the Jazz Archive, which began gathering data about jazz for use by scholars. Jazz was given some official recognition when the Jazz Museum (created by the New Orleans Jazz Club in 1961) was granted membership in the Cultural Attractions Fund.

The New Orleans Jazz Club can undoubtedly be singled out as the group that has done most to elevate the status of jazz in our city. The idea for *Jazzfest* originated in the club, but *Jazzfest* is the culmination of years of effort that opened the public's eyes to the worth of jazz and the important jazz artists who are still in town. The club had emissaries in business, social, and educational circles—people like Harry Souchon, the late Edmond Souchon, Myra Menville, and Durel Black—who helped to sell grass roots culture to those who did not understand it or saw it as a threat to their genteel notion of the arts.

But two attempts at an International Jazz Festival failed in 1965. One (again, a Jazz Club project) was canceled due to the withdrawal of investors, who feared that racial conflicts might arise similar to those that canceled out a professional football game earlier in the year. Another festival was actually held on a small scale at the Roosevelt Hotel, but it lacked both financial support and an eloquent spokesman. Its main organizer was a jive-talking attorney named Dean Andrews.

By 1968 jazz was apparently safe water—artistically, financially, and politically—and Jazzfest '68 was launched under the banner of New Orleans' 250th Anniversary Celebration with just about everybody's blessing. Although there were some minor snags and logistical errors, the festival was wildly successful. The main problem was that the night concerts were just too much of a good thing. Overly ambitious programming turned the concerts into after hours sessions, with some of the big name artists beginning their sets as late as 1:00 a.m.

The *Jazzfest* talent committee this year hired Willis Conover, last year's emcee, as talent director for the entire festival. Conover is a knowledgeable, perceptive, soft-spoken jazz enthusiast. He was musical director of THE Orchestra, a first-rate big band out of Washington, D.C., in the early 1950's. For years he has brought recorded jazz to the Iron Curtain countries via The Voice of America, for which he is currently doing twelve shows a week.

Despite a slightly scholarly, Clark Kent–like bearing, Conover can handle an audience well and is not frightened by the unexpected. During last year's program he covered skillfully for a late appearance by clarinetist Pee Wee Russell, and when some prop-shifting caused a long delay between bands he simply said, "I've never believed that an emcee has to be talking endlessly when there's not a band onstage. There'll be a brief pause while the stage is set up for the next performer."

According to Conover, planning a festival is more than "grabbing a miscellany of musicians and shooting in all directions." A festival should grow "out of a concept, into which the most appropriate elements have been fitted. Each musician, each group, is an element in that concept, if it is to grow, to develop, to lead to climaxes with maximum surety of impact."

Conover has taken the best ideas from last year's festival, shopped around town for some new angles, and come up with some surprises that promise to make *Jazzfest 1969* an exciting musical experience. Another break for this year's festival is a parallel program, the New Orleans Food Festival, which will run throughout the week of *Jazzfest*. Creole dishes will take up where jam sessions leave off, culminating in a block-long display of New Orleans foods prepared by local restaurants.

Conover has prepared a musical menu that jazz fans will find irresistible. He has organized a Jazzfest House Band that will perform in a variety of roles throughout the festival, and the musicians in it are among the most versatile and gifted in jazz. Last year's concert-dance on the Steamer *President* will be repeated, but the Jazzfest House Band and Pete Fountain's band will share the bandstand this year. Some of the "name" stars on the festival—Sarah Vaughan and Count Basie, for example—will make multiple appearances, always in different contexts. Local jazzmen, besides playing on the various concerts throughout the week, will be featured exclusively in a climactic closing concert on Saturday night, the theme of which is *New Orleans Mon Amour.*

Jazzfest 1969 will open at 2:00 p.m. on Sunday, June 1st, with *Soul Session*, a two-hour concert at Municipal Auditorium that will stress the religious roots of jazz. Sarah Vaughan will perform with the Concert Choir of New Orleans and also with a local gospel group not named as yet. Clarinetist Jimmy Giuffre, best known for his work on the West Coast in the 1950's, will play an experimental neo-Gregorian chant, and the Jazzfest House Band will be introduced with a set of jazz spirituals.

About that house band, Trumpeter Clark Terry—formerly with Duke Ellington, now a regular with the NBC Studio Orchestra on the *Tonight* show—will front the group in cooperation with tenor saxophonist Zoot Sims. Sims, who was one of the original *Four Brothers* of the Woody Herman band, is one of the greatest of the modern jazz tenor men. Jaki Byard, a veteran New York pianist currently enjoying high prestige among jazz critics, was impressive in his performance for the Mayors' Conference at Rivergate late last year. Toots Thielmans, a former George Shearing sideman seen here at the Playboy Club, is often overlooked by jazz fans because of his unorthodox combination of instruments. He is a fine guitarist and the world's only really effective jazz harmonica player. Bassist Milt Hinton is one of the solidest rhythm artists in jazz. Mention his name along with Ray Brown and a very few other universally respected bassists. Drummer Alan Dawson won over the *Jazzfest* audience last year when he had the unenviable job of filling the chair of Joe Morello on Dave Brubeck's set. He was up to the task, and the crowd will be glad to see him back with the all-star house band.

After *Soul Session* the food festival will begin with services in St. Louis Cathedral and a procession leading to the Toulouse Street wharf, where a traditional blessing of the shrimp fleet will take place. In Jackson Square booths will be set up with samples of creole food. The food festival will continue on Monday evening when a buffet at the Plimsoll Club (limited to 600 diners) will be held.

Jazzfest strikes up again on Tuesday evening with a multi-band parade beginning in the French Quarter and ending at the Steamer *President*. The marching bands—among them the Onward Band, the Olympia Band, and the Congo Square Band—will disperse at the Canal Street landing so that Pete Fountain and the Jazzfest House Band can start the session on the boat.

Wednesday night tenor saxist Stan Getz is tentatively set to appear in concert with the award-winning University of Illinois Stage Band. Getz, like Zoot Sims, was one of the original Four Brothers with Woody Herman. His style, which is at once cool and intimate, impressed the jazz world on records like *Early Autumn* with Herman, and more recently on moody bossa novas like *The Girl From Ipanema* and *Desifinado*. Getz will appear in still another light as he shares the stage with Eddie Miller, the veteran Dixieland tenor saxophone stylist with Pete Fountain's combo.

The Illinois group is a musically and showmanly band that won the *Down Beat* national collegiate stage band championship in competition with groups from all over the country. Probable late entries for the Wednesday evening program are the magnificent jazz organist, Jimmy Smith, and trombonist Kid Ory, a seminal figure in the evolution of jazz trombone. Ory is expected to return to New Orleans after an absence of many years to appear on the *Jazzfest 1969* program.

On Thursday night at the auditorium two of the most celebrated eccentrics in jazz will do a double piano concert. Willie "the Lion" Smith will join Eubie Blake for duets, chatter, and whatever else might develop. The careers of Blake, 86, and Smith, 71, span several eras in jazz, and their experience embraces vaudeville, motion pictures, extensive recording, and several world tours. The Dizzy Gillespie Quintet will be on the Thursday program, and plans are in the making for Gillespie to join forces with two other out-standing contemporary jazz trumpeters for a trumpet trio that should provide some fascinating stylistic contrasts. Sarah Vaughan will be spotlighted again, this time with the competent University of Illinois aggregation providing the background.

Friday night will be a big band bash built around the rock-solid Count Basie band. The entire first half of the program will be devoted to the Basie group, which is peerless in jazz for its unfailing drive and firmness of conception. The Jazzfest House Band will emerge from its supporting role to be featured in a set of its own on the second part of the program. A parade of ex-Basie bandsmen who were pioneers of the swing era—trumpeter Buck Clayton, trombonist Dickie Wells, tenor saxophonist Earle Warren—will appear, leading to a finale in which the former sidemen will sit in with the present Basie band. (Aside: Basie will play a little-publicized after hours dance one night, reportedly on Thursday or Friday, at a French Quarter hotel.)

On Saturday afternoon Pirates' Alley will be lined with food rather than the usual paintings by sidewalk artists. The entire block will be decked out with food displays prepared by prominent New Orleans restaurants. The restaurants, of course, will be featuring special New Orleans cuisine throughout the week of the festival, just as local night clubs will be touting their jazz groups with extra enthusiasm during *Jazzfest 1969*.

The final night's program, *New Orleans Mon Amour*, centers on New Orleans musicians and their music. Local artists who play in many jazz styles will be heard, former Orleanians will return for special appearances, and foreign bands that have been influenced by traditional jazz will play a tribute to our music. Among the returning jazzmen will be clarinetist Tony Parenti and drummer Zutty Singleton. The highly-rated Loyola University Stage Band, which won the Mobile Jazz Festival competition in 1968 and barely lost this year to the University of Illinois band, will perform. Pianist Chuck Berlin, who plays a highly stylized jazz piano in addition to his work as an Associate Professor of Otorhinolaryngology and Bio-Communication at LSU Medical School here, will be on the program. An all-star jam session with sidemen from local jazz groups will be held, and four of the famed local marching bands will appear.

A highlight of the closing show will be Pete Fountain's Clarinet Marmalade, a mini-festival in which Pete will introduce a number of fine local clarinetists who will engage in a friendly cuttin' contest. The clarinet session is another it-could-only-happen-here angle. No other city in America has such a formidable cadre of excellent clarinetists. The instrument suffered a loss of status in the jazz world after the swing era. But New Orleans, steeped in the tradition of artists like Johnny Dodds, Jimmy Noone, and Irving Fazola, continued to produce reed men who were more inclined to the clarinet than to alto or tenor saxophone.

Few cities would dare to present "local talent" at the climax of a major arts festival. New Orleans dares, because the city is fully confident that its people have shaped a new and uniquely expressive art form from their experience. Cliché has it that New Orleans is one of the few cities in America that doesn't remind you of dozens of other cities. Cliché is right. Centuries ago things began to happen in this thriving town by the river—things too complex to put into words, but not impossible to express in music; things too elusive to be predicted or created by conscious effort, but too important to escape eventual formation into the customs and art of the people. We specialize in hot food and hot jazz. Doubloons without value, doughnuts without holes. Incense and concupiscence. Citoyens, come and get it.

10

Jazzfest 1969: Review

Vieux Carre Courier, June 6, 1969

PART 1: FOOD FOR EAR AND BELLY

Jazzfest 1969 opened Sunday with a program that centered about the religious roots of jazz, and the results could be described as a mixed blessing. The crowd was disappointingly small, but generally enthusiastic. The program was carefully thought out and well paced, but it was more commercial than it needed to be. Musically, there were many fine moments but no great ones.

The Onward Brass Band opened the festivities with a mock funeral procession, playing *A Closer Walk with Thee* as a dirge. Talent director Willis Conover read a brief, tasteful narrative on an offstage mike, setting the religious theme for the afternoon's program. The Onwards broke into *Bourbon Street Parade* in the traditional manner after the mock burial, and Jazzfest was off to a salubrious start.

Jimmy Giuffre, the clarinetist who has been associated with third-stream music on the West Coast for so many years, improvised with guitarist John Stauber on a simple theme, described as "neo-Gregorian" and sung by a small choir. Giuffre played with considerable imagination, although the relationship of the performance to Gregorian chant was highly dubious. The choir sang in unison, but Giuffre's development of the theme scarcely called up the mood of chant. His absorbing interplay with Stauber's sensitive unamplified guitar was interesting precisely because it was complex, polyphonic and adventurous—none of which are characteristics of Gregorian chant.

With an ease and smoothness of pace that was typical of the entire program, the Giuffre section melded into the first appearance of the Jazzfest House Band. The all-star group, composed of trumpeter Clark Terry, tenor saxophonist Zoot Sims, pianist Jaki Byard, bassist Milt Hinton, and drummer Alan Dawson, played a coda-like extension of the Giuffre improvisation, then moved into a spiritual called *Say Amen*. The audience warmed up to the group quickly and Hinton drew heavy applause for his buoyant, down-home solo on the opening selection.

A Gospel vocal quintet—adequate but a bit more slick and sophisticated than many of the exciting groups that can be heard in this area—joined the house band on the spiritual and did a competent job on the overworked pop-Gospel classic, *Down by the Riverside*. The group's unidentified female soloist enlivened the performance with some supple phrasing and that oddly moving, shaky intonation that only Gospel and opera singers can get away with.

After intermission, pianist Jaki Byard was featured with Hinton and Dawson on a slow blues which, like most of the program, was obviously intended to move from a simple base into the gorgeous badlands of improvisation. However, the solo failed to get beyond the level of some rather ordinary explorations in three-quarter time, and it was again Hinton's solo that won the audience's approval.

Sarah Vaughan furnished the most electric performance of the afternoon and sparked the remarkable Terry to some soaring, fiery solos, most notably on an up-tempo version of *I Cried for You*. Miss Vaughan pleased the crowd with a set of jazz standards like *All of Me, Polka Dots and Moonbeams, On a Clear Day*, and *Misty*. There was little that explicitly related to Gospel sources in the selection of tunes before the finale, but her unfailing swing and rhythmic fluency provided a natural cross-reference to the Gospel group that appeared earlier on the program.

The finale was one of those everybody-on-stage rousers, yet the inevitable did not happen—nobody played *The Saints*. The vehicle was a bouncy reprise of the opener, *A Closer Walk with Thee*, and Miss Vaughan apologetically read the lyrics from a piece of paper ("I haven't sung this since I was a little girl in church"), supported by the Jazzfest House Band, the Onward band, the Giuffre duo, the Gospel group and the chorus.

Things almost got out of hand when the house band rhythm section apparently lost contact with the Onward band's formidable bass drummer, Freddy Kohlman, and Jimmy Giuffre was caught between two tempos in his strange, really strange, pseudo-Dixieland solo. Clark Terry saved the day with a let's-plunge-in-here entrance that redefined the beat and carried the musical behemoth to a unified conclusion.

Miss Vaughan's encore, performed as many were preparing to leave, was a stirring rendition of *The Lord's Prayer*. Accompanied only by New Orleans pianist Dave West, Miss Vaughan redeemed the raucous hoopla of the finale, giving the program an unexpected dimension and balance with her highly individualized (though fundamentally straight) interpretation.

This year's service at St. Louis Cathedral after the concert again failed to realize the possibilities for making religious ceremony an integral part of the week's festivities. Last year's brass and choir performance of the Jan Vermulst Mass in honor of deceased jazz musicians was a letdown because the hierarchy had rejected the idea of an actual Jazz Mass. Still, the Roman Catholic Mass is pretty good theater, and this year's amorphous ecumenical ceremony was a greater failure of imagination than was the 1968 celebration.

The ceremony featured the Crescent Community Gospel Chorus, directed by Dr. Elliot Beal, who did a workmanlike job with the mediocre materials composed by Laurinne Goreau. One wonders whether Miss Goreau's highly over-rated spirituals—not to mention her bland mis-scoring of *The Lord's Prayer*—would ever have left her escritoire if she were not a newspaper columnist. With a number of fine young jazz-oriented composers around town—Bert Braud and Roger Dickerson come to mind immediately—it seems wasteful to ornament a potentially vital part of Jazzfest with the work of a hobbyist.

The opening of the food festival in Jackson Square and the symbolic shrimp boat blessing that followed the ecumenical services were graced by several marching bands, including the Onward band, the Olympia band, the Young Tuxedo band, and the Congo Square band. It is clear from the development of the various marching bands in recent years that little attempt is being made to preserve a "pure" traditional style. For example, bass drummers play a variety of rhythms, including four-to-the-bar with an accented fourth beat. The new Congo Square band includes young trumpeters like Sam Alcorn and John Brunious, who play boppish phrases or scream out in the upper register. The result, far from bastardization, is a brisk, freewheeling sound that maintains the spirit of the old tradition but keeps it fresh and interesting. The day might come when it will be musically valid to pair Eric Dolphy with the Congo Square Marching Band on a Jazzfest program.

In a sense Jazzfest really begins with the marching bands in Jackson Square, because it is there that the self-consciousness of the mammoth festival thaws out and the people really get down to having fun, New Orleans style. The people of New Orleans still see jazz as an adjunct to social life, and for them Jazzfest is most real in the Jackson Square shenanigans and at the party on the Steamer *President*—but that is another story, and it will be reported next week.

PART 2: TO A SLOW FINISH—*VIEUX CARRE COURIER*, JUNE 13, 1969

Jazzfest activities resumed with a concert on the Steamer *President* Tuesday night, picked up momentum with the Friday Count Basie session, then ended anti-climactically in a not-so-grand finale on Saturday.

This year's concert and cruise on the *President* was not a repeat of last year's frenzied jazz band ball. The audience came to listen, not to shout and clap their hands, and as a result there was more good music but less of the party atmosphere that typifies New Orleans jazz concerts.

The Jazzfest House Band, undaunted by the heat and poor acoustics, turned in its most exciting performance of the week. There was plenty of time to stretch out on each tune, and Clark Terry and Zoot Sims took particularly good advantage of the freedom from tight scheduling that marked the performances at the Municipal Auditorium. The rhythm section was grooving along beautifully, with pianist Jaki Byard taking an unaccompanied solo on *Now's the Time* that packed decades of jazz history into a few witty blues choruses.

Pete Fountain's band continues to grow in cohesiveness, demonstrating the flexibility of a small combo despite an oversized brass section. This is largely due to the drumming of Nick Fatool, who plays tricky rudimental fills between choruses, phrases with the brass in big band style, and maintains a flowing, relaxed pulse that few uptight Dixieland drummers achieve.

Pete's solo work has never sounded better. His full, rich sound was hypnotic on jazz standards like *Tin Roof Blues*, incendiary on swingers like *China Boy*. The band's other featured soloist, veteran tenor saxophonist Eddie Miller, climbed out of his usual rut and got into some gutsy and inventive ideas on *Mood Indigo*.

Wednesday night's concert at the auditorium might have been a bomb except for the energy and ingenuity of the young musicians in the University of Illinois Jazz Band. After multiple flubs on the simple 16-bar introduction to *Basin Street* by an unidentified trumpeter in the balcony and another trumpeter who had the unenviable assignment of echoing his phrases, Jim Robinson's traditionalists played a set that was redeemed from total dullness only by the raw, exciting trumpet work of Ernie Cagnolatti.

The "name" stars—Dizzy Gillespie, Paul Desmond, and Gerry Mulligan—were no less disappointing. They drew warm applause from the audience with throwaway performances that did little more than call up fond memories of their better days. Desmond fell into his lethargic groove that is sometimes mistaken for coolness, sounding like Lee Konitz with three fingers missing. Like Mulligan, Desmond's unique sound and conception carry him with predisposed audiences when the muse fails him. Gillespie's set was slightly more interesting, thanks to some probing piano solos, but both Dizzy and tenor man James Moody have sounded far better at their appearances at Al Hirt's club here.

Marion Love, introduced as a new young vocalist, was easy to look at but burdensome to listen to. Miss Love, combining rock, jazz, blues, and Judy Garland in one of those fragile Diana Ross–type syntheses, brought cheers from the crowd; but her showmanship, not to mention her measurements, far outstripped her musicianship. Miss Love stacks up very well indeed, but not as a jazz singer.

The Illinois band was brilliant. In addition to a high standard of musicianship that is reflected in both ensemble work and solos, the band has two things that few big bands in the country can claim—a group personality and a unique approach to programming.

The Illinois band has humor (as seen in the tongue-in-cheek arrangement of *The Old Beelzebub Blues*), a sense of tradition (evident in *The Lunceford Touch*), and plenty of variety (witness Don Smith's blues vocals, Jim Knapp's thoughtful modern arrangements, Ron Dewar's splendid avant garde tenor). If conductor John Garvey continues to nurture this kind of originality in his band at Champaign-Urbana, he might well provide a new model for the development of big band jazz in our universities.

Thursday night's program was the most varied of the series and probably the most successful from the standpoint of high quality of performances. Eubie Blake, 86, proved once again that old musicians need not sound feeble or play sloppily. His vigorous ragtime piano and charming reminiscences with Willis Conover were a high point of the festival. Richard Davis, the marvelous young modern jazz bassist, performed excellently on *Summertime* and sparked the house band behind a lively set by swing era trumpet pioneer Roy Eldridge.

Multi-instrumentalist Roland Kirk was the surprise hit of the festival. Kirk (incorrectly cited as the late Eric Dolphy by this reviewer last week in a moment of aphasic stupor) is one avant garde musician who is the opposite of esoteric. Kirk, who is blind, plays three instruments at once, beats a gong, blows a vaudeville whistle, and generally supports the erratic energy of his music with wild visual devices. He obviously enjoys it all, and it is impossible to tune him out. But his musical statements are constantly threatened by his bag of tricks, and his Jazzfest set added up to a gaudy cavalcade of gimmicks.

Papa Blue's Vikings from Copenhagen played straight, contemporary Dixie without the ludicrous attempts to get an "old" sound that mars so many European jazz groups. Pianist Armand Hug played the last part of the intermission, as Ronnie Kole had done on Wednesday night. This tactic, apparently intended as a means of giving more festival exposure to local musicians, seems to be more demeaning than helpful to the artist. Certainly it proved both distracting and confusing to the audience.

Sarah Vaughan's program was not as varied as that of her Sunday Soul Session appearance, but it was a solid set made up of jazz favorites like *Bluesette* and *Day In, Day Out*. She was joined by Clark Terry (who, it should be said, was the most consistent artist of the festival) for a scat-singing exchange and by the University of Illinois band for the finale.

Count Basie headlined the Friday concert and was the biggest "draw" in a week of relatively small crowds. Basie's band is still the most powerful music machine in the business. Drummer Rufus Jones is a key figure in the band, executing deft karate chops at the cymbals and a blitzkrieg of bass drum kicks with the brass. Basie's soloists are always in character with the life force that drives the ensembles, and it was a reunion of former Basie sidemen that dominated the second half of the show.

Trombonist Dickie Wells, trumpeter Buck Clayton, tenor saxist Buddy Tate, and alto man Earle Warren joined the Basie rhythm section for several selections in which good jazz and nostalgia were too evenly mixed to be separated. However, altoist Warren was certainly on top of things, unleashing a torrent of ebullient phrases that exemplify swing, both as a noun and a verb.

Friday's show also featured the house band, the European All-Star Dixieland Band, trombonist Albert Mangelsdorff's quintet from Germany, and Rita Reyes, a vocalist from the Netherlands. Mangelsdorff's group (especially tenor saxophonist Heinz Sauer and also saxophonist Gunter Kronberg) are into the avant garde thing with much more intelligence and intensity than many American groups. The musicians were obviously stimulated by each other's work, and they provided one of the brighter sets of the festival. And someone should be congratulated for putting Miss Reyes on the program. She is a totally pleasing, unpretentious vocalist who should be seen and heard more in America.

Saturday night's *New Orleans Mon Amour* concert, dedicated almost entirely to New Orleans musicians, was a frustrating experience. The pressure of presenting over 100 performers on a single night made the programming, which was sound in itself, seem like a huge contrivance as the performers scurried off stage, Cinderella-like, when their allotted time was up. The musicians kept glancing nervously at their watches and were generally apprehensive about the possibilities of problems that might and often did arise. For example, bassist Tony Liuzza was late in getting his Ampeg bass plugged in during Armand Hug's set, and later a mike did not respond to Liuzza's vocal on *Lazy River*.

The hazards of the evening were increased by the fact that all-star groups and make-up combos seldom really play well together on concerts. Hence, Johnny Wiggs' Bayou Stompers with Zutty Singleton and Ray Burke did not sound as good as one might have predicted. (In fact, Zutty was dragging the beat constantly.) Chuck Berlin's new trio featuring James Black got by but did not really jell, and Armand Hug's make-up group (which also backed up Tony Parenti) spent half its energy just trying to keep together and communicating through subdued body English about when to end each tune.

The single entertainers and organized bands fared somewhat better. Pianist Bob Greene's solo ragtime set was 100 percent beautiful. Cousin Joe's blues vocal-and-piano set was a period piece, right out of the 1940's when cute risqué blues (*Blackberry Pickin' Time*) and novelty lyrics ("I never harmed an onion/So why do they make me cry?") were big in night clubs and lounges. A bit of Uncle Tom survives in Joe, but he has a good, throaty sound and his piano changes meter magically and with complete aplomb to suit the whims of his eccentric vocal stylings.

Sharkey Bonano's band, which opened the concert, suffered from a drab rhythm section even though vibist Godfrey Hirsch and guitarist Frank Federico were added to the group in place of a pianist. Clarinetist Harry Shields was not at his best, his usually forceful lines taking off in vague and uncertain directions. Murphy Campo's peppery combo from the Famous Door went through the usual library of clichés used by white Dixieland groups, but the routines came alive under the inspiration of Campo's powerful and spirited trumpet.

The Loyola University Jazz Band used some poor strategy in bringing on a parade of soloists in the opening number, *Down by the Riverside*. The band's strong suits are crisp ensemble work and a kicker of a rhythm section, and it would have been wiser to stick with limited solos by the best improvisers for the Jazzfest appearance. The Fred Crane–Al Belletto performance of *What's New* with the Loyola Band was a successful combination, casting everybody in their better roles.

Another strategic error on the Saturday program was the placing of pianist Dave Williams in the rhythm section to accompany the twenty-some-odd New Orleans musicians who each played a single chorus on a slow blues. Williams frequently accelerates the tempo, and since Zutty was dragging, guitarist Danny Barker and bassist Chester Zardis were left in the middle to hold the beat together.

The four clarinetists (Tony Parenti, Harry Shields, Ray Burke, Louis Cottrell) trading choruses was another good idea that suffered from cramped scheduling. The ploy was no sooner under way with a multi-clarinet rendition of *High Society* when the beat was picked up by the brass bands in back of the auditorium in preparation for the grand finale, which was—what else? —*When the Saints Go Marching In.*

Inevitably, the four brass-and-drum powerhouses could not keep together as they moved toward the stage, and the result was a muddled barrage of noise and vibrations, the sounding of brass and tinkling of cymbals. It was a spellbinding effect, not in the sense that great art inspires awe but in the manner that a man must stand numb and mute at an execution or before the burning of a city. The emotions were not engaged but hijacked, and the only honorable thing to do was leave the auditorium before someone undertook the impossible task of sorting the mess out.

Despite the absurdist strain in Saturday night's program, there was much in this year's Jazzfest that was an improvement over the 1968 festival. The production, while still basically simple and shabby around the edges, obviously had a stronger controlling intelligence. The Ed Sullivan approach was less in evidence; several programs told, or tried to tell, a story. The house band gave the concerts a kind of continuity—so much so that there were spontaneous outbursts of applause when the band showed up each night. The tight scheduling on the concerts was annoying, but it was actually an attempt to avoid last year's five-hour sessions. The pace was certainly brisk, with none of those long lulls while stage hands set up mikes and stands.

There were not as many "stars" this year, but the main problem was that many who were here simply were not playing very well. And any one who follows jazz closely knows that only God knows whether a musician is going to reach the heights of his art or grope about aimlessly on any given night. It is that capricious in a performer's art. In fact, this reviewer would have considered the festival a smashing artistic success if Gillespie, Mulligan, Desmond, Kirk, Hug, Burke, and Shields had been in top form.

As for commercial success, it is doubtful that Jazzfest broke even this year. But there will be another festival in 1970, and it is certain that Durel Black and other Jazzfest officials will search for new ways of filling the auditorium while maintaining a high quality of concert. To the credit of the festival staff, Jazzfest has not turned to the blatant commercialism of Newport. In the words of talent director Willis Conover, Jazzfest is "the world's only all-jazz jazz festival."

11

New Orleans Farewell: Louis Armstrong

Down Beat Annual, *Music* '72

No one expected that more than 10,000 persons would show up for the Louis Armstrong memorial services in New Orleans five days after his death. So the hubbub and confusion that resulted couldn't be blamed on the planners—mostly New Orleans Jazz Club members—who were prepared for neither the size nor the mood of the crowd.

As I got out of my car at O'Keefe Avenue, I felt a brisk air of anticipation in the steady stream of people walking toward Duncan Plaza near City Hall. *My God*, I thought, *do all these people love Louis? Do they know that he was not just a celebrity but a great artist and genius of our time?*

Well, some did and obviously some did not. There were dozens of tourist types (mostly white) with cameras slung on their shoulders, their eyes scanning the scene eagerly for good angles and quaint shots. Thousands of others apparently had come with the intention of paying tribute to Armstrong, our man. My motives, of course, were pure. I had come without pencil or portfolio, wanting very much to mourn Louis' death but also wanting to cheer—with the huge crowd forming in the plaza—for the life he has given us.

I moved slowly up the steps of City Hall to the speakers' area, which consisted of a badly gouged podium and a few chairs on a small patch of space already crowded by the press corps and onlookers. The squeeze was aggravated by the arrangement of the setup directly in front of the main entrance to City Hall, where people poured in and out without concern for the hassled organizers of the ceremony.

Inching back toward the crowd, I overheard two middle-aged black women talking. One had left her church services before communion with the announcement to her preacher that she was off to attend the Armstrong ceremony. Yes, her friend agreed, communion would be there every Sunday but Louis Armstrong would be commemorated only today. All of this was rendered in a gorgeous black New Orleans dialect that comes off like *Amos 'n' Andy* in print but is an elegant chunk of sound when you hear it in person.

There was commotion on the steps as the Young Christian Band, a junior marching group trained in the New Orleans tradition by guitarist Danny Barker, arrived. They played a couple of tunes—*Down by the Riverside* and *Bourbon Street Parade*—and umbrellas in the crowd around the band started bobbing artfully.

This was the first clear indication of a party mood, and the president of Local 174-496 of the Musicians' Union, Dave Winstein, announced over the mike, "We will have to ask the band not to play any more songs. We are here for memorial services and not for entertainment."

Then a great visual oxymoron, New Orleans style: blacks shouting, half angrily and half joyfully at the speakers' podium, shaking in one hand the gaily decorated umbrellas of the second line, holding the other hand out in a bold gesture of black power. Winstein seemed further annoyed at these irreverences but slipped into a showbiz motif himself a little later when he said, "After the Olympia and Onward bands arrive, we'll proceed with our feature program."

The adult marching bands never arrived, though. They were delayed by large crowds at their starting points, the railroad terminal and Basin Street at Canal. (Paul Crawford of the Olympia band later said, "It was all I could do to move the slide on my trombone.") By the time the bands got to Duncan Plaza, there was no way of getting to their appointed places on the steps of City Hall.

The "feature program" started out smoothly enough as the Right Rev. Charles Plauche of St. Francis Cabrini Church offered a brief, dignified benediction with well-chosen Biblical allusions to music. Winstein then introduced Mayor Moon Landrieu, who spoke convincingly about Armstrong as a source of pride to the community. Shouts of "Right on!" "Amen!" and "Yes, brother!" came from the crowd. Landrieu is a skilled politician, of course, but his earnestness in this matter came through as something more than political grandstanding.

Dick Allen of Tulane University's Jazz Archive was next on the program with a neat little essay on Armstrong's life and contributions, suitable for hearthside presentation but disastrous in the sprawling, open-air setting of Duncan Plaza. When Allen said ironically that young Armstrong was "a bad boy," several bloods in the audience shouted "Nooooooo!"

Ernest Wright, president of the Zulu Social Club, was the first black speaker to appear. He reminisced pleasantly about Armstrong's reign over the Zulu parade at the 1949 Mardi Gras and then stopped suddenly. The crowd around the podium got more restless as Wright appeared to be looking for part of his speech, which he finally resumed as if nothing at all had happened.

The eulogy, scheduled for delivery by Dr. E. A. Henry of the First African Baptist Church, was another snafu because Dr. Henry tried to discipline the crowd. He bellowed repeatedly: "I will not give the eulogy in the present climate." A black woman near me, summarizing the feelings of many in the crowd, said, "Thousands of people out here, and he wants pin-drop silence!"

Actually, the noise was concentrated in the area around the podium. As I moved more deeply into the crowd, most persons were listening respectfully to Dr. Henry, only slightly aware of the buzz of the background voices that had driven the speakers to exasperation.

A genuine solemnity was achieved after Henry stepped down and trumpeter Ted Riley played taps for Armstrong from the City Hall walkway that overlooks the plaza. He played very well and very feelingfully on the original cornet that Armstrong used as a boy at the Waifs Home. This was not the glossy and affected simplicity of the network-TV Armstrong tribute of the night before but a pretty moment that Orleanians savored together, certainly the finest moment in the ceremony.

Dave Winstein said, "Thank you. This ends our ceremonies." Many were taken by surprise since the ecumenical clincher—a closing prayer by Rabbi Julian Feibelman—did not go on as scheduled. But by now I was sure the crowd had no intention of rushing home like spectators scrambling to the parking lot after a football game.

In New Orleans a crowd doesn't gather just to *see* something. A crowd rapidly becomes something in itself—something for dancing, for marching, or just milling around being a crowd. So after the Louis Armstrong Memorial Services the people took to walking around the plaza. On my stroll I saw several groups dancing and chanting and innumerable persons enjoying the vibrations that are almost as palpable as summer rain in a New Orleans gathering. Although I never saw a trace of the Olympia and Onward bands, I was assured later that they played with gusto and led a rollicking, fudge-ripple second line away from Duncan Plaza.

The planners of the services had indeed forgotten about the lightheartedness, the joie de vivre of the people in this Mardi Gras city when they prepared a commemorative service for Armstrong with a beginning, a middle, and an end. From the *dirge-to-Saints* sequence of the traditional jazz funeral to the convivial atmosphere of reunion at a New Orleans Roman Catholic wake, the citizens are relentless in turning quickly from death to resurrection.

To the dismay of politicians, urbanologists, revolutionaries, and other would-be pied pipers, New Orleans is a Third World sort of environment where the people cannot be relied upon to act reverential, progressive, conservative, chic, civic-minded, or anything else in the way that Americans usually think of these terms.

As a case in point, take the school integration of 1960. At its peak, white students marched on the school board to demand that the board close the schools, defy federal court orders, etc., etc. Somewhere along the way they were no longer a mob but a New Orleans crowd, chanting and singing and cutting capers. At the school board the police ordered them to disperse. They stuck out their tongues, the fire department turned on the big hoses, and there was a frantic swimming party in the streets until everyone got tired and went home.

A case in point No. 2 was a final scene from the Armstrong ceremony: Almost unnoticed, a police car drove up to the side of City Hall as I was leaving Duncan Plaza. A severe-looking officer efficiently took a small object from a waiting functionary. It was a battered case marked "Louis Armstrong's Cornet." The crown jewels. Only in New Orleans.

SECTION II

"REVIVALS" BEAUCOUP: TRADITIONAL, DIXIELAND, AND REVIVALIST JAZZ

In the previous section I dealt with some social and institutional contexts that affected the growth of jazz and the lives of jazz musicians in the post-war years. Here the focus is on the musicians—mainly the key bands and numerous individual artists who were part of several New Orleans "revivals." These resurgences of interest in jazz have been mischaracterized, I believe, by commentators with limited perspectives or special agendas.

In sorting out the various revivals, I will discuss jazz styles—traditional New Orleans jazz, Dixieland jazz, and revivalist jazz—that call for working definitions and brief comments. As a student of language I do not believe in definitions that freeze-dry concepts and display them in immutable subject–predicate relationships. My definitions will, I hope, have shape and substance, but I offer them as negotiable ideas rather than statements about the nature of things. A working definition tells not what irreducibly "is," but "what I am talking about when I say. . . ."

My definitions of jazz styles, then, are roughly descriptive, commonsense explanations and not philosophical categories. Basically, they are lists—nonexhaustive lists—of characteristics of the different jazz styles as I see them. I believe that a given performance will embody a particular jazz style not on a yes-or-no, all-or-nothing basis, but to the extent that the performance includes and interweaves the various characteristics noted.

This approach avoids the God's-own-truth sort of definition that Al Rose proposed for jazz: "Any known melody as performed by two or more musical voices improvising collectively in 2/4 or 4/4 time and syncopating." Rose did not disguise the fact that he was trying to privilege traditional New Orleans and Dixieland jazz by carefully roping off a few elements. Diana Rose, Al's wife, states that the definition is officially cited by the city of New Orleans in response to questions about jazz. According to such a tendentious definition, the two symphony players I once heard noodling around ineptly on "The Saints" were playing jazz. By contrast, the Basie band's ensemble choruses on "One O'Clock Jump," piano solos by Art Tatum, and innumerable other candidate performances are not jazz at all.

Most jazz fans will find the thrust of my descriptions familiar and, I believe, basically acceptable. Insofar as the definitions and the accompanying discussions reflect my own biases, state or imply qualitative judgments, or include ideas that depart from common usage, they are fair game for criticism. I prefer making my perspectives and use of terms clear up front rather than bootlegging values and concepts through implications embedded in the cleavage of the discussion. In any case, the definitions provide a grounding for the vocabulary used in this section. Finally, two nits can be picked in advance: (1) many of the practitioners named as illustrative of each style have actually played in several styles over the course of their careers and (2) for reasons inferrable from the definitions, the Dixieland and revivalist practitioner lists are not limited to New Orleans musicians.

By *Traditional New Orleans Jazz (TNOJ)*, I mean certain music played by popular bands in New Orleans during the first quarter of the twentieth century, typically but not exclusively by black musicians, with qualities such as the following:

> emphasis on improvisation and mutually supportive ensemble playing
> solos by frontline players (e.g., trumpet or cornet, trombone, and clarinet) initially tending to be uncomplicated but highly expressive, played over an uncluttered 2/4 or 4/4 rhythm
> rhythm sections including some combination of guitar, banjo, tuba, bass fiddle, piano, and drums
> trumpeters, cornetists, and reed players often employing a rapid, rich vibrato
> extremely varied and individualized instrumental tone, from a raw and guttural sound to one relatively close to the tone qualities heard in nonjazz settings
> blue notes, growls, smears, irregularly placed accents, rhythmic figures deliberately delayed or otherwise manipulated, and other unconventional devices, mainly reflecting African influences, giving the music extremely intense, immediately evocative qualities

A common misconception about early TNOJ is the sentimental and ultimately patronizing assumption that it embodied a generic purity and expressive earnestness that was lost as the music changed in the 1920s and beyond. I believe that those who hold to this purist theory, which I will call the TNOJ mystique, are simply drawing a frame around some samples of the early music and declaring whatever is there to be the only true jazz. But prejazz and early jazz recordings and the testimony of musicians suggest that early players by and large combined prejazz articulation, phrasing, and nuances (e.g., staccato eighth notes and dotted eighths and sixteenths, zesty but colorless march-like rhythm, and lugubrious projection of time) with elements like those noted in the working definition above (i.e., elements that in a short time came to characterize jazz as a distinctive form).

Of course, many of the more energetic prejazz elements survived and were even cultivated in the popular music of Tin Pan Alley, various tenor ("Mickey Mouse") bands, deliberately corny bands, and some revivalist groups. Various writers recognize this prejazz strand, using phrases like "ricky-tick music," "vaudeville style," and "novelty music." But these styles are not the subject of this book. I will make further comments on prejazz and early jazz in discussing artists like Bunk Johnson, Alphonse Picou, and Oscar (Papa) Celestin below.

By including time periods as part of my working definition, I am not fudging but trying to deal with complexities that were part of the evolving art of jazz. As Gunther Schuller and others have pointed out, the music played in New Orleans by those we now call the jazz artists of the first quarter century was by all accounts a mixture of elements—those readily attributable now to jazz, on one hand, and prejazz and nonjazz elements on the other. The musicians sometimes played from written scores, sometimes from memory ("faking"). Melodies might be enriched with jazz inflections or altered through simple inventive embellishment. Extended improvisation might occur, within ensembles or in solos.

Further, at a given dance many kinds of music might be played—waltzes, mazurkas, ragtime, blues songs, and popular tunes of the day as well as materials from what we now call the jazz repertoire. These kinds of music cannot all be labeled "jazz" simply because they were played by the same musicians who were in the process of inventing the new music—unless, of course, one invokes the long-defunct notion that symphony musicians, most critics, and the general public once commonly applied, citing everything as "jazz" that is not classical music—from Gilbert and Sullivan to Tin Pan Alley hits to Kate Smith to Spike Jones to Louis Armstrong and beyond.

Far from possessing a full-blown pristine genius that suffused every note and phrase, the early players ventured tentatively, often clumsily, toward differentiation from prejazz musical conceptions, led by the most brilliant among them—Oliver, Armstrong, the Dodds brothers, Hines, Beiderbecke, and others.

Purists from the 1930s on created a mystique of TNOJ, imputing a special musical integrity and core jazz authenticity to the earliest jazz musicians and those who were reactivated in the various revivals. As the Preservation Hall article below notes, I heard some marvelous jazz at the Hall in the 1960s, but I could not lionize every musician born before 1900. Some listeners glorified whatever sounded "old"—not only prejazz elements but also phrases unfinished for lack of breath, nanny-goat vibratos without underlying firmness of tone, restraint imposed by a failing lip or loss of fingering speed, and other signs of diminished skill. This cult of archaism saddened me. The musicians deserved to be appreciated for the formidable invention they still demonstrated, not for imagined qualities of heart reflected in the very imperfection of their efforts.

Some TNOJ practitioners: Louis Armstrong, Sweet Emma Barrett, Sidney Bechet, Papa Celestin, Pops Foster, Lil Hardin, Bunk Johnson, George Lewis, King Oliver, Kid Ory, Leon Rappolo, and Tony Sparbaro (Spargo).

By *Dixieland Jazz* I mean the smoother, often more musically sophisticated styles that emerged in the 1920s and continue to be played today. Many of the qualities of TNOJ mentioned above were carried into Dixieland styles, but they tend to be characterized by more conventional tones of wind instruments, rejection of rapid vibratos, greater instrumental facility, and considerable attention to solos, which are routinely "passed around" in between opening and closing ensemble choruses. Rhythm sections rarely include banjo or tuba but might have a guitar. A feeling of 2/4 or a fluid 4/4 rhythm with a driving backbeat—especially on final ensemble choruses—is typical.

The blanket charge is often made by TNOJ purists and others that Dixieland jazz was merely the white musicians' watering down of the black players' TNOJ. It is true that early white players were slower to incorporate African influences into their music (as were the classically trained Creoles of color, like Alphonse Picou). But the Dixieland style that emerged in New Orleans, Chicago, and elsewhere was not an inept imitation but a evolved variation. Also, many bands that readily fit both my definition and common-parlance understandings of "Dixieland jazz" were racially integrated. Armstrong's All-Stars from the late 1940s on, various Muggsy Spanier and Eddie Condon combos, New Orleans bands of the 1960s led by Al Hirt, George French, and Thomas Jefferson—these make the often used "white Dixieland" term problematical. Interestingly, Leonard Feather's long-running "Blindfold Tests" in *Down Beat* made it clear that musicians listening to all jazz styles could not reliably identify musicians racially by their performance, unless they happened to know the particular artist.

The very fact that the "white Dixieland" label has a foothold in the vocabulary of jazz criticism militates against serious consideration of the best work of many bands (e.g., Bob Crosby's Bobcats, Sharkey's Kings of Dixieland, the Basin Street Six, Muggsy Spanier, various Condon units, Pete Daily, and Jimmy Dorsey's Dorseyland Jazz Band). Also, individual voices like Sidney Arodin, Raymond Burke, Irving Fazola, Armand Hug, Bill Rank, Joe Rushton, and others tend to be devalued when "white Dixieland" is a defining category in the discussion. Particular instances of this bias will be noted in the discussion of revivals below. (For a while, I recall, the French bleached certain modern jazz musicians with the same brush. They applied the term *les boppers blancs* to players like Alan Eager, Al Haig, Red Rodney, and Stan Levey. Happily, the phrase did not stick.)

A less obvious trap is also operating in the language. The term *Dixie*-land has long been rife with associations with Confederate flags, minstrelsy, de-land-ob-cotton, and worse. Its application to jazz came by chance with the fame of Nick LaRocca's Original Dixieland Jazz Band in 1917—a white group that by most accounts was neither as original nor as jazzy as the contemporary black bands that were not recorded for another half decade. Not by LaRocca's accounts, unfortunately. He spent his later years claiming that he and his cohorts, not black musicians, "invented" jazz. Besides this, there is the connotation, no, the denotation of absolute racial distinctiveness in the aforementioned phrase "*white* Dixieland jazz." It is by no means easy to cut through the miasma of association and listen to the music.

Language philosopher Kenneth Burke calls this attention-deflecting function of language a "terministic screen." Many of our observations about the world, he says, are merely "the spinning out of the possibilities implicit in our particular choice of terms," which bend our attention and response in one direction rather than another. Burke's theory is not mere academic musing. As I write this, a debate is raging in Alabama over a proposal to make the slogan "Heart of Dixie" optional on automobile license plates. For many, the word "Dixie" calls slavery and postbellum racism to mind. The etymology of the word is irrelevant. Its associative power is an oppressive reality to many citizens. Of course, one might propose a new name for the jazz that we call "Dixieland," but newly minted substitute terms seldom make it into the popular lexicon. (Remember when *Down Beat* sponsored a contest to find a new word for "jazz" in the 1950s? The winner was "crewcut.")

Another common charge is that Dixieland jazz—even as an evolved genre, whether played by black, white, or integrated bands—is facile and formulaic. Ralph Collins illustrates this bias with a vengeance in a 1996 book. Collins's broad brush paints the entire Dixieland jazz genre as crap. Ensemble choruses are "collective improvisation, which is a euphemistic way of saying every man for himself." In between such choruses is "an assembly of individual soloists held together by loud mechanical-sounding drum and cymbal beats. . . . Creativity is not required in such a methodical musical setting, indeed it might prove deleterious. . . . each man plays *fortissimo*, as loud as possible. Artistry is out of place here and originality a definite handicap." Of course, Collins's description is true of some groups, but it fails scandalously to recognize excellent Dixieland bands and musicians of the past and present, from the aforementioned Davison/Brunis, Spanier, and Bobcat groups to the recent work of George Finola, Connie Jones, Pete Fountain, and others.

Some Dixieland practitioners: Ray Bauduc, Sharkey Bonano, Eddie Condon, Wild Bill Davison, George Finola, Pete Fountain, Armand Hug, George Girard, Matty Matlock, Red Nichols, Ben Pollack, Muggsy Spanier.

By *Revivalist Jazz*, I mean music that has been produced since about 1940 in a conscious attempt to imitate or emulate elements in TNOJ. Some revivalist players select a particular band or artist as a model. Among the early bands most admired by the revivalists are the King Oliver Band with Armstrong and Jelly Roll Morton's Red Hot Peppers. Lu Watters's group in San Francisco and Claude Luter's in France in the 1940s often copied or emulated Oliver. In Boston, Bob Wilber studied with Sidney Bechet and during the postwar years played credible Bechetian soprano sax.

Revivalists as defined here range from serious students of early jazz styles to gimmicky straw hat bands and amateur groups that overstress surface aspects of TNOJ or even pick up prejazz elements to produce music that is brassily "hot" but essentially corny. As Edward Berger notes in Chip Deffaa's *Traditionalists and Revivalists*, the revivalists' approaches varied from rote, slavish recreation to freewheeling reinterpretation, for good or ill.

I do not include as revivalists the rediscovered or reactivated TNOJ artists (e.g., Bunk Johnson's band in the 1940s, Sweet Emma Barrett and others in the 1960s Preservation Hall revival). Although the music of some of those TNOJ players was no doubt affected by the jazz they heard in intervening years, they were basically playing the music of their own generation and not revisiting the past through imitation, emulation, or role-playing.

There were no revivalist bands in New Orleans during the late 1940s popular revival. Admirers of the TNOJ bands led by Bunk Johnson, Papa Celestin, and George Lewis were numerous; but as will be seen, many young white musicians formed a second line behind the Dixieland artists. In contrast, the Preservation Hall revival of the 1960s was accompanied by the growth of varied revivalist bands and a cadre of young foreign musicians, the latter discussed in an article below. The (Paul) Crawford-(Lenny) Ferguson Band was the most knowledgeable and original group. However, campy banjo-and-tuba combos like the Last Straws were more marketable.

Some revivalist practitioners: Woody Allen, Graeme Bell, Acker Bilk, Castle Jazz Band, Crawford-Ferguson Band, Clancy Hayes, Firehouse Five Plus Two, Last Straws, Humphrey Lyttelton, Turk Murphy, Bob Scobey, Lu Watters.

Again, I offer the above definitions not as statements of essence with sharp-edged examples but only as a rule-of-thumb framework for the overview below and the articles that follow it. I could easily pick apart my own definitions, and I would be hard put to use them in placing complexly situated musicians like George Brunis, Raymond Burke, Edmond Hall, Monk Hazel, Darnell Howard, Freddie King, or Santo Pecora in either a TNOJ or a Dixieland slot.

Fuzzy genres get even fuzzier, of course, as the passage of time effectively blurs and intermingles influences. "Dixieland" bands in New Orleans and elsewhere from the 1950s to the present have often included older players who were clearly in the New Orleans tradition, along with identifiable Dixieland figures hailing from just about anywhere in the country, augmented by swing musicians and even modern jazz players who found ways to adapt to small-group Dixieland improvisation settings.

Trying to sort out all of this in terms of absolute categories, setting up genres with static features and inviolable boundaries, is unwise and probably impossible. Sidney Bechet and Charlie Parker played together in 1948 at a Paris jazz festival. Pee Wee Russell played with Thelonious Monk in 1963 at Newport. Nicholas Payton recently recorded with Doc Cheatham. We can best use definitions and categories playfully, regarding jazz as part of an interesting musical hologram and applauding whatever is enjoyable and stimulating in any given performance.

THE NEW ORLEANS REVIVALS:
BUNK AND OTHER HISTORY

The articles immediately following this overview focus on some main figures in the New Orleans popular revival that took place between approximately 1947 and 1953. They are followed by an article on the second local revival—sparked in 1961 by Preservation Hall, which soon became nationally known. It is followed by two articles exploring whether young musicians will or even can carry on the styles of the early TNOJ and Dixieland artists.

The roots of the late 1940s popular revival in New Orleans are recalled by Frank Assunto and Pete Fountain. They look back at the men who were their musical role models during the revival—Sharkey's Kings of Dixieland (idols of the Dukes) and clarinetist Irving Fazola—and at their own ascent to national fame as the new generation of Dixieland jazzmen in the next decade. Fountain also recalls his work with the Basin Street Six, a group that played a role later in the revival.

Two neglected but important artists, pianist Armand Hug and clarinetist Raymond Burke, are the subjects of the next two articles. Born in 1910 and 1904, respectively, they were on the scene before, during, and after all of the revivals but are known mainly by fellow musicians and a rabid coterie of followers, mostly local. The career piece on Hug deals with his agoraphobic attachment to New Orleans and the misconception that he was basically a ragtime pianist.

The review of an odd Raymond Burke–Art Hodes concert on Bourbon Street discusses Burke's unique style. He blended well into many settings, for example, subbing for Lester Bouchon with Sharkey Bonano's Dix-ielanders in the late 1940s and playing at Preservation Hall in the 1960s. One of my most memorable gigs was a 1965 New Orleans Jazz Club concert at L'Enfant's with Burke as the sole front lineman, Hug, and bassist Sherwood Mangiapane.

The article on Al Hirt makes it clear that his musical development was on a different track during the late 1940s revival; but the revival enabled him to trade on his New Orleans origins and make a living with his flashy neo-Dixieland band at Dan's Pier 600 on Bourbon Street in 1956. In that context he was "discovered" in 1960 at age thirty-eight and became a major star with his Swingin' Dixie combo under Gerry Purcell's management.

As noted in section I, the 1947–1953 revival was passionately supported by the New Orleans Jazz Club but made a limited impression on the local Establishment. The popular revival was bracketed by negative happenings. In 1946 some high-powered leaders were burned by their allegiance to the failed local effort known as the National Jazz Foundation. In 1955 they un-doubtedly witnessed the controversy surrounding the NOJC's proposal for statues of jazz artists on Basin Street. It took the succession of national tri-umphs between 1956 and 1963 by the Dukes, Fountain, Hirt, and Preserva-tion Hall and the founding of the Tulane Jazz Archive in 1958 and the Jazz

Museum in 1961 to fully persuade local leaders that TNOJ and Dixieland jazz were truly an economic asset and cultural badge.

My view of the revivals, documented in this overview and familiar to musicians and fans who lived in New Orleans during the postwar years, is complicated by an anomaly in the literature and folklore of jazz. Curiously, the late 1940s revival that produced so much local excitement is virtually unrecognized in accounts of postwar jazz in New Orleans. *In fact, the "New Orleans Revival" commonly referred to by critics and other writers did not take place in New Orleans.* It was a national and international phenomenon that began in the early 1940s, closely linked with West Coast revivalist bands and highlighted by the rediscovery and reactivation of traditional jazz trumpeter Bunk Johnson.

Many national writers have assumed that there was no jazz activity of significance in New Orleans in the late 1940s. Others bought into the notion that the local revival, if there was one, was coextensive with the Bunk Johnson phenomenon. The respected critic Whitney Balliet is among the latter. He writes that the revival in New Orleans "first began around 1940 and petered out in the late forties, after Bunk Johnson's death." His 1940–1949 dates embrace the purists' early 1940s resurrection of Bunk Johnson and the subsequent national revival. But the local late 1940s revival is nonexistent for Balliett; in fact, he sees the years as a time of decline.

Similarly, New York *Times* jazz critic John S. Wilson states in *Jazz: The Transition Years, 1940–1960*, "In New Orleans, the revival meant little at the time. It stimulated the development of Dixieland bands, mostly made up of white musicians, who were soon catering to the limited tastes of tourists." Like Balliett, Wilson is aware of Bunk Johnson and his impact on the national New Orleans revival. But it is clear that he either devalues or is ignorant of the local activities of jazzmen like Sharkey Bonano, Papa Celestin, Irving Fazola, and George Lewis. He also implies the stereotype that white Dixieland musicians are sellouts.

William Carter, perhaps overanxious to emphasize the success of the 1960s revival in his book about Preservation Hall, evokes a sweepingly wretched image of previous years. He writes of "silence reverberating back over the decades—the musicians hungry and demoralized, the local jazz establishment virtually decreeing the old music dead."

A retrospective article on "The Revivalists" by Paul Rossiter in the London *Jazzbook 1955* emphasizes British "trad" groups and acknowledges the popularity of bands led by Lu Watters, Bob Wilber, and others in many cities in the United States. The lively postwar jazz scene in New Orleans eludes him. The same is true of the esteemed British critic Stanley Dance. *In Jazz Era: The Forties* he pays homage only to canonically accepted figures like Johnson, Ory, Watters, and the revivalists in England, France, and Australia.

Dan Morgenstern's treatment of "the New Orleans revival" in *Jazz People* and Neil Leonard's description of the 1940s "fundamentalist Dixieland revival" in *Jazz: Myth and Religion* include Bunk Johnson's national activity. But like Rossiter and Dance, they do not include the local revival in the picture.

Discographers have also contributed to neglect of the late 1940s revival in New Orleans. Mike Hazeldine's chapter titled "The New Orleans Revival" in *The Blackwell Guide to Recorded Jazz* (ed. Barry Kernfield) echoes the typical national perspectives, citing Bunk Johnson, Louis Armstrong, Lu Watters, and others. Neither Sharkey Bonano nor Papa Celestin appear in Hazeldine, in Digby Fairweather's chapter on Dixieland and swing, or in the book's index. Irving Fazola is mentioned in connection with the Bob Crosby Band, which broke up in 1942, but no reference is made to his recordings or other activities in the local revival.

Other writers slight the late 1940s revival indirectly by focusing exclusively on black musicians. Such is the case with Samuel Charters's *New Orleans, 1886–1963: An Index to the Negro Musicians of New Orleans.* Similarly, Stagg and Crump's discography, *New Orleans, The Revival,* lists recordings only by black TNOJ musicians from 1937 to 1972. Absent an accounting of Bonano, Fazola, Fountain, Girard, Hug, Wiggs, and others who were active in the 1947–1953 period, the distorted picture of those years is reinforced.

Not surprisingly, discographer Stagg is way off course when he discusses the postwar revival and a white band, the Basin Street Six, in his 1998 liner notes to the GHB reissue of the group's 1950 Circle recordings. The CD cover wrongly calls the session Pete Fountain and George Girard's first recordings, missing their well-publicized Columbia sides with Phil Zito. Stagg characterizes 1950—the peak year of the revival, as will be seen—as a year in which "dixieland was no longer popular" in New Orleans, and he shuffles earlier events into a stunted disarray.

Teizo Ikegami's discography of black New Orleans jazz artists of the 1940s, 1950s, and 1960s includes a few white band leaders (ironically, some of them non-Orleanians like Bob Havens and Barry Martyn) when their groups include black players. Inconsistently, he lists some Japanese bands. In contrast, Orin Blackstone's 1948 classic *Index to Jazz* discography is racially inclusive in its listings of jazz by New Orleans musicians. But it goes only to 1944, shedding no light on activities of the postwar years.

I found one book, Driggs and Lewine's 1995 volume *Black Beauty, White Heat: A Pictorial History of Classic Jazz, 1920–1950,* that clearly recognized the local postwar revival and acknowledged the roles of artists of many colors. These authors apparently had no trouble pinpointing the revival, stating outright that "after World War II New Orleans finally began to take pride in its music." Their text is incredibly compact, explicating well-chosen photos in a few paragraphs that recognize the influence of the New Orleans Jazz Club and the popularity of George Lewis, Sharkey Bonano, the Basin Street Six, and others.

The treatment of the postwar years in New Orleans in books by nonspecialists wanders into the surreal. In a volume promisingly subtitled *New*

Orleans Music since World War II, Jason Berry and colleagues actually focus most of the book on rhythm and blues, with an impoverished treatment of modern jazz. TNOJ and Dixieland jazz appear in a few essentially meaningless lines about night clubs in the mid-1950s. Lichtenstein and Danker's *Musical Gumbo* hints ineptly at the presence of a lively local scene during the postwar years. In a chapter that is almost intoxicating in its lack of perspective on the structure and significance of events, the treatments of Fountain, Hirt, and others are chronologically jumbled; the Basin Street Six is called Fountain's band; Hirt is labeled as a "young Dixie player"; and so on.

REVIVALS BEAUCOUP: SORTING IT OUT

In the rest of this overview I will try to paint a coherent picture of the various revivals, one that sorts out some of the confusion reflected in the comments of Whitney Balliett, John S. Wilson, and others. The reasons for misunderstandings about the national revival of the 1940s and the postwar local revival of 1947–1953 should become clear in the course of the narrative that explicates seven key points below. In connection with the last point I will summarize the reasons for historical neglect of the local revival, and I will explore the unwarranted endurance of the insular viewpoints of TNOJ purists and their reticent demigod, Bill Russell. Reasons for the decline of the revival will also be discussed.

The Preservation Hall revival began early in the 1960s. Since it has been widely celebrated and well documented elsewhere, I treat it briefly, offering some new perspectives—its relation to the earlier revivals, to the national fame gained by the non-TNOJ white artists, and to the local Establishment's belated awakening to the merits of jazz as both art and marketable product. The overview concludes with a discussion that relates to the articles on the possibility of continuation of early jazz styles in New Orleans.

I will develop the following points in regard to the national and local revivals.

- The national New Orleans revival that spanned the 1940s, hereafter referred to as the national revival, was advanced by the humble efforts of a few devoted purists (non-Orleanians like Bill Russell and Eugene Williams) who sought out and recorded the earliest living TNOJ musicians (e.g., Bunk Johnson, Big Eye Louis Nelson, Kid Shots Madison).
- Bunk Johnson's national celebrity in the mid-1940s was an unexpected, even stunning development. It was first sparked by another non-Orleanian, Rudi Blesh. He introduced Johnson to San Francisco audiences that had been supportive of West Coast revivalists and were ripe for the appearance of an authentic New Orleans originator.

- Bunk became the darling of traditional jazz fans and writers everywhere but was dismissed by many modern jazz fans and critics (e.g., Leonard Feather) as the embodiment of all that is reactionary during the nasty little jazz wars encouraged in the jazz and popular press for several years.
- Although not culturally pervasive, the national revival flourished remarkably. By the mid-1940s, revivalist and Dixieland bands were being formed and finding audiences in big cities throughout the United States and internationally.
- The national revival was virtually invisible in New Orleans before and during World War II. Neither TNOJ nor Dixieland jazz was commercially viable until the local revival began in about 1947.
- The local revival of 1947–1953 had a distinct genesis, linked only slimly with the national revival and involving many musicians who have been largely ignored by critics, historians, and discographers.
- Neglect of the local revival is rooted in a cluster of attitudes and beliefs, readily documented, that I call the TNOJ mystique.

The 1940s National New Orleans Revival

Because the music of the national New Orleans revival of the 1940s included TNOJ, Dixieland, and revivalist jazz, various writers have called it by different names—the New Orleans revival, the Dixieland revival, the fundamentalist Dixieland revival, the trad revival, and more. I simply call it the national revival. (As mentioned earlier, it became international, but that is tangential to this discussion.) My account is derived from several sources, mainly Gleason, Raeburn, and the National Jazz Foundation's *Basin Street* newsletter. Of course, I take responsibility for any errors and for my interpretations of events and critical comments about the music.

The New Orleans connection to the national revival began modestly. It was initiated by out-of-towners who were among the rabid purists/record collectors described in the overview to section I. The more passionate among them wanted to go beyond searching for rare 78rpm discs (and pre-78 technology like the Edison cuts, which were rumored to include a recording of the legendary Buddy Bolden). They set out to find early musicians who were still alive, reactivate them if they had retired from music, and make recordings, thereby belatedly expanding the library of available records of authentic traditional New Orleans jazz.

The first recordings were made in 1940 when Heywood Hale Broun came to New Orleans, hoping to record Bunk Johnson. Raeburn reports that Johnson could not make it in from New Iberia, so Broun recorded a band led by trumpeter Henry "Kid" Rena, with Alphonse Picou and Big Eye Louis Nelson on clarinets, and others.

The release of the Rena session on Delta records was not widely known, but it created tremendous excitement among purists. In a review cited by Raeburn, Bill Russell actually casts Rena's "lack of precision" in ensemble work and the musicians' diminished facility not as evidence that they were not at full strength but as a sign of utmost virility. Raeburn also quotes Rudi Blesh's rhapsodic praise of "the first recordings of pure New Orleans jazz made in modern times . . . pure, uncommercialized jazz . . . as it sounded in its first flushes of classicism . . . the music of the men . . . who never lost faith in the pure melody that speaks to the heart."

Listening to the session today (American Music CD 40), one smites one's head at the naive romance of it all. If the Rena sides sound like anything more than a pickup band muddling through music that these same pioneers must have played with greater élan and competence in previous decades, one will eat one's hat. "Lack of precision" can mean admirable spontaneity, but here Russell's phrase reveals more than he intended. Only a doctrinal purist could compare the lame 1940 Broun session to recordings actually made closer to "the first flushes of classicism" by Oliver, Armstrong, the New Orleans Rhythm Kings, and Morton—or for that matter to TNOJ records of Bunk Johnson during the national revival, Papa Celestin during the late 1940s local revival, numerous Preservation Hall bands in the 1960s revival, and George Lewis during the entire duration.

Alden Ashforth, writing in the *New Grove Dictionary of Jazz* (ed. B. Kernfeld) tells it straight: "Reports of his [Rena's] performances in the 1920s suggest he had a particularly strong tone in the upper register of the instrument for long periods; he is reputed to have developed a remarkable high obligatto for the final strain of *High Society*, later adopted by Sharkey Bonano. . . . Unfortunately, by the time he recorded [in 1940] . . . his playing had been reduced by ill-health to a cautious and straightforward lead, and exhibited only a few remnants of his former individuality."

Qualitative judgments aside, it is a fact of history that the 1940 Kid Rena session was influential. John S. Wilson calls it "the first overt step" in the national revival. Bruce Raeburn says that it "set the stage for Bunk Johnson's reception, which was destined to achieve a considerable amount of attention." And Bunk Johnson was indeed warming up in the wings—or more literally, in a rice mill in New Iberia, a city in a Cajun area about 140 miles from Bunk's hometown of New Orleans. The Johnson story has been told many times and in many ways, but I will summarize it here because it is a wonderful story and because it is in the foreground of the larger picture of the national revival of the 1940s.

Tipped off by Louis Armstrong and composer/pianist/music publisher/promoter Clarence Williams, Frederic Ramsey and Bill Russell sought out Bunk in the late 1930s as part of their research for *Jazzmen*, a book about early jazz that became a classic upon publication in 1939. Bunk was believed to be a colleague of Buddy Bolden and an influence on Oliver and Armstrong. Ramsey and Johnson engaged in correspondence that led to the trumpeter's reactivation and first recording session in 1942. Two of Johnson's moving letters to Ramsey from 1939 and 1940 are included below.

Dear Friend,

I am here, only making out now. For work, we have work only when rice harvest is in, and, that over, things go real dead until cane harvest. I drive a truck and trailer and that only pays me $1.75 a day and that do not last very long. So you all know for sure how much money that I make now. I made up my mind to work hard until I die as I have no one to tell my troubles to, and my children cannot help me out in this case.

I have been real down for about five years. My teeth went bad in 1934, so that was my finish playing music. I am just about to give it up. Now I haven't got no other ways to go but put my shoulder to the wheel and my nose to the grindstone and put my music down.

Now for the taking of the picture of mine, you can have one or six. Now six will cost five dollars, and if you care to pay for the six, I will be glad because Armstrong wants one. I would like to give Williams one, Foster one, Bechet one, and I would like to keep one, which would be six. Now, if you only want to take one, I will do so. So, you can send me what you think about it, for one or six. Now, if there is some things you would want to know about music, please let me know when you answer.

Willie Bunk Johnson

My dear kind friends,

Only a few words I want to say to you about my delay in sending you these pictures and these letters. Now, I'm pretty sure that you all know just how everything is down South with the poor colored man. The service here is really poor for colored people. We have no colored studios. This is a Cajun town and, in these little country towns, you don't have a chance like the white man, so you have to stand back and wait until your turn come. That is just the way here. So please do not think hard of me. You think hard of the other fellow.

You do all your very best for me and try and get me on my feet once more in life. Now, here is just what I mean when I say the words, "on my feet." I mean this: I wants to become able to play trumpet once more, as I know I can really stomp trumpet yet. Now, here is what it takes to stomp trumpet, that is a real good set of teeth. And that is just what I am in deep need for. Teeth and a good trumpet and old Bunk can really go.

Now, my friends, the shape that I am in at the present time I cannot help myself, so you all can judge that. Now, as I said before, that this town is very dead and it is real tough on a poor man when he do get in the shape I am in. Now, I have the very best of health and nothing but good clothes. Old Bunk is only in need for a set of teeth and a good job. Now, I truly thank you for the treat of the money. They come in need time. I did not have a penny in my house or noplace else. Do tell my dear old pal, Clarence Williams, to write me and to send a few late numbers of his. Now, I cannot play them but I can think them. O Boy, that will make me feel good anyway. If I have not got no teeth I can have something to look at when I get to thinking about the shape I am in and have no good way to go but work, just as I could get it, some weeks nothing at all.

Now, you tell Louis to please send me a trumpet, as he told me that he would, and you all do your best for me. From a good, old kind friend, as ever, and will always be so, so answer me at once.

Willie Bunk Johnson

Ramsey and Russell raised money for new teeth, fitted by Sidney Bechet's brother Leonard, who was a dentist. A $25 trumpet was provided by Lu Watters, the San Francisco trumpeter whose revivalist band grew wildly popular as the revival attracted audiences there. Johnson made recordings without fanfare in 1942 for Russell and Eugene Williams on New York–based Jazz Information label, aimed at the small population of purist collectors.

Johnson's Unexpected National Celebrity

An unanticipated break came when Rudi Blesh, one of the young intellectuals who had been championing jazz as an art form in the 1930s, brought Johnson to San Francisco Museum of Art in 1943 to perform on his lecture series. The programs were greeted like buried treasure by the liberal San Francisco arts establishment. Concerts at the Geary Street Theater followed, and soon Bunk's music and his up-from-the-rice-mill story were a hot item. He was written up in *Time* and other national journals.

Bunk recorded extensively with the group that became his regular New Orleans unit on Bill Russell's American Music label in 1944. Russell also recorded other early players, developing a list still valued as an important library of TNOJ performers. Johnson recorded for three major labels—Decca, Victor, and Columbia—in 1945–1946, and he appeared on smaller labels with a variety of other musicians as well. The Victor album, as noted in the overview to section I, was sponsored by the temporarily high-flying National Jazz Foundation (NJF) in New Orleans.

The New Orleans–based band was, on the balance, a very fine group. It included TNOJ stalwarts George Lewis on clarinet, Jim Robinson on trombone, Alton Purnell on piano, Lawrence Marrero on banjo, Alcide "Slow Drag" Pavageau on bass, and Baby Dodds on drums. In my view, Johnson at his best played a solid, driving lead, but Lewis and Dodds were more consistent and often brilliantly inventive. All of the sidemen were deeply admired by purists, but only Bunk gained national status as a minor celebrity.

Bunk: Darling of TNOJ Fans

Bunk was hailed as an untutored genius by revivalist musicians, critics who loved TNOJ, and an increasing audience of fans—some of them budding jazz aficionados, others toe-tappers who were caught up in the Johnson phenomenon. Between 1944 and 1947 he was featured—usually with local stars from the location of the gig—at New York venues like the Caravan Ballroom, Jimmy Ryan's, Orchestra Hall, and the Stuyvesant Casino, in addition to the performances in San Francisco, Boston, and elsewhere.

In one sense, the national revival could not have come at a worse time. Just as one group of jazz fans was looking back to TNOJ, revivalist bands, and Dixieland, another group was tuning into the new sounds of be-bop. The historic Charlie Parker recordings with Dizzy Gillespie, Miles Davis, Max Roach, Bud Powell, and other pioneers began in 1945—a revelation to many listeners, a hellish confusion to others.

The jazz press (and, to a lesser extent, the popular press) picked up the opposing trends all too eagerly. Fig-purists and champions of modern jazz duked it out for several years in the pages of *Metronome, Down Beat*, and other journals. Hypermodernists saw Bunk as a retrogression and the revival as reactionary—a sentimental attachment to styles long superseded, glorification of artists long past their prime, failure to comprehend the enhanced expressive range of the new forms, plain simple-mindedness, and the active cultivation of amateurism, not to mention corn.

Extreme traditionalists pointed to the directly evocative and highly expressive quality of the music they loved, to the inherent camaraderie and generosity of group improvisation, and to the roots of early jazz in shared social experiences and folk culture. The saw in modern jazz egoistic solo flights, gratuitous complexity ("all technique and no soul" was the common charge), and pretentious experimentation for its own sake. (For a crisp review of the debate, see McDonough 1995; for a historical analysis, see Gendron 1995.)

It was all very lively, even interesting, at the time. In retrospect, though, it was clearly divisive and wasteful. Those who cast the bop movement and the national revival as a meta-battle of styles and participated in the ensuing spitting contest retarded an understanding of the historical and conceptual links among the styles. They worked against the cultivation of a jazz appreciation, common today, that reaches from Bunk to Monk and beyond. By encouraging fierce loyalties to one camp and categorical rejection of the other, they discouraged a thoughtful critique of both movements. If the old jazz stinks, Bunk and Condon and the Firehouse Five are all equally bad. If bebop is slop, then Charlie Parker is indistinguishable from his wannabees, and they are all a bunch of hopheads anyway. And so it went.

To many, Bunk Johnson was a pivotal figure in the debate. If you could dig this superannuated trumpeter from a gone-with-the-wind South, you were definitely under the revival tent. This is not to say that Bunk was a passive figure in the complex unfolding of the revival. He grasped his unique situation, aware of the status he was gaining as a jazz musician, a historical resource, a folk hero, and a symbol of jazz past.

Always a great storyteller, he proved also to be a master of self-invention. His claims of working with Bolden and mentoring Armstrong were cast in doubt by later research. His stated birthdate of 1879 was discovered to be 1889. He made heavy demands on his friends and often criticized his sidemen, both in New Orleans and on the road. Some say this was because he held high musical standards. Others say that he grew intolerant as a result of his celebrity. Still others simply saw Johnson as demanding and cantankerous by temperament. Whatever the cause, he became difficult to work with. Worse, his lip was failing badly by 1947, and a year later he put down the horn. He died in 1949. Poet Norman Leer writes poignantly, *Bunk's currency /was myth. . . . In later photographs, he played the relic, /in pin-stripe suit and bowler hat. /He would make and wreck the myth /he knew they wanted.*

I believe that time and the legacy of recordings—especially the Victor and Decca sides (reissued on Document CD 1001), which demonstrate a finer unity than Bill Russell's highly touted American Music material—will reveal that George Lewis rather than Bunk Johnson was the TNOJ genius of the national revival. Of all three revivals, actually. Although Lewis was less visible than Papa Celestin or Sharkey Bonano in the local revival of the late 1940s, he was active from the early American Music records until his death in December 1968, memorialized in the brief eulogy in chapter 18.

I should note that Bunk Johnson did not wholly sever his ties with New Orleans during the national revival. As noted in the discussion of the National Jazz Foundation in section I, his band played in town for National Jazz Foundation and a few other functions, the most prominent being the aforementioned NJF/*Esquire* national radio show in 1945 with Armstrong and Bechet. The band also played all day on the NJF Mardi Gras truck in 1946, which must have been a heady event for the TNOJ fans in the group, given the quality of the band, the usual Mardi Gras levity, and Bunk's growing national reputation. His local presence, by the way, is slimly noted in Martin Williams's famous "Bunk" chapter in *Jazz Masters of New Orleans*—yet another instance of a noted critic failing to look at the local scene during the national revival.

Bunk Johnson cannot be wholly discounted, then, as an influence on the local postwar revival. But neither his limited presence nor the support of the NJF worked to transform the dreary local wartime jazz scene described below. Perhaps the NJF's strategy of promoting jazz of all styles and using big-name headliners worked against their goal of awakening Orleanians to their music. Possibly the city was not willing to accept an aging black jazzman as a cultural icon. In any case, Bunk was not lionized in New Orleans as he was elsewhere, the NJF soon fizzled, and, as we will see shortly, the hot jazz that was igniting national interest set off no sparks in the city's wartime night life.

The Flourishing National Revival

Even at the national level, the hoopla surrounding the revival and Bunk Johnson's dramatic return must be seen in perspective. Johnson never became a popular star in the manner of an Armstrong or a Goodman, or even an Eldridge or a Teagarten. Media interest in the national revival of the

1940s, of which the Johnson story is only one part, was considerable but it in no way compared with the sustained 1920s controversy over jazz in the national press (see section I), or for that matter with media coverage of subsequent popular music figures and styles, from Elvis Presley to Wynton Marsalis, from rock 'n' roll to rap lyrics.

Moreover, musical tastes in America during the 1940s and early 1950s were increasingly bland rather than jazzy or sophisticated. True, some listenable Broadway tunes (e.g., from *South Pacific*) were popular, and hip contributions from Armstrong ("La Vie en Rose") or Peggy Lee ("I'll Dance at Your Wedding") sometimes made the charts. But the public favorites were decidedly in the direction of watered-down swing (Kay Kyser, Tex Beneke), dreamy ballads ("It's Magic," "A Tree in the Meadow"), novelty tunes ("Mairzy Doats," "Managua Nicaragua"), and sanitized country and western (Jo Stafford's version of "Jambalaya"). Compared to the popularity and exposure of such Hit Parade favorites, the public awareness of Bunk Johnson and the national revival (and the concurrent emergence of be-bop) were tempests in a teapot on the back burner, with a faintly heard whistle.

The illusion of ubiquity of the national revival was created among fans, critics, and historians by the fact that so many hometown revivalist and Dixieland bands appeared and were popular in cities throughout the world. Small groups of disciples supported the groups in many American cities, but their devotion did not amount to wholesale conversion of the larger population from the tepid music that dominated the airwaves.

San Francisco was the earliest and most lively site of the revival. Lu Watters's Yerba Buena Jazz Band was organized in 1940, creating a stir that led to revivalist headliner status for sidemen Bob Scobey, Turk Murphy, Clancy Hayes, and Wally Rose. New York favored Dixieland over revivalist jazz during the decade. Transplanted Chicago-school musicians and others worked at Jimmy Ryan's, Eddie Condon's, and Nick's. The Commodore recording sessions with Wild Bill Davison, George Brunis, Edmond Hall, Pee Wee Russell, George Wettling, and others—arguably among the finest Dixieland recordings ever (reissued on Commodore CD 7011)—were cut in New York in 1943.

Los Angeles embraced Kid Ory's Creole Serenaders, mostly Orleanians, in the mid-1940s after the trombonist gave up chicken farming to return to music. Later in the decade the city supported Ben Pollack's first-rate Dixieland group and the brassy Firehouse Five Plus Two, which included Disney illustrators cutting up on weekends. At Chicago's Jazz Ltd. club the parade of artists brought in by owner/clarinetist Bill Reinhardt included Sidney Bechet, Muggsy Spanier, Miff Mole, and others.

Boston was the home of Bob Wilber's Wildcats, with TNOJ bassist Pops Foster. In Minneapolis it was cornetist Doc Evans's capable Dixieland combo. Portland came up with a brisk revivalist group called the Castle Jazz Band, which reflected the ongoing early-versus-modern jazz controversy with a song called "The No-Bop, Hop Scop Blues."

The national revival also got a boost from Louis Armstrong, Kid Ory, and a record that was actually intended as a good-natured satire on early jazz. Armstrong disbanded his large swing-style band and formed the All-Stars in 1947. The group was well named. It included jazz pioneers Barney Bigard on clarinet and Jack Teagarten on trombone; two more trailblazers, Earl Hines on piano and Sid Catlett on drums; and the excellent Arvell Shaw, then twenty-four years old, on bass. All had incorporated swing influences and musical showmanship over the years, resulting in a combination of great freewheeling Dixieland jazz and clever, crowd-pleasing head arrangements that became all too familiar with repetition. (A good example of the band's strengths and flaws can be heard on LaserLight CD 15773, a live 1948 performance.) Armstrong's performance in the 1947 United Artists movie *New Orleans* also helped the revival. His vocal on "Do You Know What It Means to Miss New Orleans?" from the movie was a hit record.

Kid Ory's Los Angeles–based band gained a national following in 1944–1945 when they were featured on Orson Welles's Mercury Theater broadcasts. The group recorded some solid TNOJ material for Columbia but tilted, not effectively, toward a flashier Dixieland style after trumpeter Mutt Carey left.

Then there was the unexplained Hit Parade status of trombonist Pee Wee Hunt's 1948 Capitol recording of "Twelfth Street Rag." Hunt's proficient Dixieland combo decided to do a transparently corny satire on 1920s jazz and near-jazz. Surprise! Listeners and dancers loved it. No surprise: Purists despised the record, and it was a bit of an embarrassment to the TNOJ musicians, revivalists, and Dixielanders who were enjoying unprecedented prestige and popularity but had not had anything resembling a major hit record.

Even so, Hunt's schmaltzy recording brought jazz-of-sorts to the attention of a wider public and probably led to a few long-term converts, myself among them. This is well and good. People should never get stuck in their first romance with bad or superficial examples of an art. I like Michael Clay's advice about entering into the universe of aesthetic experience: *Start anywhere. Never Stop.*

A more cynical—and actually hilarious—satire on early jazz was Charlie Barnet's "Darktown Strutter's Ball," circa 1948. I remember that network deejay Martin Bloch remarked, "Whenever Charlie Barnet is asked to record a Dixieland tune, he sticks out his tongue and says, NYAAAH!" The band blasted away, badly out of tune on the ensemble choruses, and the solos were wickedly clever. The record got some airplay but did not approach the success of Hunt's sendup. (The flip side, interestingly, was "Caravan," with a young Maynard Ferguson on trumpet and a percussionist named McDuffy who was soon to be a student playing with the Moods at Loyola in New Orleans.)

Finally, there were the revivalist and Dixieland bands that sprang up in other countries in the mid-1940s and beyond. England was busiest, with what was called the "trad" revival. Bands led by Jack Webb, Humphrey Lyttelton, Chris Barber, Ken Colyer, and others were popular. In Paris, clarinetist Claude Luter won dubiously merited fame with a group that mimicked early King Oliver records. Pianist Graeme Bell was a true trad pioneer in Australia. As the article below on foreign revivalists shows, many of them came to New Orleans in later years, some choosing to stay and make a living in their jazz mecca.

New Orleans before and during World War II

As I have stressed in the overviews and articles, a local jazz revival did occur in New Orleans, contrary to the views of Whitney Balliet, John S. Wilson, and others. But the revival occurred in the postwar years and was not contiguous with Bunk Johnson's reactivation or the national revival that began earlier in the decade.

Ample evidence exists for the depressed state of jazz in New Orleans before and during World War II. In his "Land of Dreams" chapter in the 1939 Ramsey and Smith classic *Jazzmen*, Charles Edward Smith laments the slim employment opportunities for jazz musicians not only in hotels and clubs but also at traditional venues such as dances, parties, and picnics.

The flood of servicemen and workforce émigrés from the southern states into the city was a major cause of the dearth of jazz during World War II, according to Ken Hulsizer. He writes in 1944 that

> the old Quarter now offers little more than a string of bars. . . . Some of these places have dull, cheap shows and some of them a piano player or a small combination, often hill-Billy, but these places with music are a minority. With hordes of people fighting to buy a drink, there is no need for the come-on of music. . . . For no valid reason, New Orleans is still the Mecca of the record collector and the hot jazz enthusiast. A half dozen came and went when I was there. I don't know for sure what all of them were looking for but if it was for Hot Jazz, most of them must have gone away disappointed. There is small inducement for New Orleans musicians to play in the joints in these days anyway. There are more lucrative jobs elsewhere. . . . The places where jazz musicians found work and got their early training no longer exist.

Through conversations "in the mephitic heat of the New Orleans summer" with Orin Blackstone, the city's primary discophile, and the already influential promoter/writer John Hammond (stationed in New Orleans), Hulsizer learned about some jazzmen playing weekends or spot gigs. But he reports that Tony Almerico, Sidney Desvignes [Desvigne], George Lewis, and Kid Rena were playing either commercial music or inconsistent, mediocre jazz. Mainly, the music was "hill-Billy," "dull orchestras in hotels," and bars with "an Irishman singing sentimental ballads." He concludes, "Jazz was born in New Orleans but it doesn't live there anymore."

The staunchest local supporters of jazz concurred with the visitors' pessimistic views, as seen in this note, titled "In Search of Jazz," in the May 1945 issue of the National Jazz Foundation's *Basin Street* newsletter.

A Chicago member asked where to hear good jazz in New Orleans. We have had requests like that before and all of them only succeed in putting us behind the 8-ball. . . . Due to the lukewarm reception jazz musicians have received in the place of its birth, jazzmen have either gone into large orchestras or given it up professionally and have taken on other jobs. . . . These men are scattered but still manage to get together now and then in private homes, or sit in with strange orchestras, just to keep their hand in. . . . They need some encouragement by our local citizens to make them take up playing hot music as a full time proposition as they did back in the 1920s.

New Orleans is just waiting (like a plum to be picked off a tree) for some enterprising business man to open a place where one could buy a good meal, a few drinks, and listen at the same time to a typical New Orleans small jazz combo. Who wants to take up the idea from here?

Raeburn has uncovered other such narratives, by both Orleanians and visitors. He reports Bill Russell's 1942 letter to friends at *Record Changer* magazine: "There isn't any jazz here, strictly speaking. Just the smell of it." He also cites Harry Lim's 1943 *Metronome* article stating that low wages and bad working conditions contributed to the lack of jazz in the French Quarter. Lim, working for Keynote Records (later called Mercury) out of New York, recorded an excellent Irving Fazola Dixieland combination. Fazola had left the Bob Crosby band in 1940, two years before the group disbanded. He returned to New Orleans in 1943, bridging the wartime jazz drought and the beginning of the local revival.

Lim was aware of the drought but apparently unimpressed by the purists' struggle to reactivate early TNOJ musicians. He saw the music of the latter as "only . . . interesting from a historical standpoint." Going against the grain of traditionalist orthodoxy, he wrote that the city "has lost almost all of its former glory to the average modern music fan, except the certain fascination it might still hold for a few record collectors who, complete with recording equipment, let their 'research consciousness' run wild."

Gus Statiras, a rabid TNOJ jazz record collector on assignment in New Orleans from the U.S. Office of War Information to film Bunk Johnson's concert for French journalists in 1945, told me that "New Orleans was dead" in terms of jazz activity during his time in the city. Raeburn notes trumpeter George Hartman's 1945 complaint in *Jazz Record* that "it is really a shame that the general public in New Orleans doesn't go for real good jazz, jazz from 'way back, the real jazz. New Orleans music has been so highly publicized and the city turned out so many good bands from the old days, but the people down there nowadays are just not educated to jazz."

Further comments on the local scene prior to the late 1940s revival appear in the fifteenth anniversary edition of the *Second Line*. The unsigned "History of the New Orleans Jazz Club" article (probably written by then NOJC president Harry Souchon) recalls that "the traditional music of New Orleans . . . had gone entirely underground. . . . Small, humble cafes and restaurants, such as Luthjens [*sic*], Mama Lou's, Happy Landings, and

'Spec's Moulin Rouge' (Marrero, La.) occasionally had traditional groups playing once or twice a week, or on weekends. But even these were not 'regular.'"

Why did the popular New Orleans revival fail to gain steam until around 1947? Some reasons were suggested in section I. Too many everyday citizens still associated jazz with corrupt environments, unable to see the lotus in the mudpond. The Establishment felt betrayed in its disastrous flirtation with jazz via the National Jazz Foundation. The "gold mine" promised by the NJF seemed to be a flash in the pan.

Ken Hulsizer's sober sociological and demographic analysis packs the most explanatory power when we look for reasons for the city's tardiness in climbing on the revival bandwagon. Hulsizer describes who was in town—military folk crowding cheap bars—and tells how their needs and tastes dominated the market. The larger picture would also include who was *not* in town and other things that were *not* happening. Many musicians and other natives were in the military service. The city's primary party, Mardi Gras, was canceled during the war years. Gus Statiras reports that the lights on Bourbon Street were painted black—an intriguing bit of symbolism as well as a practical precaution against possible air attack. The city's gaudy surface, special aromas, and unique chemistry were altered radically. But not permanently. Comes the end of the war, and the citoyens are ready to party again.

Genesis of the Local Revival

I will treat the 1947–1953 revival at some length because I believe it has been one of the most neglected and misunderstood times in jazz history. Setting an absolute date for the start of the revival would be arbitrary. I will begin, then, by indicating initial signs that seemed to precede the onset of the revival. To describe the revival in earnest, I will take two approaches. First, I will trace the development of major influences and events, focusing on jazz champions like WDSU deejay Roger Wolfe and the New Orleans Jazz Club and on several extremely popular bands. Second, I will list some jazz happenings during the peak year of the revival, 1950, giving a cross section that should demonstrate that TNOJ and Dixieland jazz were flourishing in remarkable ways. I followed a great deal of this activity closely as an zealous young jazz fan, but the materials below were also documented through various sources, including the New Orleans Jazz Club's *Second Line* publication, Orin Blackstone's *Jazzfinder* and *Playback* periodicals, and intensive interviews conducted recently and in connection with the articles that constitute chapters 12–20.

As for beginning signs of revival, the sporadic local activity of Bunk Johnson was followed by other blips on the screen. Irving Fazola's trio played live on a weekday radio program on WWL from 1943 to 1947, and he played live with pianist Ogden LaFaye in 1948. According to John Chilton, Fazola led or played in local dance combos from 1945 to 1948 and was working at the Mardi Gras lounge in the French Quarter when he died in 1949. Much of this was commercial fare, but Fazola's gifts as a jazzman were always apparent.

Fazola cut two jazz albums with local artists on Keynote and Victor in the mid-1940s. Both are worthy of close and repeated listening, but to my knowledge only a portion of the former has been rereleased on CD (*Faz*, ASV CD AJA 5279), a point that suggests a brief but useful digression. Fazola has by no means been ignored by jazz writers; but had he not died in 1949 at the age of thirty-six, his continued output might have focused attention on his unique gifts and important historic role. He has often been acknowledged as a Dixieland/swing transition figure and an original *stylist* (e.g., Chilton, Feather, Kernfeld). Yet few have recognized that Fazola possessed and projected a unique *sensibility*, being one of the first "cool" jazz musicians. His liquid tone and long, fluid lines, varied but underaccented, place him with Bix Beiderbecke as a precursor of the gorgeously easeful sonorities of Lester Young, Miles Davis, Chet Baker, and others.

To return to prerevival activity, in 1946 cornetist Johnny Wiggs succeeded in getting radio station WSMB to use an all-star Dixieland combo. It included Julian (Digger) Laine, trombone; Bujie Centobie, clarinet; Armand Hug, piano; Chink Martin, bass; and Monk Hazel, drums. Apparently, it was the "official station band" for about eighteen months; but it is not clear how often they played on the air and there is no evidence that they gained a popular following.

George Lewis played weekends at Manny's Tavern beginning in 1946. His sidemen were mainly Bunk Johnson bandsmen, except for players like Herb Morand and Elmer Talbert on trumpet and Joe Watkins on drums. Manny's was a neighborhood bar, but TNOJ fans sought Lewis out. Among those sitting in were a teenaged clarinetist named Pete La Fontaine (Pete Fountain) and banjoist Bill Huntington, not yet in his teens. Now a premier modern jazz bassist, Huntington was a serious understudy of Bunk's banjo player, Lawrence Marrero.

The event that built to a crescendo in the local revival was Roger Wolfe's one-hour *Dixieland Jazz* radio show. It began on WDSU in December 1947 and ran through mid-1952, when Wolfe took a job with a Pittsburgh television station. Wolfe, born Lassiter Yorick, was a dedicated record collector who came to New Orleans from California, where he worked under the name of Rod Whalen. He convinced the WDSU management to try the Saturday night 9:00 p.m. jazz hour by offering to do the program for no remuneration.

Despite the *Dixieland* title, Wolfe played a variety of TNOJ and Dixieland records, many of them quite rare at that time. I first heard the Original Dixieland Jazz Band, King Oliver, Armstrong's Hot 5 and Hot 7, the New Orleans Rhythm Kings, Bix Beiderbecke, the New Orleans Owls, and many out-of-print Bobcats records on his program. He also played new and recent Dixieland materials from labels like Commodore, Jump, and Jazz Man. These records (and periodicals like *Record Changer, Jazz Record, Jazzfinder*, and *Playback*) were available locally only at Orin and Harvey Blackstone's New Orleans Record Shop on Baronne Street, a gathering place for jazz fans since 1945. As mentioned earlier, the back room was the site of little-known Saturday afternoon jam sessions with contributions by established players like Raymond Burke and Johnny Wiggs as well as youngsters like George Girard and Gilbert Erskine.

Soon Wolfe had a loyal and growing constituency. He started his own record label, Bandwagon, in 1949 and recorded the two most popular bands of the revival, Sharkey's Kings of Dixieland and Papa Celestin's Original Tuxedo Orchestra. He also waxed the up-and-coming Dukes of Dixieland and a unique duo session with Armand Hug on piano and Ray Bauduc on drums.

His connection with the Bonano band was especially close. In March 1949 they organized a series of cooperative (i.e., split the proceeds evenly) Sunday afternoon concerts at a side room in the Municipal Auditorium, where kids and other non–night clubbers could hear the splendid group. One of Wolfe's often repeated comments about the band went something like this: "You know, sometimes you have a band that plays pretty well together but the guys don't get along too well. At other times you have a band that gets along just fine but doesn't really sound all that good. Well, this is a band that plays great Dixieland, and the guys really like each other, too."

I mention Wolfe's folksy tribute for two reasons. First, it reflects the genuine good feeling that one sensed among the musicians. This is noteworthy because one of the few references to Bonano is in *I Remember Jazz*, in which Al Rose summarily trashes the trumpeter as an arrogant egotist. It is true that Sharkey's growing popularity went to his head when he recorded for Capitol and was booked at the Blue Room in the Roosevelt Hotel. But the early band was a genial as well as gifted group.

Second, the avuncular tone of the Wolfe quote reflects the man's uncomplicated love for the music. Unlike the cadre of intellectual collectors of the 1930s who came to dominate jazz criticism and scholarship, Wolfe never presented himself as an expert, musicologist, historian, or theorist. He spoke regularly of "that happy Dixie beat" and had a special fondness for the one-bar tag that many bands used at the end of a tune—two beats on the cowbell and a two-beat stinger by the band.

This is not to say that Wolfe lacked understanding of or personal perspectives on jazz. In the course of introducing recordings, he made numerous intra- and interstylisic distinctions and occasional qualitative comments. He sorted out early TNOJ styles and musicians and distinguished among contemporary Dixielanders, revivalist bands, and the nearly heretical Dixieland materials that were coming out of New York. He recognized and extolled Ray Bauduc's skill at adapting parade drumming to jazz. He subtly apologized to his more knowledgeable listeners before responding to requests to play Pee Wee Hunt's "Twelfth Street Rag," sometimes substituting Armstrong's early, curiously slow version of the tune.

All in all, the music was fun for Roger Wolfe, and he enjoyed listening to and talking about it on the air—just the right temperament for a city ready to return to good times in the postwar years. A 1952 "Notes to You" item in the New Orleans Jazz Club (NOJC) journal *Second Line*, announcing Wolfe's move to Pittsburgh, stated that his was the "oldest program" and "the first to offer authentic jazz" on the air, even predating the 1948 establishment of the NOJC.

By May 1949, Orin Blackstone's *Playback* magazine could report a clear turnaround from "a year ago, [when] jazz was about dead in New Orleans, as far as the general public was concerned." Recalling that the National Jazz Foundation had died "without doing much for local talent," the article entitled "Dixie Battle" lauded the New Orleans Jazz Club's efforts and noted the Parisian Room sessions, Bonano's band at the Famous Door and Municipal Auditorium concerts, and other popular breakthroughs.

The 1948 founding of the NOJC has already been described in chapter 3, but some key specific activities must be placed within the context of the revival. Almost immediately, the club got on the radio with a half-hour weekly record show on WTPS-FM hosted by NOJC president Al Diket. In 1949 the first of the long running half-hour programs on WWL was aired. This was not another jazzfan/deejay spinning hot discs for foot-tapping listeners but a thoughtfully scripted program that focused on a particular artist, band, or period.

The club lost no time in sponsoring live music. On May 23, 1948, they rented the Parisian Room (on Royal Street just off Canal) from trumpeter Tony Almerico for Sunday afternoon concerts. The excellent makeup bands included players like Sharkey, Fazola, Digger Laine, Wiggs, and Monk Hazel. It was clear from the beginning that the sessions had a real audience and were no financial risk at all. As noted earlier, the burgeoning audience for the local revival was almost exclusively white. Upwardly mobile blacks distanced themselves from jazz. As Berry and Broven have written, rhythm and blues was rapidly becoming the popular music of choice among younger black audiences.

Recognizing the potential for profit in the Parisian Room concerts, Almerico promptly stopped renting the room to the NOJC and started sponsoring the concerts himself. I always thought of this as hijacking, but I heard no strident complaints—only frequent and conspicuous mentions of the matter from jazz club leaders over the years.

Adding cacophony to injury, Almerico soon brought in his lumbering, clunky Dixieland group as the featured band. But the Sunday sessions remained popular, and segments were soon being broadcast to the nation on WWL, the city's 50,000-watt radio station, and to audiences abroad via transcriptions. It was the Almerico band, you will recall, that was panned in England's *Melody Maker*, prompting my letter of assurance that other and better bands were active in New Orleans.

Almerico continued to run afoul of the NOJC. Tommy Griffin's August 19, 1950, "Lagniappe" column in the New Orleans *Item* reports on why Almerico's band was not invited to play on the club's summer concert series. Myra Menville said that Almerico was the only one who turned the club down in 1949, when the festival was organized on a two-day notice. He refused to play for union scale like the other bands. Menville snapped, "Now that we're getting national recognition he wants to be included, but we no longer need him." Ironically, in 1951 Almerico received the key to the city for music and activity that represented the revival so poorly.

The NOJC featured live jam sessions at its monthly meetings—albeit without pay for musicians—and got into the concert business again in the summer of 1949. Eight August outdoor concerts, two each week, were held in Beauregard (Congo) Square. The bands were fine and varied—Bonano, Celestin, Paul Barbarin, Sal Franzella, George Lewis, and Johnny Wiggs. The series was profitable in several ways—a write-up in *Newsweek*, a broadcast on ABC radio, a $3.41 surplus, and no jab in the eye with a hot stick. Each following year, through 1955, the club sponsored some sort of concert or series, none as imaginative or varied as the first. Other NOJC activities are discussed in the overview to section I and in chapter 3.

THE DIXIELAND BANDS

The bands that were most prominent in the local revival were Sharkey's Kings of Dixieland, the Dukes of Dixieland, Papa Celestin's Original Tuxedo Orchestra, and the Basin Street Six. Also visible were Paul Barbarin, Fred Kohlman, George Lewis, and Johnny Wiggs, but the contours of the revival are most strongly identified by the activities of the NOJC, Wolfe, and the four most popular groups. I will begin with the Dixielanders—Bonano, the Dukes, and the Basin Street Six—because they bore close relationships to each other; then I will discuss TNOJ trumpeter Celestin, whose band and fandom provide a revealing contrast with George Lewis during the revival.

Sharkey Bonano, born in New Orleans in 1904, spent much of his early career as a comer who did not quite arrive. His first instrument, according to Chilton's *Who's Who of Jazz,* was bought from the legendary trumpeter Buddy Petit. Bethell quotes George Lewis's statement that Bonano second-lined Kid Rena's band at parades and was "one of Rena's scholars."

Bonano circulated among top names in the 1920s and 1930s—losing to Jimmy McPartland in an audition to replace Bix with the Wolverines; working with Jimmy Durante, Jean Goldkette, Ben Pollack, and a reorganized Original Dixieland Jazz Band; coleading a big band with Louis Prima. Hadlock reports that Bonano successfully brought a Dixie combo to Nick's in New York just before Eddie Condon and other "Nixielanders" became the idols of New York fans in the national revival.

Early recordings show that Bonano's playing moved from an affirmative but crude combination of prejazz and jazz influences to a solid, no-nonsense jazz conception. In terms of my comments on jazz genres at the beginning of this overview, it is useful to listen to Bonano and the other lead horns on the pre-1926 tracks of the *New Orleans in New Orleans* collection (Jazz Archives CD N68). Most of them—Peter Bocage, Albert Brunies, Sidney Desvigne, Leon Prima, Henry Knecht—are a variation of the prejazz/jazz amalgam. Prejazz components like nanny-goat vibratos, short-clipped eighth notes/dotted eighths and sixteenths, and syrupy slurs are plentiful. I suspect that these are chief traits of what Sherwin Dunner calls "turn-of-the-century lilt" and "vaudeville effects." Gilbert Erskine calls it "ricky-tick music." Brian Wood's term is "novelty music." John T. Maher, according to Sudhalter, refers to "American syncopation" as a prejazz device that departed from European-based dance rhythms. But in the recordings noted above, the musicians are not limited to the frenetic, corny devices of popular dance and show bands. They make frequent use of bent notes, blue notes, growls, rhythmic accentuation and plasticity, and other innovations of the emerging jazz repertoire.

It is reasonable to speculate that the first Armstrong Hot Five records of 1925, the Hot Seven and Morton Red Hot Pepper sides in 1926, and the Bix Beiderbecke and His Gang releases of 1927 were a main inspiration for the looser, more fluid jazz styles that many of the above-named New Orleans players—and innumerable others—adopted later in the decade, never to return to ricky-tick devices. In fact, Bonano's 1928 track on the Jazz Archives CD (not related to the Tulane Jazz Archive, incidentally) and the 1928–1937 tracks on Bonano's feature CD (Timeless CBC 1-001 Jazz) show obvious shifts toward fleet Armstrong-like solos, a less pronounced vibrato, and more supple rhythm. The ensemble routines reflect the influence of Beiderbecke, who, as Hadlock notes, was in town with Paul Whiteman early in 1928.

By the late 1940s, then, Sharkey Bonano was a seasoned jazzman and entertainer, past his peak as a soloist but better than ever as a smooth and swinging Dixie lead trumpeter. The groundwork laid by Roger Wolfe, the New Orleans Jazz Club, and others enabled him to put together a first-rate combo called Sharkey's Kings of Dixieland around late 1948. Santo Pecora was on trombone; Lester Bouchon on clarinet; Jeff Riddick on piano; Chink Martin on bass; and Monk Hazel on drums and mellophone.

The group might well be the best Dixieland outfit ever to come out of New Orleans. Certainly, their ensemble work was a joyful collaboration. Sharkey would drive a firm lead while Pecora provided flawless tailgate backup and Bouchon played fine harmony or gorgeous contrapuntal lines to complete the lattice. Martin was unshakable on bass, Riddick sympathetically supportive on piano, and Hazel both swinging and tasteful on drums. Hazel frequently played choruses on mellophone, keeping the bass drum going while Pecora played the offbeat on his crash cymbal—great music, and a nice visual effect to boot.

The band was consistently satisfying, despite the lack of outstanding soloists. Bouchon was the most consistent and interesting soloist, and Hazel's horn was surprisingly fresh, almost "modern" in conception. Pecora projected admirable authority but had a woefully small store of ideas that made all his solos sound the same. Bonano did not solo on most tunes, and when he did he was seldom at risk of surpassing himself. Riddick's solo lines were adequate but undistinguished, a fact that became noticeable when Armand Hug sat in with the band—although Hug never meshed with the ensemble as well as Riddick.

Clearly, the whole was far more than the sum of its parts. Sharkey and the Kings of Dixieland were a perfectly balanced band, a very hot band, a band that gave the lie to the critical clichés about Dixieland jazz being a facile art or a mere framework for ego-tripping soloists.

I would like to dodge the matter of Bonano's vocals and stage manner, but these things were part of his entire career and part of the popularity of his band in the local postwar revival. He came about showmanship naturally, having an impish appearance at about 5' 4" and wearing a bowler hat. He was fond of grinding suggestively in motions that ended with a tug at his pants and a stripper's bump, punctuated by Monk Hazel's syncopations at the end of an eight-bar phrase. I found this annoying, mainly because it distracted Monk from playing straight-ahead drums behind the soloists. But it was visually irresistible, and the live audiences seemed to love it—and his singing, too.

Listening to Bonano's vocals on record, though, you might wonder why he sang at all. Without the comic visual contexts, his high-pitched voice glossing over the lyrics of up-tempo standards and novelty tunes with risqué lyrics is less affecting than, say, the recorded vocals of Kermit the Frog. (Hear, e.g., Bonano's "I'm Satisfied with My Gal" on the Timeless CD.)

But keep in mind the strong tradition of jazzmen who sang—sometimes quite wonderfully, like Armstrong and Teagarten—without conventionally "good" voices, often mugging their way through it all at live performances. Surely, the record companies heard about Bonano's popular antics and vocals and knew that his routines pleased audiences. No doubt they hoped he could follow in the footsteps of more expressive jazz entertainer/vocalists like fellow Italian-Americans Wingy Manone and Louis Prima. But he never had a hit record.

After establishing himself locally at the early New Orleans Jazz Club Parisian Room concerts in 1948, Bonano was a natural to lead a Dixieland group that would, along with Papa Celestin's traditional New Orleans jazz band, spark the revival. In late 1948 or early 1949, Sharkey's Kings of Dixieland opened at the Hyp Guinle's Famous Door, a Bourbon Street club named after the New York site of Louis Prima's 1935 success. Soon the band was doing live radio shows from the club and frequent studio spots on WDSU-TV.

The relatively early establishment of a television station in New Orleans—WDSU-TV was on the air late in 1948—had no small effect on the local revival. In the early days of TV people watched whatever was on, simply because the medium was a new miracle. And as will be seen, the Basin Street Six and Papa Celestin, like Bonano, were visually entertaining.

In April 1949 the Bonano band's cooperative Sunday concerts at a side room in the Municipal Auditorium began, with Roger Wolfe emceeing. Among those sitting in or subbing at the sessions were Ray Bauduc, Raymond Burke, Buglin' Sam Dekemel, Armand Hug, Freddie King, and my brother Don, then sixteen years old.

When Wolfe started his Bandwagon label that year, Sharkey's band cut several sides. The next year saw a real breakthrough—a record session for Capitol. None of the records (unreissued, to my knowledge) captured the band at its best, but the Capitol sides were particularly unfortunate. Sharkey sang a bland, up-tempo novelty/blues tune, "Pizza Pie Boogie," that was not even in the group's usual repertoire. (*I don't want no anchovies in my pizza tonight/ (repeat)/Just make it plain, and I'll eat it up all right.*) Wisely, the band played "Bourbon Street Bounce," a catchy melody by Harvey Blackstone. The song had been recorded earlier by Johnny Wiggs on Orin Blackstone's New Orleans label and was a surprise hit on local radio. Unwisely, Bonano accelerated the tempo, stunting the flow of Harvey's simple and graceful melody line.

Although Sharkey once again failed to make a leap to national fame, he was receiving unprecedented local popularity and getting some attractive offers. Dissension arose within the once well-bonded band as Bonano played the star and the sidemen wondered if they could do better. Santo Pecora formed his own band in 1950 and was replaced by Charlie Miller, a competent trombonist who lacked Pecora's ensemble skills. Bonano left town for excellent road engagements like the prestigious Palmer House in Chicago. He returned in triumph to play the Blue Room at the Roosevelt Hotel, a coveted gig previously reserved for dance bands from Jan Garber to Woody Herman. But as indicated on timeline chart 2 at the end of this overview, by 1952 Bonano's leadership of the local revival was effectively over. He continued to play around town, but the new generation of Dixielanders—the Dukes of Dixieland and the Basin Street Six—had picked up the torch before Bonano realized he had dropped it.

The Dukes and the Six—and Pete Fountain, who was a charter member of both groups—were in some ways the beneficiaries and sustainers of the revival rather than the creators. The Dukes made an initial splash as the Junior Dixieland Band when they won the Horace Heidt radio competition early in 1949, giving further impetus to the revival and a boost that led to their work at the Famous Door. But as the Junior Dixieland Band they were still a kid group squeezing out highly derivative performances. Other young players of equal promise did not get comparable recognition—for example, Irish channel musicians Al McCrossen, a Beiderbecke-influenced cornetist, and Johnny McGhee, a formidable reedman and pianist; Ninth Ward youngsters like trumpeter Jay Barry and clarinetists Don Suhor and Paul Vicari.

The article below is candid about the Dukes' conscious indebtedness to Sharkey's Kings, but it only hints at their immaturity. The band used many of Sharkey's head arrangements outright, with Frank Assunto modeling his lead after Bonano. Fred Assunto based his trombone style, redundant solos and all, on Santo Pecora, with results that were not pretty. As the article on Pete Fountain shows, the young clarinetist was not aping Lester Bouchon but was trying to sound like Irving Fazola—a more challenging model, but copywork nonetheless.

I was among those who thought that the Dukes of Dixieland were not well grounded in their art when they opened at the Famous Door for a forty-four month hitch in 1950. They trained on the job while fanning the flames of the local revival; and then, as the article notes, a series of fortuitous circumstances led to national popularity in 1956 before they had demonstrated their growth as jazzmen.

Pianist Stanley Mendelson was one of the most mature of the original Dukes, but even he was at the time under the spell of a veteran, emulating Armand Hug's vigorous ragtime work. Hug, unsung among jazz fans except for local near-idolaters, is featured in an article below that sees him in perspective as a jazz mutation. No mere ragtime specialist, Hug was a multifaceted musician who worked steadily through all the revivals, becoming an institution among jazz buffs but never a local or national star.

Many are surprised to learn that Al Hirt was not part of the 1947–1953 revival, so it is useful to clarify his contemporaneous activities here. The article on Hirt below includes his surprising confession in 1969 that he never saw himself as a jazzman, and certainly not as a Dixielander, despite having lead the Swingin' Dixie group with a standard Dixieland lineup since 1956.

He was partly right. It is true that during the postwar years he played powerful lead in big bands, tasteful swing with the WWL *Dawn Busters* breakout combo, and dazzling showcase solos. I played behind Hirt with the Loyola band at an outdoor concert in 1952, and his pyrotechnic display shook the quadrangle. Later that year I played my second union gig with his intermission trio at the Famous Door, and he was solidly in his swing/demo-solo groove. His Dixie group that started working full-time at Dan's Pier 600 in 1956 was formed serendipitously, well after the local revival subsided. It might not have succeeded at all but for the band's frequent departures from the Dixieland repertoire and Hirt's fleet, ever eclectic trumpet.

I have come to view Hirt differently as a jazzman, though, since writing the 1969 article. Even at the time, I knew he was downplaying the jazz image to gain acceptance for his recently introduced non-Dixieland format. Hirt dropped the trombone, added a tenor sax, and substituted an organ for the piano. Such an instrumentation had greater flexibility in backing up Hirt's hit recordings—nonjazz, bubble-gum blockbusters like "Java" and "Cotton Candy." These represented Hirt's commercial peak and his jazz nadir.

But Hirt's Swingin' Dixie bands and his later jazz groups often included rhythm sections with musicians like Fred Crane, Ronnie Dupont, or Ellis Marsalis on piano; Jay Cave, Bill Huntington, or Lowell Miller on bass; and Collin Bailey, Mel Lewis, or Jimmy Zitano on drums. With such musicians he could stretch out with bristling, well-crafted modern jazz lines. Bassist

Oliver "Stick" Felix, an ardent and able jam session bassist in the late 1940s, notes that even in the early postwar years, Hirt and Black Mike Lala had the range, speed, fire, and ideas that most closely shadowed Dizzy Gillespie's style. Jazz fan Art Scully recalls that Hirt was the trumpeter of choice to sub with the Junie Mays group, an out-of-town modern combo that played briefly at the Prevue Lounge. Pianist Frank Strazzeri recalls playing a gig in the 1950s where Hirt called up "Jordu" and showed that he had been listening carefully to Clifford Brown. Like so much of the city's early modern jazz, discussed at length in section 3, Hirt's best moments have gone unrecorded.

The bottom line is that Hirt's commercial output and his blanket "I'm no jazzman" disclaimers, aired in the New York *Times* and *Down Beat* as well as *New Orleans* in the late 1960s, in no way tell the whole story of his art. It is true that Al Hirt was not playing Dixieland jazz during the local revival, and that he was never the Dixieland player that innumerable tourists thought they were hearing in the 1960s. But neither was he a career sellout, as some critics complained. As one of his sidemen stated in my 1969 *Down Beat* cover story, "Al can do anything he wants, man. He can play anything. It's just what he wants to do for his present bag and for his present audience." In the long view, Hirt was a versatile musician who at his best played formidable jazz in many styles.

Hirt was still working various swing-based gigs in 1950 when a brand-new Dixieland band joined the revival. The Basin Street Six emerged, as will be seen, from a rebellion. The sidemen in drummer Phil Zito's International City Dixielanders fired the leader, hired Charlie Duke on drums, and set out on their own as the Six.

I did not give the rap on Phil Zito in the Fountain article, but he is a colorful figure whose role is worth explaining here. I met Zito when he sold me my first set of unmatched drums for $60 from his junk-resembling collection in 1949. I was not very sophisticated but my crap detector picked up on a compulsive eagerness in his personality. Actually, Zito was a full-fledged promoter who leaped feet first into whatever he did, somehow pulling off the improbable with great rushes of enthusiasm and a down-home New Orleans dialect. From a safe distance, though, his energy was somehow quite likable.

I appreciated Zito years later when he doggedly objected to numerous moves by musicians union president Dave Winstein. Although Dave was not a tyrant outright, many rank-and-file members were uncomfortable with his nearly complete control of the local. At union meetings Zito would plow in with contrary ideas that ranged from sound to absolutely silly, creating and then breaking tension, and bringing some perspective and humor to the situation.

Zito's career coup came in mid-1949 when he got a gig at the El Morocco club at the gateway to Bourbon Street, followed by a Columbia Records session (not reissued) for a new band that boasted two youngsters — Pete Fountain on clarinet and newcomer George Girard — and seasoned players Joe

Rotis on trombone, Roy Zimmerman on piano, and Emile Christian on bass. Christian, then fifty-four, was an interesting connection with traditional New Orleans jazz. He had played trombone locally, nationally, and internationally with the earliest jazzmen. Kernfeld's *New Grove Dictionary* places him in 1915 with Fischer's Ragtime Military Band (which included Monk Hazel's father on bass drum and members of "Papa" Jack Laine's family, according to Shafer and Kernfeld); in 1919–1921 with the Original Dixieland Jazz Band, replacing Eddie Edwards; and in 1921 with the Original Memphis Five.

Zito's drumming consisted almost exclusively of an unyielding backbeat that he apparently took to be definitive of Dixieland drumming. It was relentlessly peppy but not swinging. The jerky pulse gave the feeling of walking with one foot on the curb and the other in the street. Whether it was Zito's drumming, his run-on personality, or his plans to go on the road that caused the sidemen's rebellion is not clear, but the band did break away, subbing young Bunny Franks for Emile Christian on bass. Stung by the abandonment, Zito took a totally new tack, organizing a dance band that opened at L'Enfant's under the not quite cryptic name of the Ralph Otiz Orchestra.

Trumpeter George Girard merits particular attention here. It is tempting to romanticize his life and his art, since he died tragically of cancer at the age of twenty-six. But Girard needs no sentimental boost. He was a genuinely gifted musician. Only nineteen when he joined the Zito band, he was far ahead of the other young Dixielanders of the revival. His ensemble trumpet showed Bonano's influence, but it was more exploratory and freewheeling than Frank Assunto's or, for that matter, Bonano's. He showed greater originality, breadth, and self-assurance as a soloist than Pete Fountain did at the time. Only Don Suhor, playing weekends with Red Hott (Stuart Bergen), was as fluid a young improviser, and he was already moving toward be-bop on sax and clarinet.

Girard's style was, first and foremost, animated. He showed traces of Armstrong, Spanier, Berigan, and James but always added a personal spark that energized what was already a joy-making group. Roger Wolfe's phrase "happy Dixie beat" applies to no band more than the Basin Street Six. Unlike the Dukes, they rapidly came up with a fresh repertoire of head arrangements. The dapper Roy Zimmerman played piano—so help me, I almost wrote "tickled the ivories"—with a deadpan expression but with wonderful buoyancy. Fountain, despite consciously emulating Fazola's laid-back approach, was showing a tendency toward a hotter style. Trombonist Joe Rotis kicked the band well in ensembles and played solos that were rhythmically vigorous, if not always ideaful. Bunny Franks was a driving bassist. Drummer Charlie Duke often added to the propulsion by picking up the tempo, but he always moved with zest in a preswing groove.

To the consternation of jazz fans, the band did quite a bit of horsing around. In the liner notes to the reissue of their 1950 Circle album (George H. Buck's BCD-103), Stagg writes hyperbolically that the Six "found their niche as a funny hats band" then acknowledges that they were "still playing good dixieland jazz." Rose and Souchon's listing of the Six calls them a "dixieland-comedy band." But surely, this was no Firehouse Fire costumes-and-corn outfit. The gags were mainly visual, seldom disrupting the music, which comes across well on the reissued tracks from the Circle session.

As popular as the band was, they moved around town at a pace that kept their fans running. Between 1950 and 1953 numerous sources report the band at L'Enfant's (their main venue, and site of weekly TV broadcasts), the Belle Vista, Perez's Club Oasis, the Famous Door, the Silver Slipper Club, innumerable spot jobs, and a banana boat cruise to South America. They also played the Blue Note in Chicago, but, like so many New Orleans musicians, they were not fond of the road.

The group's demise was largely the result of internal dissension. Musicians in town had talked for years about Girard's expanding ego, his unfortunate desire to sing, and his conflicts with Fountain—the last centering less on musical differences than on competition for audience guffaws and the perception of who was leading the group onstage. In 1994 Fountain, ever a gentleman, spoke obliquely of tensions during the Zito/Six years. In Jon Pult's *Jazzbeat* interview he remarked, "In any band the trumpet always becomes the leader, they're born leaders! I always said that God put trumpet players on earth to aggravate me!"

Fountain broke away in 1953 to play for a while at the Famous Door with his Three Coins combo (no trumpet). This faded, and he sadly started the legendary nine-to-five gig, along with Al Hirt, spraying insecticides for a local pest control company. In the same year Girard led his own band at the Famous Door on a double bill with the Dukes. His replacement with the flagging Six was young Connie Jones, a talented trumpeter who had started a hot teenage group called the Dixiecats in 1950, with Larry Muhoberac on piano and Charlie (Chicken) May on bass. Jones and other youngsters of his time were coming of age as professionals. Trumpeter Murphy Campo, for example, would become a fixture on at the Famous Door and elsewhere on Bourbon Street in decades to come. But none of the post–Basin Street Six Dixieland groups captured a large audience in the mid-1950s. In fact, most of Jones's age-group had either moved to modern jazz or pursued nonmusic careers. The local Dixieland and TNOJ revival had waned in favor of rhythm and blues figures like Fats Domino, Lloyd Price, and Sam Butera, who gained increasingly wider audiences.

PAPA CELESTIN AND TNOJ IN THE REVIVAL

The other major popular band of the revival was trumpeter Oscar "Papa" Celestin's traditional New Orleans jazz group, the Original Tuxedo Orchestra. An April 1948 *Jazzfinder* article entitled "Papa Celestin Comes Back" (uncredited, but almost certainly written by editor/discographer Orin Blackstone) tells of Celestin's arrival in New Orleans in 1906 at the age of twenty-two. Born in Napoleonville, Louisiana, he had heard brass band music as a child on a showboat anchored in Bayou Lafourche. He played cornet in a brass band in St. Charles Parish before his New Orleans work, which began almost immediately with the Indiana Brass Band, followed by Henry Allen's Brass Band and the Olympia and the Tuxedo bands.

By 1910 he was leading a group at Tuxedo Hall on Franklin Street in Storyville. His bands grew in popularity between 1917 and 1927 with a repertoire of dance and novelty tunes. Surely, Celestin's early bands must have richly reflected both prejazz and jazz influences. The *Jazzfinder* names some of his stellar players during the decade: Louis Armstrong, Sweet Emma Barrett, Baby Dodds, Kid Shots Madison, Jimmy Noone, Armand Piron, Johnny St. Cyr, Zutty Singleton, and Lorenzo Tio.

Celestin was a great favorite with white audiences in the 1920s. He worked debutante parties, university dances, and the annual celebration for the king and queen of Mardi Gras. He played posh venues like the Southern Yacht Club, New Orleans Country Club, Antoine's, and the Boston Club. High society, indeed. But things started going badly for everyone during the Depression, and Celestin's musical engagements diminished. During World War II he worked in local shipyards, and in 1944 a hit-and-run accident left him with a leg injury that never fully healed.

Celestin might well have been forgotten. For reasons to be discussed, he was never the darling of Bill Russell and the other purists who recorded Kid Rena, Bunk Johnson, George Lewis, and others. But there had been talk in the National Jazz Foundation about promoting Celestin's return; and, as noted earlier, Doc Souchon claimed that the New Orleans Jazz Club had in fact supported Celestin's organization of the 1948 band.

The new band opened at Steve Valenti's Paddock Lounge on Bourbon Street in late 1948 or early 1949. Like Bonano at the Famous Door, they were soon doing regular live radio broadcasts and appearing sporadically on television. According to Nick Gagliano, Celestin recaptured his popularity with uptown white audiences, playing for a new generation of debutantes, society groups, and fraternities and sororities. The band was in and out of the Paddock, and Celestin was off due to illness from time to time, but they became identified as Valenti's club during and after the revival.

In a May 1950 article in London's *Jazz Journal* Orleanian John Provenzano wrote that Celestin "has the jazz world on its toes" and called him the "representative of the real New Orleans jazz music." A July 31, 1949, story the Chicago *Tribune* headed "Papa on Hand for the Return of Dixieland Jazz in New Orleans" gave rare exposure to the local revival and called Celestin a "leading exponent" at the Paddock.

The Celestin group included Bill Matthews, trombone; Alphonse Picou, clarinet; Octave Crosby, piano; Ricard Alexis, bass; and Happy Goldston, drums. They had a small repertoire of tunes but an interesting group conception. They seemed to straddle jazz and prejazz with ease and aplomb, achieving a exceptionally clear ensemble sound all the while. Celestin played a straight-ahead lead with an admirably raw tone and a throwback rapid vibrato. His throaty vocals carried marvelous conviction. Matthews played choppy but vigorous trombone. Picou played his famous "High Society" solo (and everything else) with a gentle sound and the staccato phrasing of an earlier era—antiquarian, certainly, but charming nonetheless.

The rhythm section had the benefit of Happy Goldston's jazzy military thrust. Perhaps his solos epitomized the band's just-across-the-line-to-jazz conception. The frequent, repetitious full-chorus solos were mainly on snare drum, consisting of rolls with march-like phrases, accented in ways that one imagines the earliest parade drummers might have executed in expanding the European rudimental vocabulary. The Celestin band was well represented on a 1950 session on Roger Wolfe's Bandwagon label.

To admit my bias, I did not like Papa Celestin's band at the time. I was justifiably bored with their repetition of the same tunes—"Didn't He Ramble," "Lil' Liza Jane," the inevitable "High Society," "Marie Laveau," "Mama Don't Allow," and a few other chestnuts. They seemed to play both less inventively and "older" than innumerable other TNOJ bands of the 1920s, 1930s, and 1940s. With the possible exception of trombonist Matthews, Celestin's group lacked the intensity and exploration, man for man, of Bunk's band.

I remember a 1949 conversation that my brother Don and I had with Lester Bouchon, Sharkey's clarinetist, during the break at a Sunday concert. We remarked that Celestin's band sounded corny to us. Lester frowned and made a comment that rebuked our attitude while partially acknowledging the point: "That's the way the music was in those days. When we were kids, that's all we had to listen to."

Celestin's 1927 "It's a Jam Up" track on the valuable *New Orleans in New Orleans* CD (Jazz Archives N68) gives some idea of "the way the music was in those days." The entire group clearly shows prejazz influences, even as they improvise and use many jazz inflections with considerable skill. Even a casual listener will recognize that the band's cluttered ensemble, ricky-tick phrasing, and wiggle-your-eyebrows reed breaks have more in common with the 1917 Original Dixieland Jazz Band session than with the fluid articulation and clear conception of the 1923 Oliver and Armstrong cuts, the Armstrong Hot 5 and 7 sessions of 1925–1926, and the Bix and his Gang recordings of 1927. Moreover, Celestin's conception, unlike Bonano's on his 1928 track on the same CD, shows little change by the time of the 1950 sessions on Bandwagon.

Even so, I admired Celestin as a jazz pioneer and disagreed with those who saw his onstage manner as Uncle Tom-ish. While his showmanship was jovial and old-timey, I recall it as virile and natural, rarely crossing the line to facial or bodily contortions that suggested minstrelsy. He had a unique way of holding his forearms parallel to the ground and moving them up and down with the rhythm, four beats to the bar, giving the impression that the whole room was shaking. It was very personal, eccentric, and, to my perception, hip.

What bothered me as a budding jazz fan was the band's prejazz/jazz synthesis, which I dismissed because it seemed to be in a self-imitating rut (which it was), and I rashly declared it unlistenable (which it was not) because of its prejazz components. It took awhile for me to loosen up and enjoy whatever is stimulating in any performance, and even longer to see mixed genres and styles in transition as particularly interesting, especially when a group carries it off skillfully, as Celestin's band certainly did.

Of course, many tourists and local fans of Celestin bought into the mystique of TNOJ—the simplistic idea, also rampant in the 1960s Preservation Hall revival, that old = authentic = great jazz. Add "quaint" and a jigger of bourbon to that formula and you have a great evening at the Paddock. This might not be the quintessential jazz experience but, tourist or jazz aesthete, one could do worse.

Papa Celestin received national recognition in 1953, the year that I mark as the last of the local revival. A short piece in *Time* magazine entitled "Papa" called him "a steady, sturdy pillar." Chilton's *Who's Who* reports that in 1953 he recorded for Columbia, the label of his "It's Jam Up" session over a quarter century earlier; played for President Dwight Eisenhower; and appeared in the wide-screen film extravaganza *Cinerama Holiday*. Celestin died in New Orleans the next year, on the very day when a bust of him was to be unveiled at the Latter Library on St. Charles Avenue.

It is useful to revisit the question of why the purists who reactivated Kid Rena, Bunk Johnson, and others basically ignored Papa Celestin's TNOJ band throughout the national and local revivals. TNOJ advocates like Broun, Russell, and Ramsey certainly did not share my distaste for Celestin's mixture of prejazz and jazz influences, since they brought back numerous musicians who, to a greater or lesser degree, were stylistically as archaic as Celestin. (Picou, in fact, was on Broun's 1940 Kid Rena session.)

Interviews in 1998 with Helen Arlt, Nick Gagliano, and Don Perry provided interesting speculations. Arlt suggested that Celestin's name might not have surfaced in Russell's research. This is unlikely, given Russell's scope as a scholar and record collector. References to Celestin abound in histories and biographical listings by Chilton, Feather, Kernfeld, Schuller, Shapiro and Hentoff, Stearns, and numerous others. The index to Rose and Souchon's *Family Album* shows sixty mentions of Celestin in the text.

Perry wondered if Russell had enough on his hands in guiding the comeback of the irascible and demanding Bunk, who became his personal friend. Arlt and Gagliano thought that the purists might have known about Celestin but simply didn't consider him to be an important pioneer. This is possible, but the purists knew that they could not fully assess the early jazz artists' skill from the meager recorded evidence; Celestin's trumpet was at least as worthy of a rehearing as Kids Howard, Rena, and Valentine. And again, many 1940s recordings made by purists on American Music, Good Time Jazz, and other labels show that they brought back some players who were less than jazz pathfinders.

Gagliano probably hit the mark when he recalled Celestin's popularity, both in the early 1920s and late 1940s, with the city's white elite. As noted in section I, the purist collectors of the 1930s were a self-described cult, many of them with vintage 1930s alliances to Marxism. A black artist kow-towing to the social set would not be an appealing figure to them, and it would not be difficult to dismiss his artistry on ideological grounds. The Ce-lestin band's long-term residency on Bourbon Street would further demon-strate betrayal of his proletarian roots. Gagliano acknowledged that he him-self "stayed as far away from Bourbon Street as possible," preferring to hear George Lewis at Manny's Tavern before Lewis himself went to Bourbon Street in 1950, the peak year of the local revival.

In describing the 1947–1953 revival, I have already hinted at some rea-sons for the neglect of that revival in popular and scholarly histories. Before making those reasons explicit, a look at the revival in profile is warranted. Some key chronological points are represented on timeline chart 2, "High-lights of the Popular Revival in New Orleans, 1947–1953" on page 159 at the end of this overview and before the vintage articles that constitute chap-ters 12–20. A different kind of depiction is presented on page 138. "The Local Revival, 1950—A Partial List of Events," though not exhaustive, lists many of the activities of Dixieland and TNOJ artists during that year.

In today's glutted music market the list might not seem impressive. But in 1950 the level of activity was quite remarkable. Some gigs lasted just a few weeks, some bands moved from club to club, and some sidemen moved from band to band, but that was part of the dynamic of the time. Swing artists like Sal Franzella and Louis Prima (with then unknown vocalist Keely Smith) played in Dixieland settings because that was where the action was. Numerous sources provided the information, the NOJC's *Second Line* and the daily New Orleans *Item* being most helpful.

Neglect of the Local Revival and the TNOJ Mystique

With such rich and varied postwar activity among Dixieland and TNOJ players in New Orleans, why did the local revival go widely unrecognized? Several explanations come to mind. One has already been discussed at length—that the impact of Bunk Johnson and some of his local bandsmen so dominated coverage in the national jazz and popular media that later writ-ers neglected to look closely at the total picture in New Orleans.

This explanation does not bail out serious commentators and historians, but it is reasonable enough when applied to the popular press of the time. Magazines like *Time* thrive on eye-catching angles: a black rice mill worker is rescued from obscurity by devoted jazz fans and his genius as a neglected pioneering artist is recaptured on record and in concerts at major sites throughout the country. Here's a snoozer: some jazz concerts, club engagements, and radio programs gain an audience in New Orleans. A *Look* reporter, as will be seen, actually started to pick up the latter emphasis in a 1950 story but was persuaded by local purists to spotlight George Lewis.

As for writers like Balliet, Dance, Hazeldine, Morgenstern, Williams, and Wilson, it appears that they simply failed to investigate what was happening locally. Accepting the mythology that surrounded sympathetic figures like Bunk Johnson and the sainted Bill Russell, they essentially equated the revival in New Orleans with Johnson's extremely limited activity there. None lived in the city at the time, and I could find no evidence that they listened to recordings of contemporaneous local artists (e.g., Bonano, Burke, Celestin) other than the select few (e.g., Johnson, Lewis, Rena) whose records were produced or endorsed by the purists. Overwhelmingly, the purists' selective perception of history has become normative in historical accounts and jazz lore. The purists created, and others perpetuated, the notion that the revival of the 1940s took place just about everywhere except New Orleans.

The purists' aesthetic doctrines—what I have been calling the mystique of traditional New Orleans jazz—also provided a perspective that dismissed the local revival. Cultivated by the 1930s record collectors, the TNOJ mystique can be described in terms of the four components discussed below. Certainly not all purists hold every component with equal fervor. In the real world, attitudes and beliefs are interrelated in complex ways. But analysis and written discourse proceed in subjects and predicates, so here we linearly go, working with the usual burdens of language.

The sine qua non of the TNOJ mystique is *(1) an apostolic devotion to early jazz as the only genuine jazz art.* Other features of the mystique, suggested in various contexts in this book, are *(2) rejection of Dixieland jazz, (3) a deep suspicion of most artists who achieve commercial success, and (4) a thinly veiled assumption that white musicians cannot play authentic jazz.*

TNOJ: The Only Jazz Art

I have written often and fondly of the extraordinary ardency of jazz fans. But TNOJ zealots cross the line of fandom into the realm of fanaticism. During the various revivals they had little use for the posttraditional styles of musicians like Bonano, Fazola, Girard, and other Dixielanders.

Raeburn cites the comments of numerous figures who were part of, or worked with, the early fundamentalists. The language of the commentators is strikingly similar in pointing to the radicalism of the true believers' stance. Ralph de Toledano, one of the original collector-historians of the 1930s, acknowledged, no, boasted, that they were virtually "a cult." Critic Stanley Finkelstein characterized Eugene Williams, another fig pioneer, as "absolutely sincere with the fanaticism of Carrie Nation wielding an axe in the saloons."

THE LOCAL REVIVAL, 1950: A PARTIAL LIST OF EVENTS

LIVE MUSIC

Tony Almerico, Sunday concerts, Parisian Room; weekends, Pontchartrain
   Plaza
Dutch Andrus, weekends, Gennaro's and Steamer *President*
Paul Barbarin, Mondays at Paddock
Jay Barry at Old Absinthe Bar
Basin Street Six at L'Enfant's, Gunga Den, Cotton Club, various sites
Sharkey Bonano at Famous Door, Blue Room; Sunday concerts, Municipal
   Auditorium side room with Roger Wolfe, host
Papa Celestin at Paddock; Sundays, Patio Royale
Dukes of Dixieland at Famous Door
Bunny Franks (Basin Street Six) at Perez's Club Oasis
Sal Franzella, weekends, Bungalow and St. Regis
Armand Hug at Absinthe House, Bayou Bar
Mike Lala Sr., weekends, St. Regis
George Lewis at El Morocco; weekends at Manny's Tavern
New Orleans Jazz Club monthly meetings/jam sessions, St. Charles Hotel;
   summer pops concerts in Congo Square; all-day Mardi Gras session,
   George Lewis, Ciro's Patio
Santo Pecora at Silver Slipper
Louis Prima, Keely Smith, Sid Davila, at Prima's 500
Various bands, weekends at Luthjen's
Johnny Wiggs at St. Charles Hotel
Phil Zito at L'Enfant's, Moulin Rouge

RECORDING SESSIONS AND/OR RELEASES

Tony Almerico on Crescent City
Paul Barbarin on Circle, GHB
Basin Street Six on Circle
Sharkey Bonano on Bandwagon, Capitol, Dixieland
Papa Celestin on Bandwagon
Armand Hug on Bandwagon (duo w/Ray Bauduc), Capitol, Good Time Jazz
George Lewis on Good Time Jazz
Herb Morand on New Orleans
Big Eye Louis Nelson on American Music
Santo Pecora on Mercury

Johnny Wiggs on New Orleans
Phil Zito on Columbia

MEDIA: BROADCAST AND PRINT

ABC Network *Battle of Bands* series from N.O.; Roger Wolfe, host
Almerico/Parisian Room on WNOE, WWL
Sharkey Bonano on WDSU-TV; on WNOE from Famous Door
Campus Dixieland Band (mainly, Loyola—Fred Assunto, G. Erskine) on
    Ted Mack's *Original Amateur Hour*
Papa Celestin on WDSU-TV; radio show from Paddock
Down Beat write-ups (G. Hoefer) on Armand Hug, Doc Souchon's 6 and
    7/8 Band
Bunny Franks (Basin St. Six)/Perez's Club Oasis on WDSU-TV
Sal Franzella on WNOE
Ed Hart, Saturday *Dixie Downbeat* record show, WTPS
Armand Hug on WDSU-TV
Jazz Journal (London) article (John Provenzano)
Irving Fazola on WTPS, five days a week
George Lewis/El Morocco Sunday on WTPS
Look magazine article by J. Roddy, June 6, "Dixieland Jazz Is Hot Again"
New Orleans Jazz Club Summer Pops concerts on ABC Network
New Orleans Jazz Club Sunday night record show, WWL
First broadcast of N.O. Jazz Club jam session on WNOE
Louis Prima, Keely Smith from Prima's 500 on WNOE
Johnny Wiggs record show on WNOE
Roger Wolfe Saturday night *Dixieland Jazz* record show, WDSU
Miscellaneous ads and mentions in daily papers, *Louisiana Weekly*

OTHER

Paul Barbarin forms his own TNOJ/Dixieland band
Jazz Pioneers Club formed
NOJC's *Jazz Club Bulletin*, first issue in April; becomes *Second Line* in May
Doc Souchon lectures at first annual joint meeting of NOJC/ New Orleans
    Art Association, Delgado Museum
Teenage Dixieland groups—Murphy Campo's band (Pee Wee Spitelera,
    Reed Vaughan) at Rex Club, Buras; Dixiecats (Connie Jones, Larry
    Muhoberac, Charlie May) formed
Johnny Wiggs recording of "Bourbon Street Bounce" a local hit

George Montgomery of *Record Changer* magazine called Bill Colburn, a Bunk Johnson and Kid Ory advocate, "the nomadic apostle of New Orleans music." Orson Welles worked with rabid jazz fans when he hosted the 1944–1945 Mercury Theater radio broadcasts of Kid Ory's band. He commented, "There's something of the opium eater in your jazz cultist. His enthusiasm affects him like a drug habit, removing him, it seems, from the uninitiated and less paranoid world about him and encouraging many of the attitudes of full-blown megalomania."

My closest personal encounter with the TNOJ extremism came in 1972, when Tom Bethell and I were both writing for the *Vieux Carre Courier.* Those who know of Bethell's later work with two conservative magazines — contributing editor for *National Review* and Washington correspondent for *American Spectator*—will not be surprised by his shintoist view of jazz. In the April 27 *Courier*, Bethell had used a review of bassist Pops Foster's autobiography as a platform for building a purist metaphysic.

In the May 19 issue I responded to his idea that only group improvisation as practiced by the masters is real, worthwhile jazz. In Bethell's words, with Louis Armstrong "the rot set in." Endless lines of soloists followed, he stated, "each less articulate than the last," their manic self-indulgence spelling the ruination of the art. I named several damned nice guys who were fine soloists and asked Bethell how he had established such sure psychological correlations between narcissism and jazz soloing. I suggested that one could love the group improvisation of the early bands *and* enjoy imaginative soloists, who might or might not be vainglorious warthogs. Bethell replied that *I* was the snob, flaunting my belief in a broader view of jazz to "impute a demonstrable superiority" to my position.

A few critics like Leonard Feather and Barry Ulanov roundly condemned purist extremism as hopelessly reactionary. Feather's *Encyclopedia* entry for Bunk Johnson called Frederic Ramsey and Bill Russell "well-meaning but misguided amateurs." Clarinetist Barney Bigard, a true New Orleans original, criticized not only revivalist players who were imitating TNOJ ("They're out of tune so bad it hurts your ears") but the early music itself. In a 1948 interview with Ernest Borneman, he said, "I try to do better. I learned a few things since I was a kid in New Orleans. . . . Who wants to play like those folds [*sic*] thirty years ago?"

At the risk of being beaten about the head and shoulders by people I have long loved and respected, I must call into question the deification of Bill Russell, which has worked considerable mischief in considerations of the 1940s national and local revivals. Without asking for the dubious honor, he became the chief guru of purists. Diana Rose (Al's wife) called him "the High Lama of Jazz" and compared him to St. Francis of Assisi. Raeburn cites critic Ralph Gleason's statement that Russell "is the nearest thing to a saint I have ever known."

A brief bio is in order. Russell was born in 1905 in Canton, Missouri, and died in New Orleans in 1992. Canton is a Mississippi River town upstream of Hannibal, so Russell was likely exposed to prejazz and jazz via riverboat bands as a youngster. Before his career as a jazz scholar, writer, and grass-roots impresario Russell was a gifted violinist. He gained a formidable reputation as a composer for percussion. B. Michael Williams reports that Russell was a colleague of John Cage and Lou Harrison, participating with the two experimentalists in the first all-percussion concerts in America in the late 1930s and early 1940s.

A charter member of the rabid fig collector-historians of the 1930s, his three chapters in the Ramsey and Smith's 1939 classic *Jazzmen* established him in the jazz community as a solid researcher and a purist icon. Russell demonstrated his selfless dedication to early jazz with the founding of American Music Records and the revival of Bunk Johnson in the 1940s. No mere promoter, he was a true friend who essentially became Bunk's caretaker during the trumpeter's final years in the late 1940s.

Russell moved to New Orleans permanently in 1956. His truthful rapport with the early jazz musicians made him the ideal, perhaps the only, choice as first curator of the Tulane Jazz Archive in 1958. To his everlasting credit, he did not enforce a purist orthodoxy at the archive. He threw a wide net, seeking interviews and artifacts from musicians and jazz watchers white and black, male and female, traditional and Dixieland, active and inactive, central and peripheral.

I met Russell and talked to him numerous times and did indeed find him to be a Christ-like man—no bull, no metaphors. A lifelong pacifist and lover of animals (hence the Assisi reference), he projected a calm, spiritual presence that inspired immediate trust. I must admit that I was awed by the man.

But let us say it, Russell venerated the archaic for its own sake and was blind to the shortcomings of the musicians he most admired, to the extent of extolling as virtues their loss of technique, careless intonation, and arrested inventive capacities. Russell's review of the 1940 Kid Rena session, quoted by Raeburn, is a case in point. Russell writes that Rena led the band "with a lack of precision in ensembles and section playing" that is at the core of "the rough and ready, knock 'em down and drag out style of music which we call New Orleans hot jazz."

Russell's admirers, unfortunately, romanticized his own romanticizing of Things Old. Diana Rose lauded his focus on "the principle of recreating the ambience of early jazz as performed by the older black musicians." She expressed genial admiration for his purist attitudes and practices, including lack of tuning up and recording on old equipment with a single microphone. The American Music recordings show that Russell's methods often succeeded all too well. Listen to Jim Robinson's painfully sharp intonation, with Johnson not far behind, on the AMCD-3 track "Darktown Strutters' Ball 1," the entire performance being encased in the fogbound sound created by Russell's primitive equipment.

Christopher Hillman also praised the poor sound quality and the fumbling, prejazz aspects of the American Music recordings. He noted with frank admiration that the AM sides were "recorded on equipment that emphasized raw vitality at the expense of subtlety." The music found Bunk and his bandsmen "playing against, as much as with, each other," with a "resulting heterophony" and "spontaneous, clashing sound" that "must have been a part of New Orleans music since the time of Buddy Bolden." Barney Bigard would no doubt have agreed with the description while wincing at the very qualities Hillman found so engaging.

It is time to put aside both Russell's hyperpurist views and the unfortunate tendency to brahamanize him. He was neither a prophet who raised the dead, as his devotees would have it, nor a deluded antiquarian, as Feather would have it. Possibly, he was a little bit of both. We need to grow comfortable with that paradox, in fairness to the man and in order to achieve a broader perspective on early jazz and the national and local revivals of the 1940s. As Bill Huntington recently commented, "Whether or not Russell's views were overly purist, he never tried to force his ideas on anyone. He was simply a genuine pioneer hero, who devoted his life to a type of New Orleans music whose documentation might have been lost without him. . . . Rather than as the masthead for the mystique, I see him as its unwitting symbol. . . . Time and misconception turned Bill's work into fodder for the purist mafia."

The deification of Russell is most powerful today among diehard figs, TNOJ researchers and discographers, and people in New Orleans who knew him personally. But in many ways he is the conscripted guru figure in the jazz community at large, embodying the TNOJ mystique—and as such, he exerts a disproportionately large influence on both scholarship and popular culture. Certainly his major role in the 1940s national revival (his obituary in the London *Times,* Masciere notes, called him "the single most influential figure in the revival of New Orleans jazz") deflected attention from the local postwar revival, which he scarcely touched.

I believe that the TNOJ mystique lives on in a curious form among jazz fans today. Although often catholic in their tastes across a broad jazz spectrum, they often lean contradictorily toward purist attitudes when looking at TNOJ and Dixieland jazz. New Orleans players from the revival years like Sweet Emma Barrett, Mutt Carey, and Jim Robinson are regarded as "truer" jazz performers than later musicians like Alvin Alcorn, Henry (Red) Allen, and Irving Fazola, who were in my view far more articulate and inventive. Which brings us to the next component of the TNOJ mystique.

Rejection of Dixieland Jazz

It is important to acknowledge again that there was some lukewarm Dixieland jazz being played during the revival. The early work of the Dukes of Dixieland was highly derivative of Sharkey's band. The Basin Street Six played wonderful Dixieland but spent a good deal of time clowning onstage. Tony Almerico's Parisian Room band lacked grace in ensembles and thoughtful, swinging exploration in solos. They were often outshone by teenaged second liners who sat in (e.g., Connie Jones's Dixiecats, trumpeters Murphy Campo and Warren Luening, clarinetist Pee Wee Spitelera, and drummer Reed Vaughan). Jones, still active in New Orleans, recently reminded me that almost all the players in those junior bands became professional musicians.

But even the good Dixieland of the time has often been ignored or put down simply for being Dixieland. This is clear from the aforementioned comments by Collins, Wilson, and others who apparently see the style as inherently shallow or commercial. Never mind that much of the TNOJ lauded by figs throughout the 1940s was unremarkable. The purist mystique attributes special excellence, prima facie, to TNOJ, even when it represents some of the players' poorest output.

An anecdote that illustrates the TNOJ mystique in action is related by Tom Bethell in his biography of George Lewis. A *Look* magazine associate editor, Joseph Roddy, was en route to New Orleans in 1950 to write a story on, of all things, the *local* revival. By chance, an old friend of Roddy's, a local TNOJ champion named Robert Greenwood, heard about the project. Greenwood's journal tells how he "immediately cornered" Roddy and learned, to his horror, that the article would "be all but the life story of Sharkey Bonano, with side articles on Phil Zito and Papa Celestin." Bonano's life story? Heaven forfend! According to Bethell, "Greenwood spent the rest of the afternoon telling him [Roddy] about George Lewis." Greenwood wrote that their trip to Manny's Tavern "completely won over Mr. Roddy."

There was still another convert to be made—a young *Look* photographer named Kubrick, yes, Stanley Kubrick, who would later be the legendary director of films like *Clockwork Orange* and *2001: A Space Odyssey.* But it turned out that Kubrick knew about Lewis from Bunk Johnson's band in the national revival. He was ready to be hip in the purist manner, shifting the focus from a report on the local revival to a paean to TNOJ in general and Lewis in particular. Indeed, Kubrick asked whether they needed to include Bonano at all, and Roddy replied that he "would have to say something about him and Celestin."

Clearly, Roddy's original intentions were right on the mark, in terms of the postwar revival as it had actually evolved. Bonano and Celestin were the true musical begetters of the revival, and Phil Zito's International City Dixielanders (the embryonic Basin Street Six) was newly hot on Bourbon Street. But the fig's-eye view won out. When "Dixieland Jazz Is 'Hot' Again" appeared in the June 6, 1950, issue of *Look,* there was a full-page lead photo of the Lewis band and another large shot that was staged in a funky backyard scene. There was a third picture, beautifully composed, of George and his mother, Alice Zeno.

Bonano and Celestin each had a photo, placed among shots of several jazzmen who were performing across the country—Eddie Condon, Art Hodes, Jack Teagarten, the Firehouse Five, Red Nichols, Sidney Bechet, and others. In giving a quick visual gloss of the national revival, Roddy was of course tardy. By 1950 that revival was by no means recent news but had stretched over most of the previous decade.

Roddy's text showed that Greenwood's view had won the day. It accurately outlined some jazz history, distinguished between the TNOJ and Dixie styles, and then treated George Lewis extensively. Lewis was quoted at length and described as "the most authentic 'New Orleans' band in the land," with Lewis "playing the very best 'New Orleans' style." The article ended with a standard purist lament. Roddy wrote that "pure 'New Orleans,'" from which Dixie derives, has not had a good year since King Oliver left. . . . With Dixieland being revived all over the country, Lewis hopes that the revival may someday get back to 'New Orleans.'"

The issue here is not whether George Lewis deserved the national attention he got in *Look*. Most certainly, he did. The point is that the TNOJ zealots hijacked what might have been the only bona fide national story on the local-revival-as-it-was, not as the purists wished it had been.

The final quotation from Roddy reveals the basic error and dishonesty in the article. The national and local revivals *did* in fact "get back to" the TNOJ style. The national revival had done so during the many years when Bunk Johnson was lionized, with Lewis, Ory, Bechet, and others highly visible as well. And in New Orleans in 1950 Papa Celestin's band was certainly playing in traditional New Orleans style. The devoted and manipulative figs simply could not acknowledge this and still depict their music as forgotten, characterize the derivative "Dixieland" as suspect, and feature Lewis as the quaint, abandoned martyr.

In the long run, I believe, serious reviews of the recorded evidence will overcome the effects of purist ideology and win a fair hearing for the entire range of the city's artists, TNOJ and Dixieland, who were performing during the national and local revivals. Of course, several things must happen first. Discographers devoted to jazz in New Orleans will need to emulate Walter Bruyninckx, Jorgen Jepsen, Tom Lord, and Brian Rust—breaking the color barrier by integrating the lists of artists and moving beyond Orin Blackstone's list that ends in 1944. More record companies will have to reissue somewhat obscure postwar sessions by artists like Paul Barbarin, Raymond Burke, Papa Celestin, and Irving Fazola. And critics will have to put aside presuppositions about genres and particular artists. By acknowledging that excellent and poor jazz performances occur in all styles, we can move toward fresh responses to the music that emerged during the revival years.

Suspicion of Commercial Success

As I have noted in several contexts, commercialism did rear its seductive head frequently during the national and local revivals. Pee Wee Hunt's "Twelfth Street Rag" proved that ersatz jazz can outsell the good stuff.

Sharkey's Capitol recordings were obviously aimed at wider audiences than his sides for Roger Wolfe's Bandwagon label, and he grew arrogant when booked at prestigious venues like the Blue Room. Tourists nudged leaders like Celestin and Almerico to rerun overly worn material. Just about everyone played "When the Saints Go Marching In" ad nauseum.

But as Holden Caulfield says, that shouldn't *ruin everything.* I have sat through many a set where Armand Hug noodled around on "Blue Tango" or "Oh!" by request, then tore into "Grandpa's Spells" or took me on a tour of "Black and Blue," and nothing but glad that I stayed for the best of it. The problem is that purists are often antiprosperity snobs, turning completely away from artists who sometimes play to the groundlings or, worse, actually become popular with the general public. This is partly from a sense of loss of insider status, I believe. The cult has been invaded by unworthy, unperceptive, everyday people. As Donne said, "'Twere profanation of our joys/ to tell the laity of our love." Contradictorily, they believe that their favorite artists are worthy of wide attention, but a chip of self-esteem falls away when the music once possessed by a few seems accessible to Neanderthals who clap on one and three.

Covert or overt Marxist attitudes are another reason for disdaining success. As noted in the discussion of Papa Celestin's band, many a left eyebrow was raised because Celestin was a favorite with the uptown crowd in both incarnations of his career, playing for white debutante parties and carnival events. In the late 1940s he compounded the offense by playing on Bourbon Street, for bloody *tourists*, no less.

Celestin, Bonano, and others who were finally making a living with their music were, seemingly for that very reason, unworthy of being heard—a narrow, sad, and hypocritical state of affairs. It seems that only a few TNOJ performers, like Bunk Johnson and Sidney Bechet, could be popular and excellent at the same time, being endorsed by true believers like Russell and Blesh.

White Guys Can't Jump—or Swing

A final possible reason for lack of attention to the local revival of 1947–1953 is unwillingness to credit white musicians with the ability to play good jazz. This attitude lives on and is debated today, but it was rampant among many white purists who spearheaded the national revival. Raeburn notes, though, that the beliefs of the fig collectors-historians need not necessarily be attributed to racism outright. The purists reflected their times, acting in line "with the emphasis on black origins of the music found in the literature of the period . . . these [black] musicians were the ones that the New Orleans revivalists wanted to document, although some young, white practitioners of the old style got into the act."

Also, as noted earlier, most early white musicians incorporated jazz techniques and inflections rooted in African music later than did the early black musicians. And it can be plausibly argued that white musicians moved more rapidly away from characteristics of TNOJ and into the stylistic qualities of swing.

But if that were the whole story, we would not see the pattern of virtual exclusion of white artists from the writings and discographies of so many purists. In fact, very few white artists "got into the act." One wonders if the term "white Dixieland" would even have emerged in the absence of baseline assumptions about who can and cannot play "real" jazz. If the white champions of black-only jazz were not racists, their choices reveal them as ideologues or sentimentalists. Their stance is ultimately uncritical and patronizing in its exclusivism.

Two 1999 works, Brian Wood's *The Song for Me* and Richard Sudhalter's *Lost Chords*, decline to take the purist line. British writer Wood's self-published alphabetic glossary of New Orleans musicians includes not only black and white TNOJ and Dixieland artists but also many swing players, a few modern musicians, many bands, nightclubs, critics, historians, and to confuse matters, a large number of musicians from other countries, mostly British trad/revivalist players.

"Quirky" is the best word to describe Wood's annotated list. He is more zealous hobbyist than scholarly historian. The Britisher acknowledges at the outset that the volume is flawed by his distance from the source materials, confesses that pleasant dalliances often overtook his need to do research during visits to New Orleans, and welcomes corrections and additions from readers. Apparently the list is on disk and will be constantly updated and revised.

The book is most comprehensive in its inclusion of the earliest black and white players, citing sources (e.g., Charters, Rose, and Souchon) more frequently than in items about later musicians. But errors abound. Wood lacks both information and perspective on numerous individuals and events, notably from the postwar years onward. But again, the author's genial self-irony softens the blow. The text is laced with Wood's opinions and *bon mots*, some of them more *bon* than others. He delights in including entries like St. Ignatius Loyola, just for the hell of it, and Lee Konitz, to annoy purists ("My little joke!"). I could not help liking the literate persona who peeks through the text and could not help being awed by the enormity (and needless overreach) of Wood's project, which after all has not been undertaken by more rigorous researchers. I will use *The Song for Me* often as a first source in seeking information about lesser-known figures in early jazz but will look for corroboration.

Sudhalter's *Lost Chords,* an 890-page scholarly volume from Oxford Press, is another matter. The subtitle *White Musicians and Their Contributions to Jazz, 1915–1945*, seems to beg for controversy. Yet Sudhalter is not abrasive in making a brief argument—an eight-page introduction and a four-page epilogue—that supports need for a book on white artists (not just New Orleans musicians) from the early years through the swing era. He notes reasonably that some critics and many in the public at large hold that jazz is essentially African music and whites cannot play it authentically. He also cites the widely accepted idea that jazz combines African and European musical elements.

Beyond this, however, Sudhalter's points are not well taken. I will not re-iterate here my views about early jazz and jazz genres advanced at the beginning of this overview. Suffice it to say Sudhalter appears to fuzz the notion that African components, skillfully integrated with European-based song-structure forms, are indisputably the most distinctive aspects of the art of jazz. He claims that there are no "litmus tests" (i.e., clear criteria) whatever for determining whether a performance is describable as "jazz" to a greater or lesser extent. Sudhalter says that a performance which lacks key African-based elements—he specifically cites influence of the blues or a concept of swing as examples—should be considered as jazz on its own terms. Surely, such a performance can be *good music* on its own terms. But blurring the question of its jazzical qualities in the name of "pluralism" ultimately equates—*as jazz*—Lily Pons singing "Basin Street Blues" (she actually did, once) with renditions by Jack Teagarten and Louis Armstrong.

Ironically, one could read the twenty-eight chapters between the introduction and epilogue with enjoyment and a critical eye without reference to the author's provocative generalizations about neglected white guys and jazz that does not swing. Sudhalter eschews the encyclopedic approach of Wood and the jazz discographers, choosing to write at length and in depth about selected individuals and groups of musicians. For example, his narrative about Orleanians Ray Lopez and Tom Brown in Chicago in 1915 and his penetrating critique of Artie Shaw as a unique clarinetist and leader would stand or fall on their own merit if they had been published separately, or perhaps as chapters in a collection that also included essays on King Oliver in Chicago and Duke Ellington's artistry and leadership.

Returning to the TNOJ mystique, I must conclude by giving due praise and credit to its early adherents. Despite their excesses, they made major contributions to the literature of jazz and raised important historical and aesthetic questions. Their earnest conviction, groundbreaking scholarship, and tenacious romanticism, rooted in part in Marxist idealism of the 1930s, still carry a power beyond mere vintage appeal. The most dedicated purists put their ideals into practice, going to considerable pains and personal expense to find, write about, or record early jazz artists like Bunk Johnson, George Lewis, Big Eye Louis Nelson, Kid Rena, Kid Shots Madison, Alphonse Picou, and others. People like Orin Blackstone, Al Rose, Bill Russell, Charles Edward Smith, and Eugene Williams contributed hugely to jazz studies and have rightfully been accorded respect by jazz historians.

THE LOCAL REVIVAL DECLINES

Just as the beginning of the popular revival in New Orleans cannot be set at an absolute date, the decline was not a sudden cessation of activity. I will point briefly to indications of change that seemed to signal that the local enthusiasm for jazz was trailing off as the mid-1950s approached. Numerous sources were used in gathering the facts below, the main one being the New Orleans Jazz Club's *Second Line* journal, which tracked jazz happenings most closely.

The NOJC's own activities are a good barometer of the revival. Although the French Quarter was lively in 1951, the NOJC expressed concern about the viability of its concerts. The June–July *Second Line* reported cryptically that the NOJC was considering "another type of entertainment" that "would be a financial success as well as in keeping with Club policy." And indeed, the NOJC's star-studded 1951 concert in Congo Square with the bands of Paul Barbarin, Papa Celestin, the Dukes of Dixieland, George Lewis, Johnny Wiggs, and guest artist Jimmy Dorsey did not do well. In 1952 a September Congo Square concert with Barbarin, Bonano, Lewis, Wiggs, and vocalist Lizzie Miles had an NBC hookup but also drew a small crowd.

A flop outright came with the May 1953 concert featuring Barbarin, saxist Sam Butera (playing pop/R&B), clarinetist Sid Davilla, drummer Freddie Kohlman, and Wiggs. *Line* editor Doc Souchon complained in the June issue that "something has to be done to remedy the situation—and soon, if we wish jazz to flourish in its own home town. It could be that people are becoming fatigued with the reptious [sic] manner in which the concerts are presented."

The NOJC tried combining local bands with out-of-town Dixie and revivalist bands—Gene Mayl's Dixieland Rhythm Kings from Dayton, Ohio, and Turk Murphy's San Francisco Jazz Band in 1954 and 1955, respectively. Poor attendance in 1954 prompted Souchon to speculate—oddly, in light of the Ohio headliners—that locals "are not interested in buying tickets to see the same bands they can see every night on Bourbon Street." On the bright side, the 1954 joint lecture/concert/meeting of the Club with the New Orleans Art Association at Delgado Museum drew a large crowd. But the event was free and open to nonmembers. Consistent with Souchon's notion, people took advantage of that fact. Another downside in 1954 was the NOJC's failed attempt to establish a jazz component in a new summer pops concert series.

The 1955 Turk Murphy concert was reported in the *Line* as the worst in the club's history. An unfortunate and indicative synchronicity: the destructive debate over jazz-related statues on Basin Street, described in section I, erupted in 1955. There was no NOJC concert in 1956, and for the rest of the decade concerts were held spottily as special events.

Of course, NOJC programs were only part of the picture. In 1952 deejay Roger Wolfe, the single most important promoter in the revival, left town for a job in Pittsburgh. Had he stayed on, he would have seen a dizzying series of shifts in the city's leading jazz groups. Sharkey Bonano took his band to the Palmer House in Chicago in 1951, returned for a Blue Room engagement, disbanded in 1952, then brought a lesser group of sidemen to the Blue Room in 1953. Papa Celestin had health problems, so he was on and off the bandstand at the Paddock and elsewhere. He died in 1954, leaving no highly visible TNOJ band (with the possible exception of Paul Barbarin units) in the city until the Preservation Hall revival in the next decade.

As described in articles below, the Dukes of Dixieland left the Famous Door for extensive gigs in Chicago and Las Vegas in 1954. After gaining national fame in 1956, they were a rarity in the city until their house band gig began at the Royal Sonesta in 1970. The Basin Street Six essentially disbanded in 1953 after Fountain and Girard left for pastures that did not turn out to be very green. Fountain's small group, Pete Fountain's Three Coins, did not draw well, and by the mid-1950s both he and Al Hirt were working day jobs at a pest control firm. In 1954 Girard led a group that did not gain a following at the Famous Door. He died in January 1957. George Lewis played the El Morocco on Bourbon Street in 1950. When the *Look* article hit the stands, his career was rejuvenated—and this resulted in leaving town for road gigs. Bethell reports that Lewis made numerous tours from 1953 to 1961, the year when Preservation Hall opened.

Other kinds of music were growing in popularity in New Orleans. Rhythm and blues, long nurtured in a black community that had virtually no interest in the Dixie/TNOJ revival, was finding audiences among young white listeners. (See Berry et al. and Broven for rich descriptions of the blues and R&B scene.) As early as 1951 there was a following for R&B artists like Roy Brown and Lloyd Price among the group called Cats at Nicholls, my Ninth Ward high school. They were sworn enemies of the "Frats," identified by the Cats as uptown pantywaists from Fortier and Jesuit high schools. The Cats wore gaudy "Hollywood" clothes with collars turned up beneath Wildroot-slick, dovetailed hair. They listened to Poppa Stoppa, the WJMR rage deejay who coined the phrase, "Man, don't worry about *nothin'!*" and they sang Price's "Lawdy, Miss Claudy" during gym classes. They were, we learned later, part of a serious underground drug culture.

More socially acceptable to middle-class whites were other nonjazz artists, mainly booted sax players. LeRoy "Bat Man" Rankins performed in the French Quarter, jumping from bar to table to floor while holding a single note, seemingly forever, through powerful breath control. The biggest favorite of young adult white audiences was tenor saxist Sam Butera. A bebopper in his early days, he was re-created with the help of promoter Joe Delaney, who tells of taking Butera to New York and introducing him to blues artists like Sam Cooke. Butera learned that building a set carefully to a rousing climax with jazz-flavored R&B pleased crowds, made money, and was fun in the bargain. Two of his sidemen, trombonist Jimmy Blount and drummer Dick Johnson, were solid jazzmen who could fall in with Butera's skilled honking and lusty vocals. Butera's group, called the Witnesses, was later the backdrop for Louis Prima's highly successful combo with vocalist Keely Smith. Their manic energy, visual appeal, and tight routines led to major TV shows, Las Vegas engagements, and hit recordings.

Even modern jazz was staking out an audience. To be sure, modern jazz was mainly a shadowy form practiced by unknown young players at jam sessions. Only the hippest of the hip knew that daring players like Ed Blackwell, Mouse Bonati, Ed Frank, Earl Palmer, Ellis Marsalis, Brew Moore,

John Probst, Mike Serpas, and others were on the scene beginning in the late 1940s and early 1950s. But one modern group became known to the general public. After developing a smooth and swinging modern jazz sound with his group in Biloxi, alto saxophonist Al Belletto caught the ear of vocalist Mel Torme in 1954, and the combo's clever vocals, clean jazz charts, and solid solos were heard on the Capitol *Stan Kenton Presents* series.

I offer more about the city's brilliant cadre of modernists in section III. The point here is that the focus of interest turned from TNOJ and Dixieland to almost everywhere else as the 1950s progressed. The local revival was spent. The Dixieland and TNOJ scene would not be rejuvenated significantly until Pete Fountain and Al Hirt returned to the city with national reputations and Preservation Hall gained local and national fame in the next decade.

THE PRESERVATION HALL REVIVAL

Most visitors to New Orleans today know nothing of the earlier national and local jazz revivals. For them the sole meaning of "traditional New Orleans jazz revival" is Preservation Hall at 726 St. Peter Street in the French Quarter, and "Dixieland" means Pete Fountain and possibly the current incarnation of the Dukes of Dixieland.

The layperson's view is basically ahistorical, but in one sense it is dead-center accurate. As noted in section I, the reimaging of New Orleans as a TNOJ and Dixieland jazz center in America resulted from the nationwide exposure achieved, in close sequence, by the Dukes of Dixieland in 1956, Pete Fountain in 1957, Al Hirt in 1960, and Preservation Hall in 1961. In the paragraphs above and the articles below I have provided local backdrops for the rise to national fame by the Dukes, Fountain, and Hirt (chapters 12–14). It remains to clarify the relationship of Preservation Hall to both the TNOJ champions of the 1940s and the local revival of 1947–1953.

The establishment of Preservation Hall and its rapid national recognition are described in the January 17, 1963, *Down Beat* article below (chapter 17). My coverage of the Hall, though, began when it was still being organized. In April 1961 I started work as New Orleans correspondent for *DB*, sending in twice-monthly "Where & When" (W&W) listings of jazz clubs and writing the brief "Strictly Ad Lib" columns. So I was hanging out in the Quarter when the young Grayson (Ken) Mills came to town in the summer of 1961 and initiated the chain of events leading to establishment of the Hall. This entry was in the August 3 Ad Lib column:

> **Ken Mills** is converting a French Quarter art gallery into a jazz club, the Slow Drag, which will feature traditional jazz by some of its earliest exponents. Among the groups that will appear are . . . **Kid Sheik** . . . **Peter Bocage** . . . the **Eureka Brass Band**, and the **Kid Thomas** Band with **George Lewis.**

The Hall was listed in August 17 W&W as "Slow Drag," the nickname of bassist Alcide Pavageau and the name Mills gave me when we talked outside the site before it opened. In the September 14 listing the transition was signaled as "Preservation Hall (Slow Drag)." Thereafter, the latter name—which probably was the one that Mills happened to like the night we spoke—was dropped.

Editor Don DeMichael printed my March 15, 1962, news story on the NBC-TV *David Brinkley's Journal* coverage of the Hall and the local jazz scene. New Orleans *States-Item* columnist Bob Sublette had rightly panned the TV story's a priori assertion that jazz was being "replaced" by strippers—the exact opposite of what was developing as a result of Fountain and Hirt's local engagements after winning national fame. Glad to see some local copy devoted to jazz, I fanned the flames by supporting Sublette locally and doing the *DB* news story. Later that year I submitted the full-length article on the Hall—the first, I believe, in a national journal.

The history of Preservation Hall is documented in detail in William Carter's 1991 book, *Preservation Hall: Music from the Heart*. As one who was pounding the pavement and making notes during the Hall's beginnings, I was surprised that Carter's research came up with some minor differences from my brief account. But in discussing my praiseful comments on the musicians and my caveats about nostalgically declaring them all to be forgotten giants of jazz, Carter generously called the *DB* piece "as wisely dimensional as anything written on the Hall, before or since."

The genesis and fame of Preservation Hall have more in common with the early 1940s ascent of Bunk Johnson than with the local revival of 1947–1953. As in the former, the TNOJ mystique dominated. The St. Peter Street phenomenon began with the efforts of fully persuaded TNOJ fans to find and record early players. Indeed, the prime mover of the 1940s, Bill Russell himself, worked with Mills until internal dissension, widely attributed to Mills's egotism, arose. Like the early revival, the emphasis at Preservation Hall was almost exclusively on aging black artists, with white jazz buffs in hot pursuit.

The Hall's appeal to the popular press was also similar to Bunk Johnson's. Come on and hear the surviving jazz pioneers, brought back for their last round—and ours—of authentic jazz. But there's more, much more. This time, it's all happening in New Orleans, the hometown of jazz. The environment is neither noxious bars nor lecture halls but a plain room in a former art gallery. Not just a handful but dozens of the originators are there, supported not by booze but by kitty donations from the audience.

This was clean copy, grabby and truthful, with little need for embellishment or an overlay of hype. Jazz fans had to love it, the media had to love it, and soon every tourist who wanted to brag about not being sucked into sleazy French Quarter tourist traps showed up, bent upon loving it.

Perhaps the main difference between the Preservation Hall revival and the return of Bunk Johnson, other than the local focus of the former, is that by

1961 civic and business leaders in New Orleans were ready to embrace jazz as a marketable art. The aforementioned national and international fame of the Dukes, Fountain, and Hirt, along with the founding of the Tulane Jazz Archive and the soon-to-open Jazz Museum, made it clear that TNOJ and Dixieland were financially profitable and culturally okay. Preservation Hall cinched it. The city would forever hail its early jazz and Dixieland artists.

In a curious way, even the tension-packed public school integration of 1960–1961 was ultimately a boon for the local jazz scene. New Orleans had always been a tertium quid of a town, a city-state sitting in southern Louisiana with its own customs, values, and varied lifestyles. During the integration crisis Governor Jimmy Davis and the legislature further isolated the city, condemning it as the awful place where southern traditions of segregation, separatism, states' rights, and white supremacism were being destroyed.

Many Orleanians figured that we could not do much better than that. We had no interest in gaining grace with the clownish Davis and racist demagogues like Leander Perez and Risley Triche. Best of all, their head-on confrontation with the U.S. Constitution resulted in the nullification of state laws against integrated performances, giving previously unknown scope to local musicians of all styles. Al Belletto, we will see, used firstrate integrated modern jazz groups when he was musical director of the Playboy Club.

One measure of the local impact of the Hall was its bevy of imitators. I tracked them for the "Where & When" listings. The Dixieland Coffee Shop, Icon Hall (Ken Mills), Perseverance Hall, Dixieland Hall, Southland Jazz Club (trumpeter George Finola), and Mahogany Hall were all variations on Preservation Hall—some combination of traditional jazz, a kitty or an inexpensive admission fee, little or no drink hustling, a non-nightclub setting, and so on. Many were short-lived, but Al Clark's Dixieland Hall ran from October 1962 until at least May 1969, when *DB* discontinued the W&W listings.

The ultimate ironic tribute to the true "hall" formats came in November 1969. The elegant Royal Sonesta Hotel audaciously opened a room called Economy Hall—a name taken from an 1885 black dance hall. The posh Sonesta site was not in the least economical, and it was given to importing nationally known artists, among them modern jazz saxist Zoot Sims.

THE BEAT GOES ON—OR DOES IT?

In the September–October 1957 *Second Line*—almost dead center between the end of the local postwar revival and the establishment of Preservation Hall—Doc Souchon wrote about the likely extinction of "authentic type archaic Negro jazz of New Orleans." He spoke of the well known fact that the younger generation of Negro boys in New Orleans (and elsewhere) were refusing en masse to play anything that smacked of minstrelsy, ragtime, or oldtime Negro musical entertainers. . . . Those who were fortunate (?) enough to obtain a good musical education immediately began to play bop or "progressive" type jazz. Those who could not attain musical proficiency necessary for those styles, switched to rock and roll. But **none**—not even the children of New Orleans [*sic*] most respected and celebrated musicians—cared to follow their internationally known forebears.

This concern was also voiced by Sam Charters in his 1963 book on black New Orleans musicians from 1886 to 1963. "There are no young musicians for these jobs, and when the older men are no longer there to play recorded music will take over." In a 1971 *Dixie Roto* article by Larry Bartlett, vocalist Blanche Thomas and guitarist Albert (Papa) French expressed the common lament about young black musicians in New Orleans denigrating early jazz. She said that they "won't come near" the older jazz. "They call it Uncle Tom music. They're into rock or modern jazz."

Souchon also believed that the second line of white Dixieland players that once included the likes of Fountain and the Assuntos was out of step.

> "Dilution"—a term which we use after much consideration—is happening right before our eyes, also, in the Dixieland (white) style. This, even though there are many, many young white musicians who are "discovering" jazz and honestly attempting to play it—and even though they have the encouragement of old Dixieland musicians and jazz clubs solidly behind them.

If the abandonment and dilution of early jazz forms held true, then the Preservation Hall revival would be the dying gasp of authentic TNOJ, and good Dixieland would also be moribund. As the decade rolled on, I reported the sad obits in *DB*—Chinee Foster, Lizzie Miles, Lester Bouchon, Papa John Joseph, Joe Robicheaux, Lester Santiago, Kid Howard, Papa Jack Laine, Pinky Vidacovich, Welman Braud, Robert Lewis, George Williams, Steve Brown, and many others.

I wrote about the long-debated questions: Will excellent TNOJ and Dixieland die out when the older generation is gone? Can sensitive younger musicians really get inside the psyche of a past generation and feel and reproduce the nuances of the music created in another time, another culture? If they do master the techniques of the older music, is their art thereby genuine, or merely a kind of Turing test that communicates an oxymoronic simulated authenticity? Is it artistically "honest" to play with an inherited voice and not seek to find one's own?

The articles below entitled "Jazz—A Festival for a Funeral?" and "New Orleans Jazz—With a Foreign Accent" (chapters 19–20) deal with those questions. The first was written just before Jazzfest '68. It is not really about the festival, though. It deals with the possible death of early jazz forms due to lack of interest by young musicians. The second focuses mainly on the work of serious young musicians from abroad who had come to the city to learn in recent years to hear and perform in the older genres. At the end I cite the indifference of local youngsters, who were being won over by modern jazz.

The problems underlying the continuance of musical traditions have many dimensions, and they merit further discussion here. Modern jazz musicians today, like Wynton Marsalis, Nicholas Payton, Herlin Riley, and Johnny Vidacovich, recognize the importance of TNOJ and show respect for the brass and marching band traditions. But even though they honor the early music and acknowledge its influence in their playing, they make no pretense about taking it up as a career. The direct heirs of the marching band traditions are said to be the numerous young brass and marching bands that have arisen since the 1960s, from Danny Barker's Fairview Baptist Church Band to the current Treme Street marching band to the New Orleans Night Crawlers to the pop-rock oriented Dirty Dozen. A critique of these bands is beyond the scope of this text, but my aural gloss of recent groups suggests that their varying levels of skill and astonishing range of styles would not please purists. Most are either amateurs happily blasting away without a sense of ensemble or young professionals who have strayed far from the music of their predecessors.

Even so, I am more optimistic today about continuation of TNOJ and Dixieland jazz. I have come to believe that questions about legitimate re-creation of early jazz are unanswerable when posed as if a categorical yes or no could be defended. Is the music of young imitators and emulators authentic? An unqualified *no* (my earlier view) is possible only if you begin with the abstract premises that an artist can only perform validly from a store of personal experiences, and that each generation of artists must draw upon their own social and psychological milieu. From those assumptions it follows that the true TNOJ and the real Dixieland will end when the old-timers are gone, and their recordings will be the sole source of the music.

An answer that proceeds from the data of actual performances will be different. The only bottom line assumption here will be Aristotle's common-sense principle—*what is, can be.* To the extent that a performance captures the letter and/or the spirit of the old music, then it will be congruent with the model, affectively successful, and authentic. Granted, the whole cloth of the earlier styles will not likely be present, but approximations and variations exist. Further, components of the performance that do not reflect the old music will dissatisfy purists but will not necessarily be distasteful to every listener. For example, most often I found the revivalist bands of the 1940s and beyond to be clumsy TNOJ imitations, generating better energy when they stretched out a little rather than when they seemed to have older texts and devices in mind.

Knowledgeable listeners who are attuned to the subtleties of the older jazz forms will be better able to sense the extent to which a particular performance re-creates the old styles. Their analyses might differ, but insights and understandings will ebb and flow through continued discussions.

Phrases like "insofar as," "partially," and "in some degree" are part of such dialogues.

As for whether skilled but highly derivative art can be "honest," we can start by acknowledging that young musicians almost invariably begin by imitating a musical idol but usually go on to develop some distinctive qualities. Early Bonano did Rena and Armstrong, early Frank Assunto did Bonano and Armstrong, early Wilber did Bechet, early Fountain did Fazola, and so on. In some cases jazz fans and critics initially failed to hear what was distinctive in a young artist's music, being misguided by their own stock responses, based on locked-in frames of reference. I recall that after the first bloom of modern jazz, many thought that Chet Baker was a carbon copy of Miles Davis, Clifford Brown a clone of Dizzy Gillespie, and Carmen McRae a Sarah Vaughan sound-alike.

The question of honesty most often comes to play when a seasoned jazz musician persists in aping an musical idol well into his or her career, locks into the style of a past generation, or switches from style to style, perhaps in order to follow the money. We can stroke our chins and talk reflectively about such things, but any conclusions we might draw are of the unprovable/unfalsifiable sort. We seldom know whether jazz musicians who continue to play like a particular artist or immerse themselves in an early jazz style have a comfortable sense of expressiveness and invention. They might well be healthily engaged in producing what they feel is their best musical effort. It would take the moral perspicacity of a Buddha or the chutzpah of a Bethell to judge the interior state of an imitator or a dyed-in-the-wool revivalist.

I know a few anecdotes that suggest the vulgarity of slavish imitation, but these do not warrant generalizations about artistic integrity. For instance, in the late 1950s a gifted Art Blakey imitator was passing through New Orleans, and we talked about what flows and rumbles inside us as we play. He explained, eyes closed and hands air-playing a cymbal and snare, "You get into a tune and you think, *I'm Art Blakey, I'm Art Blakey.*" My idols at the time were Blakey, Max Roach, and Ed Blackwell, but I found the intensity of his ego surrender unsettling. When I tried his way of simulating total identification, it was absolutely creepy. But he was a marvelous player. For the time, at least, it was working for him.

A similar story was circulating in the 1960s about a widely recorded young tenor saxist who was jamming with his idol, an innovative giant, on a night when the latter was not at his best. The young turk said, "Hey, man, you're not you—*I'm* you." The remark, even if intended in jest, was arrogant and insensitive. But again, the product, his performance, was a lyrical joy.

Style switching is another phenomenon of greater complexity than is generally acknowledged. The predominant stereotypes are those of the artistic sellout on one hand and the romantic image of the frustrated jazz musician playing in a stifling commercial context on the other. Candid discussions with individual musicians yield a different view. In the article below on the Dukes of Dixieland, Frank Assunto describes the group's brassy break-through album in 1956 as a partial put-on, giving producer Sid Frey the kind of flag-waving razzmatazz he wanted, little expecting that the Audio-Fidelity album would be a hit that would identify the band. In the Al Hirt ar-ticle the trumpeter explains, with some irritation, that he never claimed to be a probing jazzman and was happy to find ways to play different kinds of music and please the public.

In regard to other jazz figures who moved in and out of commercial con-texts, consider Nat King Cole's switch from jazz piano and vocals to popu-lar singing in the late 1940s. His best-selling recordings of songs like "Too Young," "Nature Boy," and "Mona Lisa" raised cries of crass commercial-ism from jazz fans and critics. To their utter shock, he told *Down Beat,* "I'm in it for the money." In retrospect we know it was not that simple. The hit recordings of figures like Cole, Mel Torme, Ella Fitzgerald, Peggy Lee, and, yes, Louis Armstrong, ultimately elevated popular music. Admitting that these artists occasionally did some irredeemably crappy material, in the long view they brought a depth of feeling and richness of interpretation beyond the capability of the innumerable popular crooners and torch singers who glided though dreamy ballads and punched out facile Tin Pan Alley synco-pations.

To return to New Orleans, numerous local musicians playing today at Preservation Hall and in various other TNOJ and Dixieland settings are grayheads who were raised on swing and modern jazz. They have simply learned the traditional repertoire and made stylistic adjustments in order to make a living. Whether they hate it and feel they have sold out or find en-joyment in getting into old tunes and styles is not commonly known. The matter would be an revealing area of research.

A parallel question—whether New Orleans modernists in the postwar years were compromising their musical values when playing the emerging rhythm and blues—is addressed in section III. As will be seen, Harold Bat-tiste and others answer with a resounding "no," although I also found evi-dence that other versatile performers made sharper distinctions among mu-sical styles, and many who were skilled in R&B found modern jazz more stimulating.

My interviews with New Orleans musicians suggest some interesting variations on and deviations from the myth of the uncompromising *artiste.* Several of my contemporaries who are still active, like Bill Huntington, Don Suhor, and Reed Vaughan, grew up playing early styles *and* modern jazz. They admit a preference for the latter but also take pleasure in performing in many jazz contexts. Others, like Wallace Davenport and the late Ted Riley, revisited early jazz later in their careers and learned to adapt skillfully as they got into the older styles. For musicians like these, revisiting earlier jazz forms is not like being trapped in a German Band with tight lederhosen. Jazz is a spacious and expansive art, and they can move gracefully within it.

I believe that simplistic views about pure jazz and uncompromising artistic dedication to a style are slowly fading. The purist arguments are so shopworn and judgmental that it hardly seems worthwhile to trot them out again. Recent controversy over the merits of the music of the young neoboppers—many of their leaders, like the Marsalis family and Terence Blanchard, being from New Orleans—is another variation on the purist debate.

Interestingly, their music is often called "traditional jazz," referring of course not to TNOJ but to modern jazz in the bop tradition as contrasted with postbop avant garde or fusion jazz. Their detractors generally admit that the neoboppers are fine players but fault them for lack of originality, claiming that most of their music could have been played forty years ago. Do any of them go beyond, or even match, the best bop that matured in the 1950s—Bird, Max and Clifford, Monk, Miles, Coltrane, Bud Powell, Blakey's Jazz Messengers?

The debate strikes me as halfhearted. Certainly it lacks the energy of the music, which is being played with enthusiasm and skill by many young artists. Listeners wisely seem to be dismissing the idea that trailblazing and total originality are the primary value. Implicitly, they are adopting the stance suggested above, namely, that a fine performance is a fine performance, and there is no benefit in rejecting it because it is not "new" or because it does not wholly match a model of the originators of a style.

Innumerable critics of and thoughtful listeners to classical music have long had such a performance-centered view of the music of past generations. Innovative works can be valued along with appreciation of skilled performances of music from the past. Things get tiresome, of course, when classical artists and programs dwell on the 100 best-loved melodies—the moral equivalent of jazz groups churning out "The Saints," "In the Mood," "Perdido," "Take Five," and the like. But we are refreshed by Glenn Gould's or Wendy Carlos's rereadings of Bach, excited by the revival of figures like Johannes Ockeghem, and stimulated by music played on period instruments.

With classical music and jazz alike, in the long view we can keep an open ear to evolving forms and the emergence of innovative artists. But we can also live in the moment of a given performance and take in whatever excellence it offers. Carrying the heavy artillery of assumptions about genre and history to a performance reflects a narrow view of the art, prejudges the invention of the performer, and sets up a screen that seriously limits one's enjoyment of what is going on.

Finally, jazz might well have a special advantage over composed music. Jazz improvisation can evoke human response based on its fascinating similarities to the improvisation inherent in everyday conversational language. This view is implicit in Paul Berliner's important research on thinking processes in jazz, and explicit in others' views of music/language relationships (e.g., Gunther Schuller, Ben Sidran, David Sudnow). I have argued elsewhere that three aspects of jazz improvisation—its generative nature, its rule-governed aspects, and several specific language-based qualities—are parallel to our innate language faculty (as discussed, e.g., in classic and recent writings of Noam Chomsky and other linguists).

This book is not intended to explore such a wide-ranging theoretical view. Suffice it to say here that a jazz-and-language perspective transcends parochial debates about styles, eras, traditions, and innovation. Whatever our preferences or points of entry into the music, its in-the-moment improvisational nature, along with its specific elements that directly parallel qualities of language, resonate with our hard-wired knowledge of ourselves as competent makers of language. For that reason alone, jazz from TNOJ to modern jazz is likely to be an abiding form of expression in many cultures well into the future.

Timeline chart 2, "Highlights of the Popular Revival in New Orleans, 1947–1953," notes key events in the local resurgence of TNOJ and Dixieland jazz.

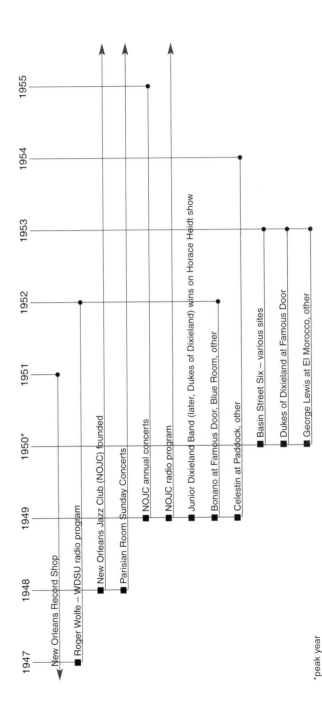

Timeline Chart 2 – Highlights of the Popular Revival in New Orleans, 1947–1953
(Underlines indicate continuation/duration)

*peak year

12

The Dukes of Dixieland: A Jazz Odyssey

New Orleans magazine, March 1970

When the Dukes of Dixieland became the house band at Economy Hall in the new Royal Sonesta Hotel, the event was much more than another jazz spot opening on Bourbon Street with a crackerjack Dixieland group. So much has happened since the Dukes started their checkered career over twenty years ago that Orleanians are likely to forget that the city—and the jazz community in particular—is deeply indebted to Frank, Papa Jac, and the late Fred Assunto.

Not only did they provide the first national thrust for New Orleans jazz in decades, paving the way and to some extent setting the pattern for Pete Fountain and Al Hirt, but they suffered numerous personal and professional setbacks along the way, the most tragic being the death of Fred, who played trombone with the group from its inception. The story of the Dukes of Dixieland is real New Orleans stuff, an epic so quaint and pathetic and beautiful that it is easy to get lost in its poetry and forget that real people lived it, suffering its pains and celebrating its joys.

The band got its start during the modest local jazz revival of the late 1940's. A handful of teenage musicians began to cluster worshipfully around Sharkey Bonano's Kings of Dixieland, the excellent group that was at the forefront of the revival. Sharkey and Papa Celestin, encouraged by a WDSU disc jockey named Roger Wolfe and the newly-formed New Orleans Jazz Club, were bringing real New Orleans music back to Bourbon Street at the Famous Door and the Paddock after a long dearth of jazz in the downtown area. Sharkey's music had a special magic for Frank and Fred Assunto, two high school boys who could claim deep roots in jazz despite their youth. Their father, Jac Assunto, had played with the Halfway House Orchestra and the Johnny Tobin Midnight Serenaders in the twenties. He had a vast record collection that he kept up to date by bringing home swing records by Ellington, Hampton, and others from Werlein's, where he worked in the early forties.

Frank, recalling his earliest memories of jazz, says, "I was about nine or ten, I guess. My brother and I used to play all kinds of things from the collection my dad had. You know, my dad gave me two trumpet lessons until he caught me trying to copy Louis Armstrong's chorus on *Shine*, and he said, 'If that's what you're going to do, you don't need me, you just need the record.' Then, naturally, in the neighborhood where we used to live—around

General Taylor and Freret Street—to get to school we had to go through a lot of old Negro neighborhoods, and occasionally we'd run into a parade or funeral of some sort and we'd second-line the band. And so it was a constant exposure to jazz."

The young Assuntos played music every chance they got, and when chance slept overtime they created their own opportunities for performing. It was on one such Huck Finn-ish episode that the Assunto brothers met Pete Fountain. Frank says, "This friend of mine, Benny Christiana—who now has a service station on Baronne and Howard—his dad was in the poultry business and he had a pickup truck. It really stunk to high heaven, but every time there was an out-of-town football game—you know, like Port Sulphur or Baton Rouge or somebody would come to town to play one of our teams—we'd decorate the truck with crepe paper in the colors of the visiting team, and we'd get Willie Perkins, a drummer, and my brother and I and Benny would drive, and we would get as many guys that play horns as we could in the back of the truck, and we'd—we wouldn't *sneak* into City Park Stadium, because they'd just *let* us in. We'd drive up and say, 'We're the visitors' band.'

"So we did that one time when some team was playing Easton. And we're playing all the jazz tunes across the field when there's about thirty people sitting on our side of the stadium, and on the Warren Easton side they were *jammed*. And the Warren Easton band was big and purple and gold, and they were wailing and Pete was playing with *that* band. He came over after they got through with their halftime thing because he wanted to play with the jazz band. And that's how we met Pete. I guess I was about 13, Pete was 14, and Fred was 15."

The Assuntos and Fountain played together sporadically for several years under the name of the Basin Street Four, Five, Six, or whatever number happened to show up for a particular gig. They were strongly under the influence of Sharkey's group when Horace Heidt brought his talent search to New Orleans in 1949. Frank tapped a rhythm section composed of drummer Perkins and pianist Stanley Mendelson to join the front line and dubbed the group the Junior Dixieland Band.

The Junior Band's victory on the Heidt show and subsequent tour was the first big break for the Assuntos and Fountain. They might have been catapulted to an early—perhaps premature—national fame if they had listened to the overtures of agent Joe Delaney, who urged them to go on the road. But they chose to remain in New Orleans, where they had become local heroes, and soon they were playing at the Famous Door under the name of the Dukes of Dixieland, a title that frankly expressed their admiration for Sharkey's Kings of Dixieland.

The four years at the Famous Door were a valuable yeoman's duty for the Dukes. They got together what Leonard Feather later called the "blend of showmanship and musicianship" that would make them one of the hottest commercial items on the lounge circuit. An argument with owner Hyp Guinle one night at the Famous Door prompted Frank to put in an impulsive phone call to Delaney, telling the agent that the Dukes were ready to go on the road.

A wildly successful Chicago engagement in 1955 won them another break, an LP with RCA Victor. But that summer the Dukes' career took a discouraging turn as Pete Fountain and the entire rhythm section gave their notice, announcing that they would return to New Orleans to work as a quartet. Frank and Fred were ready to dissolve the band, but Freddie Williamson of Associated Booking Corporation went in to a huddle with the young Assuntos. He convinced them that the core of the band was the Assunto alliance and that the Dukes could continue with a new group of sidemen built around the talented brothers.

By chance, Frank and Fred celebrated their resolution to carry on the Dukes by going to hear another family act, the Will Mastin Trio with Sammy Davis, Jr., after their crucial conference with Williamson. According to Frank, "When we left there, my brother and I got the idea about my dad. 'Why not?' we said. It's summertime, and he's not teaching. Why doesn't he come up for a month or two, and he'll play a little banjo and a little trombone and we'll make a feature out of it, and who knows?'"

Papa Jac began what was to become an eleven-year engagement, and the Dukes were in high gear again. At the Thunderbird in Las Vegas a man named Sid Frey became a great admirer of the band. Frank describes Frey alternately as a genius who pioneered stereo recordings and as a damned nuisance who wooed and harassed the Dukes into recording on the Audio-Fidelity label. "I didn't want to record for Audio-Fidelity," Frank says, "because I had never heard of them. I kept fighting with Sid Frey so bad about this album that I was really mad when we went to the session. We asked for ridiculous money and we got it. I said, 'This guy is really a stupid bird. If he's willing to pay that kind of money for a jazz band, then let's give him what he thinks he's going to get . . . *oom-cha, oom-cha* . . . Let's tuba and banjo him to death.' And that's what we did—and we built a monster."

It was a strange kind of monster indeed. The Dukes' recordings for Audio-Fidelity were best sellers; they were actually the first jazz group to record in stereophonic sound. But the highly commercial recordings gave many critics and serious jazz fans the idea that the Dukes were a funny hats band, capable of little else than the pat and pallid arrangements of the Audio-Fidelity session.

The band evolved continuously, shedding many of the contrivances of the Audio-Fidelity session to take new approaches, always with the three Assuntos at the center. Among the jazzmen who have worked as sidemen with the Dukes at one time or another are pianists Gene Schroeder and Bill Jones, drummer Buzzy Drootin, bassist Jim Atlas, and guitarist Jim Hall. The Dukes were a favorite in Las Vegas, which became their home base for twelve years. Later they worked out of Chicago's Bourbon Street Club, long identified with trumpeter Bob Scobey and pianist Art Hodes.

On April 21, 1966, Fred Assunto died of a heart ailment after a month's illness in Las Vegas. His death at the age of 36 left the Assunto family numb with grief, and it nearly caused the Dukes of Dixieland to disband. Papa Jac, who had played trombone duets almost nightly with Fred, could not play anymore. Frank, forced to carry on alone, was ready to call the show off. "For the first six months after my brother passed away I was right on the verge of quitting—just dropping it and coming back to New Orleans to start something else—you know, just sell shoes or do *something*. I was talking to a friend of mine and I told him, 'This is ridiculous. I'm batting my head against the wall. My wife is very sick. I'm sick.' I got to boozing too much—the feeling-sorry-for-yourself bit, which is what it really was. And I said, 'I think I'm just going to quit. I don't want it. No more.' He said, 'Yeah, that sounds sensible. After all, that's what Freddie would do.' Well, that was like someone throwing an arrow between my eyes. I finally got to thinking—we didn't work on this thing for twenty years just for me to walk away from it."

Frank went into a lonely huddle with himself this time, and started organizing the band that has evolved into his present group. Happily, it has the popular appeal of his earlier units, and it is one of the best musical aggregations he has ever put together. In Don Ewell he has one of the few interesting and unfailingly tasteful pre-modern jazz pianists. Rudy Aikels is a highly competent bassist with a clear sound and a strong pulse. Drummer Freddie Kohlman is equally at ease with a press roll, an extended solo, and modern jazz rhythms. Slidell clarinetist Harold Cooper, released from the clowning duties so often assigned to him in other bands, is giving new life to the Dukes' ensemble work and playing some of the freshest jazz clarinet around. Philadelphian Charlie Bornemann is increasing his command over the Dixieland genre, a task which many young trombonists scorn—and fail at miserably.

The real animating force in the band, however, is Frank himself. His strong Dixie lead marks him clearly as a trumpeter in the New Orleans tradition, yet his solos reveal that he has assimilated a variety of influences. On *Muskrat Ramble* there are traces of Bobby Hackett's lyricism, Roy Eldridge's fire. On *St. James Infirmary* he pares his tone down to that harmonica-thin, Milesian sound that is so cool and so intense. He communicates well with his audiences, both through his music and his genial patter between tunes.

Does Frank feel that he and the Dukes contributed to putting New Orleans back on the map as a jazz center? "Without being overly egotistical about it, I'd like to think so," he says. "I really think that the twenty years we put in, and all the miles and all the ballrooms in Iowa and all that kind of nonsense did add to this resurgence, or what I like to think of as an overdue recognition of New Orleans and its importance to jazz—not just traditional jazz, but all facets of jazz."

The Dukes of Dixieland are in residence for forty weeks a year at the Royal Sonesta, just across the street from the Famous Door where the band started out two decades ago. Frank will assist in shaping the year-round musical policy at the hotel, importing other jazz acts that will further enrich the New Orleans jazz scene. There are already over 100 musicians playing in every style of jazz downtown, and each owes a tip of the hat to Frank Assunto and the Dukes of Dixieland, the first band that reminded America that New Orleans is Jazztown, U.S.A.

13

Pete Fountain

Down Beat, November 23, 1961

In the variety of jazz clubs and strip joints that line Bourbon Street, a relatively isolated place enjoys the distinction of being the most sought-out night club in the Crescent City. Pete Fountain's French Quarter Inn, several blocks down the street from the main cluster of clubs, is flooded nightly by tourists and natives whose obvious enthusiasm for Fountain suggests that he might have opened a club with equal success on the banana wharves.

Fountain's success story is an unlikely one. Born in the Crescent City on July 3, 1930, Fountain's musical training began at the age of 12 when his family doctor advised him to study a wind instrument to strengthen his lungs. Pete studied with the New Orleans Symphony Orchestra's Emanuel Alessandra for several years and soon showed promise in his ability to improvise in the style of the great New Orleans clarinetist, Irving Fazola.

At an impromptu jam session after a high-school football game, he met Frank and Fred Assunto, and with them formed the Junior Dixieland Band. The youngsters were catapulted to national attention when they won on the Horace Heidt amateur show in 1949 and went on tour with the Heidt troupe.

The Juniors returned to New Orleans to discover that they were full-fledged celebrities. Within a year, Fountain left the Junior band to join an impressive roster of seniors that Phil Zito had organized for a Bourbon St. club engagement. Zito's group, copiously billed the International City Dixielanders, included trombonist Joe Rotis, pianist Roy Zimmerman, bassist Bunny Franks, peppery young trumpeter George Girard, Fountain on clarinet, and Zito on drums.

The group was highly successful. A Columbia album, Fountain's first recording, sold well; but internal dissension brought the band—or at least Zito's leadership of the band—to an end. The sidemen moved out in a body, hired Charlie Duke as drummer, and hung up their shingle as the Basin Street Six.

The inclusion of Duke proved to be a well-advised move, at least from an artistic viewpoint; Duke's style was well suited to the group's happily swinging Dixie groove.

By 1950, the Basin Street Six had become the most tightly knit Dixie group since Sharkey Bonano's band reawakened the city to Dixieland music two years before. Fountain, long compared to the city's oldest clarinetists, was establishing himself as a standard of comparison for aspiring young clarinetists.

Pete was emerging from the indebtedness to Fazola that marked his earlier playing. It was a difficult association to break, for a virtual legend had grown concerning Fountain and Fazola. Fountain had been dubbed "Little Faz" when local jazzophiles first noticed his attempts to play in the Fazola style; the night of Fazola's death, Pete, still underage, subbed for him in a Bourbon St. band; furthermore, Fazola had bequeathed his clarinet to the young Fountain.

But traces of other clarinetists were becoming evident. Fountain began to punctuate fluent Fazolian phrases with incisive, Goodman-like accents. His tone developed a brilliant edge, departing from the liquid sound identified with Fazola. And his vibrato (perhaps Fountain's most individual characteristic) took on a markedly pre-Fazolian quiver, rapid enough to reveal his roots in traditional jazz but without the annoying tremble of many of the early New Orleans clarinetists.

It is not paradoxical that Fountain should have shifted from the smoothly hewn Fazola style to a more assertive expression. Pete's earlier dedication to Fazola was not based on a happy meeting of musical sensibilities but on the simple fact that Fazola was the city's leading clarinetist and Fountain was a young musician in search of an idol.

Fazola was basically a cool musician (that term is applicable to Fazola as it is to Bix Beiderbecke), and his easeful approach could only be superficially imitated by one who did not share his essentially relaxed musical temperament. Fountain is a hot clarinetist, and he could not have remained in the Fazolian mold permanently without denying his natural propensity to play a more brusque, virile style.

As the Six popularity continued to grow, the once-inevitable appositive "Little Faz" appeared less and less frequently after Pete's name; after a while it disappeared completely.

His popularity and musical development encouraged him to put his talent to a test in a more challenging context. He opened at the Famous Door with a quartet called Pete Fountain and His Three Coins. "I liked the freedom of the quartet," he recalled. "The job with the Coins influenced my decision later to work with a small combination."

The general insecurity of the music scene in New Orleans, however, prompted him to go on tour briefly with the Assuntos, who had achieved considerable success as the Dukes of Dixieland. He returned to New Orleans when his second child, Kevin, was born. Unwilling to leave town again and concerned about the uncertainty of making a living as a musician in New Orleans, he put down his clarinet and took a job with a pest-control firm, along with Al Hirt, who then also was plagued with problems of sustenance.

Fountain soon was working weekends with Hirt at Dan's International Club on Bourbon Street. And before long, a call from Lawrence Welk changed the course of his career.

Welk had been looking for a Dixie clarinetist for his weekly television shows. Welk's son, a long-time Dixieland record collector, told him of a New Orleans clarinetist who had recorded with the Basin Street Six. Welk's offer was attractive enough to convince Fountain that it was well worth leaving his job with the pest-control company.

Fountain attributes the present success of his club directly to his tenure with Welk. "Let's face it," he mused, "when you're exposed to an audience the size of Welk's for two years, you're bound to reach a lot of people."

While performing on the Welk show, Fountain was able to function as a jazzman as such for three nights a week at the Mardi Gras Lounge in Orange County, California, with drummer Jack Sperling, pianist Stan Wrightsman, and bassist Morty Cobb. The Mardi Gras job reaffirmed his conviction that the clarinet-and-rhythm group was the most effective vehicle for his talent.

During Fountain's stay on the West Coast, his allegiance to Benny Goodman became apparent. He had long claimed Goodman as an influence but had never functioned in a musical climate that allowed the fuller development of this aspect of his style.

Yet, careless comparisons to Goodman would be even less warranted than the earlier comparisons to Fazola. Pete's admitted technical limitations and his tendency to juxtapose various influences without assimilating them suggests that the reverence with which he mentions Goodman's name is justifiably the deference of a duke before the king.

Fountain is in adamant disagreement with those who feel that his association with Welk was a prostitution of his talent. He said he feels that jazz has benefited by being offered to the layman in a palatable form on the Welk program.

"It's true that jazz was something Welk threw in to increase his audience," Fountain observed. "But a lot of people who never liked jazz before heard it on his program and said, 'You know, that's not so bad after all.'"

The itch to return to his home finally brought the clarinetist back to New Orleans in spring of 1959 to fulfill his longtime dream of opening his own club.

The group he organized in New Orleans reflects the liberality that prompted him to associate with musicians like Sperling and bassist Don Bagley on the West Coast. It consists of Berklee alumnus Dave West, piano; Paul Guma (an accomplished clarinetist in a Goodman-DeFranco mold), guitar; Lowell Miller, an unabashedly modern bassist; Paul Edwards, a drummer from Ohio who has played with every major Dixieland group in the city.

"I feel that using musicians from all schools gives me wider scope," Fountain said. "And they give the group a kind of swing that you can't really call 'Dixieland.' It isn't modern, it isn't Dixie, and it isn't exactly swing. I just like to call it 'swinging music.'"

The clarinetist's departure from head-for-the-hills-on-the-last-chorus Dixie has proved to be a commercial as well as a musical asset. Welkians who would be jarred by the blockbusting Dixie groups find the disciplined

Fountain quintet thoroughly refreshing. Fountain's audiences are a testimony to the universality of his appeal; during a single set one can find jazz fans, college students, businessmen, middle-aged couples, and elderly patrons—undoubtedly the most heterogeneous audience in town.

Fountain sees in his present success a starting point as much as a culmination. He contends that his style is still developing and gives hope that the variety of influences that constitute it will coalesce. He confesses a wide-eyed fascination with the big-band scene and said he hopes, someday, to lead a big band on a tour of one-nighters.

In the meantime, Fountain will continue to operate from his home base on Bourbon Street, depending on sporadic tours and recordings to "remind the public that I'm still here."

For the foreseeable future, the bearded clarinetist has little to fear about slipping the public's mind. A reminder to look up Pete Fountain while in New Orleans is as superfluous as a suggestion to take note of the Mississippi River.

14

Al Hirt in Perspective

New Orleans magazine, April 1969

A big man makes an easy target. Nobody knows this better than Al Hirt, New Orleans' 280-pound trumpeter who has been the object of critical pot-shots since his rise to national fame in 1960.

While Hirt was gaining a popular reputation as the greatest jazz trumpeter to come out of New Orleans since Louis Armstrong, the jazz press was attacking him with a vehemence usually reserved for Lawrence Welk. Critics zeroed in on Hirt's selection of material, his clowning onstage, his tendency to sacrifice taste for virtuosity, and his lack of originality. In short, they hurled the ultimate insult of jazz criticism at him. *Al Hirt,* they agreed, *is commercial.*

Hirt was disturbed by the extent and the intensity of the critical barbs, but his record sales continued to soar and the public continued to flock to his personal appearances. He played virtually every major TV show and night club in America, made three movies, won the *Playboy* Readers' Jazz Poll for seven years and received numerous awards from the entertainment industry (the Grammy Award, *Billboard* and *Cashbox* D.J. Polls). Just as Liberace had survived the slings and arrows of outraged classical music lovers in the 1950's, Hirt's popularity overpowered the jazz pundits' complaints about his limitations as a jazzman.

In light of such spectacular success, Hirt was under no pressure to reshape his popular image. It came as a great shock to many of his fans when he abandoned the format of his six-piece Dixieland jazz combo early in 1966. He replaced the trombone with a tenor saxophone, fired the bass player, and hired the organist and drummer from a blues-rock combo that was working at the El Morocco Club on Bourbon Street. Later the New York *Times* quoted him as saying, "I'm a pop commercial musician." Hirt turned down an offer to play for *Jazzfest '68,* and his manager, Gerry Purcell, stated that the trumpeter "is no longer a jazz musician" and would not be available for jazz festivals. In an astonishing reversal of policy, Hirt seemed to be joining the critics after he had licked them.

A look at the record, however, shows that Hirt was not betraying his native music but returning to his real *forte* when he dropped the Swingin' Dixie tag and started billing himself as America's Greatest Trumpet Show-man. Hirt has always been an outstanding instrumentalist and a lively showman. He was led by a series of accidents into the Dixieland groove, and the recent developments in his career are an honest attempt to present him in a setting that is most natural to him.

To begin with, Hirt is a conservatory-trained musician, having graduated from the Cincinnati Conservatory of Music after a brilliant record of achievement as a high school musician in New Orleans. (It is said that in citywide high school rating festivals other youngsters would beg the young Hirt to appear last on the schedule so they would not automatically draw mediocre ratings by comparison with him.) He was thereafter regarded among musicians as a double threat man: an instrumentalist capable of concert work and qualified for the lead trumpet chair in big bands.

Hirt was soon working on the road with bands like Ray McKinley, Tommy Dorsey, and Jimmy Dorsey. Reminiscing about his big band work, Hirt says, "In the bands that I played with, I never did play the jazz chair. I was always a lead trumpet player, or I'd split the lead with another player. Oh, I used to get up and play a *solo*—like if we played something at breakneck tempo, for instance, I was always the one with a lot of facility. I'd play the fast notes, I'd play the high notes—I would do that kind of thing."

The trumpeter received limited national recognition in 1950 as a winner on the Horace Heidt talent show. His feature number, *Night and Day,* was a showcase for his technical wizardry, with about 16 bars of Harry Jamesian jazz thrown in for the sake of variety.

He returned to New Orleans, where he played lead with the Dawn Busters big band on WWL radio. Although the famous morning show featured Hirt regularly with the Jive Five, a trumpet-plus-rhythm combo that was a natural context for jazz improvisation, he was not impressive in the jazzman's role. He continued to do his dazzling demonstration solos with his own dance band on weekends, and he led a trio that played adaptations of his special materials on the off night at the Famous Door.

"I never was a really good improviser," Hirt admits. "I never did blaze any trails of my own. I think I *could* jump into somebody else's bag and do a pretty fair imitation of something that's been done. But as far as originality of conception or original ideas in jazz playing, I don't fool myself in that respect."

The New Orleans jazz revival of the late 1940's actually started out as a bad break for Hirt. With a limited number of jobs for trumpet men in the city, the popularity of Dixieland jazz turned Hirt's prodigious technique and musical finesse into a liability. Economic pressure (the trumpeter's family had grown to the formidable size of eight children) forced him to take a job with a pesticide firm for a time. By sheer chance, his employer's father-in-law turned out to be Dan Levy, owner of Dan's Pier 600 on Bourbon Street. Levy happened to be looking for a Dixieland group to play at his club; so in 1956, Al Hirt suddenly found himself fronting a Dixieland jazz band.

But the Hirt combo was hardly what purists would call a Dixieland group. The band played standard Dixieland tunes at breathlessly fast tempos. Hirt's head arrangements quoted freely from swing and modern jazz sources. Non-Dixieland materials like *I Love Paris* were used when they provided a showcase for Hirt's talent. Hirt was utilizing the Dixie format with audacious freedom, making it a backdrop for his brilliant technical virtuosity.

Some called the Hirt combo eclectic, some called it progressive, and some called it chaotic. It was WWL disc jockey Dick Martin who first called it "Swingin' Dixie." Ironically, Martin's intention in coining the name was to disassociate Hirt and his group from the Dixieland jazz tradition. Hirt recalls that "when we used to do a radio show from the Pier 600, Dick Martin tabbed it [the group] that. It was a sort of a combination of swing and Dixie, because I never was a down home two-beat player. . . . So he said, 'Why not call it Swingin' Dixie?'"

When Audio-Fidelity Records wooed Hirt with a recording contract in 1958, he saw it as a chance to get important national exposure. Unfortunately, the a&r man for Audio-Fidelity called for a straight Dixieland session, with none of the pyrotechnics for which Hirt would later become famous.

"Actually, we were in the shadow of the Dukes of Dixieland, who were the big recording stars for that label at the time, and they had a lot of success with stereo sound," Hirt explains. "Remember when Sid Frey and Audio-Fidelity had the big jump on everybody with great sound? Well, when they put us on the label, of course, we were delighted to have that opportunity."

Neither the critics nor the general public took much notice of the Audio-Fidelity LP. It was in fact a good Dixieland album, but it was not distinguishable from a dozen other Dixie sessions that were on the market.

Hirt's real opportunity came when Monique Van Vooren, wife of promoter Gerard Purcell, stopped at the Pier 600 one night in 1959 after her appearance at the Blue Room. On hearing Hirt she phoned her husband in New York to give him a long distance earful of the fantastic anonymous trumpet player on Bourbon Street. Purcell flew to New Orleans to hear Hirt in person, and he immediately grasped the nature of the trumpeter's talent and its potential for commercial success.

Shortly after, Las Vegas was bombarded by cryptic signs announcing that "The King is Coming." This was Purcell's advance promotion setting up the arrival of Al ("He's the King") Hirt, who claimed his crown with a successful engagement at the Dunes. This was followed by a spot on the Dinah Shore TV show and a long-term recording contract with RCA Victor. A glance at Hirt's Victor output of more than two dozen albums shows that care was taken to represent the full range of his artistry. A few Dixieland albums are on the list, but Hirt also appears with the Boston Pops, on a double bill with vocalist Ann Margret, in a big band Carnegie Hall concert, with a string section, and in a number of popular and rock contexts.

Al Hirt came out of New Orleans and into the national limelight at a time when the Dixieland jazz revival had gained considerable momentum. The Dukes of Dixieland and Pete Fountain had re-focused national attention on

New Orleans as a jazz center, and the founding of Preservation Hall in the early sixties was another reminder of the city's rich jazz heritage. Al Hirt became a jazz musician by association, although he was never a jazzman by inclination.

Now that he has made numerous best-selling records without a jazz format, he feels he has traveled full circle and is doing the kind of thing that suits his talent best. He insists, "I never really considered myself a jazzman, but evidently some people thought I was trying to assume that image. So when I had the chance to say it like it actually is, I said it like it is—that I'm a pop commercial musician, and that's it.

"I think that what I'm doing—with the showmanship and all—is the most honest thing I can do, because I get a kick out of it. And on top of all that, I consider myself very lucky because the people dig it. It's a very happy scene."

The trumpeter's self-evaluation is far more perceptive and realistic than most critics' estimates of his talent. And a visit to the Al Hirt Club (formerly Dan's Pier 600) on Bourbon Street bears out his analysis. Al Hirt, the World's Greatest Trumpet Showman, is always the master of his horn and the servant of his audience.

In The Groove

YOUNG DONALD SUHOR, 14, 1310 Bartholomew St., shows judges the stuff that took him into the finals of the Benny Goodman trophy clarinet competition here. Listening are the judges, **DAVID WINSTEIN, IRVING FAZZOLA** and **"PINKY" VICACOVICH.** Donald will meet Don V. Lasday, 17, 2560 Mexico St., in the finals at the Pops concert tonight in the Municipal Auditorium. Benny Goodman himself will present the trophy. Other contestants in the semi-finals Thursday were Philip E. Hermann, Peter Henry Fountain, Jr., Matteo Galiano, and Jerry Boquet. Rene Douapre, instrumental supervisor of the New Orleans public schools, is chairman of the contest.

Don Suhor won the Goodman contest by playing Artie Shaw solos and later played bop. Correct surnames: Fazola, Vidacovich, Gagliano, Louapre. New Orleans *Item*, June 13, 1947. Courtesy of New Orleans *Times-Picayane*.

Orin Blackstone at rear door of New Orleans Record Shop, circa 1949. Courtesy of Hogan Jazz Archive, Howard-Tilton Memorial Library, Tulane University.

Early jazzmen at jam session at Bill Huntington's house. Steve Angrum; Huntington, 15, George Fortier; Charlie Love; Albert Jiles, 1953. Courtesy of Bill Huntington.

Chink Martin; Charles Suhor, 14; Don Suhor, 17; at New Orleans Jazz Club jam seesion, circa 1950. Courtesy of Don Suhor.

Raymond Burke, Doc Souchon, Monk Hazel, Emile Christian, Chink Martin, Knocky Parker, Doc Evans; date unknown. Courtesy of Hogan Jazz Archive, Howard-Tilton Memorial Library, Tulane University.

Louis Armstrong's birthplace on Jane Alley, razed in 1964; date unknown. Courtesy of Hogan Jazz Archive, Howard-Tilton Memorial Library, Tulane University.

Armstrong statue, unveiled 1976 in Jackson Square; placed in Congo Square, Armstrong Park, in 1980. Courtesy of Charles Suhor.

Bunk Johnson, Baby Dodds, Jim Robinson, 1944. Courtesy of Hogan Jazz Archive, Howard-Tilton Memorial Library, Tulane University.

The esteemed Bill Russel, lovingly portrayed by Al Rose, circa 1992. Courtesy of Hogan Jazz Archive, Howard-Tilton Memorial Library, Tulane University.

Irving Fazola and Bob Haggart in full strut (with Bob Crosby Band, Atlantic City, NJ), circa 1939. Courtesy of Duncan Schiedt and Hogan Jazz Archive, Howard-Tilton Memorial Library, Tulane University.

Sharkey's Kings of Dixieland. Santo Pecora, deejay/promoter Roger Wolfe, Monk Hazel, Sharkey Bonano, unidentified couple, Chink Martin, Jeff Riddick, Lester Bouchon, circa 1949. Courtesy of Hogan Jazz Archive, Howard-Tilton Memorial Library, Tulane University.

Oscar (Papa) Celestin's Band at the Paddock. Christopher (Happy) Goldston, Ricard Alexis, Bill Matthews, Alphonse Picou, Celestin, circa 1949. Courtesy of Hogan Jazz Archive, Howard-Tilton Memorial Library, Tulane University.

The Dukes of Dixieland at the Famous Door. Fred Assunto, Stan Mendelson, Frank Assunto, Chink Martin, Jr., unknown, Bill Shea, circa 1951. Courtesy of Hogan Jazz Archive, Howard-Tilton Memorial Library, Tulane University.

Basin Street Six at L'Enfant's. Roy Zimmerman, Joe Rotis, Bunny Frank, Pete Fountain, Charlie Duke, George Girard, circa 1950. Courtesy of Hogan Jazz Archive, Howard-Tilton Memorial Library, Tulane University.

George Lewis at Preservation Hall. Jim Robinson, Joe Watkins, Avery (Kid) Howard, Jerry Adams, Lewis, Dolly Adams, circa 1962. Courtesy of Hogan Jazz Archive, Howard-Tilton Memorial Library, Tulane University.

Al Hirt, circa mid-1950s. Courtesy of Hogan Jazz Archive, Howard-Tilton Memorial Library, Tulane University.

The Loyola big band toured nearby states recruiting students. From left, Don Suhor, Gerry St. Amand, Larry Valentino, vocalists Lee Voelkel and Mickey Tagliarini, and conductor John Whitlock, circa 1951. Courtesy of Don Suhor.

Dooky Chase Band. Left to right, front row: Warren Bell, Sr., Larry Smith, Charlie Gaspard, Sterling White, Hilton Carter, Curtis Trevigne; second row: Awood Johnson, Benny Powell, Chase (standing), John (Pickett) Brunious, Doris Chase, Andrew Smith; top row: Tony Moret, Ted Riley, Arnold DePass, Vernal Fournier, LeRoy (Batman) Rankins, circa late 1940s. Courtesy of Hogan Jazz Archive, Howard-Tilton Memorial Library, Tulane University.

Al Belletto Sextet. Fred Crane, Belletto, Jimmy Guinn, Willie Thomas, Skip Fawcett. Not shown: drummer Bama McKnight, 1956. Courtesy of Al Belletto.

Earl Williams band at Natal's. Red Tyler, Earl Palmer, Earl Williams, Sam Mooney, Ed Frank, circa 1953. Courtesy of Earl Palmer.

Joseph (Mouse) Bonati, circa late 1960s. Courtesy of Diane J. Bonati Meswarb.

Joe (Cheeks) Mandry, Don Suhor at Rizzo's, 1957. Courtesy of Don Suhor.

Ellis Marsalis, circa 1953. Courtesy of Ellis Marsalis.

Laverne Smith recording for Vik; Phil Darois, bass; others unknown, 1960. Courtesy of Phil Darois.

Theresa Kelly at Loyola quadrangle; Charlie McDonald, bass; Charles Suhor, bongos; looking on are John Enders, Ed Merritt, Lynn Murphy, Curtis Rome, 1953. Courtesy of Charles Suhor.

Charles Suhor with Loyola big band; brass section, from left, Curtis Rome, Carl Meyers, Kirby Bonnette, Bill Pruyn, Carl Hellmers; Theresa Kelly, piano; Bob Morgan, bass; looking on, Milson Luce, 1955. Courtesy of Loyola University.

Pianist Joe Burton's Quartet; from left, Bill Huntington, Burton, Lee Gravano, Reed Vaughan, circa 1960. Courtesy of Bill Huntington.

Biloxi-based Don Reitan group; from left, Mike Serpas, trumpet; Rusty Gilder, bass; vocalist Jackie Henderson; Lee Charlton, drums; Reitan, circa 1962. Courtesy of Lee Charlton.

AFO (All for One) Records, musicians/executives; standing: Red Tyler, tenor sax; John Boudreaux, drums; Roy Montrell, guitar; Peter (Chuck) Badie, bass; sitting: Melvin Lastie, trumpet; Harold Battiste, tenor sax, mentor, AFO founder, circa 1962. Courtesy of Harold Battiste.

Nat Perrilliat, Ed Blackwell, Alvin Batiste at Foster's, circa 1959. Courtesy of
Alvin Batiste.

Fred Crane with Al Belletto Sextet, circa 1955. Courtesy of Al Belletto.

Modernist John Probst with Pete Fountain, in Yamaha promotional pamphlet, circa 1962.

Buddy Prima Trio at the Playboy Club; Bob Ventrillo, Bill Huntington, 1964. Courtesy of Bill Huntington.

Modern Jazz Pioneers Symposium; panelists Al Belletto, Richard Payne, Germaine Bazzle, Don Suhor, Earl Palmer, Harold Battiste, Charles Suhor, 1998. Courtesy of Al Kennedy

15

Armand Hug: The Making of a Legend

Jazz, September 1966

Armand Hug occupies a unique place among jazz pianists. He is virtually unknown to a large segment of the jazz public, yet almost universally respected by jazz critics. He won his reputation as a ragtime pianist, yet he often uses modern accompanists, and he is admired by musicians of every era.

A small cult of jazz fans follows Hug with a near-fanatical dedication. His New Orleans fans have moved with him from Musso's, where he held forth for seven years, to the dozens of other clubs which he has played since 1960. The New Orleans Jazz Club sponsored Armand Hug Appreciation Day when Hug opened at the Dynasty Room in 1962. An English Hug-ite wrote an article on the pianist for a small British publication and included such minute details of Hug's life as a hand injury which once forced him to lay off for two months.

Hug is well on his way to becoming a legend like Houston's Peck Kelly. Like Kelly, he has consistently turned down offers to play in New York and other cities where his talent would receive wider exposure. Hug tells of an incident in the 20's when tenor saxist Eddie Miller hired him for an engagement at the Markham Hotel on the Mississippi Gulf Coast, some seventy-five miles from New Orleans: "I stayed over there about a week and got so homesick I said, 'Eddie, I can't stand this over here. I want to go back to New Orleans.'

"I was always a guy who stuck close to home," Hug explains; "I imagine it's the atmosphere that New Orleans offers. Not money-wise—if you're born here you know what it is. If you're ever away for a while, why, you get this urge to come back."

Hug cannot remember a time when music was not a part of his life. Born in a musically bristling New Orleans on December 6, 1910, Hug recalls having played drums in a grammar school band at the age of six. His mother, a talented amateur pianist, was his first piano teacher, and he studied formally with a Mrs. Asette for about a year when he was nine years old.

But Hug was impatient with formal study and yearned to imitate the brisk and exciting rhythms of the pianists he had heard on player pianos and Edison phonographs—Scott Joplin and Jelly Roll Morton. A piano-playing friend of the family named Edward Bordeaux would often favor young Hug with private recitals of ragtime tunes like *Chicken Reel Rag* and *Good Gravy*

Rag. "I'd go crazy listening to him play those rags," Hug says. "He played them very, very mechanical and with not much relaxation, but it was really probably one of the earliest influences that I had."

Hug's first professional experience came through an uncle named Dewey Schmede. Schmede, who worked local vaudeville houses under the name of Wilbur Leroy, was also an amateur pianist. He encouraged his nephew by introducing him to the blues and teaching him how to fake various left hand rhythms. Hug's precocious entry into the music business came when Schmede's pianist failed to appear one night at a neighborhood theater. Schmede and his partner called on the twelve-year-old Hug to back up their routine, an assignment which he executed capably, if nervously.

But Hug's first job was almost his last. After the performance Schmede took him to a speakeasy to celebrate his professional debut, and in Hug's words, "They commenced to giving me this homemade wine. By the time I got home I was some sick boy! My uncle didn't come around the house for about a month after that."

In his early teens Hug played with various high school groups, but soon he was earning a dollar a night playing with a violin-piano-drums combination at another neighborhood movie house. When Hug was fourteen years old, a drummer asked his father if the budding pianist might take the job at a downtown taxi dance hall, the Fern, for the then-fantastic salary of thirty dollars a week.

"I had just gone into long pants," Hug comments, "but my mother finally consented to let me go to work under one condition. My uncle, the brother of Dewey Schmede, was the night policeman down on Canal Street. . . . My mother says, 'As long as your Uncle George sees you home in the morning time, it's all right.' So when it would come time for me to get off, my uncle would pass around the Fern and he would see that I got on the streetcar and got home."

Hug describes the job at the Fern as "the real beginning of jazz for me." The band was composed of some solid jazz musicians, including Harry Shields (brother of Larry Shields of the Original Dixieland Jazz Band), drummer Von Gammon, banjoist Buzzy Willard, and trumpeter Bill Gillen. Gammon, the leader, would not allow Hug to use the sheet music that he naively brought on his first night. Harry Shields would call out the chords to Hug on unfamiliar tunes, and within a few nights Hug was romping confidently through the band's repertoire of Dixieland standards.

In the 20s the Fern was a meeting place for local jazzmen, and such musicians as Sharkey Bonano and the late Irving Fazola would sit in regularly. "Fazola was a little younger than me," Hug muses, "and he used to come around there in short pants and a cap. He weighed about 200 pounds. . . . He played just as wonderful then as he did later on."

Inevitably, the erratic hours and the glamour of the music world caused Hug to lose enthusiasm for his schoolwork, and he quit Warren Easton High School to become a full time musician. His reputation among New Orleans

jazzmen grew quickly; he moved to a number of jobs with top musicians—
the Valencia Club on Bourbon Street with Eddie Miller, the Silver Slipper
with clarinetist Sidney Arodin (who was later with the New Orleans Rhythm
Kings), and others.

Among jazz fans and in the slowly burgeoning field of jazz criticism,
however, only the cognoscenti knew of Hug. Unlike Eddie Miller, Louis
Prima, Wingy Manone, Georg Brunis, Ray Bauduc, and so many others
among his contemporaries, Hug stayed in New Orleans, where a small but
rabid coterie began to hail him as one of the greatest Dixieland pianists and
as the best living exponent of ragtime.

Hug's place in the history of jazz as an interpreter of ragtime is indeed secure, but it has been a mixed blessing for the pianist. Commenting on his
reputation as a ragtime specialist, Hug says, "I think the tag 'ragtime' has
put me into a certain category that has been hard for me to overcome. . . .
While I feel very flattered to have been included in this category with the
ragtime greats, I think I went a little beyond that, because I didn't stop
there."

Hug points out that in the '30s other pianists had a "terrific impact" on
him, especially Earl Hines, who "did more to revolutionize my style of playing than any other pianist that I know." He also names Fats Waller, Jess
Stacy, Art Tatum, and Teddy Wilson as important influences, and he speaks
with praise of Erroll Garner, George Shearing, Ahmad Jamal, and Bill
Evans.

Hug's playing today testifies to his ability to assimilate a wide range of
influences. The savor of Hines, Wilson, and Tatum is perhaps strongest in
his style, but traces of Garner and Shearing are unmistakable on such tunes
as *A Taste of Honey* and *Cast Your Fate to the Wind*.

Perhaps the common denominator of the many facets of Hug's style is a
distinctively light, lyrical touch. This is especially striking in Hug's ragtime.
While most ragtime pianists attack the genre with a rollicking, two-fisted
abandon, Hug approaches a ragtime composition with greater respect for its
melodic content. Yet he retains the rhythmic vitality of all the great ragtime
pianists, for he has the ability to seize the rhythmic essence of a line without cudgeling it to death. Similarly, Hug's boogie glides along gracefully
where other pianists often thunder and rumble without the redeeming quality of melodic inventiveness.

Hug's improvisational skills are most effectively displayed on lesser
heard jazz standards such as *Squeeze Me* and *Black and Blue*, played at a relaxed walking tempo. Here Hug takes a theme-and-variations approach, seldom playing more than sixteen bars without returning for at least a veiled
reference to the melody. Within the limits of this approach, Hug is capable
of gliding through chorus after chorus of rhythmic and melodic explorations, now stating a simple, basically Dixielandish line, now employing
fleet Tatumesque runs, now setting up a Garnerlike tension between right
and left hand, now toying with clever left hand contrapuntal figures.

Ironically, Hug's musical growth has resulted in a professional problem. Besides the perennial problem of passers-by who request anything from *Alley Cat* to *Warsaw Concerto*, Hug's followers have separated into two camps, each with its own taste: nostalgic Hug fans and sophisticated Hug fans. The former prefer ragtime and Dixieland, while the latter want to hear Hug's library of standards, originals, and modern tunes.

A typical set at the Golliwog Club, the plush Canal Street lounge where Hug has played for the last two years, might include such an unlikely combination as *Do You Know What It Means to Miss New Orleans, Honky Tonk Train Blues*, the fetching Cy Coleman waltz *Real Live Girl, Fly Me to the Moon*, a slightly bowdlerized version of *Rhapsody in Blue, Lazy River*, Hug's humorous *Ricky Tick Waltz, Bill Bailey*, Bix Beiderbecke's *In a Mist*, and *Little Rock Getaway*. Of these, Hug sings most of the popular material and about half of the standards, not always to the advantage of the tune or to the pleasure of the purists in his audience.

Yet Hug, like many an artist whose most immediate concern is making a living, is far less grave than his followers are in viewing his artistic problems. Through the sheer strength of his conception he brings unity and a sense of continuity to sets which seem hopelessly, even ludicrously, diverse. He seems to accept the fact that his attachment to his home town has stifled his chances for a larger income, broader popularity, and greater musical freedom.

As for the squabble among his fans over which style he plays best, the pianist dismisses the issue with typical Hugian honesty. He says, "I really believe that it can become tiresome listening to anything too long. If you play good ragtime, good Dixieland, even good swing piano, . . . if you play all of this music and combine it . . . I think you've got some good music."

Perhaps Hug's attitude is best summed up in this terse statement of his musical credo: "I feel this way—that if you're a piano player, you play piano; if you're a musician, you play music." Hug's attempts to span several eras in jazz need no fuller apology than this.

16

Raymond Burke and Art Hodes
in Concert: Review

Down Beat, September 9, 1965

Personnel: Raymond Burke, clarinet; Art Hodes, piano; Sherwood Mangia-pane, bass; Freddie King, drums

The New Orleans Jazz Club's idea of bringing Chicago pianist Hodes to-gether with New Orleans clarinetist Burke and a solid New Orleans rhythm section was a happy one. Despite some ragged endings and occasional un-certainty which inevitably spring from jam sessions, the music produced was consistently exciting, for Hodes and Burke are highly original jazzmen whose differing conceptions, rather than clashing, seemed to be sources of mutual stimulation.

Hodes' presence on the jazz scene for so many years has caused him to be taken for granted. He is one of the few genuine eccentrics in pre-modern jazz piano—one might justifiably call him the Thelonious Monk of Dix-ieland. His accompaniment, for example, is a grab-bag of approaches. Within a tune he might play four-to-the-bar, switch to modern "broken" comping, dig in with a lusty shuffle rhythm, or break into quarter-note triplets or a haunting tremolo, somehow maintaining a sense of appropriate-ness, even inevitability, throughout.

His solos, too, carry an unmistakably personal stamp. His right hand will titillate the farthest end of the keyboard while his left stretches out in search of a darkly contrasting bass line. His choruses are animated by bop licks, ro-coco rhythmic configurations, and arrestingly syncopated left-hand accents.

All of this seemed fine with Burke, who is accustomed to the most con-servative of pianists. Burke's economical solo lines, which make most ef-fective use of spacing his ideas, were quite compatible with Hodes' busy style, and on *Sleepy Time Gal* the rapport was so pleasing that Hodes burst into a lilting duet on Burke's second chorus.

Only on *Mandy, Make up Your Mind* and *Do You Know What It Means to Miss New Orleans*? did Hodes' modern voicings and relatively complex rhythms disturb Burke. Most often, the clarinetist was moved to a fluency and plasticity that is quite uncommon to him. He excelled on standards like *Lazy River, At Sundown,* and *Basin Street Blues*. And on the blues, which Burke has always played superbly, Hodes' spontaneity spurred Burke to his best playing of the session.

Burke's handling of the lower register was also impressive. He has a striking manner of beginning a chorus in the upper register—perhaps with a piercing blue note or a single incisive accent—and then moving down to a rich, mellow chalumeau. Again, Burke showed his ability to sustain the quality of his lower register by playing a full chalumeau chorus on *Wolverine Blues.*

Hodes played three solo features—*Grandpa's Spells, Chicago,* and *Maryland, My Maryland. Spells,* a Jelly Roll Morton rag, was attacked with a two-fisted vigor that drew deserved applause. Hodes tore into *Chicago* with similar gusto but failed to attain the fire of the colorful *Spells. Maryland* was a crowd-pleaser, but it showed less of Hodes' improvisational skills than did the other solos, since it leaned on a rather self-conscious gimmick in which he played melody with one hand and the familiar countermelody with the other.

Bassist Mangiapane and drummer King furnished a solid background throughout the concert. King deserves mention as a rare phenomenon—a highly creative traditional drummer-accompanist. Instead of forcing the library of drearily predictable Dixieland contrasts and climaxes on the band, he constantly listens to the instrumentalists and responds sensitively and flexibly to the musical environment that evolves from the group. He strikes a natural, tasteful balance between snare drum and cymbals, and he is one of the few remaining woodblock artists in the Baby Dodds tradition. In fact, the freedom of his playing is reminiscent of Dodds, for he avoids the rigid role-playing of the revivalists, the tedious slickness of most Dixieland drummers, and the rawness of lesser traditional drummers.

King's solos lacked the imagination of his ensemble playing, but reportedly he had been away from music since leaving New Orleans more than 10 years ago and has only become active again in recent months. The contagious honesty of his style can only be a boon to the New Orleans jazz scene.

The jazz club has promised to bring in musicians from other areas for concerts with local artists. The Hodes-Burke session proves that such combinations can be musically rewarding and that traditional jazz can indeed be played with conviction and inventiveness by jazzmen outside of the hallowed grounds of Preservation Hall.

17

Preservation Hall: New Orleans Rebirth

Down Beat, January 17, 1963

There's a New Orleans revival going on. But unlike most New Orleans revivals of the last couple of decades, it is going on in New Orleans, and its principals are not tousled-haired youngsters trying to re-create the sounds of another generation but the actual men who lived and played in New Orleans at the turn of the century.

The center of the excitement is a unique establishment in the French Quarter called Preservation Hall.

There is no cover charge or minimum at the hall; there are no waiters, drinks, or even tables. Patrons seat themselves on a collection of chairs and lounges (or on crowded nights, on the floor) and contribute to a kitty, which is the hall's main source of income. Within a given month, as many as 50 of the reactivated jazzmen might be heard, from relatively well-known musicians like clarinetist George Lewis and trombonist Jim Robinson to figures virtually unknown outside of purist circles, such as John Casimir and Peter Bocage.

The hall originated in May, 1961, when Grayson (Ken) Mills went to the Crescent City from the West Coast to record some of the older musicians for his Icon label.

Mills hoped to experiment with various combinations of instrumentalists before an audience and to give the musicians a chance to redevelop their technique. He persuaded an old friend and art dealer, Larry Bornstein, to give him the use of his St. Peter Street gallery for weekend sessions.

A group of interested jazz fans responded with promises to help organize the hall, which was tentatively named the Slow Drag in honor of bassist Alcide Pavageau. Allan and Sandra Jaffe, a young couple from Philadelphia, and Chicagoan Barbara Reid became an informal staff for the hall, and the sessions soon had a considerable following through word-of-mouth publicity and the encouragement of the New Orleans Jazz Club and Tulane University's jazz archivists Bill Russell and Dick Allen.

Soon, Mills was able to set up a regular six-night-a-week schedule of jazz, featuring seven to 10 groups a month.

Orleanians began to hear once again musicians like Punch Miller, Kid Howard, Sweet Emma Barrett, Paul Barbarin, and Billie and De De Pierce, playing with near total freedom, minus the familiar figure of an anxious club owner eyeing the cash register and urging the musicians to grimace and clown and end each set with the *Saints*.

The musicians became aware of the uniqueness of their situation. No other place in town—indeed, few places anywhere—could boast an audience whose purpose it was strictly to listen—not to talk, dance, drink, or engage a B-girl.

Their satisfaction was reflected in their playing, and a real esprit de corps grew. The bands rehearsed regularly, and the hall's staff continued to seek out older jazz musicians, sometimes furnishing instruments at its own expense. When Mills assured the union that he would pay musicians from his not-too-abundant pocket in cases of an inadequate kitty, the musicians in turn voted to turn over all tips to the hall.

By July, 1961, there was a widespread realization among jazz fans of the hall's importance. An attempt was made to assure its future by forming the New Orleans Society for the Preservation of Traditional Jazz, with Mills as president and Bill Russell as an adviser.

However, internal dissension among the hall's organizers over the financing of a recording session at the hall soon followed. Mills withdrew from the running of the hall, and the society asked Allan and Sandra Jaffe to carry on Mills' job as chief manager of the hall's activities.

The society was dissolved, but Jaffe accepted the responsibility, quitting a well-paying job to manage the hall. Jaffe's goal was to avoid future crises by finding other sources of income to act as a prop for the hall's inconsistent kitty.

This was partially accomplished with the help of several major publicity breaks. *David Brinkley's Journal* did a distorted feature on the dearth of traditional jazz in New Orleans, which was nevertheless redeemed partially by its attention to the hall's program. The Associated Press carried a story on the hall, which resulted in the exporting of four bands (Kid Howard's, Kid Sheik's, Punch Miller's, and Noon Johnson's) for engagements at the Tudor Arms Hotel in Cleveland. Nesuhi Ertegun recorded a series of albums for Atlantic called *Jazz at Preservation Hall*.

Jaffe began acting as an agent for the hall's bands on bookings and tours, bringing in money to keep the hall operating during the slack tourist season. (The Baton Rouge, La., Symphony Orchestra and Houston, Texas, Contemporary Arts Society were among those contracting for groups from the hall.) He also initiated record sales in the hall's patio, but, true to the policy of nonhustling, the records are simply made available to visitors.

The widespread recognition of the hall has not changed its essentially informal, productive atmosphere. A wider audience is being reached—including the social register, the college crowd, and an amalgam of personalities from Lucy Baird Johnson to Norman Thomas—but the admixture of rapport and respectfulness that always had characterized the hall's audiences remains. The musicians still play with a vigorous, unself-conscious abandon, reflecting their primary concern with musical expression and their lack of ensnarlment in commercial considerations.

Jaffe is highly sensitive to the combination of human and musical elements that have determined the hall's success.

Avoiding the patronizing paternalism commonly turned upon the early jazzman, he has adopted a straightforward musicians-first policy. For example, when Dixieland Hall was opened by art dealer Al Clark on Bourbon Street, in obvious imitation of Preservation, Jaffe invoked the principle of cooperative competition and helped Clark organize a schedule of bands for the hall. He also cooperated with Ken Mills in initiating Perseverance Hall on St. Louis Street last June when Mills returned temporarily to make more recordings. He even has made money available for informal loans to the hall's musicians, setting aside funds from his agent's fees and collecting on debts with no interest as musicians play in the hall.

However, it would be a mistake to view the current revival as a purist's paradise in which an idyllic past has been recaptured.

There is the palpable fact that many of the hall's musicians were not, and are not, important jazzmen. *Down Beat* reviewer Gilbert Erskine has pointed out the fallacy of the widespread romantic notion that any New Orleans musician owning a horn and playing street parades in the early 1900s must necessarily have become an important link in the chain of jazz history. Many of the reactivated musicians demonstrate a closer affinity to prejazz forms, utilizing polka and march phrasing, than to the more subtle inflections introduced by Louis Armstrong.

Moreover, even the best jazzmen show the effects of the failing lip, the waning facility, and the shortened breath. It is a tribute to the strength of their conception that their art has a high degree of realization even though their technical problems are often severe. On a good night at the hall—and there are many—a group will communicate the essential jazz spirit despite the individual weaknesses of its members, indicating that the whole is indeed greater than the sum of its parts.

And, of course, there are still the practical problems involved in keeping Preservation Hall operating without reverting to a more commercial presentation or conventional night-club format. With manager Jaffe and his wife living on past savings, and the intake of the hall still hinging largely on the problematical generosity of its customers, the hall's problems of sustenance are far from resolved.

Finally, there is the one insoluble problem that underlines both the significance and the sadness of the current revival: the generation of musicians who saw the evolution of jazz in its earliest years is slowly passing away. For two musicians—clarinetist Steve Angrum and drummer Chinee Foster—the revival at Preservation Hall was the last New Orleans revival.

18

The Last Rites of a Jazzman: George Lewis

New Orleans magazine, February 1969

To some, a jazz funeral is a quaint reminder of an innocent and colorful past. To others it is a profanation of an event that demands only prayers, tears, or silence. To those who claim it as a genuine part of their tradition, it is simply a good way to lay a brother to rest.

The problem of how to respond to death has always been a painful and embarrassing one for mankind. Few people have developed a ritual that deals effectively with the galling duality of death: it leaves the living with a sense of sadness and remorse, but at the same time it forces upon them an awareness of how fully they inhabit their bodies, of the quickness and endurance and continuity of the life that is in them.

A century ago it was fashionable to hire professional mourners to weep and moan in respectful anguish for the dead so the living could go about the less exhausting business of arranging flowers or settling the estate. The modern custom of wakes requires strict observance of grief in the funeral home, but traditionally permits renewal of old acquaintances on the gallery or even at a nearby bar.

The jazz funeral avoids the hypocrisy of the paid mourners and the gaucherie of the convivial reunion that we call a wake. In a jazz funeral the tragedy of death is symbolized clearly in the dirge played by the band on the way to the cemetery; the joy of survival is represented by the happy music that follows the ceremony after the band has left the cemetery. The jazz funeral achieves a poignant and graceful merging of both the knowledge of mortality and the spirit of mirth implicit in death.

Clarinetist George Lewis' funeral was the largest in recent years, attracting hundreds of friends, musicians, and admirers. Although the word "jazz" was not yet coined when Lewis was born in 1900, ceremonies similar to the jazz funeral had been in existence for several decades. Tulane historian Henry Kmen tells us that marching bands were so commonplace in the 19th century that they were often regarded as a public nuisance. The abundance of military bands and marching bands sponsored by fraternal organizations probably combined with the love of chant and procession found in the Catholic Church to form the unique social and religious ritual of the jazz funeral.

George Lewis was a slim, bashful man, but he stood tall in the world of jazz. Even the curiosity-seekers at his funeral seemed to know that his death was more than a single instance of human mortality. Lewis carried the classic image of the New Orleans Jazzman—the image of untutored genius, of personal and artistic integrity, of a man who could express much because he had experienced and endured much. Lewis was a living legend, and when a living legend dies the community balks at the idea of surrendering part of its essential flesh to history.

19

A Festival for a Funeral?

New Orleans magazine, January 1968

When old timers in the late 1940's shouted about the death of New Orleans Jazz, a dramatic jazz revival occurred. Under the influence of seasoned jazzmen like Sharkey Bonano, Santo Pecora, and Irving Fazola, an impressive lineup of young Dixieland musicians appeared within a decade. Frank and Fred Assunto, Pete Fountain, George Girard, Pee Wee Spitelera, Murphy Campo, and others began showing up at jam sessions and forming teenage jazz groups.

Now, twenty years later, there is a new generation of old timers and they are again talking about the death of jazz in New Orleans. But this time their predictions are probably right.

To begin with, the revival of the '40's was not as productive as it seemed to be. It did produce a number of new stars like the Dukes of Dixieland and Pete Fountain, who eventually put the city back on the map as a jazz and entertainment center. But many of the most promising young musicians turned to other musical areas after a brief flirtation with Dixieland. Pianist Larry Muhoberac, the whiz kid of a fine young Dixie group led by trumpeter Connie Jones, took up trombone and did a stint with Woody Herman before settling down to studio work in Memphis and Dallas. Don Lasday, who was playing New Orleans-style blues clarinet in the late '40's, studied at Schillinger House in Boston and became an excellent modern jazz altoist and concert clarinetist before his premature death in 1965. Drummer Reed Vaughan went from Murphy Campo's New Orleans Jazz Saints on the Ted Mack Show to the Stan Kenton Band within four years, and he is now at the Bistro with pianist Ronnie Dupont, another defector from the Dixieland generation.

Moreover, the young Negro musicians in New Orleans were almost completely untouched by the revival of the '40's. There was no second line of junior jazzmen following George Lewis at Manny's Tavern or "Papa" Celestin at the Paddock in the way that young Pete Fountain imitated Irving Fazola and the Dukes of Dixieland mimicked Sharkey's Kings of Dixieland, from whom they proudly took their name.

The young Negro musicians by and large rejected traditional jazz as Uncle Tom music. They took as their models musically sophisticated beboppers like Dizzy Gillespie, Charlie Parker, and Miles Davis, and they grew into a creative underground of modern jazz artists. To young jazzmen like drummer Ed Blackwell and clarinetist Alvin Batiste, the music of Baby Dodds and Alphonse Picou, however honest, was anachronistic. It did not speak the language of their generation, nor did it challenge their imagination and their technical proficiency. The grammar of traditional jazz was not adequate for what they had to say. For them there could be no "reviving" jazz without enriching it with new inflections and radically extending its vocabulary.

Today the accents of New Orleans jazz seem to have even less appeal for young local musicians than they did two decades ago. Most youngsters are taken up with rock and roll; some listen to folk music; a few still like modern jazz. A handful of teenage Dixieland bands has appeared at New Orleans Jazz Club sessions in recent years, but they have generally been overrehearsed groups that showed little understanding of the jazz idiom.

Actually, the jazz scene is being revitalized by the return of older musicians—veteran traditionalists like Punch Miller, Billie and "De De" Pierce, Earl Humphrey, and others who have been brought back to play at Preservation Hall after years of retirement or semi-retirement. They have won considerable critical acclaim and support from the public, and a number of out-of-town musicians (Illinois cornetist George Finola and Michigan clarinetist Jim Liscombe) and foreign musicians (British trumpeter Clive Wilson and Swedish pianist Lars Edergan) have settled in the city to study New Orleans jazz styles. But the traditionalists' influence on local musicians has been limited to a small group of young hobbyists like clarinetist Tommy Sancton and two popular "revivalist" bands, the Last Straws and the Crawford-Ferguson Night Owls.

The revivalists are the Miniver Cheevys of the jazz world. They try to revive the spirit of the traditionalists, using a banjo, tuba, and a second trumpet player to derive an "authentic" old traditional sound. Of the two local revivalist groups, the Crawford-Ferguson Night Owls (who can be heard Saturday nights on the Steamer *President*) are less prone to ancestor worship. Trombonist Paul Crawford carefully researches rare old tunes like *Bogalusa Strut* at the Tulane University Jazz Archive, but the Owls are not slavishly antiquarian in their treatment of the materials. Their 1965 album on New Orleans Originals label skillfully combines traditional instrumentation with contemporary interpretation as trumpeter Jack Bachman and clarinetist Hank Kmen play updated Dixie over the banjo cum tuba rhythm section.

The Last Straws, though much improved in recent years, typically resurrect only the elements in the old jazz that should have been left to rest in peace. They capture the brassy, chug-along qualities of the early bands without their sure sense of time and their subtle control over their materials. The result is a barrage of clumsy sounds that are closer to the boisterous and nostalgic razzmatazz at Your Father's Moustache than to the music of King Oliver and Bunk Johnson.

It is unlikely that a real revival of jazz will result from musicians whose interests in it are anthropological and sentimental. Jazzmen like Fountain and the Assuntos, who grew from the limited revival of the late '40's, were not trying to recreate the sounds of another generation. As participants in mid-twentieth century New Orleans culture, they lived in a cultural milieu that was continuous with, but different from, New Orleans culture at the turn of the century. Their music reflected their own experience, not that of their grandfathers. They were moving in the mainstream of jazz, but they did not drown in it.

Orleanians have become increasingly conscious of the need for preserving and reviving their native art of jazz. At the same time the younger generation is embracing the popular culture that is accepted by teenagers in California, London, and New York. At best, our sensitive youngsters come to appreciate the various types of New Orleans jazz as part of their cultural heritage. Yet they are not moved to play it, and no art can survive without performers. A living art is not merely preserved, it is practiced. It is not a commemoration of the past, but an interpretation of the present.

The 1950's was the decade in which the exciting new faces on the jazz scene matured and, in many cases, became famous. The 1960's so far has been a decade that looks backward. It has been the decade of the Jazz Museum, the Jazz Archive, Preservation Hall, and the revivalist bands. And this month the city begins a six-month celebration of its past that will culminate with—what else?—a jazz concert. The symbolism is painful, but inescapable: the concert might be the largest and longest jazz funeral in history.

20

New Orleans Jazz—With a Foreign Accent

New Orleans magazine, November 1972

Walking down Bourbon Street one afternoon, I heard the sound of traditional jazz coming from the patio of a restaurant. I walked in, expecting to see some of the veteran musicians from Preservation Hall or the New Orleans marching bands. To my surprise, half of the combo was Oriental—including a woman plucking earnestly on a banjo.

The trumpeter, I later learned, was a Japanese musician named Yoshio Toyama, re-dubbed Kid Claiborne in New Orleans. The banjo player was his wife, Keiko.

At a press party for the 1968 New Orleans Jazz Festival, Sharkey Bonano and his band were swinging out with *Muskrat Ramble*. All of the heads in the band—except one—were bald or snowy white. The youthful pianist had a full head of blonde hair. His name was Lars Edegran and he was a recent emigrant from Stockholm.

Marching bands like the Olympia and Tuxedo bands now show up frequently with new faces, white faces that I have not known on the local jazz scene. Paul Crawford, trombonist and leader of the Crawford-Ferguson Night Owls, told me that the newcomers were foreign-born musicians, all under thirty, who have come here to understudy the old masters of traditional jazz.

Add to these men the considerable number of foreign jazz bands and individual musicians who have passed through New Orleans, their musical mecca, in recent years (Papa Bue's Vikings, the High Society Band of Paris, Germany's Barrelhouse Jazz Band, Barry Martyn's European All-Stars, Chris Barber, Sammy Rimmington)—and you have what appears to be an astonishing phenomenon: people from all over the world playing New Orleans music while our own youngsters, with few exceptions, turn to other musical forms.

How did our music get to the ears of musicians abroad?

We should remember, with some embarrassment, that European intellectuals were the first to take jazz seriously. Leonard Feather, the dean of jazz critics, is from England. Writer Jean Cocteau and a group of French intellectuals declared in 1928 that jazz should be recognized as an art form. French critic Hugues Panassie wrote *Le Jazz Hot* in 1934 and established a jazz journal by the same name in 1935, less than a year after *Down Beat* was born in America.

More importantly, during the decade after World War II Europeans had the time to listen to rare American jazz recordings (especially Bunk Johnson's records, with George Lewis on clarinet), and they liked what they heard. A French teenager named Claude Luter put together a band that slavishly copied old King Oliver records, which made a deep impression on Moldy Figs in America. Humphrey Lyttleton's and Ken Colyer's English groups tried to capture the spirit of traditional jazz, and New Orleans–style combos were popping up throughout Europe.

Clive Wilson and John Simmons, both trumpeters from London, recall that they first heard New Orleans music on records. Wilson remembers listening to American jazz records around 1959. Simmons was nine years old in 1952 when his cousin bought some jazz records. According to Simmons, he and some musical friends started by copying records of the Bunk Johnson band note for note, "each guy copying each instrument . . . mistakes and all."

Edegran says that in Stockholm "both my father and my brother were musicians. My father played banjo and guitar, and my brother played piano. I myself took classical piano lessons for seven or eight years. . . . My father and brother had American records. . . . In 1960 I started a band with Orange Kellin [a clarinetist who is also living in New Orleans now]—it was pretty amateurish at the time—and we played in Sweden until 1964. I guess we were all trying to play like Bunk Johnson's band."

A German trombonist who lives in the French Quarter (he asked to remain anonymous) became a modern jazz buff after hearing bop records on Armed Forces Radio in the mid-fifties. In a reversal of the usual pattern, his taste moved from bop towards traditional jazz after he heard some rare records by—who else?—Bunk Johnson and George Lewis. The trombonist claims that "in Europe, the orientation was towards Bunk and King Oliver—yes, I remember Claude Luter—and we were also influenced by the British scene."

He cites jazzmen on tour and expatriates like New Orleans' Sidney Bechet and Chicago clarinetist Mezz Mezzrow as further influences on the Continent. He remembers hearing Sidney Bechet and trombonist Kid Ory in Germany as a jazz-hungry youngster.

The prototypical jazzman-migrant in America was a British seaman named Ken Colyer. Recordings were not enough for Colyer. He jumped ship in 1952 and stayed long enough to digest the trumpet styles of many of the black New Orleans traditionalists. As he developed his style, his music was thought by some to be the most authentic of the "trad revival" of the 1950's in England —especially since Humphrey Lyttleton, Chris Barber, and others tended towards Dixieland or swing styles that purists consider a bastardization of genuine New Orleans jazz.

Clive Wilson remembers "trad" in England as ". . . a big craze. There were jazz records in the Top Ten; everyone in England had heard about jazz. Of course, it was still not possible to make a living at it, unless you were a big name."

John Simmons says that the trad boom was generally good for jazz, but "it disgusted me, the way they went commercial. Young kids switched to trad in England, and that meant pop-influenced jazz as opposed to New Orleans jazz. Nobody played it [New Orleans jazz] well, even Lyttleton's band. I suppose the main influence was Ken Colyer. Since he'd been to New Orleans, he could play it straight. But he was copying the New Orleans musicians, and kids were copying him instead of going to the source."

Simmons had wisely uncovered one of several layers of irony in the postwar jazz revivals. Another is that Bunk Johnson was considered by many critics—most notably, Leonard Feather—to be well past his prime when he made his "comeback," false teeth and all, after the age of sixty. And Bunk himself called the band that made the celebrated revival recordings "an emergency band"—one that was put together too hastily, with too much advice from well-meaning advisors, for the music to be what he wanted it to be. (Feather was also hard, incidentally, on expatriates Bechet and Mezzrow. He described Bechet as "a national vaudeville figure" in France and called Mezzrow "a laughing stock among some of his contemporaries." It should be noted that Feather can be as wrongheaded and tendentious as any critic in the field.)

Another ironic note in the revival was a transcription of a jazz concert at the Parisian Room on Royal Street, sent by WWL to BBC around 1949. The Parisian Room concerts had started out with worthies like Sharkey Bonano, Irving Fazola, and Monk Hazel. But in a short time musicians like Tony Dalmado, a capable trumpeter but certainly not a New Orleans-style jazzman, and clarinetist Nina Picone—again, competent but neither traditional or especially inventive—replaced the stalwarts.

England's hip tabloid *The Melody Maker*, which knows the difference between New Orleans jazz and later forms, wrote that the Orleanians could take some lessons from Humphrey Lyttleton's band. Local figs knew that Lyttleton's band at the time was indeed in a more traditional groove than the Parisian Room band, but the latter group was by no means representative of what was happening here. I was thirteen years old and smitten with righteousness, so I filled my Eversharp with blue-black Quink and wrote a letter to *Melody Maker* (which they subsequently published) suggesting that they get transcriptions of Sharkey, Papa Celestin, and other non-revisionist jazz bands. As a final irony, the Parisian Room group evolved into one of the most plodding, undistinguished combos in the history of the art—Tony Almerico's All-Stars. But more about them later.

The jazz migrants among us insist that they long ago outgrew the stage of imitating their jazz idols, although they continue to play in the New Orleans jazz style. Clive Wilson calls it "doing your own thing while being conscious of tradition."

John Simmons' early dependence on Bunk Johnson records was broadened after he heard the many traditional trumpeters working parades, jazz halls, and dances in New Orleans. He cites Percy Humphrey, Kid Sheik, and

Kid Thomas as some of his favorites. Wilson names Kid Howard, Louis Armstrong, and Alvin Alcorn as partial influences on his style.

The German trombonist states simply, "I like them all. I used to be influenced mainly by Kid Ory and Jim Robinson. But now I try to pick up the best of all the musicians I've heard . . . Frog Joseph and Wendell Eugene, for instance . . . and come out with a style of my own."

Edegran cites Jelly Roll Morton as an abiding influence on his musical development. He points out that in Sweden when he first became interested in jazz, "Alton Purnell [with Bunk Johnson and George Lewis] was the only active New Orleans pianist whose records were available." Since settling here he has come to admire many local pianists like Jeannette Kimball, and even Baltimore-born Don Ewell, the highly eclectic pianist with the Dukes of Dixieland.

But like the others, Edegran rejects copycatting. "I like the New Orleans style," he says, "but it's stupid to continually imitate. I'll never be as good as him doing the same thing he does."

Edegran is making a name for himself among jazz fans with his New Orleans Ragtime Orchestra. The group plays ragtime and jazz arrangements and adaptations from Scott Joplin, Jelly Roll Morton, and others with an authenticity that has won the respect of the jazz press. The current mania for nostalgia has broadened the possible audience for such an orchestra, so that non-jazz audiences can dry an eye while jazz buffs hear beneath the surface of selections with titillating titles like *Pineapple Rag* and *Elite Syncopations.*

Why do young men come from afar to learn the craft of New Orleans jazz, while young musicians in New Orleans by and large turn to rock, blues, modern jazz, and classical music?

As Edegran sees it, "People like the music they *hear*. The media pushes all the latest popular music. It's continually blaring on radio and TV. Jazz is not pushed . . . although Preservation Hall has made a difference; it's opening people's ears."

The German trombonist agrees that jazz is "not the music of today, the music of the masses, like hard rock or soul."

Clive Wilson comments, "I really don't expect anybody to take it up. Most kids take up popular music or 'legit.' You can count the ones who have a serious interest in jazz on one hand. . . . It's a pity."

Simmons says that traditional jazz is "considered old hat" by local youngsters, and he is not optimistic about the likelihood of getting them interested. "The circumstances just aren't the same as they were years ago. There used to be parades and plenty of parties and little clubs where jazz could be heard."

Optimists, counting on one hand, can name the Young Christian Band from Fairview Baptist Church as a sign of hope, as well as Rick Mackie's New Leviathan Orchestra at Tulane and a few isolated instrumentalists like clarinetist Tom Sancton, Jr.

The New Leviathan group, though, does not claim to be a jazz band in the sense of group or solo improvisations. According to Mackie, the band deals with early New Orleans dance music, ragtime, and Tin Pan Alley arrange-ments. The boys at Fairview capture the marching band spirit, but as Sim-mons says, "whether they'll keep an interest in this style as they grow older is the question." And there are too few individual students of traditional music like Sancton to get up a jam session.

An even gloomier appraisal of the situation is possible—namely, that the local revival of the late 1940's and early 1950's was probably the last one that will ever produce a second line of enthusiastic young musicians in New Orleans. That revival saw the emergence of talents like Pete Fountain, Frank and Fred Assunto, George Girard, Jay Barry, Don Suhor, Stan Mendelson, Roy Liberto, Connie Jones, Bill Huntington, Larry Muhoberac, Pee Wee Spitelera, Murphy Campo, Reed Vaughan, Vinnie Trauth, Paul Ferrara, Frankie Ford, Ronnie Dupont, Warren Luening, and others—curiously, all of them white. It is true that many of these musicians moved on rapidly to other forms of jazz, but all had a period of immersion in New Orleans and/or Dixieland music at some time between 1947 and 1955.

At Tony Almerico's dreadful Parisian Room concerts, it was not uncom-mon to hear "youth bands" play almost half of the sessions. A group of kids like Connie Jones, Larry Muhoberac, Ronnie Dupont, and Reed Vaughan would sound a little rough around the edges in those days, but they invari-ably outsparkled Almerico's enervated, unswinging combo.

The large number of local musicians between 30 and 40 years old playing jazz in New Orleans today is deceptive. *Down Beat* editor Dan Morgenstern said it all in a review of the predominantly black Storyville Jazz Band at the 1972 Jazz and Heritage Festival: "Before traditionalists become too heart-ened, let me state my conviction that they [the Storyville Band] are in it mainly because it offers steady employment. Nothing in the band's approach indicated that they consider the form a living mold still capable of stimulat-ing creative expression. They . . . have learned to play it for a living."

And few second liners are in evidence behind the Storyville Band or Wal-lace Davenport or Murphy Campo or the more "purist" bands at Preserva-tion Hall. Traditional and Dixieland jazz pleases audiences but it does not inspire young musicians here as it does, apparently, in other parts of the world. For the musical emigrants, our music is indeed seen as "a living mold." For our native sons, it's a gig.

SECTION III

AN INVISIBLE GENERATION: EARLY MODERN JAZZ ARTISTS

Jazz fans today generally think of New Orleans as the home of the young lions of contemporary jazz artists like Wynton Marsalis, the articulate spokesman for "neotraditional" modern jazz, Branford, Delfayo, and Jason Marsalis, Terence Blanchard, Marlon and Kent Jordan, Nicholas Payton, and others. Harry Connick Jr. has become not only a jazz celebrity but a popular icon and talk-show personality through movie roles and television appearances.

The popular assumption is that this rush of creativity is a new phenomenon, bringing the city's jazz community into the modern jazz orbit a full generation late. Some fans remember that alto saxist Al Belletto had a popular modern jazz sextet that recorded hip, polished vocals in the mid-1950s. And the current fame of Ellis Marsalis, the excellent modern jazz pianist who is father of the young jazzmen, suggests that *some* jazz that was not in Dixieland and traditional New Orleans jazz (TNOJ) styles must have played in the city during the postwar emergence of be-bop and other modern jazz.

As a New Orleans native who played with or heard dozens of excellent modern jazz artists in the late 1940s and beyond, I was always annoyed by the stereotype of New Orleans as the city that jazz left behind. Harold Battiste, a key artist and mentor in the development of modern jazz in New Orleans, has spoken out for decades on this point. In his excellent 1976 *New Orleans Heritage* text, he lamented the fact that "musicians of the late 1940s, 1950s, and 1960s were being completely overlooked" by historians and insisted that the city's modern jazz musicians have been "continuing the tradition of creativity that started nearly a century ago." Battiste quoted his 1963 liner notes for one of the first vintage AFO (All for One) albums.

> When people who are Jazz lovers, followers, critics, etc., think of New Orleans, they almost invariably think of its past. Many are the legends about the great New Orleans musicians, and the contributions they have made. . . . But they are all in the past tense. Somewhere along the way, while Jazz was growing from infancy to puberty and possibly to adolescence, it seems to have wandered away from home. . . . At least, we are led to believe that if you want to hear the latest or if a musician is really on to something on his ax, N.Y. is the place to find him. In reality, however, the spark that ignited jazz in the first place did not leave home.

I confronted the same negativism during my army stint in 1958–1959. Most fellow bandsmen laughingly identified jazz in New Orleans with the Dukes of Dixieland's blatantly commercial Audio-Fidelity albums. A few, though, had been there and had heard the new jazz. They would marvel, "Man, what a great town!" and talk about musicians like Mouse Bonati and Earl Palmer.

No one would make the claim that be-bop originated in New Orleans in the same sense that the city was the focal point for the growth of early jazz. The history of modern jazz and its revolutionary initiators like Charlie Parker, Dizzy Gillespie, Miles Davis, Bud Powell, Thelonious Monk, Kenny Clarke, Max Roach, and others—the list is well known—is amply documented. The Parker recordings with Gillespie, Davis, Catlett Roach, and others that yielded classics like "Groovin' High," "Hot House," "Billie's Bounce," and "Now's the Time" were made in 1945, the same year that marked the end of World War II.

The early New Orleans modernists in the following symposium (chapter 26) talk about the influence of the founders with an excitement that is still vibrant after more than half a century. They also warmly acknowledge the presence of out of towners like Joseph (Mouse) Bonati, Ornette Coleman, Brew Moore, Joe Pass, and others in the local postwar jazz community. The point is that modern jazz was a revelation to dozens of young players in New Orleans, and they immediately saw it as a challenging and enthralling means of expression. TNOJ and Dixieland jazz were enjoying a popular revival in the late 1940s and early 1950s, but a parallel track of development of modern jazz was under way, unknown to the public at large and slimly acknowledged in writings about the postwar years.

Clearly, the new music was not easily found. Be-bop and other modern jazz had to be sought out at strip clubs, after-hours jam sessions, and other uncommon venues. It was essentially an underground music, an invisible art supported by the musicians themselves, a small number of serious listeners, and a few Beat Generation wannabees.

As noted in section I, TNOJ and Dixieland jazz were still highly suspect among civic leaders after World War II. It is not surprising, then, that the city's modern jazz pioneers were scarcely on the Establishment's mental map. Some were picked up in police raids related to B-drinking, prostitution, drugs, or integrated performances. Like their predecessors in Storyville, the modernists were regarded not as musical innovators but as part and parcel of bad environments.

Frustrated by widespread misunderstandings about modern jazz in the New Orleans, in 1960 I wrote to *Down Beat* about doing an article on the subject. As noted in chapter 1, the query was put aside at first, but it led to an assignment as New Orleans correspondent. Shortly after, editor Don DeMichael okayed the article proposal. The two-part "New Jazz in the Cradle" article was published in the August 18 and 31, 1961, issues (chapters 21 and 22 below).

I knew that the article was only a few drops of data in a bucket of myth-information, but it got a new historical perspective on the record in what was then the premier national jazz journal. Since the New Orleans press did not give a damn about contemporary jazz, *DB* might, ironically, be a resource for making some historical points about the music and for keeping tabs, through the twice-monthly "Ad Libs" and "Where and When" features, on current activities of local jazz artists in all styles. And so it went. During the 1960s *Down Beat* was essentially the magazine of record for jazz of all styles in New Orleans.

This section will present what I believe is the most comprehensive picture to date of early modern jazz artists in New Orleans. I hope to correct popular misconceptions about the postwar years and counter nonsense contentions like Lichtenstein and Danker's 1993 statement in *Musical Gumbo: The Music of New Orleans* that other than Ellis Marsalis "there were not many other be-boppers around New Orleans in the mid-fifties."

I will also expand on the limited view of postwar modernists presented in *Up from the Cradle of Jazz: New Orleans Music since World War II,* by Jason Berry, Jonathan Foose, and Tad Jones. As noted earlier, this 1986 book is not mainly about jazz but the growth of blues/rhythm and blues and early rock 'n' roll in New Orleans. It sidesteps postwar TNOJ and Dixieland jazz almost completely and devotes one chapter to modern jazz, titled "The New Jazz and AFO," giving considerable follow-up in the next chapter, "Jazz and Blues Kept Coming."

To give due credit, the materials in *Cradle* are a serious attempt to portray at least part of the evolution of modern jazz in New Orleans. The problem is that the varied and diffuse early modern jazz scene is not easily described. Little was written about the musicians at the time, and they gathered in innumerable combinations, some subsets overlapping with others, some relatively isolated, often gigging and jamming at remote and unlikely places. How are we to get a handle on all this?

The *Cradle* authors manage to achieve focus and narrative coherence, but at great expense. They select and concentrate on a few of the truly worthy figures and institutions—among them, Harold Battiste, Al Belletto, James Black, Ellis Marsalis, AFO (All For One) Records, and the American Jazz Quintet—and treat others as spin-offs, incidental data, or not at all. As a result dozens of gifted artists and important sites of development are slighted or omitted.

This approach radically contracts not only the number of players but also the range of modern jazz activity and the musical leadership exercised by other early artists in postwar New Orleans. Regarding range, little is reported in *Cradle* about the work or the culture of early white jazz modernists, other than Belletto's extremely valuable experiences—mainly as a student at LSU in Baton Rouge and with his Biloxi-based sextet. Musical leadership is a highly subjective matter, but it is certainly arguable that Alvin Batiste, Ed Blackwell, Mouse Bonati, Fred Crane, Bill Huntington, Nat Perrilliat, and Mike Serpas were among the most probing musicians in New Orleans or elsewhere in the 1950s. (See the comments about these artists by their contemporaries in the symposium, chapter 26, and the 1961 *Down Beat* articles, chapters 21–22.)

Curiously, the *Cradle* authors quote writer/pianist Rhodes Spedale and pianist/vocalist Jimmy Drew as authoritative voices on pre-1960 jazz. Both are able commentators, but Spedale noted in a 1999 interview that he came to town in 1959, and he stated accurately that Drew arrived during the 1960s. Their comments in *Cradle* seriously misrepresent the early modern jazz culture—citing, for instance, a dominance of "the West Coast influence" on white musicians. Key popularizers like the Belletto sextet on the Gulf Coast and pianists Joe Burton and Ronnie Kole in New Orleans were sometimes subdued in their approach to jazz. But the generalization about West Coast approaches does not apply to white musicians like Joseph (Mouse) Bonati, Bill Huntington, Mike (Black Mike) Lala, Joe (Cheeks) Mandry, John Probst, Mike Serpas, and numerous others who played be-bop or, in some instances, were influenced by the Tristano-Konitz school.

I will try to give a fuller account of the early New Orleans modern jazz scene in five ways. First, this overview will provide a broad discussion of issues and some specific points as well. Events did not lay themselves out in tidy narratives, but I hope to paint a reasonably coherent picture without straining the data. Following a prelude about swing in postwar New Orleans, I will describe in contour some of the clusters of modern jazz players who were active in the late 1940s through the 1960s. Many sites of modern jazz, from jam sessions to strip joints to concerts and club gigs, will be described, as will pertinent activities at local and nearby educational institutions and at venues in the Biloxi, Mississippi, area. Biloxi was a revolving door for many New Orleans modernists and a unique site for the new music in its own right.

Throughout the overview I will deal with themes parallel to those I explored in relation to TNOJ and Dixieland jazz—the struggle for acceptance in the community and for recognition by the Establishment, with attention to musicians who advanced the cause; racial issues pertinent to that struggle; relationships among black and white musicians; and attitudes in the educational community. Occasionally I will embark on brief digressions in order to relate local to national action (e.g., the Beat Generation movement), to deal with anomalies (e.g., the curious Junie Mays band), or to describe the influence of particular figures not treated elsewhere in this book (e.g., clarinetist Alvin Batiste, alto saxist Mouse Bonati, deejay Dick Martin).

Second, timeline chart 3, entitled "Highlights of Early Modern Jazz in New Orleans, 1945–1970 " (page 250) will give a visual depiction of key events.

Third, the articles and reviews from *Down Beat* and *New Orleans* (chapters 21–25) will present contemporaneous views, starting with the 1961 *DB* two-part article "New Jazz in the Cradle," which itself begins with a historical perspective harking back to the previous decade. The 1967 "Problems of Modern Jazz in New Orleans" is a progress report of sorts, written for a local audience. Another *New Orleans* magazine piece, the 1969 "Jazz Off Bourbon Street" article, shows signs of growth in the number and variety of modern jazz groups working in the city. A review of a trio led by pianist/ vocalist Buddy Prima at the groundbreaking Playboy Club in 1964 will bring a further sense of presence in the lively 1960s scene.

Fourth, the transcript of a 1998 gathering of early New Orleans modern jazz artists, "Modern Jazz Pioneers in New Orleans: A Symposium" (chapter 26) is an extraordinary source of information and insight. I organized the panel for the second New Orleans International Music Colloquium, a cooperative project of the University of New Orleans and Loyola University. I set some goals for the symposium but did not ride shotgun on the discussion, preferring a relaxed exchange to a linear Q&A approach that might have bogged down in minutiae. As a result, the discussion ranged freely and included mention of musicians and teachers from numerous contexts over many years. I believe that the perspectives presented in the overview, timeline, and articles provide the basis for a grounded reading of the informal symposium proceedings. Also, the wonderful anecdotes and the respect and affection demonstrated by the participants, even amid occasional disagreements, were as revealing as the who/what/where data that emerged.

Fifth, appendix 2 presents a list of modern jazz musicians who were active in the postwar years to about 1960. Their number—some 125 plus—is in itself a statement about the size of the local modern jazz community in the early years. Of course, many of the musicians are deceased. The list was derived from one-on-one interviews with numerous musicians and fans, the symposium, my own recollections, Harold Battiste's *New Orleans Heritage*, and a few other printed materials.

Lists in isolation are a hieroglyphic of interest mainly to scholars, but the interpretive materials in this section, the articles, and the introduction to appendix 2 give a context for the names. In any case, I include the list for purposes of research and reasons of heart. Some readers will properly read it for accuracy and thoroughness, others for curiosity, and all, I hope, as a tribute. At a practical level, the list serves to identify instruments played by the modern jazz artists mentioned in the text below. When the instruments are omitted from the text, either inadvertently or to avoid repetition, the appendix is helpful.

NOTES ON SWING IN POSTWAR NEW ORLEANS

Bassist Bill Huntington once remarked, "You know, the swing era just about bypassed New Orleans." The comment was an exaggeration, but not by much. Interestingly, the Berry book, *Up From the Cradle of Jazz: New Orleans Music since World War II,* extensively treats the growth of rhythm and blues in postwar New Orleans, makes an attempt at dealing with early modern jazz, and brushes aside traditional and Dixieland jazz. Swing? The word is not even in the index.

The complete omission of swing is unwarranted, but it is mitigated somewhat by the postwar focus of the book. New Orleans musicians who came to national prominence during the swing era—from early transition figures like Barney Bigard and Henry "Red" Allen to later artists like Joe Newman, Benny Powell, and Louis Prima—were absent from or not dominant in the local postwar scene.

Also problematical are squiggly definitions of styles. Which instrumentalists were playing "swing" and which were playing "Dixieland" in New Orleans during the postwar years? Fuzzy genres confound us again if we insist on discrete categories. At the beginning of section II, I noted that the movement from prejazz to jazz was a matter of degree, as was the movement from traditional New Orleans jazz to Dixieland. Yes, Johnny Dodds and Bunk Johnson were TNOJ players, and Sharkey Bonano and Lester Bouchon were Dixielanders, but what about George Brunis and Raymond Burke?

A description of the transition from Dixieland to swing (in terms of individual players rather than ensembles) is also an inexact art. In fact, the earlier movement from TNOJ to Dixieland is describable in terms of the more "swing-like" qualities of tone, rhythm, and instrumental technique of the Dixieland artists. The line between a "Dixieland" solo and a "swing" solo can be very blurry. Again, Bonano and Bouchon were Dixieland jazzmen, and vibist Godfrey Hirsch and drummer Frank Vicari were swing artists, but what about clarinetist Irving Fazola and trumpeter Thomas Jefferson?

Further, New Orleans bands that played swing in the postwar years ranged from excellent to unlistenable. Virtually all thought of themselves as dance bands that played some big band jazz arrangements. As veteran trumpeter Wallace Davenport recalls it, most such bands played commercial music and would "slip jazz in" when they could. In the terms still in use at the time, dance bands played in styles both "sweet" (e.g., Harry James's "You Made Me Love You") and "hot" (e.g., Basie's "One O'Clock Jump"). Many black bands in New Orleans played rhythm and blues as well, and as R&B grew in popularity the white bands also played it. Soloists might be swing musicians like trombonist Benny Powell or fledgling boppers like trumpeter Herb Tassin.

Even acknowledging such complexities, I believe that some swing-oriented big bands, combos, and individual artists of the late 1940s and early 1950s are worth noting. To begin with the most visible group, the Dawn Busters band played weekday mornings on WWL radio for eighteen years (from 1941 to 1959, according to Aiges and McCusker) as part of a unique homespun variety show. It is a bit of stretch to call this competent studio group a swing band, but it came close. The Dawn Busters played decent but undistinguished swing arrangements and backups for pop vocalists like Margie O'Dair and for faux-Cajun songs by reedman Pinky Vidacovich. Their most interesting swing contribution came in the early 1950s. A band within the band, the Jive Five, featured Al Hirt and vibist/drummer Godfrey Hirsch.

Small swing combos were heard frequently on spot gigs and on other live daytime radio shows in postwar years. The latter included trios led by pianist Ogden Lafaye and clarinetists Irving Fazola, Liston Johnson, and Johnny Reininger. Live broadcasts of Dave Bartholomew's band, then playing swing and early R&B charts, were heard on WJBW. There were a few swing-specific deejay shows, notably WJBW's "Jive at 5:05." It opened daily with Roy Eldridge's burning solo on "After You've Gone" with the Gene Krupa band and featured kickers like Tommy Dorsey's "Well, Get It" and Erskine Hawkins's "Tippin' In."

When the musicians in the 1998 modern jazz symposium and other interviewees were asked specifically about local bands that played some good swing arrangements and/or included gifted swing musicians, they fondly recalled groups they had heard of or worked with before or during the postwar years. Lloyd Alexander, Dave Bartholomew, Earl Bostic, Dooky Chase, Sidney Desvigne, Clyde Kerr Sr., Herbert Leary, the Loyola Moods, Fats Pichon, and others were named. By all accounts, the group led by trumpeter Dooky Chase (now owner of a celebrated restaurant) merits particular attention. Chase describes the sixteen-piece group he led from 1944 until 1949 as a "transitional band" from swing to modern jazz, "the most progressive in the South." Clarinetist Alvin Batiste calls Chase's group "the first be-bop big band" in New Orleans.

In Harold Battiste's *New Orleans Heritage*, alto saxist Warren Bell tells of his work as a teenager with the Chase band, praising the group's close attention to ensemble work and fine instrumentalists like trombonist Benny Powell and trumpeters Big Emery Thompson (Umar Uthman Sharif) and Ted Riley. Chase names those players plus Bell, guitarist Curtis Trevigne, and drummer Vernel Fournier as the jazz nucleus of the band and cites trumpeter Clyde Kerr Sr. and pianist John (Pickett) Brunious as the group's forward-looking arrangers.

The group was the house band at the Coliseum Arena, which brought such stars as Billy Eckstine, Dizzy Gillespie, and Earl Hines to New Orleans. Chase tells an interesting anecdote involving a Gillespie concert. The Chase band was playing as the warm-up act when Gillespie ran in, anxious and panting. Hearing Chase's group from a distance, he thought that he was late and his band had started the concert without him. Chase declines to overstate the band's jazz activity, noting that they played for diverse functions and had a varied book. Dance music was a large part of his repertoire, and he brought vocalist Andy Brown (Smith) and reedman Le Roy "Batman" Rankins forward for rhythm and blues tunes.

Other big bands of the postwar years—the Loyola Moods, Lloyd Alexander, Al Hirt's short-lived big band—were highly versatile. The Alexander band began in the late 1930s and continued as an excellent swing/dance band well into the 1960s. But none embodied a transition to modern jazz or boasted so many soloists of the quality of the Dooky Chase band.

And again, there were dozens of dance bands that were interchangeably mediocre. They played stock arrangements of hit parade tunes and transcriptions from recordings of tunes that had by the postwar years become swing classics—"In the Mood," "Eager Beaver," "One O'Clock Jump," and the like. The bands did provide a valuable starting point for young musicians who could read music adequately, but they were no place to hone improvisational skills, nor were they very rewarding to seasoned swing-based players.

Among the first-rate swing artists in the white postwar big bands were trumpeters Woody Guidry and Richard (Bing) Crosby, reedmen Paul Guma, Frank Mannino, and Jack King, trombonist Larry Valentino, vibist/trumpeter/arranger Louis Escobedo, and drummer Frank Vicari. Many were fine improvisers who played splendidly on combo gigs that included popular tunes, good standards, and some Dixieland numbers. They were in great demand as section players in show bands and Lombardo-style society bands. (The latter were also known as Mickey Mouse or simply Mickey bands, and their characteristic buoyant tempo was called "the businessman's bounce.")

But swing musicians rarely participated in far-flung, early morning jam sessions with the emerging modernists. The latter tended to be younger, with fewer World War II veterans among them. Almost certainly, those who were at home during the war years were more in touch with the be-bop movement; and it is reasonable to speculate that those who were not on the battle lines were more prone to seek adventurous musical paths and new life experiences after the war.

The postwar jam sessions will be discussed at length later, but a point relevant to the discussion of swing was brought out in interviews with drummer Lou Timken, bassist Oliver (Stick) Felix, and clarinetist Tony Mitchell, three modernists who were active at jam sessions. Timken, arguably the first white modern jazz drummer in New Orleans, was on the scene before and after his 1950–1952 army service. Felix was similarly active, jamming with white and black artists before and after his 1945–1947 military stint. Mitchell moved to New Orleans from Massachusetts in 1949 and was immediately admired as a pacesetter on clarinet at jam sessions, despite the fact that clarinet was not in vogue in modern jazz. All testify that after the musical drought during the war, Dixieland and TNOJ were dominant in the popular local revival (see section II), and the underground art of the times was modern jazz. Swing was a verb, not a noun.

It is accurate to say that after World War II, New Orleans music was moving in many exciting directions—the Dixieland/TNOJ revival, modern jazz, rhythm and blues—but for the most part the swing era as a creative force had peaked, both nationally and locally. Interestingly, not one of the modern jazz artists I interviewed mentioned swing until I brought it up—this despite the fact that swing was dominant when they were in high school. At an impressionable age, some of their earliest experiences as listeners and as players were with big bands and swing combos. Both Ellis Marsalis and Don Suhor, for example, were keen admirers of Artie Shaw, particularly the Gramercy Five recordings.

I first learned about Al Belletto's early experiences with swing not from Al himself but from the mid-1940s issues of *Basin Street,* the newsletter of the NJF (National Jazz Foundation—a local group, despite its name; see section I). The June 1946 *Basin Street* reported that Belletto, then eighteen years old, led an all-city teenage swing band that took first place in the southern regional *Look* magazine national amateur teenage band contest, cosponsored by the NJF and held at Municipal Auditorium. Belletto adds that the group went to Carnegie Hall in New York for the national competition under the sponsorship of Werlein's Music Store. The New Orleans big band took first place, and the smaller (nine-piece) swing unit ranked third in combo competition. Significantly, Belletto recalls that the victories were largely due to lack of good soloists in the other bands. The top individual instrumentalist award of the competition went to tenor saxist Sam Butera. About eight other New Orleans players, including Belletto on clarinet, were among some twenty-two who won all-American awards as the best performers on their instruments—a tribute to the city's transmission of the value of improvisation.

Earlier, the NJF had sponsored a local high school jazz band contest. The five entrants—from Easton, Fortier, Nicholls, Maumus, and Peters—were Dixieland groups rather than swing bands, according to Oliver (Stick) Felix. The December 1945 *Basin Street* reported that the Peters group won. It included modernists-to-be like Benny Clement on trumpet, Chick Power on clarinet and tenor sax, and Felix, now a bassist, on trombone.

So swing did not bypass New Orleans in its heyday, and it was still visible in after-image during the postwar years. Nevertheless, Huntington's statement has a rule-of-thumb rightness. To transplant Bunk Johnson's phrase, swing never had the city of New Orleans Real Crazy and Running Wild over it.

The chief reason for lack of a vital postwar swing community is clear from the testimony of the then-young musicians. Almost all of them experienced the emergence of modern jazz as an epiphany. They were not disrespectful of their swing seniors, and most continued to work in varied contexts with bands that played swing, rhythm and blues, hit parade favorites, Dixieland, and what have you. But from the mid-1940s to the early 1950s, the music of Charlie Parker, Dizzy Gillespie, Bud Powell, Max Roach, and others effected life-defining changes. The challenge of modern jazz was a thrilling experience that they still speak of with an invigorating joy and wonder.

I believe that a factor deeply embedded in the local jazz culture—the sheer love of improvisation—contributed powerfully to the relatively faint image of swing in the postwar years. In New Orleans the resonance of the early group improvisation of traditional jazz was powerful and enduring. Further, the liberating force of individual solos that was so stunning in the Armstrong Hot Five recordings (only two decades old in 1946) and in many subsequent TNOJ and Dixieland groups was afloat in the jazz culture. While many New Orleans musicians of all generations were competent readers and could play well in a variety of styles, the ability to "fake" melodies and harmonies in ensemble and to "jam" improvised choruses was a highly respected skill.

Moreover, the economic prudence of hiring combos over big bands meant that the city provided a continuing market for spot gigs that called for some fake/jam skills. Even in the early postwar years, when steady employment for jazz players was rare, casual engagements or weekend club gigs found TNOJ, Dixieland, and swing players going through a common repertoire of standards and popular tunes of the day. A comment in Orin Blackstone's *Jazz-finder* in May 1948 reflects this situation: "Jazz is still played in New Orleans, but it takes time and effort—and luck—to find it." Harry Souchon's "History of the New Orleans Jazz Club" article in the May–June 1963 *Second Line* noted that jazz was elusive before the late 1940s revival but could still be heard at "humble cafes and restaurants."

Beginning in 1949, I played drums on weekends at lounges and for dances with numerous fake/jam combos and dance bands that played stock arrangements. The former included a few well-known pioneers like trombonist/bassist Tom Brown and some unheralded second-generation players like guitarists Angie Palmisano and Coco Hymel, alto saxist Joe Helwick, and trumpeter Milton Bauer. Part of the pleasure of fake/jam gigs was due to the fact that jazz had not become overcodefed. In the great New Orleans tradition of the gifted amateur, the players could set their music out to sail without an overcultivated sense of genre or era. Were these musicians playing TNOJ, Dixieland, or swing? Well, Palmisano played electric guitar with an odd Dixieland sensibility, reminding me of George Van Eps with an amplifier. I used brushes all night behind Hymel, who played a hypnotic, bluesy, unamplified guitar through an alcoholic haze. Helwick echoed Trambauer but loved to leap across registers in ways that reminded me of Boyce Brown. Bauer played fiery trumpet somewhere between the cracks of Armstrong and Eldridge.

On dance band gigs I enjoyed learning to kick jazz phrases with the brass section and appreciated section players like Bobby Falcon and Bill Scarlato, who played lead trumpet warmly and with rich interpretive skill. But as Al Belletto points out in the symposium, the soloists in the white dance bands were often painfully inept. This is still the case, of course, in many semi-professional dance bands that play the swing repertoire. And as Wynton Marsalis commented in a 1998 *JazzTimes* interview with Willard Jenkins, helping students in school jazz programs to become good soloists as well as expressive section players remains a key problem in jazz education.

Playing fake/jam engagements was a constant exercise in ear training. Musicians who cut their teeth on such gigs were widely admired and in great demand. The common hyperbolic tribute was, "Man, he knows every tune ever written!" Even the young fake/jam musicians who were not skilled readers were highly respected, with no trace of patronization, by read-only players. Conversely, many improvisers who read music well were not attracted to working with the bland, stock-reading dance bands of the day.

Even after sightreading the challenging book of an excellent group like the Lloyd Alexander Band, a jazz player might remark, "It's a good band, but you don't get much chance to play."

Since this book focuses on postwar jazz in New Orleans, I only touch on possibilities for exploration of swing bands and individual instrumentalists in the earliest years of swing through its heyday—from the late 1920s through World War II. Local bands and artists during the peak years of swing were discussed at the April 9–10, 1999, program of the New Orleans International Music Colloquium. Among the participating musicians were saxophonist Ed Lewis Clements, veteran of the Tulanians; trombonist Waldren "Frog" Joseph, who played with Joe Robichaux's big band; and Frank Vicari, known for his many years with the Lloyd Alexander Band. Driggs and Lewine's pictorial history briefly discusses local swing artists but omits some noteworthy names, such as Lloyd Alexander and Dooky Chase.

To summarize, I have stressed here that swing activity, although diminished, endured somewhat during the postwar years. The swing groups included a small number of solid combos and big bands, but the latter were mostly stock-reading dance bands that ranged from competent to simply awful. I have argued that the traditional love of improvisation in the New Orleans musical culture and the economy of hiring small groups favored eclectic fake/jam combos over big bands. The revival of popular interest in traditional and Dixieland jazz between 1947 and 1953, discussed in section II, also downplayed swing. So did the growing popularity of rhythm and blues—first in the black community, then among white audiences. And for many young musicians, the emergence of be-bop and other modern jazz was transformative, providing expanded models of improvisation that flourished in the underground settings described below.

The emergence of modern jazz in New Orleans will be treated in two segments. First I will describe the early years, from the late 1940s to 1960—a period in which many of the unsung pioneers, as well as a few musicians who have been rightly recognized, were cultivating their art. The second segment, from 1960 to 1970, saw considerable development. Some musicians who survived the early years became more visible, new artists appeared, and modern jazz began to capture a small popular audience.

HOUSE JAMS, STRIP CLUBS, AFTER-HOURS SESSIONS, AND GIGS

I recall a handmade sign at a seedy 1950s weekend after-hours club in the Quarter: "IT'S A GIG." The environment was depressing, the pay was low, and the small audience was composed of a few fans, some aspiring beatniks, and other musicians. The written word does not capture vocal inflections, but you can imagine the derisive tone of Ed Frank's comment, "*Yeah*, man, it's a *gig!"* Even so, Frank and his friends—Ed Blackwell, Chuck Badie, and Nat Perrilliat—came to play, and play they did, quite marvelously.

The fact is that bona fide, steady modern-jazz *gigs* were practically nonexistent. I attempt to get a handle on postwar gigs later in this section. It is essential first to show that most early modern jazz was played for other musicians or smuggled into indifferent or even hostile settings. Playing the new jazz in New Orleans during the late 1940s and 1950s typically meant jamming at somebody's house or at an educational institution (usually furtively), working a strip club, playing an after-hours session where few if any musicians were paid, or having a weekend or spot job that included some jazz but emphasized hit parade or R&B tunes for dancing.

Bear in mind that from about 1947 to 1953, many of the city's traditional New Orleans and Dixieland jazz musicians were making a living and gaining popularity due to the local revival. The display on pages 138–39 depicts the peak year of the revival, 1950, when an astonishing number of Dixieland and traditional New Orleans jazz artists were playing regularly and making records for local and national labels.

Also, recognition was arising for local artists who were developing the music that became known as rhythm and blues. My examination of the *Louisiana Weekly* from 1945 to 1950 shows a jumping R&B scene in the black community, discussed below in relation to some key modern jazz musicians. Berry points to "the flurry of recordings from 1947 to 1952," five years that were "a prelude to rock-and-roll." Paul Gayten, Roy Brown, Fats Domino, Shirley and Lee, Lloyd Price, and others were recorded and became local celebrities, some breaking through to national fame. Even tenor saxist-vocalist Sam Butera, the white bopper-turned-blues/rocker, copped an RCA contract in 1953 and did well with his gritty rendition of "Chicken Scratch." Sam Butera and the Witnesses later became the backup combo for Louis Prima and Keely Smith's hit recordings and frantic and famous Las Vegas act.

The rarity of recordings of the postwar New Orleans modernists, like the unrepresentativeness of recordings of many of the TNOJ and Dixieland artists of the time, is frustrating to listeners who heard the musicians at their best. True, the 1954 Al Belletto Sextet sides for Capitol captured the group doing its excellent vocal and instrumental program, but they were not intended to showcase improvisational flight. A local mid-1950s session organized by WDSU staffer and sometime bass trumpeter Tom Hicks featured Jack Martin's original *New Orleans Suite* composition on one side of a Patio LP. The other side might have been formidable. It featured reedmen Joseph (Mouse) Bonati and Chick Power, trumpeter Benny Clement, pianist Ed Frank, bassist Jimmy Johnson, and drummer Earl Palmer. But the group played unremarkable charts and took disappointingly brief solos.

Bassist Phil Darois recalls a 1956 album for Vik (a subsidiary of RCA Victor) by vocalist Laverne Smith, with liner notes by George C. Simon. It featured standards by the excellent singer and a jazz backup combo that included Darois, guitarist Ernest McLean, trumpeter Wallace Davenport, drummer

Earl Palmer, and others. The album might have been a career launcher, but it did not catch on. Fortunately, AFO has preserved some fine jazz of the decade, releasing two CDs of the American Jazz Quintet, "In the Beginning" (1956) and "Boogie [Ed Blackwell] Live" (1958), to be discussed later. These give a relatively early glimpse of the work of Alvin Batiste, Harold Battiste, Ed Blackwell, Ellis Marsalis, Richard Payne, and others.

In the mid-1950s and beyond, a considerable number of tapes and vinyl discs were made by the city's Dean Benedetti, WTPS deejay/jazz fan/bassist Bill Bise. Unfortunately, Bise dropped out of sight and it is not known whether he still has invaluable examples of players like trumpeter Mike Serpas, tenor saxist Joe (Cheeks) Mandry, and pianist Buddy Prima. I played on at least two informal Bise sessions with those musicians and others. Tom Hicks taped some jam sessions of sets by Benny Clement, Don Suhor, and others at Rizzo's. Possibly these and other underground tapes of early modernists will someday be traced so that a performance legacy can be established.

I do not believe, though, that the absence of recordings negates the argument of this section and appendix 2, that is, that New Orleans was the site of rich and inventive modern jazz artistry in the postwar years. Brian Priestly laments the fact that writers claiming to present jazz history are all too often writing *only* about what was recorded, with the implication that nothing else is worth discussing. Jed Rasula is positively suspicious of "the sonic legend, inscribed in the obstinately material medium of recordings." He calls for broader and more contextualized evidence, noting that "historians are virtually incapable of getting a history of jazz under way without using recordings to provide traction."

In this book I am relying largely on a community of credible testimony — the comments of musicians and listeners who were on the scene sometime between 1945 and 1970. A few written resources are also revealing or corroborative, and the vintage articles and reviews below view the data from yet another point in time. I could wish for more recordings of the modernists, but other kinds of documentation would be needed, in any case, to build a coherent account of the times. Let us turn, then, to an investigation of where the modern pioneers were playing, and who they were.

House Jams

In Antoinette Handy's biography of Ellis Marsalis, the pianist notes that "the jam session, where people used to learn, is no longer a common occurrence or part of the social fabric of young players." Since modern jazz had captivated so many young musicians but had virtually no popular audience in New Orleans during the early postwar years, jam sessions in various settings were essential to the development of the music.

But casual, home-cooked jam sessions are not readily recalled. Undoubtedly many modern jazz house jams that occurred during the postwar years have been forgotten. Others have no survivors to tell of the sites and the fledgling players who felt free to risk stretching out with the new music among friends. Even so, it is clear that jamming at individual musicians' houses was an important early recourse for local modern jazz musicians, as it had been for previous generations of TNOJ and Dixieland players.

In the symposium (chapter 26) Earl Palmer and Al Belletto tell of sessions as early as the mid-1940s at Benny Clement's house in the French Quarter. The visibility of the site of their interracial jams resulted in arrests that amounted to tweaks of harassment in laissez-faire New Orleans. Their stories carry warmth and nostalgia, even humor, today. But they also illustrate the framework of legal oppression in Louisiana that had far more serious consequences: Earl Palmer and Ed Blackwell, the city's two greatest modern drummers, were virtually banished. Both were pressured into leaving town because of relationships with white women. Palmer left for California in 1956 with New York–born Susan Weidenspech, who became his second wife. Blackwell married a white woman, Frances Cobble (the sister of jazz drummer-to-be Earl Cobble) and went to New York in 1959.

Many a rehearsal of a dance combo or rhythm and blues group would end up in a jam session. Also, "woodshedding"—a general term that refers to going into seclusion (i.e., "out to the woodshed") for intensive practice of one or more musical skills—had various jazz realizations. Individuals practiced improvising alone, sometimes with recordings, or worked intensively with friends to develop modern jazz improvisation skills, either at home or surreptitiously in school settings.

Harold Battiste's *New Orleans Heritage* describes how the brilliant Edward Frank enlisted Ellis Marsalis, who began as a saxophonist, in a woodshedding routine at the Xavier school for young musicians around 1947.

> Edward Frank . . . was a very promising young violinist who wanted to play and experiment with the piano and experiment with jazz. He taught Ellis his first three chords, a D-Minor, a D-Flat, and a C-Major. Whereas Ellis didn't really understand what he was playing, he just mimicked what Edward showed him, and he would play those chords over and over while Edward Frank ad-libbed on the right hand. Of course, Ellis didn't know what Edward was doing at the top of the piano, but was enjoying playing those three chords at the bottom end of the piano.

During most of the decade between 1947 and 1957, Don Suhor and I were playing duos almost daily in the living room of our shotgun double house in the Ninth Ward. I played on cardboard boxes, pot covers, and a wooden stool until I got some real drums, and Don was on alto sax, clarinet, and self-taught piano. We started out playing swing standards from the Goodman and Shaw repertoires and Dixieland tunes. As Don's improvisation moved toward modern jazz, influenced mainly by Lee Konitz and Charlie Parker, I followed suit, digging Max Roach, Shelly Manne, and Ed Blackwell.

Don did a woodshedding exercise that stimulated me. He would jam on a blues or a standard like "I Got Rhythm," starting in the key of C and then going up a half step after a drum interlude or full chorus until he had explored the changes at length in every key. Sometimes instead of trading fours on a twelve-bar blues we would trade six-bar solos as an exercise in visualizing different phrase lengths. For reasons I never dared try to discover, our neighbors never complained during a decade of nearly constant record playing and jamming.

Alto saxist Ornette Coleman and trumpeter Melvin Lastie spent many hours in cordial exploratory jazz duets, according to Berry. Lastie was nineteen years old in 1949 when he moved into his Ninth Ward home after they played a gig in Natchez, Mississippi. In 1949 and 1950 Coleman jammed with other young modern jazzmen, finding particularly kindred spirits in clarinetist Alvin Batiste and Ed Blackwell. Tenor saxophonist Edward (Kidd) Jordan recalls sessions at Blackwell's house with trumpeter Billy White in the mid-1950s. All were reaching out toward what became known as avant garde jazz. White went to California; Jordan, to Chicago. Blackwell, of course, joined Coleman's revolutionary combo in 1960. Berry reports later jam sessions at Ed Frank's house in the Magnolia Project with Blackwell, bassist Chuck Badie, and others. After early morning sessions at the Dream Room in the French Quarter, they would go to Frank's house and "put on a pot of beans and sit around and play all day."

Several interviewees in the Battiste volume talk about house jams. Battiste heard Nat Perrilliat playing tenor sax and piano in the mid-1950s at sessions in the homes of trumpeters Johnny Fernandez and Melvin Lastie. Drummer John Boudreaux tells how he and drummer James Black, then playing piano, jammed at Boudreaux's house. Pianist Frank Strazerri told me about sessions at his French Quarter house, not far from Benny Clement's place, with Mouse Bonati when they arrived in town around 1951. In the mid-1950s I jammed with pianist Buddy Prima, trombonist Al Hermann, guitarist Bill Huntington, and others at Buddy's house and Al's garage.

Strip Clubs

In postwar New Orleans, striptease clubs were sites of both employment and after-hours jam sessions for early modernists. Most of the clubs, aptly called strip joints, were a sorry mess. To understand this we must beam back imaginatively to the cultural milieu and physical environment of the late 1940s. In recent years we have grown accustomed to partially or totally nude waitresses and dancers in supposedly sophisticated, even posh, settings for middle-class and wealthy patrons. The contemporary idea that nice folks will frequently stare at bare boobs during a power lunch or that lap dancing is okay as an occasional lark would have been incomprehensible to all but a few safely closeted intellectuals in New Orleans of the 1940s. Yes, a solid citizen might take out-of-town friends to a strip club under the guise of slumming or seeing how the wicked and wretched live. But there was no patina of urbanity or justification by reference to consenting adults or alternative lifestyles.

The settings were typically dingy and the dancing artless. Strippers disrobed while walking arhthymically across the stage, embellishing the stroll with bumps and grinds. B-girls and prostitutes worked the dark, ill-smelling rooms, soliciting watered-down drinks and sometimes "rolling" hapless customers (i.e., robbing them after drugging or clobbering them). Various narcotics were available, and they took their toll on musicians, entertainers, and prostitutes.

Around the turn of the decade a few clubs, led by the Sho'Bar and Prima's 500 Club, aspired to the dubious status of classy exotic dance nitery. On the theory that gauche is a step up from sordid, they featured better-known strippers or those who had a gimmick—Candy Barr, Lily Christine (the Cat Girl), Evangeline (the Oyster Girl—the slimy mollusks would slide seductively down her body), Kalantan, Allouette (who twirled tassels that were affixed to pasties on her nipples), Sally Rand, Blaze Starr (Governor Earl K. Long's mistress), and Stormy, whose success led to a follow-up act, Stormy's Mother. Only in New Orleans: in the squeaky-clean 1950s, the Sho'Bar had a radio show in which comedian/emcee Lenny Gale touted the club's ecdysiasts and vulgarian red-hot-momma Carrie Finnell with the energy and aplomb of today's infomercial hosts. (A David Cuthbert interview of comedian Frankie Ray suggests that the evolution of strip clubs is a source of rich local lore. Ray describes the Latin Quarter of 1949 as "a real den of iniquity" and the Treasure Chest as "the worst _____ house on the street. They had five-minute intermissions to carry out the wounded." He later worked the Casino Royal, and with fellow comic Shecky Greene he opened the Wit's End.)

Not every strip club in the Quarter hired jazz musicians, of course, but among those where modern jazz was played behind dancers or at after-hours sessions were the Gunga Den, Prima's 500 Club, French Opera House, Old Opera House, Puppy House (later called the Sho'Bar), Stormy's Casino Royal (later Dan's Pier 600, then Al Hirt's), Club Slipper (later the Dream Room). Another club, the French Casino, was away from the river on Canal Street between Rampart and Claiborne, near the Texas Lounge jazz club and the Brass Rail, the early rhythm and blues site where Paul Gayten held forth.

For a variety of reasons, modern jazz was acceptable accompaniment behind the dancers and between introductions and chasers for the comics and other postvaudeville acts at the strip clubs. Since there was seldom any attempt to depict the stripping as a species of terpsichorean art, it mattered little what the background music was like as long as the drummer caught the bumps and grinds. Also, there was an aptness of sorts in the very unfamiliarity of the new music. Its heavily accented phrases and "weird" harmonies became part of the decidedly countercultural, borderline verboten ambience. In the absence of musical freedom of any sort in most other venues, many modern jazz artists chose to make a living in the strip clubs.

Jazz-for-strippers has some built-in musical problems, of course. Some dancers and club owners allowed little or no freedom. They wanted to hear the clichés of exotic pit band music—a slurpingly seductive sax, a growling trumpet—as if the customers were actually listening. And as anyone who has ever seen a classic strip show knows, the drummer's role is inherently invasive. The music, whatever the style, is pitted against rim shots, rolls, cymbal crashes, and tom-tom and bass drum thrusts that must be coordinated with the dancer's gyrations, all without losing the basic beat. Percussively, a challenge. Musically, a triple-forte nuisance.

But not a stopper. Amazingly, jazz accompanists were relentless and could often play wonderfully amid the random percussion accents. It appeared to me that they were not so much mentally blocking out the din as visualizing it as an asymmetrical phenomenon that was part of the performance, like the Kafka tale in which the frequent disruption of a ceremony by a leopard was handled by making the leopard a part of the event.

Among the early modern jazz musicians who worked at the strip clubs were Al Belletto, Mouse Bonati, Sam Butera, Benny Clement, Fred Crane, Tony D'Amore, Johnny Elgin, Bill Evans, Don Guidry, Pete Kowchak, Black Mike Lala, Tony Mitchell, Brew Moore, Bruce Lippincott, Joe (Cheeks) Mandry, Joe Morton, Fred Nesbitt, Earl Palmer, Joe Pass, Bill Patey, Chick Power, Pete Monteleone, Mike Serpas, Frank Strazerri, Don Suhor, Bob Teeters, and Louis Timken.

Drummer Timken, born in 1928, was a thorough player in the early bebop years—strong conception, fine left hand and bass drum control, plenty of speed, good reading skills, adept in combo or big band playing. He remembers hearing Mississippian Brew Moore (later one of Woody Herman's celebrated "Four Brothers" saxmen) at the Gunga Den in the late 1940s, with New Jersey–born Joe Pass (known, among other things, for his later recordings with Oscar Peterson) running a bass line on guitar in the lower register to compensate for lack of a string bass.

Pass is cited by Spedale as stating that he stayed in New Orleans for ten months in 1949 to play for strippers. Pass said that after 3 a.m. "we could jam, and that's what kept me here. . . . In 1949 there was as much good jazz and good players happening here as in, say, Chicago; 'cause you could live here relatively cheap and you could play—all night and all day!" Tenor saxophonist Jerry Boquet, who as a leader hired players like Moore and Mandry, recalls integrated jam sessions in 1948–1949, broken up by the police, only to move down the street and start again at another club.

After Hours Sessions; Jazz and R&B Connections

Boquet's comments underline the fact that there were numerous venues other than strip joints where modern jazz jam sessions were held in the postwar years. Most were short-lived. Club owners did not make much money by staying open after 3 a.m., and the musicians union discouraged the essentially free entertainment that jam sessions provided. Pianist Frank Strazerri tells of his unflagging attempts to find places to jam when he and alto man Mouse Bonati came to town. "We would just go into a joint that had a piano and start playing," he said, "but the union would fine us if they caught us."

The after-hours sessions were by far the most free and exploratory sites, despite some grim environments. Bonati became the musical leader of a clique of excellent white musicians active in the French Quarter in the 1950s. (See timeline chart 3.) A small-framed, wiry man with a dark mustache, Bonati came to New Orleans around 1951 from Buffalo, New York, after a stop to play a strip club on the Mississippi Gulf Coast, according to Strazerri. An upstate New Yorker from Rochester, Strazerri met Bonati in Biloxi, where Strazerri was stationed at Keesler Field.

He describes Bonati as his best friend and an extreme introvert. Musically, Bonati was "one of the greats . . . a be-bopper, but very lyrical. He used a plastic reed that gave him a different sound, somewhere between an alto, a soprano, and an English horn—an Indian, nasal sound." Don Suhor, his worshipful protege in the 1950s, agrees that Bonati was a highly original artist in the Parker tradition. "He had his own thing going, his own sound (that didn't record well), his own phrasing—natural, virile, not pretentious or contrived."

Bonati was instinctively antisocial and "oddly conceited," possessing an inner confidence in his unique artistic gifts, Suhor says. Bonati served nine months in Parish Prison after a drug bust around 1955. When his wife Rhoda had a child, he decided to seek steady work. In 1957 he left town as quietly as he arrived. He ultimately followed Strazerri to Las Vegas and the West Coast, where he did pit band work and played other gigs until his death in 1983.

Among the French Quarter jam session sites in the late 1940s and 1950s were Danny's Inferno, Dominic's Jazz Room, Fuzzy's, the Hidden Door, Kilroy's, Mambo Joe's, the Monkey Bar, the Pendulum, the Puppy House, Rizzo's, the Three Deuces, and Wit's End. At some clubs, a few musicians were paid a small amount to assure the basis for players who might come to sit in.

One after-hours session around 1956 produced a memorable anecdote. A dapper, mustachioed man walked in with a tenor sax case during a break and introduced himself as Lester Parker. *Lester Parker? . . . Well, okay.* He had just arrived from New York, he said, and wanted to sit in. His eager edge did not seem quite right for the early morning hour and the undulating cigarette smoke, but the locals welcomed him, Manhattan swagger and all. It was not a hard test—something like "Indiana" at a fast clip—and in fact, Lester was very competent in a Vido Musso sort of way. He took the first solo for about five choruses and was followed by a string of players that included Joe Mandry, Mike Serpas, and Don Suhor. Lester's jaw dropped and his shoulders slumped as he realized that these southern boys were giving a clinic in improvisation. We later learned without surprise that his name was something like Tony Gianfalgo.

The French Quarter clubs of the early postwar years were almost exclusively for white audiences, and white musicians had most of the jobs at strip clubs. Some exceptions are recalled by Richard Payne and Earl Palmer. Payne remembers trumpeter Thomas Jefferson's description of a gig where a black band played for strippers from behind a curtain, invisible to the audience. Palmer's biography (*Backbeat*, a fine book by Tony Scherman) tells of Palmer playing at the Old Opera House with Harold Dejan's band in the late 1940s. Always living on the edge, he had a steamy year-long affair with Stormy, the white stripper who became a local celebrity with wacky publicity stunts. Stormy was also linked, you will recall, with *Item* columnist/jazz entrepreneur John Lester of the National Jazz Foundation in 1947–1948. (See section I.)

Musicians like Fats Pichon, Pickett Brunious, and Lavergne Smith played at music clubs like the Absinthe House, Three Deuces, and Tony Bacino's early on, and black modern jazz and R&B artists later played after-hours jam sessions at the strip clubs. Melvin Lastie played sessions at the Sho'Bar in 1955, Harold Battiste reports—probably the same sessions mentioned by Alvin Batiste, who recalls jamming there after hours as a teenager with Earl Palmer, Ed Frank, Lee Allen, Paul Gayten, and others.

But again, black customers were discouraged or kept out. Journalist Tex Stephens, a social and musical activist who wrote for the *Louisiana Weekly* and other newspapers for decades after World War II, says that he avoided Quarter sites where black musicians were working because of hostile "backdoor" treatment at the clubs. Deejay Dr. Daddy-O (Vernon Winslow) wrote in his August 10, 1950, "Boogie-beat" column in *Louisiana Weekly,* "Since the ofays have restricted the French Quarter to their own tourists, why don't sepia businessmen get together and develop Rampart Street for colored tourists?"

Of course, numerous black clubs outside the French Quarter were well-known as jam session venues. The Dew Drop Inn on La Salle at Washington and the Tiajuana on Sarartoga Street are described in Berry and Broven as the sites of legendary sessions. Tex Stephens recalls that the music at such sessions was "a combination of rhythm and blues and modern jazz," with R&B predominating—although the term "rhythm and blues" was not in use when the music first emerged. (See Berry for the evolution of the terms "race music," "rhythm and blues," and "rock 'n' roll.")

Berry reports that the Tiajuana "almost enshrined rhythm and blues" while the Dew Drop "leaned toward hot jazz," but only in the late hours. Both showbills during regular hours highlighted R&B music and variety shows—comedians, dancers (including strippers at the Tiajuana), female impersonators, novelty skits, and many imported headliners and local acts that later became nationally famous. According to Stephens, a group of musicians informally dubbed themselves the Dawn Patrol beginning in the early 1950s. They would jam all night, moving from one club to another—the Hurricane, Robin Hood, Club Desire, and the Golden Leaf.

Some panelists on the symposium noted that many of the early black rhythm and blues musicians and modern jazz players were the same people, playing in a variety of settings. Rigid dichotomies are ill-advised, perhaps even elitist, as Harold Battiste states. Indeed, outstanding jazzmen like the Lastie brothers, Ernest McLean, Roy Montrell, James Rivers, and Red Tyler are among those who played at the Dew Drop and other R&B venues over the years. I recall 78 rpm records on which alto saxist Earl Bostic would bend his swing-based combo toward the "jump" style of Louis Jordan, R&B, or popular dance music. His solos were heartily eclectic, often using extended harmonies which, according to the Bostic bio in Kernfeld's *New Grove Dictionary of Jazz*, strongly influenced John Coltrane.

But the overlap of early R&B and modern jazz in New Orleans—the musicians, performance venues, and the music itself—should not be overstated. Certainly not all of the early rhythm and blues artists were modernists, or vice versa. Granting Battiste's point about the value of all music that is well played, it is clear that there was differentiation among the evolving musical genres. Further, many musicians who excelled in R&B were not exploratory modern jazz players in the traditions that were being cultivated by Alvin Batiste, Warren Bell, Earl Palmer, Ellis Marsalis, and others. A review of the dozens of early R&B artists advertised or mentioned in the pages of *Louisiana Weekly* in the postwar years shows slight correlation indeed with the black modernists of the time. In short, most of the early black modernists played R&B, but many R&B innovators did not go into modern jazz.

There is abundant evidence that the musicians themselves made distinctions among the kinds of music in which various artists performed and excelled. As noted earlier, Dooky Chase described specializations within his big band of the 1940s, identifying players like Warren Bell and Vernel Fournier as upcoming modernists and LeRoy "Batman" Rankins and Andy Brown as expert rhythm and blues artists. Scherman's biography of Earl Palmer cites the drummer's comment that R&B giant Lee Allen "was a honking tenor player. . . . He played the shit out of the blues; any other tunes, he had trouble with the chords. He didn't have the knowledge of chords to be a first-rate bebop player." Bill Huntington recalls guitarist Roy Montrell's comment about being bored with doubling the R&B bass lines with Fats Domino's band. Broven cites trumpeter Wallace Davenport's statement that in 1948 he had two bands in New Orleans, "one for playing Dixieland and the other [the Be-Bop Jockeys] for playing modern jazz."

Woody Thompson quotes Red Tyler's comment that Ed Blackwell, who was universally admired as a jazzman, "didn't work out" on local R&B recording sessions "because he didn't want to play the backbeat." This view is seconded in Broven's citation of Dr. John's (Mac Rebennack's) comment that Blackwell "was too hip, too jazzy" for the local R&B sessions. And when young Rebennack wanted to learn R&B, he tuned in most intensively to Professor Longhair, Paul Gayten, and others who were trailblazing that music.

Earl Palmer's fascinating *New Orleans Drumming* video reveals that the young black musicians of the postwar years were keenly conscious of the need to provide a danceable music for public consumption, even as many of them were deeply involved in playing the new jazz at house jams and after-hours sessions. Bear in mind that Palmer, who preceded Ed Blackwell as the city's premier modern jazz drummer, has been credited with virtually inventing what came to be known as rock 'n' roll drumming. He explains that the strong snare drum backbeat and adaptations of bass drum marching rhythms were overlaid on the popular Louis Jordan shuffle/jump rhythms. Little Richard and others added a straight eighth-note feeling to the basic rhythm, opening still more possibilities for funky rhythmic propulsion. For slower tunes, the backbeat, a triplet rhythm on the cymbal, and bass drum variations provided an energy that was absent from the bland hit parade ballads of the day.

And that, of course, is just a particle of the story of the evolution of R&B in New Orleans in the 1940s and beyond. (See Broven and Berry for more.) It was a time of tremendous invention in both R&B and jazz, and while the musics that were evolving were complexly interrelated through common cultural and spiritual roots, Palmer's narrative indicates that differing lines of development were under way, and the musicians involved had a technical and commonsense awareness of the differences.

In the mid-1950s I attended an interesting American Jazz Quintet concert that featured a "battle of the drummers" between Ed Blackwell and Fats Domino sideman Cornelius (Tenoo) Coleman. It was clear from the outset that the drummers were mining different musical lodes, albeit from the same rich soil. Blackwell swung lightly but passionately through complex polyrhythmic lines, a brilliant colorist and phrase maker with swift wit embedded in daringly sculpted solos. Coleman was the slasher, juxtaposing thickly accented snare and tom rhythms with familiar Afro-Cuban beats of the day, all of it bristling with prefunk R&B energy that contrasted with Blackwell's Max Roach/Shelly Manne–style of improvisation. The crowd responded more strongly to Coleman, but I could not help feeling that this was a matchup between apples and oranges, and I knew clearly where my tastes lay in the matter.

The distance between the new jazz and other forms even took the form of satire, both nationally and locally. In Battiste's *New Orleans Heritage,* drummer John Boudreaux describes the brilliant modern tenor saxist Nat Perrilliat in a whimsical mood, "running around the floor clowning, imitating those guys like Illinois Jacquet." Earlier, I recall Don Suhor tweaking swing-era clarinetists like Herman and Shaw. He would end a flashy cadenza on a high note, holding what was called the licorice stick in one hand, the bell pointed skyward, the other hand extended in a grandiose gesture of achievement.

The gags were sometimes good-natured, sometimes mean-spirited. The West Coast–based Jimmy Giuffre wrote a raunchy put-on called "Little

Girl" for a 1953 Howard Rumsey's *Lighthouse All-Stars* LP. There was plenty of honking and growling and a heavy backbeat by Shelly Manne (who, ironically, dragged the tempo). Manne was the vocalist on the snide Stan Kenton blues send-up in the mid-1950s. The recording found Manne shouting variations of the old lyric, "I'd rather drink muddy water/ Sleep in a hollow log" while Kenton's band played intentionally out of tune, recalling Charlie Barnet's earlier razzing of traditional jazz on "Darktown Strutters' Ball." I was astonished to hear the popular New Orleans R&B disc jockey Poppa Stoppa taking the record seriously, telling listeners that they shouldn't be put off by the Kenton name because "Jivers [a compliment in those days], *this* Stan Kenton record is *different*."

Lester Young pulled off a more subtle, actually ingenious, satiric variation in his solo on "The Closer," an up-tempo blues that constituted one side of a ten-inch LP recorded at Norman Granz Jazz at the Philharmonic concert. Primarily wide-open jam sessions, the Granz all-star concerts had room not only for thrilling jazz that pushed the boundaries of improvisational art but also for great swing and booted, crowd-pleasing, honking tenors and screaming trumpets that guaranteed immediate, visceral response. To get the audience shouting "*Blow, blow!*" or "*Go, go, go!*" tenor saxists would punch out a simple riff or play a phrase around one accented note for a full chorus or more. On "The Closer," tenor man Flip Phillips began with some routine blues choruses that led to the expected squawking and grandstand hurrahs. When Young came in, he cunningly turned the clichés on their head by leading into honked notes with wildly inventive phrases and bending notes with excruciating beauty within the context of clever riffs.

New Orleans modern jazz artists continued to reflect acute awareness of stylistic differences in the 1960s. Broven notes the Turbinton brothers' distinctions between their jazz efforts and their rhythm and blues and rock work. "Willie is a man of high principle who considers himself more of a jazzman rather than an R&B artist. Earl Turbinton admits: 'I think we were a little impracticable, we had a hit rock record out there but we opened up by playing . . . some jazz tune that we wanted to play, and we went through a whole period of really playing supposedly in a rock setting but playing what we wanted to play, and we felt like we were forced to play the other things because we had to survive.'"

The Beats, Bird, and Drugs

One might expect that New Orleans would have been a fertile ground for the jazz-oriented Beat Generation movement that began in the 1950s. The Beat hipsters are widely viewed as the spiritual foreparents of the hippies of the late 1960s and early 1970s, although Jack Kerouac and some of his fellow nomads disavowed the kinship.

As a student and later a teacher of literature, I admired works like Kerouac's *On the Road* and Allen Ginsberg's *Howl,* so my mind and ears were open to any signs of Beat literary invention, especially jazz and poetry performance. Research by New Orleans poet Dennis Formento, editor of *Mesechabe: The Journal of Surregionalism*, is now uncovering some local bohemian writers of the postwar years, notably Robert Cass and other social activists/artists who became regulars at the Quorum Club coffee house at 611 Esplanade in the 1960s.

But the Beat activity I saw in the late 1950s was thin gruel. In August 1961 I wrote to critic Ralph J. Gleason about the tardy appearance of a Beat culture in New Orleans:

> Coffee houses have popped up in the last couple of years, but haven't altered the tone of the Quarter, which attracted genuine Bohemians long before the Beats moved into town with their Zen, outrage, and self-conscious hipness. They offer poetry readings, folk singing, and . . . combinations like flute and bongos. Few of these have musical interest. Although the coffee houses seem to be holding their own (I seldom make them), their influence outside of the Beat circle appears slight. Big-eyed college kids seem to support them; the general public treats them like curio shops; musicians ignore them. (Believe it or not, I am trying to be objective.)

I was unaware that in 1960 the newly opened Vernon's had featured a jazz and poetry group led by flutist/poet Eluard Burt. Burt recalls that he had been in San Francisco the previous two or three years, hearing numerous black and white jazz artists and poets who were at the forefront of the evolving West Coast culture. At Vernon's, Burt and Marty Most (Maurice Martinez) read poetry and the combo featured Afro-Cuban percussion and jazz stalwarts like bassist Chuck Badie and drummer Smoky Johnson. Burt was later a habitué of the Quorum Club with other poets like Cass, Lee Grue, and James Nolan.

I first heard Most's poems—not "Beat poetry" but a fine personal blending of wit and social protest—at a sophisticated 1963 jazz/poetry performance with Roger Dickerson, Ellis Marsalis, and others. Like Sybil Kein's sensitive collaborations later in the decade, Most's work was well beyond the faux-Beat efforts I heard in white clubs during my casual rounds in the 1950s. I recall hearing one or two dharma-bum wannabees lamely aping poets like Ginsberg, Ferlinghetti, and Corso at jam sessions where the musicians did not take them seriously. With good reason, I thought. It was as if they had read Mailer's "White Negro" essay and set themselves to playing the hipster, an archetype brazenly fashioned in Mailer's heaving imagination. I concluded that New Orleans does food, jazz, architecture, and cemeteries splendidly, but it does not do San Francisco very well.

Only Bruce Lippincott, the poet/tenor saxist known for his work with poets on the West Coast, seemed to authentically represent the Beat movement as codified in the 1950s. Codifications aside, though, one might describe passionate strugglers like alto saxophonist Mouse Bonati and pianist Triggs Morgan (who once said that his improvisation was a form of prayer) as unself-conscious Beats whom Kerouac would have celebrated. Similarly, unrecognized painters, writers, and other seekers who were not labeled Beats had long dwelt in the city's garrets and slave quarters or squatted illegally on the batture—the river side of the levee—at the St. Charles and Carrollton Avenue bend of the river. I met batture dwellers Arthur Jackson and his wife, Glug, through my sister Mary Lou, a journalist. Jackson was a former carnival magician who became a labor union advocate and wrote a liberal column called "Our Stand" for the not-so-liberal local weekly, *Catholic Action.* These people were originals who had discovered what was later called "alternative lifestyles" (a phrase they would have loathed) long before the hip literature of the mid-1950s delineated the way of the Beats.

I would prefer to downplay the drug culture that was part of the modern jazz scene, but drugs were a fact of life (and often of death) among jazz musicians in New Orleans and elsewhere. Heroin, marijuana, and upper/downer pills were not hard to find in the Quarter underground, and drug use was exacerbated by the knowledge of Charlie Parker's addiction to heroin. I suspect that the influence of Bird's bad example has been exaggerated. Certainly it cannot be proved or disproved, and accepting the common lore as tragic-romantic fact is ultimately a form of scapegoating.

It is true, though, that young modernists in New Orleans and elsewhere were stunned by Parker's innovative genius. There is abundant anecdotal evidence that some admirers drew destructive inferences from his use of drugs. Drummer Roy Porter, who was on the tragic 1947 Dial recording session where Parker went to pieces while playing "The Gypsy," says on the *Celebrating Bird* video, "During that time, heroin was the thing. And if Bird got high, all the musicians and fans figured that was the thing to do. That's how much people idolized him. They would do it because Charlie Parker did it."

Alto saxist Mouse Bonati, trumpeter Benny Clement, tenor saxists Don Guidry and Chick Power, bassist Jimmy Johnson, and pianists Triggs Morgan and Red Fredd were among the gifted Quarter habitués who suffered from addiction. Bonati's apartment came to be known as "Mouse's Shooting Gallery," a transparent allusion to shooting up heroin. Among the black modernists, guitarist Sam Mooney, drummer James Black, tenor saxist Nat Perriliat, and others had serious drug problems.

Surely, the oppressive social environment and the conditions under which the young modern jazz musicians worked were more powerful than Charlie Parker's alleged influence. In *New Orleans Heritage*, Harold Battiste is rightfully and eloquently indignant about the death of Nat Perrilliat.

But that was just his physical death, for the real Nat . . . the spiritual soul, the tender, happy and Creative Child . . . the Artist has already been killed. The real Nat was murdered by a social-political structure that has little regard for the Arts. Nat was overpowered by an economic system that reduces artistry and creativity to craftsmanship and then to assembly-line drudgery.

It would cheapen the tragedy of these artists to simplistically label them as conscious Beat Generation figures. But Ginsberg's *Howl* is close to the mark in describing their plight—the best minds of their generation, destroyed, "looking for an angry fix, . . . burning for the ancient heavenly connection to the starry dynamo in the machinery of night."

I was a French Quarter drop-in and a scrupulously straight arrow, which is to say a thoroughly repressed Catholic, which had its own comeuppance later on but shielded me from participation in the drug culture. My greatest fears were for my older brother, Don, who was at the epicenter of the hazardous environment. As it turned out, Don settled in on pills like benzedrine and dexedrine, washed down with a beer or other potable.

At one after-hours session at a Canal Street club in the late 1950s, I got an insight into why Don did not go more deeply into other drugs. We were playing "Strike Up the Band" at a rapid clip, amid pot fumes and the smell of stale beer. Tenor saxist Chick Power was stoned. Usually an effectively laid back, Lester Young–type player, he was beyond cool and well into lugubrious, bordering on comatose. From behind the drums I saw Don step up and play three or four truly strange bars on alto sax. He took the horn from his lips, put it back disgustedly in the case, and sat with the case on his lap for the rest of the session. Later he explained, "I had some marijuana and I thought I was playing tenor sax, so started my solo in the tenor sax key."

A confrontation with an amateur trumpeter who was strung out on heroin almost got violent at one strip club jam session. The skinny, blond-haired junky, eyes underbagged with deep gray circles, asked the trumpeter—I do not recall who it was—if he could sit in. The answer was a polite but transparent brush-off: "Well, this is a union group and you need to be in the union. Do you have a union card?" The yellow face turned red and a double-forte response came, "No, man, I don't, but I have a UNION *GUN*. Do you want me to go home and GET MY UNION *GUN*?" The consensus was, he should sit in and call up the next tune.

Modern Jazz Gigs

While strip clubs and jam sessions were genuine sites for early modern jazz in New Orleans, bona fide modern jazz gigs—where the audience came primarily to listen to the music rather than dance, see a show, or find a partner of the opposite, same, or ambiguous sex—were infrequent in the late 1940s and 1950s. Most of the engagements described below, then, involved jazz that was reined in by commercial considerations. Even so, modernists welcomed a chance to play gigs that went beyond ordinary popular music fare.

Unfettered modern jazz that involved remuneration, however slight, was heard mainly at the handful of concerts, weekend jobs, and a few paid after-hours sessions. Various musicians and *Louisiana Weekly* cite concerts by black artists at the Labor Union Hall, YWCA, and Booker T. Washington High School, often sponsored by the musicians and promoters like Clinton

Scott and Tex Stephens. In the mid and late 1950s, concerts by the American Jazz Quintet (AJQ) were heard at Hayes' Chicken Shack, Lincoln Beach, and elsewhere.

I have already mentioned the American Jazz Quintet and its members in several contexts, but their excellence warrants further comment here. To my knowledge the AJQ never played a full-time gig, but it was the city's best modern jazz group of the 1950s. The band that I heard several times included Nat Perrilliat on tenor sax, Alvin Batiste on clarinet, Ed Frank on piano, Chuck Badie on bass, and Ed Blackwell on drums. Other musicians who played with the AJQ were the group's founder, Harold Battiste, tenor sax; Ellis Marsalis, piano; Richard Payne, Otis Deverney, and William Swanson, bass; and James Black, drums. Like the Ellis Marsalis Quartet and the short-lived Fred Crane Trio in the next decade, they were unafraid of experimentation on the cutting edge of jazz, and capable of pulling off mind-bending explorations.

Two CDs by the American Jazz Quintet on AFO label, *In the Beginning* (AFO CD 91-1028, mostly from a Cosimo's Recording Studio session in 1956) and *Boogie* [Ed Blackwell's nickname]—*Live, 1958* (AFO CD 92-1228) do not show the group in peak form, but they are indispensable disks. Most of the charts are interesting originals by Harold Battiste or Alvin Batiste, with a lovely ballad contribution, "Toni," by Ellis Marsalis. Batiste's "Three Musketeers" is one of my favorites, a blues followed by sixteen bars that seem to flow naturally from the twelve-bar structure, holding the listener's attention all the way as the soloists explore twenty-eight-bar choruses with skill and daring.

Most of the players sound like themselves rather than clones of then-current innovators. In discussing the music, though, I will use other artists as points of reference—not an easy task in describing the two most distinctive voices, Alvin Batiste and Ed Blackwell. Batiste does not sound like Buddy DeFranco, the premier modern clarinetist of the time. On the 1956 session he reminds me of an update of traditionalist Tony Parenti, crossed with Swedish modern jazzman Arne Domnerus. On the 1958 session Alvin Batiste is Alvin Batiste, moving more fluently and confidently through the set. His work on the Marsalis ballad, played on both CDs, is a splendid tour de force.

The AJQ's ensemble work in the earlier session is slightly stiff but far more precise than on the live concert. Harold Battiste projects both a cool and boppishly hot feeling on tenor, self-assured and firmly Rollins-like. On both disks Ellis Marsalis is in the Bud Powell school, showing tinges of Horace Silver as well, emulating rather than plagiarizing. His solo work is strong though underrecorded throughout the live program at B. T. Washington Auditorium, where the piano was not in tune. Marsalis's comping is a delight. He even lays down occasional chords as place markers behind Blackwell's complex solos. His solo on "You Don't Know What Love Is" provides the high point of the studio session.

Blackwell is constantly inventive. He takes charge and takes chances at the 1958 concert, always thinking and listening as he stretches out. His work in the rhythm section is both contrapuntal and complementary. He often plays busy tom-tom/bass drum lines that should not come off behind a soloist—but they do. At this point in his career his own solo work owed much to Max Roach and perhaps Shelly Manne—in my view, the only two comparable drum soloists of the day. But again, his ideas have a personal cast, and he gets a highly African sound from his drums. (See chapter 22 for more about Blackwell.)

Nat Perrilliat shows early signs of his great Coltrane-based style, although the 1958 concert preceded the landmark Coltrane quartet of 1960. Rollins and early Coltrane are evident influences as Perrilliat moves through multiple choruses on several tunes. (Everyone gets to play at the concert; four of the six tracks go nine minutes or longer.) On "Fourth Month," a fine Alvin Batiste chart based on "I Remember April," only Perrilliat, Marsalis, and Blackwell seem comfortable with the breakneck tempo. Perrilliat is propelled through stunning chorus after chorus on this track, and he is a joy to hear on the rest of the CD, rough-edged as it is.

To return to jazz gigs in the 1950s, a few sites in the French Quarter provided genuine space for young improvisers, such as weekend sessions at Dominic's Jazz Room and after-hours gigs at Rizzo's. Most often, though, modernists working at relatively hip commercial venues or playing spot jobs around town would hold back, trying to mix jazz and popular music without angering the management or losing the audience. For example, early in the decade John (Pickett) Brunious had a trio at the Three Deuces in that was strongly bent toward jazz, according to drummer Lou Timken.

To get a fuller picture of the various kinds of remunerative modern jazz gigs before 1960—again, beyond strip clubs and unpaid jam sessions—I will do a brief survey of weekend club work, spot jobs, and full-time gigs.

Weekend Club Gigs

Between 1945 and 1960, weekend club gigs where modern jazz was featured were generally short-lived, with changes in personnel and unpredictable audience response affecting the musicians' latitude in choosing the kinds of music they would play. A complete accounting of the amorphous world of come-and-go clubs and bands would scarcely be possible and would certainly be uninteresting. Bands led by Gerry Boquet played hip materials for dancers at the Midway in Algiers and the St. Regis on Airline Highway, with sidemen like Mike Serpas, Joe (Cheeks) Mandry, and Brew Moore. Nelson's in Algiers featured pianist Jack Hebert and others playing jazz and cocktail music. Pianists Theresa Kelly and Lee Burton worked with small groups at the Swamp Room on Canal Street and Ched's on Mirabeau, respectively. Neither played adventurous piano, but their striking beauty and meltdown jazz vocals had great appeal to musicians and hip audiences.

In *New Orleans Heritage* Battiste notes that alto saxist Warren Bell and others played with few restraints at the Caravan off Freret Street. Ed Blackwell and other AJQ musicians worked at Foster's Green Room and the Gypsy Tea Room. At Melvin Lastie's High Hat Club, the trumpeter's show band included irrepressibles like Nat Perrilliat and Johnny Fernandez, not to mention Lastie himself.

Pianist Buddy Prima led a weekend group for about nine months beginning in September 1957 at Prima's Fountain Lounge. I believe that the gig and Prima himself are in some ways a window on the early tug-of-war between modern jazz and entertainment, so I will tell the story. Buddy's father, trumpeter Leon Prima, remodeled a small house at the corner of Harrison Avenue and Milne Street—a mainly residential area close to Canal Boulevard. Because Leon owned Prima's 500 Club, the well-known French Quarter strip club, there was understandable concern at first about what the new club was to be. A neighbor complained that it would "bring Bourbon Street into our backyard." In fact, Leon opened the club mainly for the purpose of providing a venue for his son.

Buddy Prima was the emcee, pianist, vocalist, and trumpeter. Bill Huntington played guitar, Clinton Montz was on bass, and I was the drummer. Still in his teens, Prima was a fine modern pianist and witty vocalist with an engaging on-mike manner. His teddy-bear appearance and easy humor did not disguise a keen, inquiring intellect. The quartet attracted jazz fans and musicians like trumpeter Herb Tassin, tenor saxist/historian Hank Kmen, and drummer Randy Baunton, who loved sitting in with the group. We cut a few radio shows for WWL in 1957 and 1958.

The music was mostly danceable, but the tiny dance floor was not inviting. The group shunned requests for hit parade tunes, favoring standards and Prima's original material. But we would rev up two-beat backgrounds when Leon sat in with his solid Dixieland trumpet or when his wife, Madeline, Buddy's stepmother, came on stage to belt out Sophie Tucker songs. All good music, but it played strangely in the mellow jazz lounge environment, and the gig ended in May 1958.

Buddy was conflicted by his immense gifts for jazz and composition and his daunting show-biz heritage. His uncle Louis—the swing trumpeter star of the 1930s, composer of the Goodman classic "Sing, Sing, Sing," and popular novelty vocalist/big band leader in the 1940s—was at the top of the pop charts in the 1950s. The Louis Prima/Keely Smith duets and a frenetic backup band led by Sam Butera were wildly popular. So Buddy was pulled toward the Las Vegas get-it-on mentality even as he cultivated his talents in jazz and contemporary classical composition.

Prima was simply born too soon. If he were starting out today as a young Orleanian, his jazz lineage and varied talents would surely be tremendous assets, not obstacles. Given the national mania for the city's music, he would be on a fast track to stardom as a versatile, jazz-based artist with impeccable cultural and musical credentials. This is not to say that he threw in his hand and became an aluminum siding salesman. Prima graduated from Loyola and went on to study composition at UCLA. Then he returned to New Orleans, where he played for a while at the Playboy Club and elsewhere in the 1960s (see the *Down Beat* review, chapter 25). He also worked as a composer and arranger in New York, California, and Las Vegas for several years. Later he chose a reclusive life, making infrequent contact with local musicians.

Spot Jobs

Besides weekend club dates with different kinds of bands, many New Orleans musicians moved freely in and out of spot jobs, including dances, weddings, parties, picnics, and concerts. These one-shot engagements were sometimes with organized bands, large or small, other times with makeup bands consisting of players who knew the same basic repertoire of tunes.

It was common for young modernists to be chastised or even fired for venturing into more complex harmonies and rhythms. A classic story in national jazz lore, reported in Shapiro and Hentoff, concerns Dizzy Gillespie's work with Cab Calloway at the Cotton Club in Harlem in the early 1940s. Calloway was constantly vexed by Gillespie's personal antics and musical experimentation. After an adventurous solo that involved harmonic collusion with bassist Milt Hinton and guitarist Danny Barker, Calloway said, "Whoever is doing that, the so-and-so should stop it." Pointing to Dizzy, he added, "And you, I don't want any of that Chinese music in my band."

Similar scenes were played out in New Orleans. For example, Earl Palmer was drumming with Dave Bartholomew beginning in March 1947. In Scherman's biography, Palmer says, "Dave kept that band commercial. He didn't want no be-bop rhythm section. . . . People were dancing out there. . . . I'd sneak in a bomb and Dave would flash me a dirty look and say, 'Uh-uh, chief.' I knew I was doing wrong, but I was bending him." Some leaders were not perceptive enough to know the difference. Bassist Red Schroeder, leader of a novelty dance combo in the 1950s, would say, "Man, that bop is nowhere! Nobody in town can play that shit!" His trumpeter, Gerry St. Amand, was threading bop into his solos at every opportunity.

In my experience the hardest taskmasters were leaders who were enamored of swing. In Dixieland-based combos led by Dutch Andrus, Chuck Credo, Armand Hug, Blue Prestopnik, and others, the leaders did not object to bass drum bombs and left hand interplay as long as the rhythm section was generating good jazz energy. But swing-oriented leaders like Paul Guma, Irwin Knight, and Frankie Mann did not see drummers as potential colorists. They tended to want a 4/4 bass drum and predictable backup kicks phrased with the ensemble.

Of course, freedom has its downside. On one spot job around 1950, a combo of young modernists was turning the gig into a jam session, leaving the audience bewildered. Accordionist/vibist Joe Tarantino, himself often an instigator, saw what was happening and tried to bring us back to earth. He called up "Stardust" and asked trumpeter Bruce Ahrens to start with Billy Butterfield's universally known three-note pickup and first chorus (from the Artie Shaw recording). His back to the audience, Bruce obliged—with the three notes—then left no trace of melody as he jammed boppishly to the end.

Full-Time Gigs

Curiously, the first documented six-night-a-week modern jazz gig in New Orleans, discovered at the Tulane Jazz Archive by Charles Chamberlain, was an anomaly. Anomaly, at best. The April 1947 issue of *Metronome*, then a competitor with *Down Beat* for leading national jazz journal, carried an article-length review by Chet Lane titled "Mays Is Amazin'!" A traveling group led by pianist Junie Mays was playing at the Prevue Lounge on Carondelet and Canal Street. The group was not nationally known, but the premise of the review, stated in the subhead, had considerable glitter value: "Junie's little band leads the way in New Orleans, and there's nary a trace of dixieland in it."

Lane combines a put-down of New Orleans musicians and music with rave commentary on the Mays band and left-handed compliments for bebop (then often called "re-bop"). He writes of "the shameful dearth of jazz musicians around the city" and says that "the one shining light in this otherwise dark picture has been provided, ironically enough, by six musicians who neither hail from the Crescent City nor have anything in common with the archaic jazz bearing the 'New Orleans' label, still lionized by so many jazz reactionaries." Ironically, indeed. The Mays band itself would have been unknown but for Lane's *Metronome* article. Members of the combo, all pictured in mug shot, were Mays, a former sideman in Al Donahue's dance band, piano; Ralph (Red) Clemson, trumpet; Jimmy James, tenor sax; Gil Stancourt, trombone; Frank Marcy, bass; and Larry Callahan, drums.

Lane's review is an epidemic of superlatives and fuzzy comparisons. He predicts "an important role in the future of American jazz" for Mays's brand of music. The group's sound as a whole is compared to Eddie Heywood's swing combo, but its style is "based principally on the re-bop school of thought," although they "sift out the bad elements of the modern style." Trumpeter Clemson's versatile solos make him "another Billy Butterfield," yet "at various times he sounds like James, Elman, and Eldridge" and "he is probably best suited to the Dizzy style." Drummer Callahan "could give many of the 52nd Street's re-bop drummers some needed lessons."

Of course, Mays and his sidemen did not become jazz giants, and their Prevue Lounge stint did not register in the memory of any local musicians I spoke to. But there is no reason to believe that the group was not extremely able. Jazz fan Art Scully recalls hearing Mays's band and finding it impressive. Scully notes that when trumpeter Clemson was out for awhile, Al Hirt subbed with the band. Unfortunately, Hirt died before I could interview him about the engagement.

Lane's antipathy toward "reactionary" jazz styles is off-putting, but remember that the context is the Dixieland versus be-bop war that was rampant in the jazz press at the time. Certainly, Lane was in line with *Metronome*'s editorial stance. Former editor Barry Ulanov recalls finding the angle of the article appealing and consistent with the magazine's championing of modern jazz and new artists.

Lane's blanket dismissal of New Orleans musicians was inaccurate but understandable. An article published in April 1947 was probably written in late 1946, just as the postwar musical cultures were beginning to find their form. As noted earlier, even traditional and Dixieland jazz groups were heard infrequently and at offbeat sites before the 1947–1953 revival in New Orleans. Only a diligent seeker would find preswing artists. Lane (who was from all appearances a visitor, although I could not confirm this) was clearly not interested in early jazz and was unaware of the city's nascent modern jazz.

If Lane had explored the French Quarter and linked up with the black community, he would have discovered "re-bop" at strip clubs, house jams, or after-hours sessions. Of course, this would have run counter to the article's assumption that only a carpetbagger combo could be playing modern jazz in New Orleans. But it would have broken immensely valuable ground by demonstrating at an early date that a local modern jazz culture was evolving in the city. As it stands, the *Metronome* paean to the Junie Mays combo is an interesting mutation in the slim reportage of postwar modern jazz in New Orleans.

One of the city's most memorable early modern groups was a quintet formed by Earl Williams in the early 1950s. They became a staple at the Texas Lounge on Canal Street but Williams also worked over the years at Club Slipper, Natal's, the Safari Room, and the Sho'Bar. The personnel were Williams, leader/vocals/bass; Alvin (Red) Tyler, tenor sax; Sam Mooney, guitar; Ed Frank, piano; and Earl Palmer, drums. Palmer has often called the Texas Lounge the best gig in town, while acknowledging its drawbacks. In Scherman's book the drummer explains, "Three of us in the group were the best [modern] jazz players in New Orleans at the time: Edward Frank, Red, and me. Sam Mooney never became well known, but he was a good guitar player. Ellis Marsalis used to sub for Frank and sometimes for Tyler; sometimes he'd even pick up Earl's bass. We welcomed that, because Earl couldn't play. We used to cheer every time he hit a note that was actually in the chord. . . . Earl had never gone near a bass, he just didn't want to hire a bass player."

I was about sixteen years old when I first heard the group—there was virtually no age checking at New Orleans bars in those days—and it was a thrilling experience. I had started listening to modern jazz records but had never heard it played live with such skill, drive, and intensity. The images are still vivid in my mind. Ed Frank hunched over the piano, his impaired left hand comping-pecking away while the right hand sang out lyrically. Williams, perspiring, pulling at the bass strings as if he knew exactly what he was doing, shouting "work, work, work!" behind the soloists, who grinned in half-annoyance at the intrusion. Palmer laying down left-hand/bass drum bop interplay and trading fours that seemed hopelessly abstract until I learned to "read" be-bop drumming.

In the late 1950s Joe Burton came to town. Burton was a pianist from New York with an attitude and a determination not only to play modern jazz in New Orleans but also to win a popular audience and dominate the local jazz scene. He started out in a small club on Royal Street around 1958, and within a year he opened his own club on Canal Street and Jefferson Davis Parkway—away from the tourists' path but accessible to the sophisticated clientele he was hoping to attract. He was not a musical trailblazer but he was the first in town to court (and win) a sizable white audience for modern jazz. Burton built then lost his following, but his odd story plays out in the sixties. At this point I will simply note his appearance as a datum and a prefiguring of the decade of inroads.

EDUCATIONAL INSTITUTIONS AND NEARBY SITES

While Bonati, Mandry, and others among the postwar modernists were decidedly bohemian in lifestyle, many of the early players were enrolled in local and nearby colleges and universities or were studying at Grunewald's School of Music. In this section I will give an overview of activities at key educational institutions in and near New Orleans. The discussion of LSU and Southern University in Baton Rouge and Southeastern College (now Southeastern University) in Hammond will segue into a treatment of jazz in the hottest nearby site of them all—Biloxi, Mississippi, and the Gulf Coast area.

Not surprisingly, no local university formally embraced jazz of any kind in the postwar period. Students who played modern jazz considered themselves fortunate if individual faculty members respected their efforts or if the administration winked at their attempts to jam on campus. Always a minority, the modernists were tenacious, even relentless, in their pursuit of minimal recognition and a place to play.

One of the most influential postwar schools was a private institution that was not connected to a university but to a music store. Grunewald's School of Music at 829 Camp Street in downtown New Orleans was not taken seriously by the higher education leaders. But it attracted many GIs and other aspiring musicians with its expert teachers on individual instruments, instruction in theory, arranging, and other areas, and tight sense of community for musicians with varied interests. A *Louisiana Weekly* advertisement on August 6, 1949, headed "Why Grunewald's?" described it as "the only school where an entire curriculum is devoted to music in the modern idiom. . . . Every member of the faculty is an approved instructor as well as a successful professional in his own right."

Just about everyone from the postwar era remembers Grunewald's as a gathering place for dedicated young musicians. Among those who studied there—the black students upstairs, the white students downstairs—were Chuck Badie, Warren Bell, Al Belletto, Fred Crane, Earl Palmer, Richard Payne, and Red Tyler. Quentin Baptiste and Jack Martin taught composition and arranging, the former incorporating the then-innovative Schillinger system into his instruction. Numerous musicians speak of the camaraderie of the black and white musicians at Grunewald's, despite formal segregation. Some recall jazz sessions at the school. Lou Timken states that drumming great "Papa" Joe Jones was passing through town and played an impromptu jam session with pianist Fred Crane.

Turning to the universities, Xavier is discussed at length in the symposium (chapter 26). The climate there went from fair in bassist Richard Payne's years to very chilly indeed during Germaine Bazzle's time. Like Loyola, Xavier took particular pride in its voice department. Unlike Loyola, Xavier did not try to suppress jazz, at least in the early postwar years. Elaborating on his symposium comments, Payne says that between 1949 and 1952 "the nuns and priests and others at Xavier encouraged us to play music in African-American traditions." Gospel music was valued in its authentic form and not in the bland renditions popular at the time. Band director Solomon Spencer, himself a multi-instrumentalist, had a broad vision that embraced jazz as well as classical music. Payne laments the changes that came in later years, when music at Xavier was neglected in favor of the sciences and pharmacy.

Among the Xavier players cited by Payne in the late 1940s and the 1950s (not all of them modernists) are trumpeter Joe Phillips; reedmen Lee Allen, Percy Humphrey Jr., Carey Levine, and Plas Johnson; and trumpeter/saxist/keyboardist Raymond Collins. Bazzle adds trumpeter John Fernandez, tenor saxist Bill Fisher, and drummer Al Fielder. It was Fernandez, a tenor man (Fisher, Bazzle speculates), and a pianist from Xavier who joined me, bassist Louis Pendarvis, and vocalist Theresa Kelly at a Xavier/Loyola/Dominican College interracial program at Jesuit High School Auditorium in 1955. The event was technically illegal, but it went off without a hitch.

The symposium touches lightly on Dillard University. Rightly, in one sense, because modern jazz was very limited there. Wrongly, in another, because two Dillard students—Harold Battiste and Ellis Marsalis—had a profound influence on the course of modern jazz history in New Orleans in the postwar years and beyond. Marsalis recalls that "there was no jazz clique," no pesky jam sessions for the faculty to squelch, because there simply were not many students who were interested in jazz. Dallas-born pianist Cedar Walton was at Dillard for a while, and band director C. Melville Bryant informally encouraged both Battiste's jazz development and the formation of a student dance band. Roger Dickerson, now a broad-gauged composer and performer, was mainly interested in classical music during his student days at Dillard, and pianist-vocalist Laverne Smith was a blossoming talent. The remarkable point is that a private university with small enrollment and no formal commitment to jazz was the place from which two major figures emerged.

Certainly, the symposium does not adequately describe Harold Battiste's seminal, long-range influence. In his senior year, 1952, he met Marsalis, whose quartet would become one of the most exciting local groups of the 1960s. Battiste was also founder of the American Jazz Quintet. As will be noted later, in the 1960s he organized AFO (All For One) Records, a cooperative composed of versatile black musicians who made now-classic R&B sides and some jazz recordings as well.

Battiste was in California in 1956 and from 1963 to 1989. During the latter period he was on a fast-track career in Hollywood. Among other jobs, he was musical director for superstars Sonny and Cher. Always mindful of talented unsung musicians of New Orleans, in 1967 he wrote *New Orleans Heritage—Jazz: 1956–1966*, a collection of brief biographical sketches of twelve artists, most of them stalwarts of both jazz and R&B in the city. His role as historian continued today as he taught jazz history in the University of New Orleans Jazz Studies program.

A fairly detailed picture of the restless dynamic at Loyola University is given in section I ("The Stage Band Movement at Loyola," chapter 7). There was a mixture of World War II veterans, most of them solid swing-era players who formed the nucleus of the Loyola Moods, and a cadre of passionate younger modernists. While the former were regarded with extreme ambivalence by the conservative administration, the latter were branded as confounded subversives. Gallingly, they would hold impromptu jam sessions (sometimes joined by nonstudents) in the practice rooms of the music school basement.

Among the students and drop-ins at these sessions were trumpeters Jerry St. Amand and Black Mike Lala; reedmen Al Belletto, Charlie (Chicken) May, and Don Suhor; bassists Herbie Hollman, Jimmy Laborde, Bobby Morgan, and Lou Pendarvis; pianists Fred Crane, Dave West, Theresa Kelly, and F. A. Cassanova; and drummers Lou Timken and me. By my sophomore year (1953–1954) most of the fluent improvisers were gone, leaving the big band (called Campus Capers), a pale descendant of the postwar Moods.

In the late 1950s students like Buddy Prima, Charlie Blancq, and Joe Hebert arrived to give new energy to the school. A fine alumni-based rehearsal band was organized by then up-and-coming composer/arranger/pianist Bert Braud and tenor saxist/arranger John Celestin in 1961. As things loosened up administratively, students-turned-faculty like Hebert and Braud and new faces like drummer Johnny Vidacovich (my student at Campo's Music Store during his high school years) and pianist/vocalist Angelle Trosclair continued the jazz tradition at Loyola.

The action next door at Tulane was nil. True, Tulane was the first local university to take traditional New Orleans jazz seriously when it established the Jazz Archive in 1958. (See section I.) But *jazz performance in the curriculum* or as an *endorsed* cocurricular program at the aspiring Harvard of the South? Cripes, no. Tulane's honoring of jazz as history did not translate to teaching the art and craft of the music.

Some local fans remember an active big band called the Tulanians. Ed Lewis Clements, who played tenor sax with the band both before and after World War II, describes the group as a good fourteen-piece dance band that had no official connection with the university and included students and nonstudents. Bassist/leader Ike Greer occasionally hired jazz-oriented players (e.g., a teenaged Sam Butera, drummer Lou Dillon) but the Tulanians' book was composed of stock arrangements, swing classics, and a number of specials from the Hal Kemp band's sweet-and-hot swing book.

Trumpeter Richard (Bing) Crosby, a Loyola student from 1946 to 1950, began teaching at Tulane in 1951. There was no music school, he notes. Music students in the School of Fine Arts were served by a small music faculty and played in the concert band. "John Morrisey's concert band was the big thing," Crosby recalls. Composer/conductor Morrisey had built an extremely popular band that specialized in clean rendering of pops-concert fare. Each year a new Morrisey work—always engaging, unpretentious, and lightweight—was featured.

Louis Berndt, a Tulane reed player in the early and mid-1950s, remembers a few outstanding individual student improvisers like trumpeter Bill Pruyn and also saxist/arranger/teacher Don Lasday (who could somehow meld Benny Carter and Lee Konitz in imaginative solos). But he agrees that no continuing thread of big band or modern jazz activity was to be found on campus. Crosby tells of faculty trombonist Ted Demuth's unsuccessful attempt at starting an informal lab band. He concludes, "There was no real jazz feeling about the place at all."

Some nearby university towns—notably, Baton Rouge and Hammond—had many young modern jazz players, students and nonstudents. A long and solid tradition of modern jazz began at LSU after World War II. Some of the best of the early white Baton Rouge modernists—pianist/vocalist Mose Allison, trombonist Carl Fontana, trumpeter/leader Lee Fortier, and underrated drummer Paul Logos—were rarely on the New Orleans scene, but they formed a jazz culture of their own. New Orleans reedman Phil Hermann, older brother of trombonist Al Hermann, was an LSU undergraduate from 1949–1952. He tells of what was probably the first full-time modern jazz job in the area—a gig he played around 1950 at a Baton Rouge restaurant/gambling club named La Louisiane. The combo included Fortier, Fontana, Logos, bassist Richard Alexis, and others. Along with Orleanians like Al Belletto, who went to LSU in 1951 for graduate work after finishing Loyola, trumpeter Benny Clement, and tenor saxist Chick Power, they set a high standard for jazz excellence at the university.

The mammoth Louisiana State University is about eighty miles north of New Orleans. Unlike Loyola, LSU had no bourgeois anxieties about being identified with Storyville's brothel music. As Belletto notes in the symposium, the LSU administration simply looked the other way instead of bearing down on the modernists. Hermann says that Lee Fortier started a big band that was benignly ignored by the faculty. A highly indicative anecdote is told by Belletto in Berry's book. At his performance audition for the master's program at LSU, a professor said, "Boy you play with such spirit. I don't believe it. You play like a whore!"

In the mid and late 1950s a new wave of gifted jazz players was at LSU. Drummer Reed Vaughan, pianist/trombonist Larry Muhoberac, trumpeter Vinney Trauth, bassist Bobby Alexis (Richard's brother)—all Orleanians—and pianist Rusty Mayne and alto saxist Eddie Hubbard were among them. By then, Lee Fortier's big band was by all reports hipper than any in New Orleans. Mayne, who later became a regular in New Orleans as a Red Garland–style pianist, told how Fortier would loosen up the group by kicking off the tempo and letting the rhythm section lock in for an opening chorus or two. "Rev up the *machine!*" Fortier would say, bringing the powerhouse band in on the propulsion created by Mayne and his cohorts.

Clarinetist Alvin Batiste was a student at Southern University in Baton Rouge from 1951 to 1955. He and tenor saxist Edward (Kidd) Jordan recall that jamming was frowned upon by the administration. Things loosened up under band director T. Leroy Davis, Batiste says, but not until the late 1960s did jazz become accepted as part of the curriculum—a timeline similar to that of Loyola. As with the unauthorized Tulanians, a band called the Southern University Collegians played for popular audiences, the Southern group emphasizing rhythm and blues.

Batiste tells of many capable black jazz players at Southern and in the Baton Rouge area over the years. Kidd Jordan, trumpeter Big Emery Thompson (Umar Sharif), and alto saxist Earl Turbinton are among the best known. None, though, is more distinguished that Batiste himself. When I heard him in live performances with the American Jazz Quintet in the 1950s, he was one of the most distinctive clarinetists in jazz. Eschewing hard-edged phrases imitative of jazz saxophonists, he played thoughtful, original lines with a lovely tone. Fluid and cool, he was a marvelous foil for tenor man Nat Perrilliat, who was cultivating a Coltrane-based style. And he both complemented and contrasted with the rhythm section. Chuck Badie kept a firmly swinging pulse on bass. Ed Frank and Ed Blackwell played heavily accented backgrounds, but their asymmetrical comping was projected with relaxation, sometimes reaching resolution over several bars of complex interplay.

I regret that I never heard Umar Sharif. He is virtually a legend among local musicians. If he had been white, he might well have attracted attention and won the fame that Al Hirt gained. Sharif is described as a powerful, versatile trumpeter with great technique and range. He could improvise beautifully or lead a section in a big band. According to his 1988 obituary in the *Times-Picayune* ("Umar Uthman Sharif"), his career included work with Louis Armstrong, Dooky Chase, Jimmy Lunceford, Lionel Hampton, Broadway pit bands, and—in the final performance before his death—a Lincoln Center program with a band led by Wynton Marsalis.

Other early jazz instrumentalists at Southern cited by Batiste are trumpeters Edward Sawyer and Ludwig Freeman, reedmen Burt Robinson and George Andrews, trombonist Curtis Godchaux, vibist Don Dillon, bassist Bernard Beaco, pianist Sigmund Walker, and drummer Edward Duplessis. The tradition continued in later years, Batiste says, when drummer James Black, reedmen Alvin Thomas and Leonard Evans, trumpeter Herb Taylor, and others went to Southern. Assistant band director John Banks encouraged the young players by setting up a practice schedule for a jazz group. It was Batiste, though, who returned as a teacher in 1969 to found the Southern University Jazz Institute, bringing jazz from the margins into the main text of the university's music program.

The Baton Rouge jazz culture was not as varied, subterranean, or outright strange as the New Orleans scene. But the reports above and the symposium below testify that lively gigs and jam sessions did exist. New Orleans-based players even traveled to Baton Rouge for occasional jobs and sessions. Ornette Coleman and Melvin Lastee went upriver for a gig, as did Brew Moore, who played there with Mose Allison. I made the trip in 1955 with pianist-vocalist Theresa Kelly for an all-night jam session with Reed Vaughan, Larry Muhoberac, and others. Batiste tells of sessions at black venues where white jazzmen like Lee Fortier, Bud Brazier, and Oscar Davis sometimes joined in. As in New Orleans in the early days of modern jazz, white musicians were typically welcomed as customers or sit-in artists at black clubs, but the management at white clubs rarely reciprocated.

Hammond, Louisiana, the home of Southeastern Louisiana University, is less than sixty miles from New Orleans, but the city was not a hot spot for jazz. The school's most famous alumnus—Southeastern College '50—was New Jersey–born pianist Bill Evans, who would later become a sideman with Miles Davis and a major innovator with his own trio. Southeastern can justly claim Evans, and there was some interaction with early modernists in New Orleans. Peter Pettinger's biography of Evans notes that the pianist had "a base on Magnolia Street" in uptown New Orleans and "went jamming almost nightly around the Crescent City and the surrounding countryside with his regular group, the Casuals."

The connection with New Orleans appears to be overstated, since almost no one recalls Evans's time in the city. Some confusion might exist because of a popular local dance combo called the Casuals in the 1950s, unconnected with Evans's group. But Al Belletto clearly recalls working with Evans at a strip club around 1947. Evans, probably the off-night pianist, was really impressive, Belletto says, "although we had no idea of what he would come to be." Belletto adds that Fred Crane was the first real modern jazz pianist he heard in New Orleans. It is certain that Crane and Evans met, since Evans later told Belletto that Crane was his favorite pianist. During visits in Dallas (where Crane later settled) they would play four-handed piano improvisations.

Don Nelson's 1960 *Down Beat* article mentions Evans's gigs around New Orleans, but the extended anecdotes are about Evans's work in outlying areas—a Mississippi roadhouse where a shooting took place amid the gambling without apparent ado, and an outdoor Louisiana party with jambalaya aplenty and a bandstand protected by chicken wire. Nelson reports Evans's comment that "I once heard this trumpet player in New Orleans who used to put down his horn and comp at the piano. . . . When he did, he got that deep, moving feeling I've always wanted, and it dragged me because I couldn't reach it." This is almost certainly Mike Serpas, who jammed with Evans in Hammond and remembers a session in New Orleans. Serpas says, "He was beautiful . . . knocked me out."

Two of Evans's close friends in Hammond, trumpet/French horn player Ralph Pottle Jr. and trombonist Ron Nethercutt, told me that Evans played extensively in and around Hammond with his trio of New Jersey imports (Condit Atkin, bass, and Frank Wrobel, drums) and with the school's dance band, which was the source of a partial scholarship. Pottle, a contemporary of Evans as a student, recalls that Evans developed his jazz style while in Hammond even though "there were no real be-boppers" at Southeastern in the early postwar years, and most gigs involved straight dance music fare.

The fact that the school gave scholarships for the dance band testifies that the Southeastern administration was not rabidly antijazz. Pottle's father, head of the music department and its primary recruiter, was a vigorous, respected, open-minded leader. When Evans graduated, Pottle *père* wrote a letter on behalf of the young pianist to commercial dance band leader Freddy Martin. Pettinger reports Pottle's high praise of Evans as "an intent student of the modern idioms in piano playing" and "perhaps the best all around dance pianist I have heard in the profession." Nethercutt, who arrived at Southeastern in 1954, says that jazz was "tacitly approved" by the administration but jamming was an after-hours activity. He named the Brown Door and the Crescent as local jam session sites.

Pottle, Nethercutt, and the symposium panelists named several other jazz musicians who were at Southeastern or in Hammond over the years. In prebop days bassist Red Mitchell and guitarist Mundell Lowe were there. Modernists of the postwar years include Evans, trombonist Al Chemay, bassist Lou Chemay, saxophonist Oscar Davis, drummer Bobby DeSio, and trumpeters Mike Serpas and Herb Tassin. Of these, only Serpas, Tassin, Davis, and DeSio are remembered as active modernists in postwar New Orleans.

Mike Serpas went to Southeastern in 1955, already a veteran of early postwar New Orleans jam sessions and a hitch in the U.S. Navy. At weekend sessions with French Quarter boppers Mouse Bonati, Don Suhor, Reed Vaughan, and others, Serpas was extraordinary. At those sessions I often heard Davis, an able alto saxist, and DeSio, a drummer with a driving pulse and fine endurance. DeSio had an odd conception—a pronounced 4/4 thrust combined with be-bop phrasing—that contrasted with Reed Vaughan's loose, almost spiritual projection of time. Bill Huntington, in his "Roll Call" discussion of drummers, calls Vaughan "a child prodigy" with a "light and crisp" touch. Vaughan went on to play with Ira Sullivan, Art Pepper, Hampton Hawes, and Stan Kenton in the late 1950s.

For a large number of white musicians, the most vital nearby modern jazz site was not a university town but the Mississippi Gulf Coast. Biloxi was the center of a string of night clubs, gambling places, motels, hotels, and restaurants that functioned as though they were on a different planet from inland Mississippi. Keesler Field (later Keesler Air Force Base) furnished a steady supply of lusty young men in search of entertainment after the terrible war years. The gentle and inviting Gulf waters attracted visitors from nearby states. Economic benefits of the military and tourist trade prompted politicians to look the other way as booze, gambling, strip clubs, and prostitution held sway in the breezy coastal area. Just as New Orleans was often regarded as a city-state in southern Louisiana, Biloxi and its environs were a mini-Riviera hanging like a fold of fat beneath the Bible belt.

In this laissez-faire atmosphere, modern jazz had a chance of infiltrating. Al Belletto and Lee Charlton report that jazz musicians from New Orleans and elsewhere were working and hanging out in Biloxi beginning in the early 1950s and continuing through the next decade. Among the formidable group of modernists who were part of both the Gulf Coast and New Orleans jazz scenes were trumpeters Benny Clement, Mike Serpas, and Bob Teeters; leader/alto saxist Al Belletto; tenor saxist Joe (Cheeks) Mandry; pianists Fred Crane, Carrol Cunningham, Johnny Elgin, Ed Fenasci, Rusty Mayne, and John Probst; guitarist Linc Luddington; bassist Jay Cave; bassist/trumpeter Rusty Gilder; drummers Lee Charlton, Lee Johnson, Bill Patey, and Reed Vaughn; and arranger Jack Martin. Not highly visible in New Orleans but playing in the Biloxi area were trumpeter Willie Thomas; reedmen Rick Bell, Tater Dahnke, and Don Menza; trombonists Carl Fontana, Urbie Green, and Jimmy Guinn; pianists Don Reitan and Sam Spivey; bassists Skip Fawcett and Gary Miller; drummers Bama McKnight, Buddy Fountain, Tom Montgomery, and Kenny Ward; and vocalist Jackie Henderson.

Al Belletto and Don Reitan established well-organized combos that merit particular attention. Belletto played summers as a sideman before starting his own combo in 1951. Their first break came when the group was backing up vocalist Mel Torme's show at Gus Stevens' club. "He thought he'd be out on the boondocks and was surprised to find a jazz group backing him up," Belletto recalls. "He wrote some five-part vocal arrangement for us. That's how we got started singing. I taught [pianist] Fred Crane to play baritone sax for the ensembles. It was a seven-night-a-week job. We'd rehearse in the afternoons and play six hours a night. All of this happened within a few weeks."

Torme connected them with a New York booking agency, and they went on the road. The next break came when Stan Kenton heard the combo. Kenton was the most ambitious and controversial big band leader of the day, coining the term "progressive jazz" for orchestrations that ranged from garishly pretentious to genuinely interesting. Kenton made flashy use of soloists like Maynard Ferguson, Frank Rosolino, Art Pepper, and Shelly

Manne. He was producing a *Stan Kenton Presents* series for Capitol Records, and in 1954 Belletto's sextet cut their first fine pop/jazz album.

The sextet included Belletto on alto sax; Willie Thomas, trumpet; Jimmy Guinn, trombone; Fred Crane, piano and baritone sax; Skip Fawcett, bass; and Bama McKnight, drums. Most of the arrangements were by Jack Martin. The sextet had the appeal of superhip vocal groups like the Hi-Los and well-oiled modern jazz combos like Shorty Rogers. Those looking for out-and-out-bop or other exploratory jazz would have to look elsewhere. But no serious listener could dismiss the group's exceptional craft and the intense jazz conception of soloists like Crane and Guinn. It was quite a combination. Arguably, there was no better singing jazz group in the world.

Belletto's success had an impact on the New Orleans scene, bringing modern jazz to the attention of wider audiences in the city and the entire Gulf area for the first time. Deejay Dick Martin was a constant booster of the sextet. He provided both local and national exposure on his latenight show, *Moonglow with Martin*. The program was heard throughout the country on Loyola-owned WWL radio, billed as the city's "50,000 watt clear channel station." The smooth-voiced Martin specialized in sophisticated jazz and moody vocals. I recall hearing some of the best of Ella Fitzgerald, Peggy Lee, and Sara Vaughan on the program—and plenty of the Al Belletto sextet.

Since many jazz fans in the city and elsewhere have lionized Martin, a brief digression is warranted here. I agree with those who see Martin as a unique and creative figure who should be remembered in a survey of those who influenced postwar jazz in New Orleans. But I disagree with those who describe him as a major boon for local music and musicians. To his credit, Martin had helped the New Orleans Jazz Club get its WWL Sunday evening radio slot in 1949, and his promotion of Belletto's work in the 1950s was exceptional. But as Belletto notes, Martin had little traffic with other local jazz artists. There was rarely a mention of New Orleans musicians—traditional, Dixieland, or modern, black or white—who did not fit his nice-and-easy style and taste. At a time when so many local musicians could have benefited greatly from the informal promotion Martin had to offer, he walked a narrow path.

Martin had another platform that he failed to use to the benefit of New Orleans musicians. When I wrote a query to *Down Beat* in 1960 about doing an article on modern jazz in the city, the then-long established deejay was listed as New Orleans correspondent for the magazine. Editor Don DeMichael later offered me the correspondent's role, commenting that Martin had not been sending in copy. Undoubtedly, Dick Martin improved the quality of life in America by playing excellent popular and jazz recordings nightly for over a decade. But a champion of the rich local jazz culture he was not. Martin either did not know about or did not appreciate the variety and energy of the music that was being played only blocks away from the Roosevelt Hotel radio station. He left town in 1961 to become regional director for Dot Records.

None of which detracts from Martin's great support of the Belletto sextet. He used Belletto's "Relaxin'" as an interlude after key station breaks and announced the group's touring schedule regularly. Belletto's road work gradually dwindled, though. Berry describes an unexpected rescue by none other than Woody Herman in 1957. Herman, of course, was a jazz legend, leader of the longest-running and most uncompromising white band in the profession. He heard the sextet in Denver and learned from Belletto that the group was about to disband. He proposed that they join his Thundering Herd as sidemen and as a featured band within a band.

There were some precedents for such an arrangement, such as the Bobcats within the Bob Crosby big band, Woody Herman's Dixie combo within the Band That Plays the Blues, both in the late 1930s; and the underrated Dorseyland Band within Jimmy Dorsey's band in the late 1950s. Those were all Dixieland insets, aped by innumerable dance bands (including the postwar Loyola big bands). As for swing combos within bands, Benny Goodman pulled out key sidemen for his now classic small-group numbers. Drummer Chick Webb's band featured the Little Chicks, a lively flute, clarinet, and rhythm combination. The New Orleans Dawn Busters band had its Jive Five, with Al Hirt on trumpet. But the Herman-Belletto collaboration was unique. It gave the spotlight over to a different band leader and an intact modern jazz group that had earlier established its own identity. The connection continued through 1959. The next year, Belletto was playing at the Playboy Club in Chicago, which led to his work at the New Orleans Playboy, an important inroad to be discussed shortly.

Pianist Don Reitan led a quintet in Biloxi that received no national recognition, although it was far more in the modern jazz mainstream than Belletto's group. In his *Gulf Coast Jazz Scene* liner notes, Alabama-born drummer Lee Charlton tells of his arrival in Biloxi in 1957 to play for floor shows and dancing with a trio headed by Reitan, whom he knew from earlier gigs in the pianist's home state of North Carolina. The Biloxi site was Gus Stevens's club, where Al Belletto's career was launched a few years earlier. Belletto was long gone, but the divinely decadent Gulf Coast subculture was still intact and modernists found room to practice their art.

Charlton recalls that Biloxi was "a true mecca for young, talented jazz musicians" with clubs like Chez Joey, the Key Club, the Prelude, and the Downbeat as sites of gigs and after-hours sessions. He continues, "The rhythm of our musical day began with our evening and club performances, followed by sessions at the Downbeat until 3:00 or 4:00 a.m., when we took a break to sleep until noon. After breakfast there was nearly always a.m./p.m. jam sessions at Country Mettina's house." The Mississippi coast was less inviting to black musicians, he notes. There were occasional gigs and concerts, and even integrated jam sessions at the Key Club, but the area was not a wellspring of opportunities for black musicians.

Reitan's group reached a peak when it expanded to a quintet. In 1959 Jay Cave left Red Rodney's band to play in New Orleans, but after a trip to

Biloxi he joined Reitan, Charlton, and trumpeter Mike Serpas. Tenor saxist Rick Bell from Atlanta rounded out the group, described by Cave in Charlton's liner notes as "the best band I ever played with." Fortunately, they made live recordings at Chez Joey. A 1961 session, engineered by a technician from Cosimo's studio in New Orleans, was released by Charlton in 1999 on the Music in the Vines label (MIV-289).

The CD is in some ways a landmark. It is a culmination of fifteen years of modern jazz on the Gulf Coast, and it shows musicians like Reitan, Charlton, and Serpas to some advantage. The charts and ensemble work are relentlessly funky, showing the influence of the Jazz Messengers and Horace Silver's groups. ("Sister Sadie" is one of the charts.) A nice tension is created as Charlton and Cave swing hard on top of the beat while the soloists are typically more laid back. Cave plays mainly a supportive role here, although he came to be known also as a superior soloist in New Orleans at the Playboy Club and elsewhere in the 1960s.

Six of the twelve tracks are originals, five by Reitan and one by Bell. "Minority Report" is Bell's piece, an engaging melody in 3/4 with well-placed syncopations. Bell's tenor is a wonderful surprise. He has a dark sound that has a slightly hard edge, but he generally projects a cool feeling that is a fine foil for the burning rhythm section. Reitan writes ever energetic lines ("The Boss," "All-American," "Out & Out") and is fond of hot interludes that break up the feeling of yet another a-b-b-a, thirty-two-bar jazz vehicle. His comping and solos are eclectic, ranging from an understated Tommy Flanagan–style bop on "All-American" to pianistic gutbucket on "Sandcrab Blues." In the latter he works hand in glove with Charlton, who demonstrates a thorough rapport with the soloists throughout the CD. Charlton's own solos are well sculpted along the lines of Jimmy Cobb.

Serpas, always a normative player at jam sessions, shows his adaptability in a tightly organized group. Solo space is somewhat rationed, the longest track being almost nine minutes ("More Than You Know," played at an excruciatingly slow forty-five beats per minute). Serpas told me that the CD does not feature the band's best all-out jazz work. Tracks like "Poinciana" and "Lover" bear him out, yet he soars on the up-tempo "Out and Out" and is outstanding on loping, down-home renditions of "Somebody Loves Me" and "Shoo Fly Pie" and "Apple Pan Dowdy." His soulful, original style is in evidence on the two standards, bringing to mind (to my mind, at least) that if Bix had lived to play modern jazz, on a good day he would have sounded like this. These two tracks are the only vocals on the CD. A marvelous Floridian named Jackie Henderson, later married to Serpas, is up to the task of the slow-paced "Somebody," and Serpas tweaks "Shoo Fly" with fine wit.

Reviewing the postwar years through 1960, I confess a special fondness for the artists and the music of the time. The first generation of New Orleans modernists was the only one to experience the new music when it was new—not just to themselves but to the entire world. There is a singular excitement when a new movement emerges among artists—musicians, painters, writers, architects, dancers, whatever. The nature of the project and its boundaries are not clear at the outset, and a special daring is required of practitioners, who communicate the thrill of shaping fresh artistic expression. Some of the musicians of the early years left the city before I was able to hear them (e.g., Joe Pass, Frank Strazerri, Emery Thompson). Others were in town but I did not hear them until the 1960s (e.g., Ellis Marsalis, Bob Teeters, Earl and Willie Turbinton). The ones I heard who moved me most were clarinetists Alvin Batiste and Don Suhor, tenor saxists Joe (Cheeks) Mandry and Nat Perrilliat, alto saxists Joseph (Mouse) Bonati and Don Suhor, trumpeter Mike Serpas, pianists Fred Crane, Ed Frank, and John Probst, guitarist Bill Huntington, and drummers Ed Blackwell, Earl Palmer, and Reed Vaughan.

Knowing the price that the early modernists paid for venturing into the new music—rejection of their efforts, economic hardship, police harassment, the menace of drugs—I have tried to avoid romanticizing the times. Even so, I was a teenager between 1948 and 1955 and an admiring protégé of the modern jazz elders. "Elders" meant those who were a few years older than I was, young discoverers who were passionately, often recklessly, dedicated to the music. There is genuine wonder in that, and I hope the wonder has threaded the lines of this section.

THE 1960s: SOME INROADS

In the 1960s modern jazz gained some momentum in New Orleans. No single group received the national exposure to jazz fans that Al Belletto's Biloxi-based sextet had in the previous decade, but there were modest inroads on several fronts. Leaders like Belletto at the Playboy, pianists Joe Burton and Ronnie Kole at their own clubs, Ronnie Dupont at the Bistro, and Ellis Marsalis at various clubs won small but loyal local followings. Some cutting-edge combos were formed—notably, the short-lived Fred Crane trio at the Black Knight, Marsalis's quartet at several sites, and Willie and Earl Turbinton's group at the Jazz Workshop. All of these combos moved beyond the vocabulary and stylistic dimensions of be-bop. Each of the popularizing and pace-setting leaders and groups will be discussed below or in the vintage articles that follow.

I was able to chronicle virtually all of the developments of the 1960s as New Orleans correspondent for *Down Beat* beginning with the May 11, 1961, issue. The twice-monthly journal started a "Where & When" page— listings of bands and night clubs in six or seven cities. Additionally, I sent copy frequently for "Strictly Ad Lib," a column that consisted of information items from various cities. The W&W and Ad Libs materials and interviews with numerous musicians are the sources for most of the information below.

The local dailies were basically tone-deaf when it came to jazz. Mainly, activities of popular artists like Fountain, Hirt, Celestin, the Dukes of Dixieland, and Ronnie Kole were mentioned in chitchat columns like Tommy Griffin's "Lagniappe." In the letters to the editor column of the September 3, 1966, *States-Item* I wrote angrily that "talent outside of the areas of traditional jazz goes unrecognized unless a 'name' modernist comes to a popular night club. Has the New Orleans press ever heard of, much less given exposure to, gifted local modernists like James Black, Bill Huntington, Ellis Marsalis, or Jimmy Zitano?" (See the overview to section I, "Jazz and the Establishment," and chapters 2–11 for the context of this lamentable situation.)

Five general observations furnish a backdrop for modern jazz in the 1960s. First, during the decade an increasing number of sites took a chance on featuring modern jazz, mainly on weekends. Jam sessions continued, but more pay gigs became available. Some of the 1950s regulars and numerous new faces appeared at clubs (many of them short-lived) such as the Backstage Lounge (annex of Al Hirt's Club), Birdland Lounge, Bistro, Blackbeard, Black Knight, Blue Note, Cabaret Club, Cellar, Chandelle Lounge (at the Fontainebleau Hotel), Checkmate Lounge, Ched's Tower Lounge, Club Continental, Club 77, Cosimo's (no relation to recording pioneer Cosimo Matassa), Cozy Kole's, Devil's Den, Devil's Dungeon, Dominic's Jazz Room, Downs Lounge, Dream Room, Farhad Grotto, Haven (Claiborne Avenue), Holiday House, Hollie's, House of Zin, Hurricane #2, Jamaican Village, Jazz Corner, Jazz Room, Jazz Woodshed, Jazz Workshop/Listening Eye Gallery, Jewel Room, Joe Burton's, Jory's, Joy Tavern, Kole's Corner, Laura's, La Strada, Music Haven (at Marsalis's Mansion), Nero's Nook, Off Limits, Pepe's, Playboy, Rendezvous Room, Sheriff's Office, Spotty's, Stereo, Sylvia's, Vernon's, and the VIP Lounge (at Mason's).

This was not a groundswell but sporadic activity that gradually increased during the 1960s. Early in the decade (August 1961) I wrote to critic Ralph J. Gleason that

> modern clubs lead a tenuous existence for the most part, even on weekends. Joe Burton's trio (only 6-nite-a-week modern gig in town) draws on [the] college crowd and professional people, but it's rough going. Exception: Joy Tavern, where Alvin Tyler has taken root. Currently operating: Cosimo's. . . . The non-Dixie clubs and coffee houses are most often ephemeral.

My first "Where & When" listing for *Down Beat* in the May 25, 1961, issue included twelve clubs, five of them featuring modern jazz: Joe Burton at his own club, Ditymus at Spotty's, Ellis Marsalis at the Jazz Room, Buddy Prima at the Jazz Woodshed (Slidell), and Alvin (Red) Tyler at the Joy Tavern. The traditional and Dixieland sites, all in the downtown area, included the two French Quarter clubs that had been at the center of the 1947–1953 revival: the Famous Door, with bands led by Murphy Campo and Mike Lala, and the Paddock, where a group headed by Papa Celestin's former pianist, Octave Crosby, was playing. Established star Pete Fountain was at his French Quarter Inn, and Al Hirt, just into his ascent to national fame, was at Dan's Pier 600. Veteran trombonist Santo Pecora led a Dixieland group at the Dream Room. All of these clubs were on Bourbon Street, all of the bands playing full-time. Pianist Armand Hug had a steady job as a single at the Prince Conti. The sole weekend-only gig for traditional or Dixieland bands was the River Queen, where Leon Prima, the Last Straws, and Papa Albert French were playing.

To illustrate the change during the decade, fast forward to the March 6, 1969, issue. The "Where & When" list contained thirty-three items, eighteen of them modern jazz-oriented; of those, half were full-time. Al Belletto at the Playboy, Ronnie Dupont at the Bistro, and Ronnie Kole at Kole's Corner had the largest popular audiences. Savvy listeners could also seek out groups led by Jay Cave, Roger Dickerson, Porgy Jones, June Gardner, David Lastie, Tony Mitchell, James Rivers, Don Suhor, Willie and Earl Turbinton, and others. Vocalists Germaine Bazzle, C. J. Cheramie, Betty Farmer, and Lavergne Smith were also performing.

Although smaller in number than the modern jazz entries on the W&W list, Dixieland and traditional New Orleans bands were the most popular attractions—overwhelmingly. Al Hirt's and Pete Fountain's clubs were still the big-draw Dixieland hotspots. Preservation Hall, a mere curiosity in 1961, had long since become a must-see institution for locals and visitors alike. Its sole surviving imitator, Dixieland Hall, was doing well, and the venerable Famous Door and Paddock were still in business. Even so, modern jazz musicians were finding employment, and a subset of the populace was latching on to a variety of modern styles, from commercial to unrestrained avant garde, that were offered at the end of the 1960s.

It is clear that collectively, the TNOJ/Dixieland and modern jazz scenes made a quantum leap between 1945 and the mid-1960s. At first glance, one wonders how Broven could possibly generalize that "in 1964, New Orleans was a depressed area, musically" and refer to that time as "the Dark Ages." Like Berry, Broven is strongly focused on rhythm and blues in the city and pays insufficient attention to the growth of jazz in the postwar years. From Broven's perspective as an R&B historian, his pessimistic statement is plausible. He cites AFO's lack of business acumen and cliquish organization as a partial cause of "the mess which the New Orleans music scene became." Nationally, he sees the "onslaught of the Beatles" and the dominance of guitar bands, soul, and Motown as part of the "overturn of the existing order" in rhythm and blues. But from the perspective of jazz performance, the 1960s were, if not a new golden age, a time of relatively high prosperity and popularity for rediscovered TNOJ old-timers, Dixieland superstars, and daring young modern artists as well.

A second factor in boosting jazz activity in the 1960s was the demise of Louisiana's segregation laws. Integrated bands appeared with increasing frequency once the legal barriers were down in the mid-1960s. As will be seen, Al Belletto broke through at the Playboy Club in 1964, bringing in the excellent Richard Payne on bass. Other instances: Don Suhor included Smokey Johnson as drummer in his be-bop pit band at the Sho'Bar in 1966.

Dixieland trombonist Santo Pecora used Thomas Jefferson on trumpet at the Dream Room in 1968. The two musicians unions, Local 174 (white) and Local 496 (black), were formally integrated in 1969.

I hasten to add that examples of integration do not imply an absence of prejudice. Instant conversions did not occur once the legal bans were lifted. Mainly, those who were initially interested in the quality of music rather than the skin color of musicians were allowed to go their own way. Some biased club owners continued to discourage integrated bands. Some white musicians, especially older ones, were threatened by loss of economic and social advantages they had enjoyed for years. And when the Black Power movement emerged in the 1960s, it was the white musicians and customers who felt a draft at some of the black clubs where they had been welcomed in the years when liberals were keenly (and automatically) valued as allies.

Third, a crackdown on strip clubs in 1964 by District Attorney Jim Garrison (who grew notorious as a conspiracy theorist and prosecutor of Clay Shaw in the Kennedy assassination case) had mixed results for modernists. Employment of musicians at strip clubs had already diminished as dancers turned to blaring stereo accompaniment. The police action aggravated the employment problem at strip clubs. In one Keystone Cops raid, police avoided early detection by boarding a bus that went down Bourbon Street and ordering it to stop directly in front of the targeted club. Scurry, scurry. Busted. Padlock on the door. Headlines for Garrison.

The positive side of the crackdown was that some former strip club owners decided to offer music (not necessarily jazz) as the main entertainment fare. In the June 4, 1964, *Down Beat* "Ad Libs" column I quoted Joe Trovato and James Clayton, two Bourbon Street club owners who declared that "stripping is dead in New Orleans" and announced a switch to a live music policy. To paraphrase Mark Twain, the death of stripping was greatly exaggerated; but the musical climate that had been growing since 1959 with Fountain, Hirt, Preservation Hall, and the Playboy was further enhanced by Garrison's high profile operation.

Fourth, the practice of modernists playing with varying degrees of freedom in Dixieland bands, though by no means unprecedented, grew rapidly in the 1960s. Pete Fountain hired pianists John Probst and Dave West and drummer Lou Timken. Santo Pecora featured Pete Monteleone on piano at the Famous Door. Even the Dukes of Dixieland brought in a modern bassist, Rudy Aikels.

Al Hirt was by far the most consistent employer of modern jazz sidemen in Dixieland lineups. He hired pianists Fred Crane, Ronnie Dupont, and Ellis Marsalis; bassists Jay Cave, Bill Huntington, and Lowell Miller. Hirt made another important contribution. He brought major jazz groups led by Cannonball Adderley, Dizzy Gillespie, Lionel Hampton, Ramsey Lewis, Buddy Rich, and others into his Bourbon Street club when he was on tour. This was not totally innovative. According to *Louisiana Weekly,* Gillespie, Hampton, and a host of others—Count Basie, Billy Eckstine, Mercer Ellington, Johnny Hartman, Helen Humes, Ella Fitzgerald, Jimmy Lunceford, Jay

McShann, Dinah Washington, and Jazz at the Philharmonic — had played between 1945 and 1950 at black venues like the Coliseum Arena and Booker T. Washington High School (a point I missed in my *Down Beat* article on modern jazz in New Orleans). Hirt blazed new trails, though, by featuring big name modernists on a regular basis at a celebrated tourist-path night club for integrated audiences.

Finally, a few modern jazz recordings were made in the decade. As in previous years, the recordings did not adequately document the excellence or the range of the music being performed. But there was some action. In an interesting act of entrepreneurship, Harold Battiste and a core of other first-rate black jazz artists establish AFO (All For One) Records. They formed a studio band that backed up some fine R&B artists and cut a few jazz sides as well — most notably, a session by Ellis Marsalis's quartet that is discussed below. A compendium album by the AFO studio/jazz band — Melvin Lastie, cornet; Alvin (Red) Tyler, tenor sax; Harold Battiste, alto sax and piano; Peter (Chuck) Badie, bass; and John Boudreaux, drums — with vocalist Tammy Lynn, showcased versatility more than jazzmanship (reissued as AFO CD 92-1028). Some fine jazz moments are provided by the group, though, with surprisingly funky piano by Battiste, and Boudreaux drumming flawlessly in many styles.

In 1962 Nat Adderley invited Marsalis and two of his sidemen, Nat Perrilliat and James Black, to record a Riverside LP with Cannonball Adderley and bassist Sam Jones. It was a fine effort, but it did not launch a national career for the locals. Ronnie Kole had a hit record, the *Batman* TV show theme, on the ABC Paramount label. Buddy Prima cut some sides with Bill Huntington and Charlie Blancq on Dot. Singer Tony Page, a Sinatra-based stylist, did an undistinguished LP on Empire with Ronnie Dupont and a makeup big band. Possibly, some privately owned tapes of other groups are still around. One that I received recently from composer/pianist/arranger Bert Braud is an excellent 1961 rehearsal band led by Braud and tenor saxist/arranger John Celestin. The big band, kicked by Charlie Blancq's crisp drumming and Joe Hebert's strong bass, features tight ensembles and some brilliant solos by Charlie Miller on trumpet. Drummer Lee Charlton, who recently released the above-mentioned 1961 Don Reitan Quintet recordings made in Biloxi, has other tapes that include players like Earl Cobble, Joe (Cheeks) Mandry, Ellis Marsalis, John Probst, and Bob Teeters.

The stronger public presence of modern jazz in the 1960s should not be mistaken for a mass conversion of the local populace. Few of the city's growing cadre of modernists were making a living at modern jazz at any given time. But there was a definite increase in listeners, from no-nonsense fans to a new in crowd for whom modern jazz was part of a calculatedly sophisticated image.

The sophisticates furnish a useful starting point for an account of key groups of the 1960s. They were part of the predominantly middle-class, white audience that supported Joe Burton. I recall hearing Burton's trio at a tiny Royal Street club around May 1958. I had been working weekends on the Steamer *President* with Dixieland trumpeter Dutch Andrus, tenor man Hank Kmen, and others. Burton was a finger-popping, laid-back pianist who liked supportive bassists and drummers who could swing softly with brushes à la Denzel Best. And indeed, he set out to hire the best sidemen in the area.

Burton's understated style struck me from the beginning as subtle and original, but one-dimensional and prone to repetition. At his best, his improvisations were interesting enough to hold the attention of musicians and serious lay listeners. His stage persona, which I never once saw him abandon, was that of the *artiste* who came down from New York, Baby, to bring hip and cool sounds to the provinces.

I was drafted after the *President* gig. During my army stint Burton opened his own club at Canal Street and Jefferson Davis Parkway—a good move because the French Quarter was not ready for subdued jazz, and he was not a tourist attraction. Burton once boasted that he would soon control modern jazz within a hundred-mile radius of New Orleans. That was typical hyperbole, but Bill Huntington stated that Burton was "definitely dominating." He had, after all, found financial backing to open a modern jazz club, no small feat in a city that had basically ignored post-Dixieland jazz. In October 1959 I received an early release from the army because of a shortage of public school teachers and found that Burton had gained momentum.

There was an offbeat charisma in Burton's moody posing that attracted those who romanticized the modern jazz artist as a misunderstood hero. Admirably, he demanded quiet while performing. Not so admirably, his demands soon extended to quirky, unpredictable tirades. (See the Al Belletto anecdote in the symposium in chapter 26.) Listeners who were initially attracted to his music came back to see if he would pull off some sort of zany tantrum.

But there is limited charm in zany tantrums. Customers ultimately did not want to run the risk of being insulted, and business dropped off. Sought-after sidemen like bassists Huntington and Jay Cave and drummers Earl Cobble and Reed Vaughan had been fired or had quit as a result of Burton's mood swings and tardiness in paying wages.

I played several nights at Burton's club and did a TV spot with him in fall of 1960. (He was adept at promoting radio programs and occasional TV spots from his club.) I was in my third year of English teaching and was no longer equipped to sustain a modern jazz gig. Bassist Carl Hellmers was wholly out of his element, merely guessing at lines when Burton played tunes like "I'm Getting Sentimental over You." Carl and I did a double-take when Burton sent out for beer at a convenience store to stock a bar that wholesalers no longer serviced due to unpaid bills. But we got cash at the end of the gig each night, and Burton treated us with respect, knowing that we were putting forth our best effort, such as it was, for some very long evenings—and that there were few players who would work with him if we bolted.

In the summer of 1962 Burton left town suddenly, apparently burdened with debts and a considerable store of ill will. I remember that he made a recording shortly after, and it was reviewed with high praise in *Down Beat.* In the spring of 1966 he found financial backing again and returned to New Orleans to open an after-hours club on Toulouse Street in the French Quarter.

Prospects were not bad. The Quarter was more open to modern jazz. Despite a history of problems with keeping good sidemen, Burton was able to get top-drawer players like Huntington and Cave and drummers James Black and Jimmy Zitano. Why? "We needed a gig," shrugs Huntington. Burton's highly mannered piano style had not changed, and it did not wear well with musicians. Huntington recalls James Black's comment after a typically gingerly rendition of a tune: "What's the matter, is the piano too hot for him to touch?"

Burton cannot be faulted for lack of hustle in trying to establish a base of fans. He again did radio shows on several local stations and later a TV spot from the Top of the Mart lounge. My *Down Beat* materials show that at one point in 1967 he was playing at three different clubs. But the city's modern jazz fans had heard a lot of good music during his four years in Chicago, Miami, and Las Vegas. Moreover, their choice of venues continued to grow during Burton's second crack at the slim modern jazz market. Jazz lovers had heard dig-in and stretch-out players like Nat Perrilliat and Ellis Marsalis. The Playboy Club had become a powerful magnet for both party-line sophisticates and true-blue fans. Ronnie Kole's Trio was modeling polite, showmanly jazz with a smile for popular audiences at Al Hirt's. Good jazz for dancing was provided by Jack Hebert's Encores at Ched's Tower Lounge, Ronnie Dupont at the Bistro, and Tony Mitchell at the Fontainebleau. Weekend modern jazz clubs were not hard to find. For those who had ears to hear, modernists in Dixieland groups were playing "bopsieland," an amalgam that was often interesting.

So Burton left town again when the Top of the Mart gig ended in mid-1968. His legacy as a crusader for modern jazz in New Orleans is genuine. But early on, his complex, self-destructive temperament sabotaged both his artistic and commercial projects, and in the long run the New Yorker was eclipsed by "local talent"—always a loaded phrase when applied to New Orleans musicians.

The Ellis Marsalis Quartet did not set out to capture Burton's easy-listening jazz lovers. Marsalis and tenor saxist Nat Perrilliat had played with Alvin Batiste and several bassists in various incarnations of the horizon-busting American Jazz Quintet. In the summer of 1961, a late if not final edition of the AJQ—Batiste, Marsalis, Perrilliat, bassist Richard Payne, and recently added drummer James Black—conducted a summer clinic for young musicians.

Marsalis's trio worked two trio gigs in small French Quarter clubs in 1961 before becoming one of the earliest groups to play full-time at the new Playboy Club on Bienville Street, just off Bourbon. The job lasted six months.

From late 1962 through spring of 1963 his quartet (Perrilliat, Black, and bassist Marshall Smith) got into gear with a full-time job at the Music Haven. The club was part of a Marsalis's Mansion, a motel on River Road owned by Ellis's father. The group had a radio show on WJMR and was attracting both white and black jazz fans.

Interestingly, James Black saw the white audiences as a hindrance. In Battiste's *New Orleans Heritage* he says that "around that time segregation was happening . . . black against white and white against black and all that shit. . . . When the brothers and sisters would come to the door and see all them white people there, they figured it was a white joint and turned around. So we never did get no black exposure, and gradually the shit began to slack off."

A major event occurred in New Orleans around the time of the Music Haven gig. Late in 1962, Vernon's brought the John Coltrane Quartet to New Orleans. The revolutionary group included McCoy Tyner on piano, Jimmy Garrison on bass, and Elvin Jones on drums. Berry quotes Earl Turbinton's comment: "This was like God was in town. The whole music community turned out."

Hearing Coltrane live at Vernon's was even more stunning than hearing his innovative recordings that begin in 1960. The new sounds bounced off the walls, curled around each other in deliciously puzzling ways, stretched across time like a gorgeous run-on poem, throbbed so that your shirt trembled against your chest. As with the first hearing of be-bop fifteen years earlier, we were listening to a new music for the first time. Quite a privilege. It occurred to me that if life were fair, everyone in every generation would have the benefit of experiencing the first taste of an innovative art.

My impression as a frequent listener to local artists was that the impact of Coltrane's visit was powerful and highly salutary. Turbinton visited with Trane for several days and was tutored in the saxophonist's daring new approaches. In Marsalis's group, drummer Black, previously influenced most strongly by Ed Blackwell, began working with Jones's thundering asymmetries. Marsalis expanded his range along the lines of Tyner. Perrilliat, already an admirer of Coltrane's work with Miles Davis, had the imagination and technique to emulate Coltrane's cascading "sheets of sound."

Early in 1963 the Marsalis quartet made an album in the studio for AFO, now reissued with additional on-the-gig tracks as AFO CD 91-0428, *The Classic Ellis Marsalis.* The studio tracks are most remarkable for Black's compositions, especially "Monkey Puzzle," "Dee Wee," and "Magnolia Triangle." All employ 3/4 or 5/4 time signatures, posing challenges that the soloists accept with relish. But the studio set was not geared toward extended solos, and the group had not yet absorbed the influence of Coltrane's quartet. The risk-taking, powerful accentuation and pure passion of Perrilliat's sax are not strongly evident. Marsalis is warmly eclectic, playing more sparely than on the late 1950s American Jazz Quintet sessions. Echoes of Hank Jones, Tommy Flanagan, and Wynton Kelly are blended in a personal synthesis. Black is sometimes solidly in the Blackwell mode (hear his malletson-toms comping on "'Round about Midnight"), but his solo work also reflects Max Roach and Jimmy Cobb.

The quartet digs in and reaches out on two live tracks from the Music Haven. The aforementioned "Midnight" and "A Night in Tunisia" each run over ten minutes. The balance is poor, but the playing is rich. Perrilliat is turned loose for fluent, scorching chorus after chorus, Rollins-like, recalling his live performances at Cosimo's with bassist Richard Payne and Black or John Boudreaux on drums. Black's up-tempo backing recalls the best of Blackwell. And as Kalamu ya Salaam points out in the liner notes, Marsalis is in a driving be-bop mode.

After the Music Haven gig the quartet continued to play concerts around town and on the Gulf Coast. There was an after-hours stretch on weekends at the Blue Note on Rampart Street for about two months in 1963. The group disbanded the next year. Battiste reports that Black got work in New York, first in commercial settings but later with Yusef Lateef, Horace Silver, and other pace-setting jazz groups. Perrilliat went on the road with Junior Parker. Smith returned to Dallas. Marsalis took a teaching job in a rural Louisiana town. When Black and Marsalis returned around 1966, they were briefly reunited with Perrilliat when the latter played at Al Hirt's Club with the Fats Domino band. Black then went with Joe Burton, Marsalis with Hirt. Later in the decade they worked together at Mason's, and, according to Black, with bassist Richard Payne at Lu and Charlie's.

The Playboy Club was a major force in the growth of modern jazz in New Orleans the 1960s. The symposium participants rightly praise Al Belletto's leadership as musical director. He consistently hired modern jazz combos, as many as three groups playing full-time in the club's different rooms. Belletto began by hiring both white and black combos. In 1964 he presented the first highly visible, full-time integrated combo in the city.

The music at the Playboy might have sounded like the West Coast jazz—a more subdued, less propulsive style—to some. A recent TV documentary on Playboy bunnies described the jazz at the Playboy chain as "mellow." But those labels did not describe the basic orientation of most of the musicians who played at the New Orleans club. Indeed, Bill Huntington recalls that the musicians at that club could often "just play" without restraint.

Nevertheless, the Joe Cool atmosphere did not encourage the kind of unfettered improvisation that artists like Fred Crane, Ellis Marsalis, and John Probst were capable of. During my visits as a listener or as an off-night drummer, there were no ten-minute romps through "A Night in Tunisia." More like "Lullaby of Birdland." But the overriding point in the context of the growth of modern jazz in New Orleans is that many local modernists were working steadily and being heard by the large number of patrons at the club.

In my review of Buddy Prima's trio for *Down Beat* (chapter 25 below) and the cross-section articles in appendix 1, I did not hide my distaste for the bourgeois hipness and upscale erotic gaucherie that the club was peddling. In retrospect this seems excessive, but not by much. After all, one purchased

Playboy club membership and was given one's personal key to enter the building, plus perks like the bunny decal for one's car window. Once inside, one's name was posted as a guest who was present.

The "Playboy philosophy" articulated by Hugh Hefner in the magazine struck me as especially phony—an aggregate of impulses slickly alchemized into then-liberal pop philosophy. This is not to say that no one read the excellent fiction and essays in the softcore magazine (the nudity being mild by today's standards; pubic hair was even airbrushed out of the idealized T&A photos) or that no one who patronized the club went to hear the music. But many malleable young men of my generation became good-living snobs, devoted to the shallowest sort of cosmopolitanism, caught up in a Hefnerian value system that included sports cars, James Bond movies, foreign films, expensive stereo equipment, sexism masquerading as sexual liberation, misquotations from Nietzche, and, yes, modern jazz.

Al Hirt commented indirectly on the Playboy mentality in a *DB* cover story of September 4, 1969. I pointed out that *Playboy* readers had often voted him as the top jazz trumpeter in the magazine's annual poll. Hirt protested, "How embarrassing for a guy like me, for God's sake, to finish ahead of Miles Davis and Dizzy Gillespie as a jazz player. Miles and I . . . and Dizzy and I are very close friends, and the first time that happened I wrote them both and apologized." Wisely, the magazine had changed the name from "Jazz Poll" to "Pop Poll," diminishing the absurdity when Herb Alpert was voted top trumpeter. Hirt, usually a gentle critic, marveled, "Now Herb Alpert is a successful business man, he's got a sound that's popular with the public, and *good*—I'm all for him for that. But I mean, as far as a trumpet player, he doesn't know how to play."

One takes one's victories where they are found, though, and throughout the 1960s I celebrated the musical, economic, and publicity benefits of the Playboy Club for the local modern jazz scene. My "Ad Libs" column of December 7, 1961, notes that Belletto's first house band consisted of Ed Fenasci, piano; Jay Cave, bass; and Charlie Blancq, drums. Another house band, Ellis Marsalis's trio, included James Black. A third group played only a few weeks. A Dixieland band led by the Cooper twins did not quite go with the drapes. The "Where & When" *DB* listings for the Playboy between 1961 and May 15, 1969 (after which *DB* dropped the W&W page) showed a remarkable array of modern performers at the club. Among the leaders, besides Belletto, Marsalis, and Prima, were Fred Crane, Carrol Cunningham, Ed Fenasci, Rusty Mayne, Pete Monteleone, Joe Morton, Bill Newkirk, John Probst, Phil Reudy, and Dave West. Others played the club before it closed in March 1973.

The first racially integrated full-time combo, discussed at length in the symposium (chapter 26), was hired by Al Belletto as his backup group. Richard Payne sets the date as October 1964. My "Ad Libs" column of April 22, 1965, included this item: "For the first time in recent memory, an integrated combo is playing full time in a New Orleans club—**Dave West**'s trio at the Playboy, which now includes bassist **Richard Payne**." I suspect that the delay in my reportage was an intentional attempt to lay low and watch for possible reactions to Belletto's bold action, taken with the admirable personal support of Hugh Hefner.

As it turned out, there were no protests, no arrests, no lawsuits. But the caution was not paranoid. As James Black pointed out in discussing the Marsalis gig at the Music Haven, race relations were tense at the time. And in late 1964 the city had been embarrassed by the cancellation of a prestigious American League all-star football game because of allegations of discrimination in New Orleans. As noted in section I, the attendant bad press resulted in abandonment of plans for a mammoth jazz festival that George Wein would have produced. As with the integration of public transportation in 1958, accomplishing the integration of a band without fanfare was prudent and effective.

The 1969 "Jazz Off Bourbon Street" article from *New Orleans* magazine (chapter 24) gives further evidence of the growth of modern jazz venues in the 1960s. The title is a slight misnomer, on two counts. First, the article includes some nonjazz clubs and artists. Second, the phrase "off Bourbon Street" cannot be taken too literally. In common parlance, Bourbon Street activity included nearby clubs on intersecting streets, like Preservation Hall and the Playboy, each a few paces away on St. Peter and Bienville Streets, respectively. The article does not regard such locations as "off" the Street.

The article focuses on the city's expanding ecology of entertainment and names several then-leading modern jazz pioneers and popularizers on Decatur Street in the Quarter, North Claiborne Avenue, and Tulane near Carrollton. Young Orleanians and visitors today will find it difficult to visualize lower Decatur Street as a "haven for winos" greatly in need of rescue. But it was exactly that when a group of artists and entrepreneurs ventured into the area. The New Orleans Studio School of Fine Art, headed by L. S. Carstater, set up shop for nontraditional painters at 1100 Decatur. The unique Jazz Workshop and Listening Eye Gallery combined photography exhibits with avant garde jazz provided by an absolutely brilliant quartet—Willie Tee and the Souls, led by Earl and Wilson (Willie Tee) Turbinton. Earl played alto sax; Willie, organ; George Davis was on guitar and David Lee on drums. Willie was a fine rhythm and blues vocalist, and the group had an R&B repertoire that had won them a following a few years earlier with Willie's Atlantic label hit, "Teasin' You." In 1968 Willie had a brush with R&B stardom. He did a session for Capitol supervised by Cannonball Adderley, but it was never released.

At the Jazz Workshop, Willie and the Souls were following their bliss—playing amazing avant garde jazz and seeking to create a learning environment for young musicians. Though the group was influenced by artists like John Coltrane and Rahsaan Roland Kirk, their instrumentation gave them a unique sound and nudged them toward their own postbop sound and feeling. Earl Turbinton moved through ever fresh explorations of the changes on standards, modal materials, and original tunes. Willie's keyboarding was richly inventive and funky. Davis was full of surprises, both in his accompaniment and solos. Lee had digested many influences, laying down a hard-swinging groove while invoking the spirit of Elvin Jones. The band could be intimately soft or thunderously loud, but whatever happened seemed to proceed as if it were inevitable, unfolding like the cadences of great free verse.

Decatur Street ultimately became hostile to winos and friendly to jazz clubs, restaurants, tourists, and the arts. But neither the Studio School of Fine Art nor the Jazz Workshop and Listening Eye Gallery was sustainable in 1969. Carstater wrote to me that the Studio School was working counter to the "sociopolitical art establishment which exists in New Orleans, steadfastly maintaining a tight circle against anyone not willing to advance along its pecking-order." Berry notes that the jazz workshop concept was proposed to public school officials as a possible focus for an expanded music curriculum. The idea was rejected but reshaped in the next decade when a workshop-oriented jazz program taught by Ellis Marsalis became part of the now famous New Orleans Center for the Creative Arts (NOCCA). As English supervisor for the public schools, I was able to get a modest grant in 1970 to produce a black poetry audiotape that used the nucleus of the Tee group. Several tracks were jazz/poetry combinations, accompanied by the Turbintons, David Lee, and bassist Richard Payne. Poet Sybil Kein, then a high school English teacher in the district, was one of the readers.

After the Decatur Street site folded, Willie's sidemen went on to some wonderful things. Lee and Davis were hired by Dizzy Gillespie. Earl went to New York, where he recorded with Joe Zawinul, who was soon to become the keyboardist with Weather Report. He toured Japan with B. B. King before returning to New Orleans.

Another emerging off–Bourbon Street area cited in the article was the Tulane/Carrollton Avenue intersection. Pianist Ronnie Dupont's quartet at the Bistro had no intention of breaking new ground musically. They tried and succeeded at playing listenable and danceable jazz, with a bit of blues to boot, provided by tenor saxist Iggy Campisi. And the group never failed to swing.

Dupont, a longtime Hirt pianist, was supported by Al Bernard on bass and Reed Vaughan on drums. Vaughan was past the prime of his stellar be-bop performances of the 1950s, but it was great to hear him laying it down with taste and grit in the Dupont quartet. The combo reserved its best moments for vocalist Betty Farmer, a liberated lady who sang with sensitivity and authority night after night. A male vocalist named Tony Page was competent and popular but a mood buster, doing mainly Sinatra songs in Sinatra style while claiming not to. The gig began in the summer of 1966 and lasted three years—a strong contribution to the popularization of modern jazz in New Orleans.

Just as Dupont was beginning his run at the Bistro, pianist Fred Crane's trio was concluding a five-month engagement *way* off Bourbon Street—at the Black Knight on Veterans Highway in suburban Jefferson Parish, an unlikely spot for jazz. Yet for ten months in 1965 and 1966 the club featured modern jazz exclusively, starting with Houston pianist Bill Gannon, followed by Crane.

A native of South Carolina, Crane had been a strong presence in the New Orleans and Biloxi jazz scenes since the early postwar years. He studied at both Grunewald's and Loyola. In the late 1940s he played the Prevue Lounge (Junie Mays's venue) with Al Hirt. He was part of the Belletto sextet—the best part, some would say—in the 1950s, and a ubiquitous figure in the 1960s. At the Playboy and with Hirt's neo-Dixieland group he showed remarkable adaptability without canceling the stamp of his style. At afterhours sessions at Hirt's club in the mid-1960s with bassists Jay Cave, Mickey Gozilio, or Bill Huntington and drummer Jimmy Zitano, Crane was a hard-swinging soloist and artful rhythmic conversationalist.

Bostonian Zitano was an ideal partner in these conversations. He was one of the most intuitive musicians I ever heard—possibly the most underrated modern drummer of the postwar years. With technical flexibility that gave him every choice of where and how to comp, place fill-ins, and build solos, he went where the spirit took him, and with Crane the spirit was consistently inspired. Bill Huntington recalls playing one night with Zitano when Tony Williams came in. Williams sent a note to Zitano: "You were my teacher."

When I heard Crane's trio at the Black Knight, he was moving in a different direction. The music was powerfully ethereal, a combination of intense conception, subtle swing, and delicate abstraction. Bill Evans's trio comes to mind as the closest model. But Crane was a mature artist with a personal voice, and he had exquisite backing from Bill Huntington and Miami-based drummer Don Hesterberg. (Later, Zitano joined the group.) The trio played standards at a wide range of tempos, but often the pulse became implied as Huntington and Hesterberg slipped gracefully out of the timekeeping and comping roles. They became part of an ensemble that played sly and thoughtful counterpoint, keeping flawlessly faithful to the beat that was insinuated. It was a sheer joy to wait for an understated resolution to subtly generated tensions. I recall a super slow rendition of "My Funny Valentine" that forced me to shift from the stock response of tracking the horizontal motion of time. The pulse was there, but I found it more interesting to let the waves of sound wash over me without holding on to familiar rhythmic moorings.

I was frankly surprised that Crane's trio lasted as long as it did at the Black Knight, if their music was always as uncompromising as it was on the nights I heard them. Even the Playboy catered to the audience impulse for finger popping and head shaking along with the music. My *Down Beat* listings show that vocalist Jan Allison was with the group, perhaps providing a more popular edge. But I do not recall hearing her—either because she was absent when I was there or because the trio's instrumentals made such an overpowering impression. Sadly, Crane died of a heart attack while leaving a Texas gig with Al Hirt in 1984.

Pianist Ronnie Kole, like Al Belletto, was a successful popularizer of modern jazz in New Orleans in the 1960s. Kole was not the jazzman that Belletto was, but then he never claimed to be. He found a niche as a jazzman/entertainer, flashy technician, and civic-minded leader. Where Joe Burton became known for alienating audiences, Kole played the role of, indeed was, Mister Nice Guy. Sporting a beard that gave him a mock-rakish appearance, Kole led bassist Everett Link and drummer Dickie Taylor through crisp, well-structured sets.

I have heard musicians say that Kole could dig in with solid modern jazz at jam sessions. His career was best served, though, by accentuating the palatable. Each set was carefully paced for showmanly value, each tune enlivened by catchy head arrangements, each improvisation marked by clean lines that incorporated quotations from familiar melodies: jazz that a Montovanni fan could love. Kole was rewarded with a surprise record hit, a jazz/rock treatment of the *Batman* theme from the popular television series. Jazz that a teenager could love.

Kole came to New Orleans with the Heavyweights, a novelty band that played a long run at Dan's Pier 600 during Al Hirt's many absences for national appearances. In 1964 Kole became leader of the house trio under his own name. When Hirt bought and renamed the club, Kole was also named musical director, bringing in big name bands. With sidemen Link and Taylor, Kole developed an appealing approach not unlike that of Peter Nero, then a nationally known popularizer. Within a few months Kole opened his own club, Kole's Corner, behind the Old Absinthe House. Soon the energetic pianist was everywhere—at Pops concerts, youth benefits, society parities, whatever. I once was at a shopping mall and heard his trio at a shoe store opening. All the while, Kole was gaining the respect of social and political leaders, particularly in the white Establishment. In 1969 he and Pete Fountain testified at a city council hearing in opposition to store-window sales of food and drink on Bourbon Street. Kole gave modern jazz a presence and respectability among people who would have been bewildered by Crane's deadpan brilliance, mowed down by Marsalis's unremitting drive.

When the first Jazzfest was produced in 1968, Kole and Belletto were the two active modern jazz musicians who influenced selection of bands for the event. Journalists Doug Ramsey of WDSU-TV and Tex Stephens of the *Louisiana Weekly* were also highly knowledgeable advisers on local and national modernists. In fact, modern jazz dominated the program's national headliners, and local modernists were not absent. Included during the six days of programming were groups led by Belletto, Kole, drummer June Gardner, and Willie Tee. The following year found Belletto on the Jazzfest Executive Committee and Belletto, Kole, and Ramsey on the board of directors and hospitality committee. Local modern groups on the seven-day 1969 Jazz and Food Festival were Belletto, Kole, trumpeter Sam Alcorn, pianist Chuck Berlin, guitarist George Davis, the Loyola University Stage Band, and Willie Tee. (See the overview to section I for a detailed discussion of the evolution of the Jazzfest, and chapters 8 and 10 for contemporaneous reviews of the 1968 and 1969 festivals.)

There were some interesting efforts that did not get off the ground in the 1960s, like the Daliet-Jeanjacques Atonalists in 1961 and trumpeter Warren Luening in 1967. The Atonalists played original compositions that adapted twelve-tone "rows" to the jazz idiom, a venture that might have ignited an Ornette Coleman-type controversy. Despite atypically strong publicity, the group did not make a breakthrough in either New Orleans or a Los Angeles concert. I wrote about the Atonalists twice in "Ad Libs" but did not hear persuasive jazz in the imaginative twelve-tone compositions. Their work on standard jazz materials, moreover, was not in the same league as the city's exciting combos and individual improvisers of the time.

I reported a more modest (and more successful) twelve-tone experiment at a Gulf Coast Jazz Club concert late in 1963. Pianist Roger Dickerson composed a "row" inspired by a Marty Most poem. Ellis Marsalis's quartet then used the row impressionistically as the basis for improvisations behind Most's reading.

Warren Luening was an extraordinarily talented trumpeter who had come up as a teenage Dixieland prodigy sitting in at Tony Almerico's Parisian Room concerts. (See the overview to section II.) He followed Pete Fountain's footsteps as a featured New Orleans instrumentalist on Lawrence Welk's national TV show. But in fact, Luening had become an eclectic jazzman with clear gifts for modernism in the style of Clifford Brown. Fountain further supported Luening's bid for fame by featuring him at Pete Fountain's Storyville, a new club on Esplanade Avenue. It did not sell. Musically, the trumpeter was pulled in too many directions. Commercially, he was low concept. There was no single handle, like Fountain's ebullient projection of hot Dixie clarinet licks or Al Hirt's pyrotechnics, for launching a career as the next New Orleans pop/jazz star.

To summarize the inroads of the 1960s, it cannot be said that Orleanians rushed to embrace modern jazz and its practitioners as audiences had done in Los Angeles, New York, and elsewhere a decade earlier. But the support was substantial. Certainly, the idea was afoot that the music was chic, complex, enjoyable, and perhaps worthy of serious attention. During the earlier postwar years local modernists were heard mainly at after hours sessions, strip clubs, out-of-the-way lounges, and occasional concerts. In the 1960s modern jazz was also performed at well-publicized venues like Al Hirt's Club, Kole's Corner, and the Playboy. And as noted in the section I discussion of jazz and the Establishment, by the late 1960s the music was gaining limited recognition at Loyola, Southern, and other universities.

As in the 1950s, there were several of the 1960s players whom I heard more frequently and especially admired. Among them were trumpeter Bob Teeters; reedmen Nat Perrilliat, Don Suhor, and Earl Turbinton; keyboardists Fred Crane, Ellis Marsalis, John Probst, and Willie (Tee) Turbinton; bassists Bill Huntington and Richard Payne; guitarist George Davis;

drummers James Black, John Boudreaux, David Lee, and Jimmy Zitano; and vocalist Betty Farmer.

It is true that these and many other fine modern jazz artists of the decade seldom did their most adventurous work in the popular clubs. The blind piano wizard John Probst, for example, had a unique touch and original conception that came through at the Playboy and with Pete Fountain. But at freewheeling jam sessions he played some of the most astonishing jazz piano I have ever heard. Nevertheless, in a town internationally known for Fountain, Hirt, and Preservation Hall, it was marvelous that some modern jazz musicians were working full-time and gaining a modicum of respect from civic, educational, and social leaders.

Another decade or two would pass before the city's new generation of modernists—the Marsalis brothers, Harry Connick Jr., Terence Blanchard, Nicholas Payton, and others—would gain worldwide fame and win fans who had no hint of the struggles of their brilliant musical foreparents. The articles in chapters 21–25, written when the exciting postwar years were strongly resonant in the minds and hearts of New Orleans musicians, should give a fuller picture of the music and the times. The symposium, a joyful collective memory-jogging session by some key surviving modernists, also conveys a sense of the postwar years. Timeline chart 3, "Highlights of Early Modern Jazz in New Orleans, 1945–1970," is a visual representation of the period.

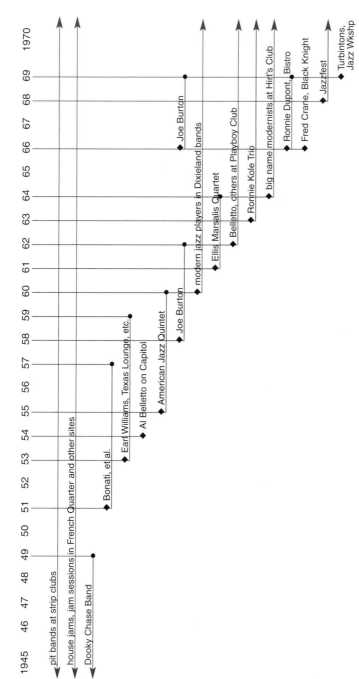

Timeline Chart 3 – Highlights of Early Modern Jazz in New Orleans, 1945–1970
(Underlines indicate continuation/duration)

21

New Jazz in the Cradle, Part I

Down Beat, August 17, 1961

Ask the average jazz fan to name several cities producing good modern jazzmen in abundance. It will probably not even occur to him to mention New Orleans.

Suggest to him that New Orleans today is the begetter of not only a substantial force of competent modernists, but is still producing major talents who are carrying jazz forward in the manner of their musical progenitors of half a century ago, and you will most likely encounter incredulity, scorn, or mild amusement.

On the surface, it might indeed seem contradictory to expect a crew of creative modernists from a city whose most widely publicized musical exports in recent years have been the Dukes of Dixieland, Pete Fountain, Al Hirt, *et al*. And yet, it would be an even greater enigma if a city that showed the remarkable vitality and unique cultural flavor of New Orleans in the early 20th century were to become utterly sterile after bringing forth its most brilliant issue.

New Orleans, in fact, is not a living anachronism. It is fertile, complex, contemporary, and still possesses the subtle qualities of soul which create a distinctive personality and an artist of deep sensitivity. The cultural milieu that produced Buddy Bolden, Bunk Johnson, Louis Armstrong, and the others is still here. It is modified, of course, influenced by the flux and tensions of modern life, but it still retains the basic combination of casualness and intensity reflected in the music of the earliest jazz men.

Those who believe that the "New Orleans era" ended when jazz went up the river in the 1920s are guilty of historical error. Leonard Feather's *Encyclopedia of Jazz* lists Lester Young, Joe Newman, Benny Powell, and Mundell Lowe as either New Orleans–born or dwellers in the Crescent City during impressionable periods in their lives. And in recent memory, modern musicians like Brew Moore, Ornette Coleman, Bruce Lippincot, and Roy Burns have absorbed the city's many moods.

Why, then, has New Orleans remained in the background as a significant jazz city while the "major" jazz areas continue to grow in repute? There are a number of reasons for this, some obvious; others require elucidation.

New Orleans, being about as far south as one can go without dipping into the Gulf of Mexico, is at a geographic disadvantage. The city is isolated from the regular band and show routes on which musicians so often make connections, switch bands, and are heard at important sessions that can lead to work with more influential groups.

The cost of bringing name bands and package shows to the Deep South is generally prohibitive. Nail-biting promoters bring name jazz groups into New Orleans about once a year; hotels which use any bands at all use New Orleans–based society groups; and only one Bourbon Street club follows a policy of bringing in out-of-town jazz talent. The situation is complicated by state legal barriers against interracial performances and integrated audiences, which keep many groups and shows away.

It is the musician who suffers most from these circumstances. Since traveling bands are not marketable in New Orleans, he must try breaking into the bands in a city where a heavy band and combo traffic exists, and this in competition with established favorite sons whose goals are identical with his—and who have the added luxury of living at home until the opportunity to move out presents itself.

"What for?" the jazzman will ask when he is confronted with the argument that he should bring his talent to an area where it is more likely to receive recognition. Drummer James Black, playing with the American Jazz Quintet in New Orleans, retorts, "In New York or Chicago, you're just a playing cat among a thousand other playing cats. Your chances of making it are small, unless you know someone or have a gig lined up."

Many musicians of Black's caliber share his distaste for the starving-artist role. For them, the problem becomes one of acquiring sustenance and achieving fulfillment as a modern jazzman in New Orleans.

On this point, the suspicions of the layman are confirmed; there are in New Orleans virtually no full-time gigs where the modern jazzman can develop his talent unfettered by commercial considerations. The tourist trade demands Dixieland bands and strip shows. Since the young modernists are generally the best improvisers and reading musicians available, they are constrained to brave the anarchy of the neo-Dixie groups and the boredom of the belly dancers in order to make a living. So it is that musicians like bassist Oliver Felix turn up in Al Hirt's hell-bent-for-leather Dixie group, and talents like those of alto saxophonist Don Lasday provide backgrounds for the bump-and-grind queens of Bourbon Street.

Nor does the musician have the sympathy of the public at large. Local citizens traditionally have felt that the close connection between jazz and New Orleans is a lamentable fact of history that might eventually be forgotten if no official notice were taken of it. The intensity—and influence—of this anti-jazz feeling comes ludicrously to light every so often, as it did several years ago when Mayor de Lesseps Morrison considered a proposal to erect a statue of a jazz band at the foot of Basin Street. Objections poured in from irate citizens who were scandalized that the city's "shameful past" should be put on display. One sardonic letter in a local newspaper suggested that a memorial might be erected with equal propriety to Lulu White.

Today a statue of Simón Bolívar, the South American liberator, stands at the corner of Basin and Canal Street, and if the traveler is unable to relate this to the historical importance of Basin Street, he is referred to Bill Russell and Dick Allen, Ford Foundation jazz researchers at Tulane University, who are still unable to confirm reports of a clandestine meeting of Bolívar and Jean Lafite at Mahogany Hall.

Recently the city has grown more tolerant of its Dixieland musicians. This is probably attributable to a potpourri of largely unrelated factors: the healthy images created by Fountain, Hirt, and the Assuntos in their public appearances, the establishment of a New Orleans jazz museum, the tireless work of the New Orleans Jazz Club, the realization that the city's jazz stars can enhance tourist trade, and the greater acceptance generally that jazz has achieved at the national level.

But the stamp of approval has not been extended to modern musicians or to other forms of jazz, and the likelihood of the city's deserving corps of modernists' finding in-town gigs is small, in the city's current psychological climate. (Even the highly marketable Al Belletto group, which was based on the Gulf Coast, seldom worked in New Orleans.)

With few exceptions, the jazz gig available to the local modernist is a weekend job in a depressing bar usually owned by a well-meaning hipster who wants to provide a place for jazzmen to blow and break even in the money department at the same time. The illusion in such places—and there has been at least one in tenuous existence somewhere in the Quarter since time immemorial—is that the dreary atmosphere can be transformed into hipness by hanging morbid pseudo-modern paintings on the wall and allowing dust to collect on the top of the inevitably out-of-tune upright piano.

This is, of course, the brand of "hipness" musicians deplore. But experience has insulated them from such calculated inanity, and they proceed relentlessly to produce some memorable sounds in these ephemeral surroundings.

Charlie Ducharme, Canadian-born owner of Cosimo's lounge, is trying to break the jinx of the now-you-see-it-now-you-don't Quarter jazz rooms by operating on the assumption that he is primarily a businessman and only secondarily a crusader for jazz. He is currently offering a stimulating trio led by Nat Perrilliat (Perrilliat, tenor saxophone; Richard Payne, bass; James Black, drums) on weekends, and is looking forward to expanding his activities in a new club shortly.

"Bourbon St. has gone commercial," Ducharme contends. "Even the tourists are looking for a place off the beaten track where they can hear good jazz." Perrilliat himself concurs that a hip proprietorship and an attractively kept club could successfully provide full-time work for a modern group in the French Quarter. Whether Ducharme's efforts will go the same way as the Hidden Door, the Playboy, Mambo Joe's, the Pendulum, and countless others is a question of great interest to Orleans jazz fans and musicians.

At least two clubs, the Joy Tavern and Joe Burton's, have been able to sustain a modern jazz policy. Alvin Tyler's tightly knit quintet has appeared at the former club on weekends for more than a year. And Burton, a New York pianist who migrated to the Crescent City in 1958 with the express purpose of selling modern jazz to Orleaneans, soon begins his fifth year as the only six-night-a-week modern jazz attraction in the city.

Although Burton's admirable dedication to restraint has often miscarried his groups in the direction of jazz-flavored cocktail music, his best group in 1958 showcased two of the city's outstanding jazz talents, guitarist Bill Huntington and onetime Stan Kenton and Ira Sullivan drummer Reed Vaughan. Burton scored an important break-through with this group last summer when the New Orleans Pops Orchestra featured his quartet on its annual jazz night, the first modern combo to be so honored.

Guitarist Huntington and Ed Blackwell, the remarkable drummer who came to prominence with Ornette Coleman, are deserving of special comment. In these men, the city boasts two musicians who rise above mere competence to levels of creativity that put them in the company of the few who are developing the insights which will set the standards for jazz to come.

It is not, I think, partisan to suggest that they may be the most probing musicians on their instruments today. For this reason, they required extended comment, which will be made in Part II of this essay in the next issue of *Down Beat*.

22

New Jazz in the Cradle, Part II

Down Beat, August 31, 1961

Of the group of modern jazz musicians playing in New Orleans during the last few years, two have reached high levels of creativity—drummer Ed Blackwell and guitarist Bill Huntington. It would not be partisan to suggest that they may be among the most probing musicians on their instruments today.

Of the two, Blackwell has the wider reputation, having played with Wardell Gray and Ray Charles before returning to New Orleans, where he met Ornette Coleman, who was impressed by the drummer's imagination.

The first time I heard of Blackwell was when I was talking to two Xavier University students in 1955 about another local drummer, Earl Palmer. Palmer was then with Earl Williams' group but has since settled on the West Coast, where he has gigged with Buddy Collette and now is doing studio work. I ventured the opinion that Palmer was probably the finest jazz drummer in New Orleans. The students smiled and shook their heads, saying, "I don't know, man. . . . That Blackwell. . . ."

I didn't hear "that Blackwell . . ." until almost two years later, but it was clear then why the students' tribute to him had not been a profusion of words but only an amazed shaking of the head.

Blackwell not only had prodigious technique and exceptional coordination, but he was the most inventive drummer I had ever heard. His solos, executed with what only can be described paradoxically as icy abandon, were gems of asymmetry. It was a challenging delight to follow Blackwell's lines down devious paths and then back again to home base. Even more refreshing was his instinct for deviating from standard practices at the right time to stimulate the soloist with ingenious devices that would be tasteless distractions or affectations in the hands of the less perceptive.

It is possible, however, that the exposure Blackwell is receiving in the Coleman group is not the most favorable kind. Not that he is unable to conform to the group's standard of nonconformity. Certainly he is capable of going as far into orbit as his companions, but Blackwell's is basically a mainstream talent, building on the past rather than breaking from it, and it is best viewed against the relief of an adventurous but not anarchic group.

Furthermore, the hotly controversial nature of the Coleman group has tended to divide the critics and public into two camps. In this rigid critical atmosphere, categorical damnation or praise of the group is more common than cool evaluation of the merits of its individual members.

While Blackwell's importance is clouded by his association with the highly publicized Coleman, the problem of guitarist Huntington is quite different: he is virtually unknown outside the Crescent City. And yet Huntington, at the age of 23, has a background with all the makings of a jazz legend, for his development is practically a recapitulation of the history of jazz itself.

When Huntington was 12 he became a protege of Lawrence Marrero, the famed banjoist with Bunk Johnson's band. His mastery of the blues-drenched Marrero feeling brought him to the attention of the New Orleans Jazz Club, where he became a regular at the club's monthly sessions.

When 15 years old, he was recorded with Ken Colyer, the British traditionalist trumpeter who was visiting the city. Young Huntington subsequently appeared with George Lewis and other veteran New Orleans bands at private sessions and dances.

Then the young banjoist began to listen to later jazz musicians. He next became attracted to swing-era figures, such as Teddy Wilson, Coleman Hawkins, and Benny Carter. Inevitably, he became aware of the modernists, most notably Charlie Christian and Charlie Parker. Although it was a long way from New Orleans banjo to Christian, Huntington set out on a Herculean program of self-education to master a new instrument and digest the nuances of three decades of jazz.

The metamorphosis was not an easy one. Beset by illness, Huntington dropped out of school for a few months before graduation and rededicated his energies to the task of assimilating the later jazz forms. Within three years he became as precocious a modern musician as he had been a traditional one.

Pianist Buddy Prima (Louis' nephew and a comer among the city's young modernists) describes his reaction on first hearing Huntington in 1954: "I was amazed by Bill's free conception of time. He wasn't all tied up with *try·ing* to swing; he would just swing along naturally with fine-free-flowing lines."

Gradually, the city's young jazzmen became aware of the comprehensiveness of Huntington's background. Each job on which Huntington appeared became an object lesson in how to project a natural, relaxed jazz feeling. Musicians dedicated to fad, frothy technical display, and popular clichés came to realize that the absence of these devices in Huntington's playing was really the presence of a conceptual maturity that was self-contained and whole and did not draw its power to excite from notions of hip phraseology.

Huntington's stature as a jazz guitarist continued to grow as he worked with Prima, Joe Burton, and Dave West. He cut a memorable series of radio shows for Loyola University with Prima and made a brief tour as a bassist with Al Belletto's sextet.

Huntington has in fact achieved a synthesis of widely varied elements in the jazz tradition—the rootsy qualities of Marrero's rich blues banjo; the warm and natural vibrato of Django Reinhardt; the communicative power of Charlie Christian; the rhythmic plasticity of Charlie Parker; and the adventurous spirit that releases these elements in ever-fresh combinations to fulfill the one inalienable right of the listener—the right to be surprised without being jarred.

A final point, and perhaps the most telling and central point, remains to be made about the presence of modern jazz musicians in New Orleans. Many musicians choose to remain in the city for a reason so basic that it tends to be overlooked: they want to live there.

New Orleans does possess, as one musician phrased it, "some sort of power," which, like Buddy Bolden's legendary trumpet, keeps "calling its chillun' home." To a native this is a truism that does not require explanation; to him it is easier to experience the city's unique cultural savor than it is to verbalize it.

Speaking of the distinctive mood that permeates the city, bassist Richard Payne says, "It would probably take an outsider to explain it. I guess it's just that in places like New York, they have a fast thing going. Down here it's a relaxed thing, and it's different from anywhere else— something in the way of living that's unique . . . in other words, *hip*, when the word is correctly used."

There is near-unanimity on this point among native musicians, who will complain bitterly that the city is square in its musical tastes and then turn around and say that something about the tone of life is appealing, vibrant, and productive.

So it is that many musicians would prefer to live in the relaxed atmosphere of New Orleans, getting a day gig and taking their musical kicks where they can be found (much in the manner of the city's earliest jazzmen), rather than entering the arena of insecurity and entanglement that offers a nebulous promise of artistic fulfillment and immortality but most often proffers prolonged periods of hassle and fruitless sacrifice.

Even those who have traveled successfully "up North" or to the West Coast often have retired from enviable chairs in big bands and combos to return to New Orleans.

Pianist Pete Monteleone, who has traveled full circle and returned to New Orleans permanently, sums it up in this way:

"New Orleans still has the kind of soul that produces good jazz musicians. People expect a New Orleans musician to absorb some of this soul, and they're right—except that they don't realize that the musician today has the desire to express himself in a different way from the musicians who lived here 20 years ago. New Orleans still turns out some of the best musicians anywhere, but unless the people come to enjoy what good musicians of every era have to say, our young jazz musicians won't get the kind of recognition they deserve."

If New Orleans creates fine jazz musicians and then frustrates them, this is regrettable. However, the very fact of the city's fecundity, coupled with the irrepressibility of the musicians' desire for musical expression under the most adverse circumstances, suggests that the third essential party—the public—might be brought to an awareness of its neglected grandchildren, the line behind the second line that followed the early marching bands through the city's narrow streets.

If jazz can progress from a word of dubious etymology to a widely accepted art form in 40 years, it might not be too optimistic to hope that the city that nurtured it will embrace it in all its forms in our generation.

The Problems of Modern Jazz in New Orleans

New Orleans magazine, August 1967

New Orleans is one of the few cities in the world where a tourist with a free evening, a hefty wallet, and a high capacity for liquor can program his own jazz festival. In the Bourbon Street area alone, he would find almost 150 musicians playing in dozens of night clubs, all within walking distance of each other. He would hear plenty of traditional jazz, an abundance of Dixieland, a few brass and banjo groups, and enough rock-and-roll to send him screaming back to Minerva, Ohio. But he would find only three clubs in the entire city—the Playboy, Joe Burton's, and the Bistro—that promote a modern jazz policy.

Even these clubs provide an unsympathetic setting for modern jazz. At the Playboy, jazz is part of the sophisticated Playboy image; it is there because Playboys are supposed to dig modern jazz, along with sports cars, foreign movies, and the foldout of the month. Al Belletto's group tries valiantly to come to terms with the audience, but it is distressingly obvious that jazz at the Playboy is background music for banter and bunny-watching.

The rapid turnover in sidemen in Joe Burton's trio prevents the pianist from developing the kind of tightly-knit group he had a decade ago at his Canal Street club. Burton's unpredictable personality usually assures an eventful evening, but the music is seldom as colorful as the leader's offbeat stage manner.

At the Bistro, pianist Ronnie Dupont has no personnel problems—his quartet is not only stable, it is rock solid. But the Bistro is a showplace, and the jazz is diluted for the sake of dancing and entertainment. Still, Dupont leads the group skillfully through its many roles. The group plays tasteful and swinging dance sets, drawing from the better pop tunes and standards; they provide unshakable support for Tony Page, who delivers Frank Sinatra imitations with ring-a-ding credibility; and they respond sensitively to their most demanding assignment—accompanying Betty Farmer, a gifted jazz vocalist with a magnetism that attracts non-jazz audiences as well as hipsters.

Dupont's quartet demonstrates that modern jazz can be made commercially acceptable. But the groups that have set out to explore the frontiers of contemporary jazz have inevitably been forced to retreat to safe ground. At least two such groups, the American Jazz Quintet and the Fred Crane Trio, have been starved out of existence in New Orleans in recent years. The

American Jazz Quintet was a superlative modern combo that played a series of memorable concerts and weekend sessions in the mid-fifties. Paced by the brilliant drummer Ed Blackwell, the quintet (Nat Perrilliat, tenor saxophone; Alvin Batiste, clarinet; Ed Frank, piano; Chuck Badie, bass; and Blackwell, drums), pushed past the boundaries set by the bop movement in the previous decade.

But the quintet never received adequate exposure in a setting worthy of its talent. One by one, its members began to leave. Pianist Ed Frank moved to Dallas; Blackwell went to New York, where he joined Ornette Coleman's avant garde combo in 1961. Perrilliat stayed in New Orleans to become a key member of an excellent quartet led by pianist Ellis Marsalis, but within a few years the latter group had disbanded as well—despite the fact that in 1962 alto saxophonist Cannonball Adderley featured Marsalis, Perrilliat, and drummer James Black on a Riverside LP, which was well received nationally by jazz critics.

Today New Orleans' cadre of talented modernists is scattered about in a variety of unlikely bands. Some, like Huntington, Marsalis, and Perrilliat, can only be caught on the run. Huntington played briefly with Joe Burton after the Black Knight engagement, then left town, joined Al Hirt on the road—only to quit after several weeks of traveling with the *Java* sound. Marsalis made an appearance at the Playboy recently, but by the time the word got around he was no longer on the scene. Perrilliat is back in New Orleans freelancing after a long tour with singer Fats Domino.

Other modernists are less elusive, but an outsider would not find their names on a marquee. For example, at the Sho'Bar, alto saxist Don Suhor and trumpeter Bob Teeters play unabashed bop in the Parker-Gillespie tradition while the strippers go through their usual calisthenics. Trumpeter Mike Serpas is in the brass section of Pete Fountain's newly expanded Dixieland group. Another solid trumpeter, Sam Alcorn, is playing casual engagements with Preacher John's blues and rock band. Numerous other Dixieland bands and blues combos in the city have a modernist-in-residence, and even Leon Kelner's Blue Room band is well stocked with modern jazz musicians.

Why can't New Orleans, a city with a rich jazz tradition and over a million people, support a single group that is interested in experimenting freely in contemporary jazz? Perhaps it is because the city's unique jazz tradition has conditioned the public to think of jazz as something more than a mere musical experience.

Jazz grew in New Orleans as a folk art. As such, it was inseparable from the city's rich and varied social life. Jazz was a part of picnics at Milneberg, taxi-dancing at the Fern, Mardi Gras reveling, whoring in Storyville, and neighborhood parties. It accentuated the joy at a celebration or sharpened the sense of grief at a funeral.

Modern jazz evolved from earlier jazz forms, but it did not grow as a simple extension of community life. In fact, its originators—men like Charlie Parker, Dizzy Gillespie, Thelonious Monk, and Max Roach—found that the freedom of expression they sought was incompatible with the traditional function of jazz as an adjunct to social life. To them, jazz was a field of artistic exploration; the listener's reward did not consist in getting in on the performance but in following the daring flights of the jazzman's imagination.

Modern jazz undeniably demands more of its listener than most jazz forms. If the traditional jazz fan brings the same expectation to a modern jazz session as he brings to Preservation Hall, he is certain to be frustrated and bored. He must re-educate his responses, focusing his attention more on the music than on the life and excitement surrounding it. He must refine his listening skills, sensitizing himself to the subtler and more complex shades of emotion in modern jazz. He must see the communication between the artist and his audience as an aesthetic rather than a social interaction.

Creative and spontaneous communication of emotion is, after all, the essential element in all good jazz. A traditional jazz fan is potentially a modern jazz fan. If the New Orleans jazz audience can accept the idea that the artistry of jazz is not identical with its nostalgic appeal or its value as a catalyst in promoting good fellowship, modern jazz will emerge as an important part of our musical culture.

24

Jazz Off Bourbon Street

New Orleans magazine, June 1969

Everybody knows that a walk of a few blocks in the Bourbon Street area will put you within earshot of more jazz than you can find in any other city in America. Traditional jazz, Dixieland, swing, modern jazz, and even blues and rock can be heard in the area, which undoubtedly offers the most varied musical bill of fare in the South—or the North, or the East, or the West.

This is plenty enough to keep tourists busy, but the local music buff should know that there is plenty of exciting music that can't be heard on The Street because it isn't there. Three clusters of clubs have grown in different parts of town, each stressing some aspect of contemporary music that is only sampled on Bourbon Street.

Closest to Bourbon Street is the Decatur Street cluster, most promising of the new areas because it is bolstered by the conscious effort of artists in several fields to transform the street into an arts center. A black modern jazz, blues, and avant garde cluster is growing on North Claiborne Avenue between Orleans and Esplanade. Tulane at Carrollton is the third entertainment mini-center, where jazz for dancing has been successfully featured for several years.

The Decatur area across from the French Market, long known as a haven for winos, now boasts the only avant garde jazz in the Quarter at the Jazz Workshop and Listening Eye Gallery. The gallery features rotating photographic exhibits while the theater-style workshop spotlights Willie Tee and the Souls six nights a week. The workshop activities are being expanded to include teaching of jazz improvisation to young musicians. Further up the street two rock clubs, the Bank and Bonaparte's Retreat, have been established. Galo Diaz and Benito Gomez, owners of the Bank, are interested in acid rock, blues, and jazz. They hope to create a valid rock showplace, importing quality rock combos like Gum and Nectar, two groups from other parts of the state, in the absence of exciting local rock bands.

Bill McConnell, owner of a recently opened coffee house called the Sphinx on Decatur Street, comments on why he chose to locate in the area. "I wanted to be close to the Quarter element—people prone to the arts. . . . I'll have a high quality of folk singer at the Sphinx. New Orleans will have a genuine coffee house." McConnell insists that there is a vast difference between the "people prone to the arts" in the neighborhood and the assortment of hippies, alcoholics, and hangers-on who have long been associated with the Quarter Riverfront. A new breed of serious artists is beginning to dominate the area. They may or may not have long hair and beards, but they can be identified by their involvement in endeavors like the Jazz Workshop, the New Orleans Studio School of Fine Arts, and any of the several theater groups in the area. Look for an alliance of these artists soon in the form of an organization that will call the public's attention to the productiveness of many of our lesser known local artists.

The Claiborne Avenue cluster is composed of several clubs that have adopted a jazz or blues policy in recent months. At press time, the black community in the area was supporting live music at three clubs: Club 77, where trumpeter Porgy Jones leads an after-hours jazz combo; the Desert Sands, which features Sam Henry, Aaron Neville, and Cyril Neville; and the Off Limits, where after hours weekend sessions feature David Lastie's modern group.

The action on Claiborne Avenue is impressive because it is composed of several clubs that function in a kind of cooperative competition relationship. However, the tradition of black jazz and blues artists playing their music in predominantly Negro neighborhood lounges is by no means a new element on the local jazz scene. Promoter Clinton Scott, who has been constantly in touch with modern jazz and blues in the black community here, puts the current activity at the North Claiborne Avenue cluster in perspective.

"Actually, live (modern) jazz started uptown with concerts at places like the old Elks' Club, the Caravan, and Hayes' Chicken Shack, and at clubs like the Dew Drop," he explains. "La Salle Street was the thing uptown for a long time because of the Dew Drop Inn. The Joy Tavern was another uptown club. Alvin Tyler's group was there, and they drew a lot of students from Xavier University to the Joy."

Speculating on why a concentration of clubs grew in the downtown area, Scott hypothesizes that "the downtown people seldom came to the uptown clubs, so maybe they needed to get their own thing going. Then, also, Whitney Barkoney, the man at Club 77 on North Claiborne was originally at the 808 on Cadiz Street uptown, and Club 77 was the leader among the downtown clubs that have live jazz now."

Tulane Avenue, dotted with motels and snack bars, might well become a large entertainment sub-center. The Fontainebleau Motel's longstanding nightly music policy provided the thrust for what will probably be a continuing trend towards commercial jazz in a modern vein on the Tulane Avenue strip. Years ago, the Fontainebleau offered pianist Fred Nesbitt's interesting and eccentric brand of modern jazz at the Chandelle Lounge, but the audiences were not in tune with far-out sounds. Clarinetist Tony Mitchell's combo, which is thoroughly flexible and eclectic, came in on a two-week contract, caught on, and has been in residence with a varied program of danceable jazz since 1961. A new group, the Frank Sparcello Trio, is alternating with Mitchell's group and emphasizing jazz-tinged materials.

The Bistro started out attracting the overflow crowds from the Fontainebleau but has long since become established on its own as a first rate jazz-for-dancing club. Pianist Ronnie Dupont's quartet, though troubled by shifting personnel in recent months, is sparked by the excellent modern trumpet of Warren Luening, who many will remember as a kid star in the early 1950's at Tony Almerico's Parisian Room Dixieland sessions. The Bistro's Sunday night feature, Dave West's trio, is more of a straight jazz trip with occasional concessions to the cha-cha crowd. Owner Lou Angelo has added more show biz glitter to Tulane Avenue by dabbling with imported name acts from Las Vegas, but the club's consistent strength is still in the house group's successful merging of jazz, popular, and dance music.

Elsewhere on Tulane Avenue, club-owners have tried danceable jazz with mixed results. Caesar's Palace featured trumpeter Jay Barry with Paul Ferrara on drums for a while, then went back to selling steaks exclusively. A new club called the Cage is currently using a rock group called the Del Rays on weekends. However, the ecology is set, at least for the foreseeable future. Considered back o'town in Louis Armstrong's time and thought of as suburban until the 1950's, Tulane Avenue is the doorway to Fun Town, a natural for a sophisticated dine and dance strip in New Orleans.

Bourbon Street provides the most thorough musical walking tour in the jazz world. The three club sections emerging in various parts of town each have a different musical accent. Besides these, though, there are several places relatively isolated from each other where jazz can be heard. If you're looking for individual clubs with avant garde and modern jazz uptown, try the VIP at Mason's on South Claiborne, where drummer June Gardner and vocalist Germaine Bazzle are heard nightly, and Sylvia's on Freret Street, which brings reed man James Rivers in for after hours weekend sessions at the end of trumpeter Porgy Jones' evening sets. Downtown it's James Rivers playing the early sets on weekends at Laura's on North Dorgenois and vocalist Billy Tircuit in a jazz and popular context at the Sugar Plum on Ursuline Street. Just off the Bourbon Street network of jazz clubs, Armand Hug is playing the best ragtime and swing piano in town at the Touché Lounge in the Royal Orleans. Another single, pianist-vocalist Laverne Smith, is worth a detour to the Sheriff's Office on Dauphine and Conti.

A jazz fan touring New Orleans will probably want to see Bourbon Street first, but to stop there would be like sitting through Mardi Gras on a reviewing stand. A little legwork will yield a far broader picture of what's going on, and only the off–Bourbon Street jazz clubs tell what's really new on the New Orleans music scene.

25

Buddy Prima Trio: Review

Down Beat, October 22, 1964

Playboy Club, New Orleans; Personnel: Prima, piano, trumpet, vocals; Bill Huntington, bass; Bob Ventrulla, drums

Prima, son of New Orleans trumpeter Leon Prima and Louis' nephew, has organized a group that is trying to bridge the gap between entertainment, down-home jazz, and the "new thing." Of course, he has set himself a Herculean (if not downright presumptuous) task, but there is in fact something of interest in the group for any listener, and in its best moments it moves toward an arresting synthesis of the slick, the rootsy, and the abstruse.

Prima's tendency to encompass too much is most evident in his vocals on standards like *That Old Black Magic* and *I've Got You under My Skin*. He has a witty, showmanly appeal that wins an audience effectively; but his piano choruses between his vocals mark an abrupt change in gesture and musical texture as he extends himself, quite capably—if shockingly—in a meditative and penetrating Bill Evans-ish mood.

The shift is less jarring when Prima plays trumpet, as he did on *Yes Sir, That's My Baby*, for his warm, buoyant trumpet work affords a greater continuity with the vocal choruses.

Prima's piano style is highly eclectic, showing the influence of Oscar Peterson, Bud Powell, Red Garland, and Evans. Yet the strain toward individuality is unmistakable, especially in the paradoxical tension between ebullience and restraint that generates a peculiar excitement in his playing.

Prima's right-hand lines have a bubbling, spastic energy that reflects, at a more serious level, the extroverted Prima-on-mike, while his left hand lays down chords with transporting ease and beauty. Even when he is block-chording in the Evans groove—an all too common crutch with young pianists—his phrases tend to be more strongly accented than Evans'.

Often, as on a disjointed *I Get a Kick Out of You*, Prima fails to unify the elements in his style, and a musical pastiche results.

Prima seems to respond best to the more challenging materials in his library. His multitempo version of *Lollipops and Roses*, the lovely ballad *My Ship*, and two originals, *Miss Cottontail* and *Puddin' Tane*, were developed with fine balance and control. The originals are from Prima's *Louisiana Suite*, and they suggest a strong compositional talent. The savor of Louisiana culture is there, along with the Prima wit, rhythmic intensity, and thoughtfulness.

Huntington and Ventrulla are an excellent rhythm team.

Huntington is an extremely creative bassist. A former guitarist, he seems hell-bent on making the instrument behave as flexibly as a guitar. His strongly conceived solos on *I Believe in You* and *My Ship* were most adventurous, employing fluent technique and achieving remarkable color through use of a wide vibrato, slurs, and almost harplike effects in the thumb positions.

Ventrulla is a thinking man's drummer. He is always aware of his role as timekeeper, yet he is quite up to the challenge of entering into complex interplay with Prima and Huntington, as in the free-wheeling 12/8 patterns on *Puddin' Tane*. His sensitive mallet work on cymbals and tom-toms behind Prima's poignant vocalizing on *Lazy Afternoon* was also a fine demonstration of taste and control.

Prima's group is enthusiastic, well rehearsed, and at times highly inventive. Prima might not achieve his goal of pleasing all of the people all of the time, but he is a versatile performer who will bear watching in his development both as a pianist and as a showman.

26

Modern Jazz Pioneers in New Orleans: A Symposium

Loyola University, New Orleans, April 22, 1998

This symposium of modern jazz pioneers in New Orleans was part of a two-day conference of the New Orleans International Music Colloquium (NOIMC) at Loyola University. Administered by Loyola and the University of New Orleans (UNO) faculty and staff, the program's theme was "Roots and Revolutions: New Generations in Jazz."

I heard about plans for the consortium in 1997 and contacted Connie Atkinson of UNO about the possibility of organizing a panel composed of some of the city's early modern jazz artists to discuss their work and others' during the postwar years. She was immediately receptive, and I began contacting some key musicians. Many of the panelists' activities are revealed below or have been noted earlier in this section, so I will do minimal introductions here.

Three scheduled panelists were unable to attend—clarinetist Alvin Batiste, a member of the brilliant American Jazz Quintet; Bill Huntington, who began as a traditional New Orleans Jazz banjoist then became a marvelous modern guitarist, then bassist; pianist Ellis Marsalis, widely known as a New Orleans modern jazz innovator and father of the multitalented young lions of today, Wynton, Branford, Delfayo, and Jason.

The panelists who participated included myself as chair; Harold Battiste, versatile reed player, mentor, arranger, and entrepreneur; Germaine Bazzle, a seminal jazz vocalist in New Orleans; alto saxist Al Belletto, whose sextet was the first successful modern group to come out of the city; drummer Earl Palmer, the city's first great modern jazz drummer and major innovator of rhythm and blues drumming; bassist Richard Payne, another American Jazz Quintet veteran and fecund anecdotist; and clarinetist/alto saxist Don Suhor, who worked the early jazz underground's strip clubs and jam sessions.

As the loosely structured discussion progressed, I was pleased to learn the extent to which these artists had far more experiences in common than I expected. Although living in a segregated society, the black musicians—Battiste, Bazzle, Payne, and Palmer—had known, jammed with, and sometimes been arrested alongside the white musicians—Belletto, Don Suhor, and myself. The age span was considerable, but this served to bring out interesting influences, adjustments of perceptions, and contrasts, as in Payne's and Bazzle's engaging joust about the influences of "the good nuns" at Xavier University. In addition to furnishing new perspectives, many of the musicians' comments corroborated other sources and provided leads that resulted in information that is fleshed out in greater detail in the overview to this section.

My gratitude to Connie Atkinson and Joseph Logsdon of the UNO History Department goes beyond agreeing to the symposium idea. They and other UNO leaders oversaw the acquisition of grants that brought Earl Palmer in from California for the program. They also handled the program logistics, from audiotapes and videotapes to the transcriptions from which the text below was derived.

Editing of typed transcriptions is usually tedious and demanding work. So it was here. In checking the transcripts against the tapes, I labored mightily to maintain both the language and the intentions of the speakers. I used ellipses in dealing with routine repetitions and to indicate omission of digressive materials (which were few). Occasionally, I attempted clarification through bracketed and italicized words. More rarely, I used brackets and italics to deal with an erroneous statement that I researched after the program. In punctuation and paragraphing, I tried to respect the sense and contours of the spoken word. I hope that the fine New Orleans cadence of the speakers comes through.

Harold Battiste: First of all, there's Don Suhor. Don is the one up here I know least. Why is that, Don?

Don Suhor: Well, first of all, when did you leave New Orleans?

Battiste: I left in 1956.

D. Suhor: Okay. I was at the 500 Club. I had just been out of the army for a year, and you had a lot of irons in the fire. You were playing for a while, though, across the street. You had a sound like Sonny Rollins—you were playing tenor—I think it was at Rizzo's or one of those spaghetti houses. They told me it was you. I knew all the people you know; I worked with Ed Frank and Red Tyler, all of them—Germaine, all these guys. But for some reason you left town and I stayed here.

Battiste: I left because some cats wanted a ride to California. They knew I had a car. And they said, "Man, we ought to go to California!"

D. Suhor: I was rubbing elbows with other jazz players in those days after the strip tease shows. I played for Lily Christine, the Cat Girl, at the 500 Club for seven years. I was the official Lily Christine clarinet player. It didn't pay much but the scale.

Battiste: Was there anything that paid much?

D. Suhor: And after the 500 Club I would go play the jam sessions with Mouse Bonati and those kind of people. You remember them? Al will remember. We played at little holes in the wall.

Battiste: Next on the panel is Mr. Richard Payne, who was one of the original American Jazz Quintet players. He was the bass player with that group, and I knew Richard probably even before that because it seems as though I can remember Richard coming by the Robin Hood Club with a bassoon, or something.

Richard Payne: I had one of everything.

Battiste: Yeah, trumpet, too. You never knew what Richard was going to come around to play. Next to Richard is our premier jazz vocalist, who has invented the style of jazz vocals for New Orleans, Ms. Germaine Bazzle. I remember in fact, while Richard was running around playing bassoon and trumpet, Germaine was playing bass. And my earliest remembrance of her is playing at a place on Louisiana Avenue—was it Hayes' Chicken Shack?

Germaine Bazzle: Vernon's. *[Editor's note: Same building; Hayes' became Vernon's.]*

Battiste: Our first ambassador of modern jazz was Al Belletto. Al was one of the first cats to get on a national label.

Al Belletto: Stan Kenton had discovered the band in Ohio and we were signed on Capitol Records for four albums, as they called them at that time.

Battiste: Yeah. I'll never forget that. Man, I didn't know what that was. I got the record of the Al Belletto Sextet and I thought it was somebody from California.

Belletto: Well, you see, you and I left New Orleans about the same time. I started that group over in Biloxi, Mississippi—the sextet—in around '53, and then from '53 until I opened the Playboy Club in '62, I was just on the road playing jazz. That's it.

Battiste: That's right. We'll talk about that Playboy thing. Next on the panel is—let me see now, are you the eldest up here? Anyway, this is of course the most renowned percussionist to ever be here—Earl Palmer. When you speak of setting standards, Earl Palmer has set the standard for recordings at every level, from Little Richard to Frank Sinatra. He set the standard that studio people would call and say, "Well, if you can't get Earl, see if you can get somebody that sounds like Earl." He set the standard. And here is our moderator, Charlie Suhor. You got it.

Charles Suhor: Okay.

Earl Palmer: May I say something?

C. Suhor: Please do.

Palmer: There are some very important things that have been said here earlier that I know something about, since I'm probably one of the oldest, if not the oldest guy up here. Anyway, I was told by Charles when we first talked about this conference that he had read an article that said few New Orleans musicians of our era were playing modern jazz or playing be-bop. And as you know, the whole American art form started right here—so why would us young guys coming up *not* be wanting to play whatever is new? Whoever wrote this was somebody who just writes for a paycheck. Every one of us up here, regardless of what we have achieved now, we *all* were struggling on our jobs at night, and not playing Dixieland. We weren't playing rock 'n' roll, because rock 'n' roll hadn't started then, but I'm supposed to have been the drummer that started rhythm and blues, which became rock 'n' roll.

What was I playing prior to that? Being from New Orleans, what else but jazz of some sort? But at any rate, he *[pointing to Don Suhor]* was trying to play jazz; Richard was; all of us were trying to play like Charlie Parker, Max

Roach, Ray Brown or somebody like that. And Germaine, I didn't know her too well until recent trips coming back. I met her through my dear brother and friend Red Tyler, and she is a wonderful artist, and I was so glad to hear about her background. I said, "Here is a lady that not only sounds good, she knows what she is doing." I really appreciate meeting her, and I am proud to be on the panel with her. Here *[pointing to Belletto]* is a man that had one of the favorite groups I've heard. I knew most of the personnel—yourself, Bama McKnight, Benny Clement. They're all pretty much dead, except you and I.

Belletto: You know, I want to add just one thing in line with what Earl is saying. In 1944 and '45 is when the Bird and Diz Records came out. I remember Benny Clement and myself spending eight hours playing the records over and over copying down the charts. Today a youngster can buy anything that was ever played by anyone. But that's to prove that there was be-bop going on in New Orleans around 1944.

Palmer: One last thing. Whether you know it or not, during the time we are talking about we all started to play be-bop and modern music, and so forth. There were times in that particular era, some of us would remember, we *[black and white players]* used to go to jail for playing together, for having jam sessions. And I distinctly remember the cops, whenever they'd so choose to, they knew where to come to find us—at 912 Toulouse, which is where Benny Clement lived. And we would go to jail quite often for just jamming together. And it got to be, we didn't mind.

Belletto: Also the Texas Lounge. We used to get busted there.

Palmer: And they'd say, "Why you guys keep doing this? We are going to take you to jail." Yeah, we know. But he *[pointing to Belletto]* had his uncle on the police force, who was his benefactor. My benefactor was the late Judge Ed Haggerty. He was a young attorney here in those days. I had met him years earlier working at the Whitney Bank, where my job was pulling those towels. Anyway, I won't belabor that. We'll talk about that later.

C. Suhor: Thank you, Earl and Al, for setting up the program so wonderfully, and thank you, Harold, for introducing the panel. There's one thing that Earl mentioned before we came here which I think is very important. There is an empty chair at the table. A couple of panelists couldn't make it, but one person is not here because he is no longer with us and we'd like to dedicate the program to Alvin Red Tyler, who died recently. *[applause]* If Alvin Batiste or Ellis Marsalis comes into the auditorium, please push them down toward the head table. I just heard that Bill Huntington is in the hospital unexpectedly. I don't know what's wrong, but I'm hoping he'll be well, and I know we send him our healing intentions. *[Editor's note: the ailment was not a serious one.]*

Now, when I wrote to these folks, I told them that this panel is not a reading gig. But I am going to read something just so that I start off the program in a way that stops me from babbling on. Then I'm hoping the panelists will talk fluently while I take notes and come in with questions and comments here and again. As I was saying to Earl earlier, very little has been written—

written correctly, accurately—about jazz in New Orleans in the postwar years of the late forties and the fifties, the years when the musicians on this platform and so many others were first playing be-bop and other modern jazz. At best, there was deserved mention of groups like Al Belletto's Sextet and their recordings on Capitol in the mid-fifties. And there has been some recognition of the wonderful American Jazz Quintet, which Harold Battiste and Richard Payne were members of. This was the group that ultimately, I think, grew to be members of the AFO, the All for One label in the sixties.

But the modern jazz community that was here in the late forties and early fifties was composed of dozens of jazz pioneers. They came together in different settings to play a music that was mainly invisible to the general public, and apparently to later writers and researchers who didn't do their homework. I hope that today we can get a better picture both of the range of modern jazz artistry that existed in those years, and also some specifics—for example, some nightclubs and other venues where gigs and jam sessions took place.

We've already heard about a couple of them—the Texas Lounge and French Quarter strip clubs. There was jazz backup for strippers because the strip joints were among the few places you could get away with playing be-bop in those days. And there were after-hour jam sessions in the Quarter and elsewhere. But was modern jazz being played at the blues and the rhythm and blues clubs in those days? At people's garages or in their front rooms? We are hoping that we'll find out what the hidden venues were for modern jazz, since there weren't a lot of gigs.

I hope we'll also hear about some specific institutional settings where the musicians met. Universities, yes, but also places like Grunewald's Music Store, where many apparently met each other as young jazz musicians and studied after World War II. I think it would be interesting and valuable to know if the playing of modern jazz was encouraged, tolerated, or flat put down in educational settings in the late forties and early fifties.

We might find out about some specific clusters of musicians who hung out together and played the new music and encouraged each other by sort of woodshedding in ensemble. Which musicians were particularly helpful as mentors in bringing others along in the new music? Which were helpful simply because they were just inspiring players?—helpful because they just blew your mind when you heard them, and made you want to play better?

So to start off, I'd like to pose the question to the panelists in terms of gathering-places. What were some of the earliest gathering-places in New Orleans where you first heard or played modern jazz?

Palmer: Well, first of all one of the earliest things I remember was hearing Al Belletto's group. . . . Then prior to that, we had some players like Harold, Alvin Batiste, and Edward Blackwell, as far back as I can remember. They were younger than me. We were already going on to play commercial jobs and they were starting to play be-bop and modern jazz and avant garde and those kinds of things. There was Harold and Blackwell and Nat Perrilliat—another wonderful saxophonist who passed away. These were great modern jazz players. We couldn't play that on the job, but they persisted and played it anyway. . . . Al's group was known for playing jazz, so he had no problem playing it.

Belletto: But see, that was later—in the fifties. My earliest recollection was a guy named Johnny Elgin, who was a self-taught bass player and piano player. The earliest be-bop jam sessions that I can remember were in Johnny Elgin's home, which was down in the French Quarter. And it was more like a shack, but that was the only place that I know in the late forties that be-bop was allowed to be played.

C. Suhor: Who was playing with Johnny and you? Who were the other players around then?

Belletto: Well, usually it was very difficult finding a drummer at that time. So sometimes we would play without a bass, sometimes we would play without a drum. Benny Clement was really the only one that I can remember in that group, and I searched my memory last night. These were like sort of like part-time musicians, you know.

Palmer: Earl Cobble, for one, and Louis Timken.

Belletto: Man, I was trying to think—Earl Cobble and Louis Timken were playing drums with me, that's right. *[Editor's note: Timken was playing in the late 1940s, but Cobble began in the mid-fifties, first influenced by Reed Vaughan.]*

D. Suhor: Linc Luddington—guitar. Remember Linc?

Belletto: Man, I was searching last night for those names.

D. Suhor: Now that's going back to Mouse Bonati.

Belletto: I had Mouse coming in around 1950.

D. Suhor: He was one of my biggest influences. I had just come back from Washington, D.C., and I was disillusioned. The only thing to play down here was Dixieland or strip shows. In order to keep my chops up on clarinet and alto, I chose the strip shows. We would go after hours to Danny's Inferno. . . . Ed Frank would come in every now and then. But Linc Luddington, he later went up to Baltimore.

Belletto: I had forgotten that name.

D. Suhor: I was a disillusioned cause I came from playing with Shirley Horn in Washington, D.C. We were all kids in our twenties. I was just out of the army and I came back home and I said, "What? This is what we've got to play for a living?"

Belletto: That was the mid-fifties?

D. Suhor: This is mid-fifties, right. The early fifties, before I went in the Army, is what you were talking about. I was just out of Loyola, about to get drafted. I'd hang out with Linc Luddington and Mouse and Frank Strazzari, the piano player, excellent piano player—went out to California.

Palmer: The first jazz album that I ever worked on was a thing by Jack Martin, the trumpet player and pianist. He wrote this *New Orleans Suite*, and that was the first thing I ever played on that was an organized session where we were reading the parts and so forth. I remember the personnel on that was Mouse Bonati and . . .

D. Suhor: Chick Power.

Palmer: Chick Power. Freddie Crane was on that, and Benny Clement. I still see Strazzari, and we often reminisce in Los Angeles. I see him all the time. As a matter of fact, my second wife used to babysit for Frank and his wife when they were living here. She died not long ago. That was around the same time we would go to jail. You never knew who was going to jail with you!

Belletto: Jack Martin wrote all the original arrangements for my sextet. The things that we recorded for Capitol were written by this Jack Martin, who couldn't play very well, but my goodness, he could sure write!

Payne: He was also a good teacher. I took his place years later at Colton Junior High. Well, let me backtrack a little. I was introduced to what we call be-bop about 1943 when this young man came on the scene who was known as Birks—John Birks (Dizzy) Gillespie—and another young man named Fats Navarro. They were outgrowths in my view of what was going on with Roy Eldridge and other guys. It seemed like that was the necessary evolutionary step to take.

Now, I was attending Xavier Prep at that time, and our band teacher was Clyde Kerr Sr. And I must tell you, I didn't hear his name mentioned, but he was responsible for many, many successful players, including Red Tyler. Somehow or another he touched Wallace Davenport. Another person nobody ever talks about is Manuel Crusto. Some incredibly great player! There was a Solomon who played bass and another Solomon—Solomon Spencer, who played all of the instruments, especially the woodwinds. And I just happened to be the "junior-junior" member of that grouping. Wardell Quezergue was our lead trumpet player and junior arranger. I could just go on and on. It would take another fifty minutes to call all their names, and I hope they don't hold it against me that I don't have them on the tip of my tongue. But right at that time is when things changed. Right at 1944, '45, '46 and by '47 I was on the road playing with different bands.

There was also Dooky Chase. He had eighteen players on tap at any time. What was the guitar player that he used to hang with? Yeah, Curtis Trevigne. . . . And there was a guy that played piano with him. Yeah, Edward Santina. There was a drummer in that band from time to time.

Palmer: But the main one was Vernel Fournier.

Payne: I met Vernel that year, and the next year we were in high school at Booker T. But that was only for a fleeting moment, because we went to McDonogh 35.

D. Suhor: What about the Adams brothers?

Payne: Oh, those were some good players. The whole family. There was a band called Miss Flossie and her Marvelous Kids or something like that, and everyone of those Adamses could play. Only one could not play. . . .

That was the youngest one. He was the schlepper for the band. He was what we call a roadie now; I don't remember his name.

D. Suhor: I still work with Gerald Adams. I worked last week with him.

C. Suhor: Richard, you said something about a change in 1946. . . . What was the nature of the change?

Payne: The change was not as obvious as the Fats Navarro thing. How I was introduced to Fats and Chick Webb and Jimmy Lunceford—who were real be-bop players, be-bop bands—was by listening to radio late at night, because you couldn't get the stations here until late. . . . I couldn't believe it. There was one band that was known to play hotel music—Claude Thornhill. Once in a while, we'd get live from Chicago, live from Minneapolis, or wherever they were. Claude Thornhill.

C. Suhor: Lee Konitz was playing with him.

Payne: Lee Konitz was his lead alto player. What was the other guy that played tenor, went with Herman? Dave Pell . . . and Vido Vespucci played alto in that band, also.

Palmer: Bruce Raeburn's father had a terrific big jazz band—Boyd Raeburn.

C. Suhor: So you guys were listening to the records and to the radio, and that was a big influence in terms of your being motivated to play jazz, right?

Belletto: That radio era, though, was just a few years, unfortunately. You used to get live broadcasts from the Cotton Club on the weekends and even from places like Minneapolis. People would say, "How can they have jazz broadcasts from there?" Well, they sure did.

D. Suhor: Birdland, too, from New York.

Palmer: Yeah, they had broadcasts from here, too—from the Blue Room of the Roosevelt Hotel.

Charlie and I were talking on the phone about various big bands in town, jazz bands even before be-bop came along. It wasn't Dixieland and it was something a little more than *[swing]*. I would say it was modern jazz, even then—bands like Fats Pichon and John Brunious. Pickett Brunious, Wendell's father, was a trumpet player and an arranger in that band, besides Pichon's arranger, and they had another great drummer who was in that band. . . . Nobody seems to remember him. They say, "Who was he?" It was a guy named Stan Williams.

Payne: Yeah, I remember Stan. I played with Stanley.

D. Suhor: I worked with Stanley at the Paddock Lounge.

Payne: That's where you and I worked with Stanley, yes.

Palmer: He seems to be forgotten. They would only be remembered by guys who remembered Pichon's band, and guys in that band. He was a great drummer, and Emmanuel Simms, who appeared for many years, who left here with Buddy Johnson.

Payne: "Foots" Johnson.

Palmer: I wonder how his foot stayed on that pedal, because he had feet that long. *[gestures]* Great drummer. People need to know about who were some of the musicians in this particular phase of music. These were the guys who were forerunners. We were all kids when these guys were playing. It wasn't be-bop yet, but it was something in between.

Belletto: Modern swing, really.

Palmer: Sidney Desvigne's Band, Herbert Leary's band. I don't know very much about the white bands, because at that time I wasn't even playing. I was tap dancing in the French Quarter for tips at that time.

Payne: Wait, there is another guy—talk about tap dancing. . . . There was a guy named Maurice Hines, Chink Hines.

Palmer: That whole family was in vaudeville with my mother, my aunt, and myself.

Payne: Dorothy Mae, and whatever the other lady's name was. This guy Chink Hines—I've got to tell you, have you ever heard of Hines, Hines, and Dad? This is the father. Gregory Hines is the younger of the two brothers. Maurice Jr. is the older.

Palmer: And Edna was their mother . . .

Payne: One more thing, and you can have it. The Playboy Club put together more players in one spot in New Orleans in modern times than I can remember at any other place. And on the up and up and legit, we got very few calls from the police. And we need to really thank Al Belletto for that. *[applause]* He did it when it wasn't nice.

Palmer: And when it was not popular.

Belletto: You know, one of the things I remembered last night was that we had Nat Perriliat as the off-night band leader. We had the two showrooms. And Nat's band subbed for both those. I had known about him, but Ellis Marsalis's trio was one of the bands in the opening of the Playboy Club here in New Orleans. Ellis told me about Nat Perriliat, and I just couldn't believe that we had a tenor player down in New Orleans that could play like that.

D. Suhor: Charlie Fairley, too. Did you know Charlie Fairley? I've got to say something else about Al that he probably forgot. Before the Playboy, he was doing things. I was still in high school. You've got a few years on me, Al. I was about to go to Loyola and my older sister, Mary Lou, said, "Come on and hear this band at Loyola." You had a Woody Herman type band, right? And you had a white Brillhart mouthpiece on clarinet . . .

Belletto: It was called the Loyola Moods.

D. Suhor: Right, I heard a concert and I was really impressed. That was what—mid-forties, late forties?

Belletto: That was probably around '46 or '47.

D. Suhor: Right, because I was still in high school, and I was getting ready to go to Loyola. And I heard you, Mike Caruba and people like that, and Rupert Copponex playing the Miles-style trumpet in that band.

Belletto: And Buddy Bishop was also playing trumpet.

D. Suhor: And Woody Guidry on trumpet.

Payne: And Rupert Surcof on bass.

C. Suhor: The Moods are a band that was talked about even later, when I was at Loyola. There were resonances of the Moods. "There'll never be another big band at Loyola like the Moods," people said. I heard them once or twice when I was a kid. I think Mary Lou must have brought me, too. They were quite a wonderful band. The other bands—help me out, Don and Al— the other white big bands that were playing around town were mostly playing, you know, Johnny Warrington's stock arrangements and transcriptions of *Eager Beaver* and stuff.

Belletto: And poorly. I mean, I realize I was young and I was a rebel, but you talk about bad bands. Lloyd Alexander had the only band that sounded good.

D. Suhor: Jack Martin arrangements, that's why. Jack Martin did arrangements for that band, and they weren't easy to cut, either, at sight.

C. Suhor: When did the Alexander band start? I played with them occasionally in the fifties but I think they predated that, didn't they? They played mostly specials, which were good—a lot of swing influence more than modern, but it was a good jazz-flavored big band, one of the few that I heard in town.

Belletto: Well, really, as for big bands, there were three or four black bands, and they were it—if you were able to sneak in and get to hear those bands. It wasn't necessarily rehearsed, or anything. The thing was, like it was really swing, hard swing. And they had jazz soloists. Well, in the white bands nobody could play solos.

D. Suhor: Don't forget Emery Thompson. Big Emery?

Battiste: That's what I was just about to ask. Did anybody know Emery Thompson?

Payne: Well, while we are reminiscing, really reminiscing, there was this one teacher who had three bands, full-sized dance bands, just in your neighborhood, Valmour Victor.

Palmer: Professor Victor.

Payne: Yeah, I studied jazz with him when I was like seven years old. We used to play for kids, in and out of school. I had attended school at Blessed Sacrament, officially. And I'd catch the streetcar or bus and go over to Thomy Lafon School to play to kids in school, go back and do my schoolwork, and in the evenings we would play to kids out of school. And my bosom buddy was Ed Blackwell. I won't tell you what year that was . . . but I will—it was '38 or '39. Nobody mentions Valmour Victor.

Battiste: Under the heading of trying to find the teachers, there has been one man who recently did his dissertation on the teachers. And I think he tried to find all of them, like Mr. Victor and another guy named Mr. Wilson, and so on down the line, to finally discover the teachers who sort of laid the groundwork for all of us. And also a lot of *[other]* musicians like Emery Thompson. The first cat I heard was a cat named Sterling White.

Payne: Oh yeah, he lived in the court by Ed Frank.

Battiste: He really inspired me to want to be a musician. He was dating one of my little buddies' big sisters and he would bring a saxophone in and he would play like anything—like a Lester Young record. He would play anything Lester was playing. And I couldn't believe it.

Payne: I'm glad you brought his name up. People don't know that Lester Young is from here. Yeah. And I was playing with Earl Bostic, another of the alumni from Xavier University. I attended Xavier and I taught there. I also taught here *[at Loyola]*, thanks to Al Belletto. And we had so much fun coming through in that time. How it happened has passed from people's memories. We had the Junior School of Music at that same time—1938, right? Germaine was too young.

Bazzle: I wasn't there. *[laughter]*

Payne: She's a baby. She, Ed Frank, and who was the guy that played violin so well?

Bazzle: Edward. Edward Frank played violin.

Payne: Another guy, there was another guy who played violin.

Bazzle: Sam Henry?

Payne: No, this is before Sam.

Bazzle: Frances Gonzales.

Payne: Frances Gonzales. Well, we could go on and on but I'm thinking in these little pieces that have been in my heart.

Bazzle: Ellis Marsalis was there, too.

Payne: Ellis came later, in 1940 or 1941, something like that.

C. Suhor: While we're talking about schools, this might be a good time to get a little survey of what the institutional attitudes were toward jazz. Harold, can you tell us a little bit about how Dillard was? You were a jazzman at Dillard, and I think Ellis was the person you taught there when you were a senior. . . . Tell us a little bit about who was with you at Dillard and whether the school encouraged, discouraged, or ignored your efforts in the way of jazz.

Battiste: At this point, no. We weren't at a point where jazz was acceptable to the community. I mean to "decent people," so to speak. In fact, in my personal life my mother tried to keep me from being a musician when we moved into the project. She said, "They don't allow pianos in the project." So we left the piano. And I understand it very well because a mother, even now, is sort of skeptical, if you're going to play jazz—"But what are you going to really do for a living?" *[laughter]* So the institutions, particularly the black universities—that's where I went—we were way behind because our people were still in the process of trying to find acceptability. In the black universities European music had more status than music that we were creating. So when I went to school, fortunately we had a music director named Melville C. Bryant who had been a warrant officer in the service. And he had a little different attitude than the university.

C. Suhor: At Dillard?

Battiste: At Dillard. He allowed me to do some things. Not officially; I could do things as long as I did my other stuff. So by the time Ellis and Roger Dickerson came together, when I was a senior, I had been able to establish a band that would play just at little dances, and so forth. So we were able to do what we wanted to do, but we could not get any credit for it.

C. Suhor: Maybe, Germaine, you can tell us a little bit about your sense of how Xavier viewed jazz in your days there, and Richard can help with this as well.

Bazzle: Well, it was pretty much the same as it was at Dillard. Please remember that this was an institution that was owned, operated, and run by the good nuns, so there was definitely a difference. However, we did have some of us . . . Johnny Fernandez was there at the time. Bill Fisher was there at the time, and Al Fielder. Al wasn't in the music department, he was a pharmacy major, but he was a drummer. We were sort of tolerated as long as we didn't do it all day long. And we didn't have the—how should I say it—we didn't have the enthusiasm from the campus as much as we would have liked. I think that it was the same kind of thing—this was not the *[accepted]* kind of music.

I was into it then not so much as a performer, but I started listening at around that time. And because of my brother, who introduced me to this kind of music, I got to know a lot of the guys because we had listening sessions at my home. I'd be the only girl in this room with about ten boys and it would be so quiet because the music is playing. My mom used to come and peep to see what was going on because there was no talking. I mean it was a *class*, actually, listening to these people . . . . But on the campus itself jazz was not the priority. Opera was the thing.

C. Suhor: Do you want to add anything to that, Richard? You were at Xavier a little earlier.

Payne: Yeah, I was quite a bit earlier than her. I was just behind William Houston and Earl Bostic and Omaha Jones and some of the other guys. I'm not that old, but I have a cousin who attended school with them—Irvin Payne, who played with Jimmy Lunceford and Andy Kirk and a couple of other bands—so he brought things home to us.

But right at that point there was a nun who came from Philadelphia named Sister Mary Letitia, and she was extremely tolerant—as long as you did your work, because we had a certain amount of things that we had to do. Just after her came Sister Elise, and Sister Elise would get angry with anybody who would *not* tolerate everything. The only time I ever had her angry at me was when I said something about, "How dare they put me in an integrated physical science class with some Neanderthals?" She said, "Well, what do you mean?" I said "Well, these poor chaps can't even read and write but you've got them in here with me and my other buddies who are going to be doctors and lawyers and Indian chiefs." She said, "My dear Richard, how terrible of you to say that! Don't you ever let me hear you say that! Everybody has a place in life and every human activity has a place in life." That changed my outlook. So from that point on I started being a whole lot more tolerant of all of the other activities of humanity.

But, I don't know, maybe a lady sees another thing, especially, a person who comes just two three years later has another outlook. But we had some nice bands. We had some good jams. Solomon Spencer was our band leader at one time. He had just gotten out of the military. . . . Just as the war ended I was at Xavier, just getting in. And we had a couple of good bands. You had a lot of so-called catching up to do, because gentrification seems to be the way of the world. But I played my first symphony at nine, which is real, real good because that prepared me for all of the things that happened, and I happened to play at ten in a jazz band, and before that I played with Valmour Victor.

So we had a little bit of everything and a lot of the European influence. I can't knock it because my life was saved by being able to play the bassoon, and the French horn, and being able to conduct. And to know the nine Beethoven symphonies and do the Brahms requiems, and all. Those were second nature to me because I had started way back. Those ladies and gentlemen gave their lives for the blacks and the Indians and Asians and all. So I cannot under the pain, of as we say, mortal sin knock them. And I say it in all fairness. They provided a very necessary steppingstone for humanity as we know it.

If we look back in our history books, we will find out that many of the people who were influential did it through one of those kinds of institutions. Even if we had to play in a cellar or somewhere else, it was wonderful. And I wish I had that kind of influence for my young people now. And I speak for all young people. Once in a while, I'll have some influence over somebody. I just gave my wife a record of Jeremy Davenport. If anybody wants to hear a young trumpet player who is unsung and beautiful, listen to Jeremy Davenport. Nicholas Payton, Chris Seversan . . .

Palmer: Jimmy Sharif.

Payne: Sharif came a little later, but he is another one.

Palmer: Eric Jacobsen.

Payne: Eric, yeah. But my dream, first of all, I wanted to be a Mozart. I've got to tell you that. I wanted to sit down and write a thousand works, right? I didn't have that ability. After that I wanted to play as well as Mozart and that took me around all the instruments. So here I am now. But I had to throw that in there because I am starting to feel as though what the good nuns and the good brothers and priests did was not acceptable.

Bazzle: Well, I don't know, but that's *not* what I meant to imply at all. My point was that on the campus jazz was not accepted. The question was about jazz, or what part the university played in that. When I was at Xavier, we had all of this positive influence you are talking about, but we did not have the great support for the jazz in the department when I was there. It takes nothing away from the nuns. It takes nothing away from anybody. It takes nothing away from the university. It's just that that was a fact, you see. And those of us who played jazz or were involved with it, we did it off campus. That's what I'm saying.

Payne: Some of us did, but not all of us.

Bazzle: We are not talking about all. You just asked my point.

Payne: I didn't ask what your point was.

Bazzle: We are not going through that.

Payne: Excuse me, please. I don't intend to make anybody less happy. I only want to add to the happiness, okay? I want to add to the joy because it is important that we enjoy this moment. I am enjoying being here with you and I wouldn't knock you or anything else, to break down the joy.

Bazzle: O.K. we're not going to put it that way.

D. Suhor: Germaine, in support of what you're saying . . . Nowadays kids can major in jazz—you know, it's encouraged. But in those days everything had to be "legit." You couldn't even major in saxophone then. It had to be clarinet, which was my basic instrument. As you know, Charlie used to accompany me on boxes at home; that's the way he started being a drummer. And he turned out to be a fine teacher. He taught Johnny Vidacovich and several other great drummers in the city. But in those days it was frowned upon. It was sometimes encouraged, like the Campus Capers radio bands at Loyola, just to drum up trade. Very vanilla-type bands. Just to drum up new students, you know, there were Saturday afternoon radio broadcasts. But I was in good company. Freddie Crane was there, and we'd go down to the basement to jam. The dean would come down and say "vot is dees booogie-wooogie," like an old Hollywood movie. It was frowned upon. But I can understand that point of view; everything was approached from a legit standpoint until Paul Guma came in. He was fine musician. He encouraged jazz, but still you had to approach the instrument from a legitimate standpoint.

C. Suhor: You'd be doing a jam session in the basement, and maybe you'd get into *Pennies from Heaven.* That was fine. But somebody might storm in and say, "Cease!"

D. Suhor: That's it.

Bazzle: Yeah.

Belletto: Well, a little prior to that we were suspended here. *[at Loyola]* But the jazz musicians here had a great friend in the dean of men, and his name was Father Gutteril. He also drove the bus for the Loyola Moods when we played out of town. Very quickly, anybody that was playing jazz in the music school building was automatically suspended by Dr. Schuyten, and thanks to Father Gutteril, we were reinstated fifteen minutes later. *[laughter]*

C. Suhor: While you've got the mike, Al, will you talk a little bit about LSU? There was a great cadre of jazz players there in your day. Give us some years and some players there, if you would.

Belletto: Well, in our little group we had Mose Allison, Carl Fontana, Benny Clement, and myself. We all lived in the same brand-new apartment building right off campus, and we did a lot of playing. I mean a lot of *jazz* playing. There were other guys there that weren't as interested, but it was tolerated there even though there were no jazz studies at that time. But at LSU it was tolerated because you had some of the professors like Dr. Timm. And those people, they just knew that something good was happening, so they said, "Let's leave it alone."

Palmer: I don't know how much longer we have, but there are many people that you have mentioned, and there are many people that many of you here know, who are playing around town in various places and you may hear them in certain situations, and they give no indication as to what they started out playing. I'd like very much to run over some of these names. Some of them you will know and some you won't; for example, guys who are from New Orleans for that matter and who were very prominent in this modern jazz music of New Orleans at that particular time.

For example, Vernel Fournier. I don't know how many of you know him, but you may know him by his great recording of *Poinciana* with the Ahmad Jamal Trio. He lived around Dumaine and Galvez Streets, St. Ann and Galvez. . . . He was with that great Dooky Chase Band. He was the drummer there. Henry Nance, who is still playing here right now—another wonderful guy playing jazz. June Gardner Sr., who's still playing here, but what you might hear him playing now wasn't where he began. And Johnny Vidacovich. Some of you may remember Pinky Vidacovich, his grandfather.

C. Suhor: Uncle, I think.

Palmer: His uncle, yes, was always was known more or less for Dixieland. Johnny could play everything but I have never heard him play any Dixieland. All I ever heard him play was *[modern]* jazz—marvelous drummer. He was here today, as a matter of fact. *[Editor's note: Vidacovich began playing in the 1960s; as a young teen he played with Dixieland groups.]* On trumpet, there were guys like Dalton Rousseau, Herman Gagne, and Johnny Fernandez, who Germaine mentioned earlier. Tony Moret. Jack Willis, who was one of professor Victor's main students, and Wallace Davenport, who was mentioned earlier.

And on sax there was one young man here who, I think, Charlie Parker wanted. He was in the service in New Jersey. In those days guys like Charlie Parker would take young guys in to stay with them so they could learn. Thank God, many of them didn't get involved like Bird did, in unfortunate situations. But one guy that was invited to stay was Warren Bell. How many of you knew Warren Bell? Hilton Carter. Larry Gilbert. They were a part of that great Dooky Chase band. Another guy who was out in the Quarter, and I am sure Al will remember, was a great tenor saxophone player, and he had a kind of comedic personality but it didn't take away from his playing, if you were listening to him. He was a big fat guy, we called him "Cheeks." Remember him?

D. Suhor: Yeah. Joe "Cheeks" Mandry.

Palmer: Now we had a piano player here, one of the first guys to render be-bop on piano. Ironically enough, his name was Thelonious—Thelonious Pernell, remember him? And Burnell Santiago was a genius—phenomenal. He was a creole; looked kind of Mexican.

D. Suhor: That was the Brunious's relative—uncle, wasn't it?—that got killed by the police? *[Editor's note: Brian Wood cites no sources but disputes this "persistent rumor" of Santiago's death, claiming he died in 1944 of high blood pressure and kidney failure.]*

Palmer: Yeah, related to John and Wendell.

Payne: Also, do you also remember Pajo? Pajo that played piano and moved to Oakland?

Palmer: Frank Campbell, another great saxophone player that moved to Oakland, since you mention it. On the other hand it was Burnell Santiago and he had a brother named Black. Now what Black's first name was, I don't know. But there was a rumor—and I have heard from older musicians that it was true—that Paul Whiteman wanted Burnell to come on the road with his band as kind of added attraction and Burnell said, "Look man, I'm black, man, I can't go." And he said, "We'll call you Cuban." *[laughter]* It never happened.

And Roger Dickerson, of course, who has always been the studious one of the musicians that played jazz with us—always very clinical jazz, but nevertheless good jazz. He is also still active here, more in teaching now than playing, from what I understand. Chuck Badie was always a jazz bassist—we all know him. Many times you see these guys playing on *[commercial]* jobs and you think that's all they ever played.

D. Suhor: Chuck's still playing. I worked with him about a month ago at the Palm Court Cafe.

Palmer: That's why I wanted to mention their names, because they all had the same beginnings we had but they are not here on this panel.

D. Suhor: Don't forget Snookum Russell. Snookum had Charlie Parker and J.J. Johnson in his band at one time.

Palmer: Ray Brown was in Snookum Russell's band, too.

Belletto: I'll tell you one more we have to remember. He's not with us anymore, but he really blazed the trail in this town and his name was James Black. We had him at the Playboy Club and he and I used to almost have physical fights because of his attitude, but my goodness, when he played the drums!

Palmer: And a great arranger, also. James, he was one of the guys besides Tyler that instilled in me the idea to go to music school. Tyler had said to me, "Brother, you need to go to music school with those G.I. rights you have." I said, "Why? They tell me I'm the best drummer in town. I've got the best job." He said, "But you don't know what you're doing." And that's what got me to music school. And then I said, "That's right."

James Black was younger than me. He not only played drums, he was another Louis Bellson. He could arrange, write songs, play the drums and everything. I said, "Yeah, that's what I want to do." And thank God for those two guys, one my age the other younger, who were very instrumental in me going to music school. And the guitarists. One of them we mentioned was Curtis Trevigne. Now Curtis came up playing *[modern]* jazz. He didn't know anything about Dixieland or traditional or anything like that. But another guy that came up—and his father was one of the great clarinet players in this town—was Ernest McLean. A great jazz player. He has been playing Dixieland at Disneyland for the last thirty-five years now. But he was another great writer of those jazz tunes at Grunewald's. He would give concerts at the Y on Claiborne and Cleveland every Sunday. Different ones played there. First it was Red Tyler and Frank and I, and then it was Harold and Nat and Alvin—they'd have concerts there. They were playing a little more modern avant garde type music. Many other guys from the school would have the specific groups that would give the concerts, too. . . . Now speaking of vocals, Germaine, there was young woman who went down famous as a blues singer, but she started off trying to sing jazz and be-bop and scat singing, and she was wonderful at it—Blanche Thomas.

Bazzle: Right.

Palmer: That was Blanche's beginning. She wasn't a blues singer when she started. She was trying to sing like Ella Fitzgerald, and kind of looked like her, too.

Belletto: She was the first one in this city to do that kind of scat singing, to my memory.

C. Suhor: What about Laverne Smith? She was a very moody singer, as I remember.

Payne: A moody person, though she was.

Bazzle: Laverne was the person that kind of got me into doing gigs. We used to have the Musicians' Union Hall down on Claiborne and Columbus, and there was a thing there every Friday night. You could go in and get all the seafood that you wanted. I wasn't in the union or anything like that, but some friends and I were walking down the street and they saw this Musicians' Union sign. . . . When I saw the free food, I said, "Well, let's go in." And they said, "But you're not in there *[the union]*." I said, "But I can play something." I walked in and Laverne was playing on this upright piano and there was a bass on the floor beside her. And I walked up to her and said, "Who plays the bass?" and she says, "Nobody." I said, "May I play it?" She says, "Sure." So I picked up the bass and we played some tunes. My friends did all of the eating—I never did get to eat. *[laughter]* But because of doing that with her, then she started getting gigs around town and I was the bass player with her for about three years, at least.

C. Suhor: Earl, you mentioned that Blanche Thomas started out singing jazz, not blues, at first. One question I wanted to ask is whether or not there was much interaction among the jazz players and the blues players who have been written about quite a bit—Professor Longhair and the bands at the Dew Drop Inn, etc. Were the people who were playing in these bands jazzers? Did they interact with the jazz musicians? What was the relationship of the blues community to the jazz community?

Battiste: May I?

C. Suhor: Please.

Battiste: There are a couple of things that have been on my mind since we started talking. One of them addresses that issue of names that we give to the music. It seems that my perception of what I was doing when I was young was not in a category. I just liked to play music.

Bazzle: To play music, right.

Battiste: I really liked to play music, and I was just as excited about Louis Jordan, when I first learned a little lick off Louis Jordan. All of it was just music, and I really had a good time with all of it. The names over the years seem to have put up barriers not only to music but between people. When we went to Los Angeles the problem we had was that they'd say, "What do you all play? You all blues band? You a jazz band? What you play?" Well, I couldn't answer that, because we played everything and we enjoyed playing.

Bazzle: Well, most times when you had these gigs that's what you had to play—everything.

Battiste: The names, the words come easy to people who aie not playing the music. I don't know of any musician who said, "Well we're going to call this 'jazz.'" You know what I mean. It was usually someone else who determined what we are going to call it. And over time we begin incorporating that and saying, "I am a jazzman." That's not what I am. And my history can prove that, that I'm not a category like that. So the question is, "What about the interaction between these people?" There was always interaction because we were all . . .

Palmer: We are all the same people.

C. Suhor: I agree that categories limit us and sort of dictate our speech in ways that they shouldn't. I guess if I had to have some kind of an acid test I would say that a jazz musician might be somebody who could play blues very well and whose music is influenced by blues, no matter what they are playing; but they can also play a tune like *All the Things You Are* at an up tempo, or *Cherokee* at that tempo, which a very good blues player might not be able to play. Is that a rule of thumb that you can live with, in terms of posing a question that relates to jazz and blues communities?

Battiste: I understand what has evolved to give definitions to these terms. However—and this is just personal—I continue to look for the thing that brings it together. If Gatemouth Brown can't play *Cherokee* at a tempo like that, that does not mean he can't do what jazz players do—and that's express himself and use his voice for, whatever. And from that springs the creativity. When it gets to be how fast you can play, or how many notes, it becomes elitist. It closes out the people who have a natural creativity. I've heard many guys who really had something to say but then would cap it with, "But I can't read"—as though him not being able to read excludes him or makes him less.

Belletto: Good point.

Payne: Can I say something now? Because I keep backtracking—I have not said much about this. But on October 6, 1964, a young man who is sitting with us—and I am very proud of—he and I together integrated music. Before that day you would be arrested for playing *[in an integrated band]*. Al Belletto. . . . He said, "Would you come with me?" And I said, "How much are you paying?" And he told me, and I said, "I'll be there tomorrow."

Even when I go to the union, people want to pat me on the back. It was not that—it was that music needs to break down all those barriers. Music.

Belletto: Well, the one point about that Richie left out is that you were one of three people who auditioned for the gig. Richie was by far the best bass player. And I called Hugh Hefner and asked if there was going to be a problem because of Louisiana state law. And he said, "If that's the guy you want, yeah, hire him. I have better lawyers than the state of Louisiana." *[laughter]*

Payne: I just had to say that.

Palmer: He was really one of guys who had that kind of heart—never had that kind of problem. At any rate, there is one thing I want to say about defining music and separating it that was always done by the press. For example, rock 'n' roll was *[first]* called "race music," then it became "rhythm and blues" until the disc jockeys in New York put a name on it—"rock 'n' roll"—so that all of the children's families would accept them listening to this music. Without the name "rock 'n' roll" on it, it probably would still have been black people—race music and rhythm and blues.

C. Suhor: What his name—the disc jockey?

Battiste: Alan Freed.

Palmer: Alan Freed, *Moon Dog.* He put the label of "rock 'n' roll" on that early music, and that's why it spread so wide. Because *[before that]* the kids who were listening to it, bootlegging listening to the music, couldn't tell their parents they were listening to it. They would be grounded and so forth. Charlie Parker was asked once how do you define be-bop. Charlie was known to have quite a sense of humor. He was a very brilliant young man. He said, "Be-bop is a series of one miraculous recovery after another." *[laughter]* . . . Charlie Parker, when I first met him, came in with Jay McShann. When I run into Jay in various festivals in California I always say to him, "You know, you may not have never hired Charlie Parker if you had any understanding of what he was doing at the time when he was in your band, when he played that great solo on *Confessing the Blues*." He said, "You're right. I just said, 'This young man is playing something I don't quite know what it is.'" But he let him play it. . . . Jay McShann, being a band leader could have very easily said, "You're trying to revolutionize my music. I don't want to hear you playing this anymore." But he didn't. He decided to listen and see what he thought. He ventured a little bit. And as far as I am concerned, he's largely responsible for Charlie Parker by doing that.

C. Suhor: Earl, I'd like to get back to something we talked about on the phone here because I think it has to be mentioned as an educational institution that apparently influenced a lot of musicians after World War II and that was Grunewald's. Were any of the other panelists at Grunewald's?

Belletto: I was at Grunewald's.

Palmer: Jack Martin was the teacher downstairs. The races were separated then.

C. Suhor: Apparently, a lot of great musicians learned there. . . . Tell us a little bit more about it.

Palmer: Upstairs, there were guys like Quentin Baptiste, who later became an instructor around town. Shirley Goon was a teacher who never could play jazz, but she encouraged us to play it all the time. And they had an old bassist, an old German man, I don't remember his name.

Payne: Finch. Otto Finch.

Palmer: Otto Finch. You remember that, Richard. I remember us laughing, bringing him the sheet music to a Ray Brown solo with Dizzy Gillespie on "One Bass Hit" and "Two Bass Hit." We brought it to him just to see how he would interpret it. And the man didn't miss one accidental, not one note. He played it very strict, very Germanic, but the man played it excellently. This old man didn't have to reach for anything. With the proper speed, with the proper execution, he played both of those solos one behind the other. And Red Tyler and I—and another guy—three of us just turned away from Professor Finch, and he ambled away with his big pants and didn't make anything of it. He didn't realize what he was doing—what we considered the greatest bass player we had ever heard, he had just mastered two of his solos.

And that school was another point of integration here in New Orleans because we . . . were able to play together. I remember Freddie Crane and Jack Martin and a few other guys downstairs. At any rate, that was also an opportunity for us, where musicians could meet without the threat of going to jail. To perform together and enjoy the music and learn from each other, learn the music together, we didn't have to worry about that aspect of it. And so it became very much accepted that we could get together. The only thing that kept us from getting together more was scheduling. . . . There were some guys you wanted to play with, but you couldn't get them because their classes were scheduled different. . . . But that was a wonderful place for the music in this town. There were some people there who were studying "seriously," so to speak, but I don't know anyone there that wasn't trying to play jazz or trying to play be-bop, upstairs and downstairs.

C. Suhor: The other institutions that we don't have much information on would be Tulane after the war and in the fifties, and Southern, which Alvin Batiste I'm sure can illuminate for us. I will be sure to interview him. And there was Southeastern in Hammond. I did talk to Mike Serpas, one of the best of the postwar generation, about that.

Belletto: What a player he was.

C. Suhor: He's been ill, by the way, but he was telling about how he used to come and play in the Quarter at jam sessions in the strip clubs. He brought in a drummer named Bobby DeSio from Southeastern, I remember. He used to jam with Mouse Bonati and Reed Vaughan and the group in the Quarter. Bobby DeSio was a very good drummer.

D. Suhor: With Mike Serpas we were playing Clifford Brown things like *Joy Spring.* Herb Tassin was in on that too, but Mike Serpas continued on in the jazz mode. Herb went more the commercial route, but he still likes to play jazz.

C. Suhor: As far as Tulane goes, I talked to Louis Berndt who was here in the fifties, and he said that there simply wasn't a jazz culture at Tulane. I have to talk to a few more people, but I'm wondering if anybody here knows what was happening in Tulane's music department. I'll call Richard Crosby, who was teaching there at the time, to find out more about that. Does anybody know the Southern University jazz scene? Was there a jazz group at Southern? Southern in Baton Rouge, I'm talking about.

Battiste: I didn't know of anything until Alvin went there. Alvin had a fabulous band even when I went to college, and that was four years before Alvin. Whenever there would be football games you know, like the big Bayou Classic, Florida A&M would come here and bring their band. So there were always cats who would jam. Cannonball and Nat Adderley were at Florida A&M at the time and they came and met with Southern and would always look forward to jam sessions with the musicians, although it wasn't "offered" in the school.

Belletto: Don't you feel those big marching bands were influenced a little bit by jazz?

Battiste: Sure.

Belletto: Because the first one I ever heard was Florida A&M and they were coming down the street doing Dizzy things, and stuff like that.

Battiste: Those youngsters like that are always at the front end of whatever is going on. They are at the front end. And whatever style you do it in, they wanted to be in the forefront.

C. Suhor: Well, Bill Huntington isn't here but he was in on a lot of early modern jazz activity. I can't speak for Bill—he's so eloquent. But we used to hang out with each other and a lot of the same musicians. This was the mid-fifties approximately, and we did a lot of jamming at Buddy Prima's house and Al Hermann's back shed. It was Buddy Prima, Bill Huntington, Al Hermann, the trombonist. His brother Phil Hermann, who left town, was a very good alto man. And we used to have sessions in different parts of town. Then a little after that, Charlie Blancq came along playing drums with Buddy. There was also Bruce Ahrens, a very good trumpet player. So that was another group that kind of clustered together for a while. Reed Vaughan, of course, was with that group. Reed was playing exceptionally well in the mid-fifties in the Quarter with a piano man that is almost never heard of— Triggs Morgan.

D. Suhor: From Chicago. He came down here with Johnny Scott Davis's Band.

C. Suhor: Around 1957 Reed played with Stan Kenton. He came back to town and worked with pianist Joe Burton. Burton used to hire the best jazz drummers he could find, and then antagonize them—then I would get the gig! Burton was part of the scene, and he did get a popular audience for jazz. I think people often came to see him because they never knew what he was going to do, and because he hired guys like Bill Huntington and Reed.

Bazzle: For a while Joe Burton had a little thing on television.

C. Suhor: He was a promoter. I've heard him play brilliantly, but he did strange things, and then he would get angry . . .

D. Suhor: . . . And make up his own bridges to songs. . . . I played with him, not regularly, but after I would get off the strip gigs I would sit in with him and Jay Cave, a good bass player. James Black was with him, and Jimmy Zitano, another excellent drummer.

C. Suhor: Al, you have a story?

Belletto: Well, one night after an early gig I walked into Joe Burton's place, and as I got through the front door he was on the microphone and he said, "Get the hell out of here, Al Belletto!" I said, "Oh gee, what did I do?" So I just never went back in there again—obviously.

C. Suhor: Harold, do you have anything to say in summary? I think we're out of time; in fact, we're running a little overtime.

Payne: Can I say one more thing, please?

C. Suhor: Please.

Payne: We passed over Hammond—Southeastern—too quickly. There were two brothers, Lou and Frank Chemay, bass and trombone, who were incredible. And there is a third brother in that Chemay family.

Payne: And Bill Evans, who wrote a lot of stuff for Miles Davis and many other bands, played piano there. And someone else—Ralph Pottle, who was an incredibly good bass player.

D. Suhor: He was a teacher.

Payne: Right, and he had a son named Frank Pottle who played French horn in another band. And last, but not least, the best saxophone player that I had heard from the Middle West—was a guy named Arthur Lauer. He was my roommate in the air force when I was in Air Force Orchestra.

C. Suhor: Oscar Davis was from Hammond too, wasn't he?

Payne: Right, Oscar Davis was from Hammond. I played a lot with him. He played sax, clarinet, flute, oboe, bassoon.

Belletto: You've got to mention Tony Mitchell. I wrote his name down last night. He was playing a lot of clarinet, be-bop, in New Orleans for a long time. He wasn't born here. But we can't leave him out.

C. Suhor: We've probably left out all kinds of people. There are others, like Don Guidry, a tenor saxist who died on drugs. . . . There are so many who are gone, and many who are still with us.

Palmer: Wilbur Hogan, too.

C. Suhor: Yes, we've only touched the surface today. But I think that in touching the surface, we've come up with a lot of information—so many people, so many experiences, that I'm hoping that we won't hear as much in the future about how few modern jazz players there were after World War II in this city. It was a wonderful jazz community.

Belletto: Please don't underplay the importance of Bill Huntington in the fifties. Because basically, of those people that you all mentioned, Bill has become a worldwide, accomplished bass player. In New York a couple of months ago, Ellis and I were talking with a whole bunch of New York musicians. The first thing out of their mouth is, "What is Bill Huntington doing?" He doesn't get the recognition in town here that he really deserves.

Payne: Also, he is about three times as good on the guitar.

C. Suhor: My first article for *Down Beat* in 1961 was on modern jazz in New Orleans. I talked about the local modern jazz scene and in general the fact that there were many good players here. I focused in the second part of the article on my two favorite local modern jazz musicians—Ed Blackwell and Bill Huntington. They were playing drums and guitar, respectively, in very, very unique ways. And that article just touched the surface. So much has been learned since then. I hope that others will take this topic up and carry it further.

Palmer: Charlie, I always like to say when speaking of Bill Huntington, that he never blows his own horn. . . . I like being able to say that somebody is a wonderful musician and is also—just as important, if not more important—he's a wonderful man. I also want to thank the old-timers. I made the suggestion about honoring Red Tyler to Alvin *[Batiste]*, to Charlie, and also to Connie Atkinson, not knowing what the setup would be at this meeting. But I just hoped that there would be in some way to do what little we can to perpetuate the name of Red Tyler, because we have been sitting here forgetting a lot of people that we know very, very well. In New Orleans we are fortunate enough to have so many people coming along all the time—good young musicians—but we would not want to forget some of the greats, and I am so happy for what you did what you did on behalf of Red Tyler and his family. Thank you. *[applause]*

Joe Logsdon: I want to thank all you for coming, especially this panel. One of the things that you might forget about them—they didn't talk very much about themselves. They are the teachers, now in the jazz programs—this generation of whatever they want to call themselves, be-boppers, or what, but I think the best thing is, the thing that started these conferences was Sidney Bechet, who said in his autobiography, *Treat It Gentle*, it is not *jazz*—which was too small for him—but *New Orleans music*. They are keeping it alive, and they are now the teachers in the jazz programs launching the young lions . . . all over the world again and keeping New Orleans music alive. I want to mention one thing to you. You were trying to think of the name of the person who has written about the earlier teachers like Valmour Victor and Clyde Kerr Sr. and Yvonne Bush. That's Al Kennedy, who finished a dissertation. . . . So we are remembering the teachers and remembering this wonderful era of music in New Orleans, and we hope we can keep it going. What we call this is not the jazz conference, but the New Orleans International Music Conference, and we did that purposely in the spirit that all of you from Sidney Bechet to everyone else, are talking about. . . .

D. Suhor: I have to say something about our moderator, and not just because he's my brother. But Charlie has done so much for jazz. He was writing articles for *Down Beat* and *New Orleans* magazine. As a matter of fact, he has got seven hundred pages of articles and letters that he donated to the

Tulane Jazz Archive. He was pushing guys like Blackwell and all these musicians here way back in the fifties when it was a no-no, and I think he deserves a lot of credit. *[applause]*

C. Suhor: All my respect to these musicians. Thank you. Harold, do you have some remarks to conclude with?

Battiste: I want to make people aware of some interviews in a book. This is a small book *[Editor's note: New Orleans Heritage—Jazz, 1956–1966 available through Battiste's AFO Records, New Orleans.]* . . . that carries interviews with some of the people that we have been dealing with—Chuck Badie, Warren Bell, James Black, Edward Blackwell, Melvin Lastie, Alvin (Red) Tyler. Several of the musicians were interviewed at that point. So what we are talking about today, we've got each one of their opinions on it. I learned from this experiment, when I got all these different viewpoints, that history is something that is very, very difficult to get accurate, and it's almost impossible to get "truth." It's almost impossible, because all these people see things from different angles. I'd see two or three people who had been in the same circumstance, and they all saw something different, and that's what gets recorded. Somebody's view. It really is "his-story"—whoever writes it. It's his story and so you should bear in mind when you read so-called history that there are several other true viewpoints, true versions of it.

Logdson: Come to the crawfish boil. We're going to have a French band influenced by Sidney Bechet bringing it all back home.

Appendix 1

The Jazz Scene: Four Cross Sections

As stated in the text of this book, jazz activity in New Orleans grew impressively during the 1960s. Due largely to the national fame of the Dukes of Dixieland, Pete Fountain, Al Hirt, and Preservation Hall, civic leaders finally saw jazz as a boon—i.e., a marketable commodity, and maybe even an art—rather than as a part of the city's shameful past. Even modern jazz made inroads as local fans frequented chic venues like the Playboy and out-of-the-way clubs like the Black Knight and Marsalis' Mansion.

Various publications were interested in this mini-renaissance in the hometown of jazz. So between 1965 and 1970 I wrote four quick-gloss articles for very different kinds of magazines—*Jazz Journal* (London); *Delta Review*, a Southern regional magazine; the first Jazzfest program, titled *Jazzfest '68;* and *Gentlemen's Quarterly*, a.k.a. *GQ*, the men's style magazine.

The cross-section articles are somewhat formulaic and lacking in elaboration. I needed to pack much information and commentary into limited space, often for general audiences. But the cross-sections provide a different angle on the materials in this book insofar as each article juxtaposes the traditional New Orleans, Dixieland, and modern jazz activities in the city at a given time. Placed in sequence, the articles show a definite growth of the local jazz scene. The February 1965 *Jazz Journal* piece (written in 1964) described the rising but not brimful local offerings for readers of the hip and handsome British magazine. The article is basically an explication of the *Down Beat* "Where & When" list of the time, with some interpretive and critical comments. *Delta Review* sounds like the name of one of those little academic journals, but it was actually a slick regional magazine aimed at a popular audience, the niche being literate people interested in credible reports on different aspects of Southern culture. I did a short historical introduction that led into the considerably brighter jazz picture of 1966. The less jazz-oriented audience allowed brief mention of blues, folk, and rock activity. The printed program for first Jazzfest in 1968 returns to the expanded W&W list model, this time reflecting much livelier action than the 1965 article. The *GQ* piece was geared toward that magazine's cosmopolitan audience. The editors asked for a breezy narrative about the New Orleans lifestyle in general, and I was able to include enthusiastic comments about the jazz scene of 1970.

NEW ORLEANS TODAY
JAZZ JOURNAL **(LONDON), FEBRUARY, 1965**

Jazz in New Orleans today is much like New Orleans food. If you know where the best chefs are cooking, you will find it a tasty combination of indigenous ingredients. Maybe it will lack a few of the homey spices of the past, but it is still highly distinctive, and few would turn it down just because the figs are not quite as mouldy as they once were.

For most jazz gourmets the greatest feast at present is at the two revival centers in the French Quarter, Preservation Hall and its imitator Dixieland Hall. At both places one can hear the most genuine traditional jazz, although Preservation Hall still projects the warmest atmosphere and has been sterner in retaining policies of non-commercialism and freedom for the musicians. The halls feature such stalwarts as George Lewis, Punch Miller, Billie and De De Pierce, and the Eureka Brass Band, with different groups each night and only a nominal kitty charge for admission.

But there is other jazz of varying degrees of interest in the Quarter, and regrettably, many purists pass up the opportunity of hearing the exciting trumpet of Thomas Jefferson at the Paddock, or Snooks Eaglin's rootsy guitar and blues singing at the Playboy simply because of the commercial setting and a dread of hearing the *Saints* at the end of each set. In fact, it is worth the price of a drink (about 11 shillings to keyholders) to witness the sheer sociological irony of Snooks chanting his compelling blues verse among the Playboy Bunnies and party line sophisticates who frequent the club.

Even among the white Dixieland groups there is much to interest the discriminating listener. Pete Fountain's conception never loses its intensity, although his ideas are still cast too familiarly in a Goodman-Fazola mold. Fountain's rhythm section tends towards timidity—he only uses powerhouse drummer Jack Sperling on recording sessions and road dates—but bassist Oliver Felix and pianist Earl Viuovich rescue it from the sluggish four-to-the-bar feeling that many swing era type rhythm sections fall into. Al Hirt's group offers the solidly traditional clarinet of Pee Wee Spitelera, and if your tastes are sufficiently catholic you can enjoy the well-seasoned rhythmic cuisine of ex–Al Belletto pianist Fred Crane, bassist Lowell Miller, and Boston drummer Jimmy Zitano. Hirt himself has been known to swing furiously at times, but he is seldom inclined to put aside the trick bag and play jazz for its own sake.

Less can be said for the two Dixieland bands at the Famous Door, led by trumpeter Mike Lala and trombonist Santo Pecora. Lala does not play a strong Dixie lead, and the personnel of both groups changes so regularly that the musicians do not attain a unity beyond that of a slick Dixie jam session. Of course, everyone should hear Santo Pecora for much the same reason that everyone visits Congo Square—he is an important figure among the early jazz trombonists, and he is still playing an affirmative, if unimaginative horn.

Armand Hug at the Golliwog Lounge on Canal Street is the city's outstanding solo attraction. Hug is best known as a ragtime specialist, but depending on the complexion of his audience he might be heard playing ragtime, cocktail music, or an eclectic adaptation of Hines, Tatum, and Teddy Wilson. Hug has been forced to musical compromise for years because he refuses to leave town for a more sympathetic environment, yet on the rare occasions when he appears in concert, his technical fluency and impeccable sense of time are outstanding. Hug prefers modern musicians as accompanists, and he is a particular favourite of several modern drummers, most notably Dick Johnson and Louis Timken, who feel that the critics have pegged him too narrowly as a ragtime pianist.

The young revivalist (traditional) groups in New Orleans, like the young revivalists elsewhere, seldom produce anything more than good time jazz, a congenial razzmatazz that lacks the intensity of the genuine traditional groups and the respect for order of the Dixieland bands. The most interesting of the groups, the Crawford-Ferguson Night Owls, could probably be a better-than-average freewheeling Dixie band; unfortunately, they have chosen to ape the music of another generation. The Owls tend to play somewhat updated versions of old, rarely heard tunes instead of copying the original traditionalists' styles, and the presence of the inevitable banjo bogs the group down rhythmically and restricts the soloists.

Paul Crawford, trombonist and co-leader, is a talented arranger in a Duke Ellington vein; yet he seems to be the instrumentalist in the group most strongly bent on ancestor worship. It does not work, for Crawford is cosmopolitan in his temperament and he fails to capture the raw, lusty expressiveness of the Ory-influenced trombonists. Raymond Burke was once a member of the band, but the brilliant blues clarinetist sounded like a parody of himself in the cloying environment of the Owls. His replacement, Hank Kmen, is a competent musician who role-plays effectively along with drummer Lenny Ferguson and the other members of the group.

The city's most popular young revivalist band, the Last Straws, is far inferior to the Night Owls. The front line sounds coarse and amateurish, and the rhythm section lumbers along tediously. As a matter of fact, the members of the band do not take themselves seriously, for no one in the group has ever made his living in jazz. When the group is at its best, it does indeed project the footstomping gusto of hobbyists on a weekend pass from the office.

Modern jazz in New Orleans is most consistently found at the Playboy Club. Al Belletto plays nightly with either of the two house groups, the Dave West Trio and the John Probst Trio. Both groups contain first rate musicians; but the house policy calls for a subdued approach, and the music is seldom more exciting than the conversation.

In the recent past New Orleans has produced some remarkable modernists. Employment is so irregular, however, that groups have been forced to break up, with some members going on the road and others accepting work in Dixieland or commercial bands. In the former category is the magnificent drummer Ed Blackwell, who has been heard since leaving New Orleans with Ornette Coleman and various other *avant garde* groups. Still about town is Bill Huntington, a guitarist who began as a teenage understudy of banjoist Lawrence Marrero. (Huntington played banjo on the famous recording session that Ken Colyer made in New Orleans in 1952.) Due to the lack of demand for jazz guitarists, Huntington has also become the city's most interesting bassist as well.

Other formidable talents include pianist Ellis Marsalis, tenor saxist Nat Perrilliat, and drummer James Black, all of whom so impressed Cannonball Adderley that he and his brother Nat did a recording session with the three locals and bassist Sam Jones. Black and Perrilliat are on the road, while Marsalis is still in New Orleans, appearing occasionally at afterhours sessions at the Blue Note.

The jazz menu in New Orleans is probably richer than it has been since Storyville was closed in 1917, and it is certainly more varied. But most musicians and jazz fans feel that today's multi-course jazz banquet will be followed by a bitter demi-tasse. A majority of the older musicians of the revival will be dead or unable to play within ten years. (Almost a dozen have died since the founding of Preservation Hall two years ago.) Moreover, the young musicians who might be forming a second line behind such artists as Blackwell and Huntington have often been misled down the blind alley of rock and roll.

And worst of all, the unique character of New Orleans culture has been threatened by suburban industrial development, which is bringing a new mood to the city—the dreary mood of organisation life that inflates incomes and deflates cultural distinctiveness in cities that expand too rapidly in a short period of time. New Orleans faces a crucial test of cultural stamina in the next decade. If the flavour of old New Orleans can be preserved beneath the myriad of changes the city is undergoing, jazz connoisseurs will be nourished by another generation of jazzmen who will continue to translate the Oliver-Armstrong tradition into terms of contemporary society.

JAZZ IN NEW ORLEANS—A NEW GOLDEN AGE
DELTA REVIEW, NOVEMBER–DECEMBER, 1966

In the 1940s the word was around New Orleans that jazz was dead. If not dead, no longer commercially marketable.

The city that was a hothouse of musical activity at the turn of the century had become a musical wasteland. Storyville, a focal point in the growth of jazz, had been closed in 1917 because of vice and crime. Bourbon Street, a pale successor to Basin Street, was a depressing row of strip clubs and nondescript lounges featuring juke boxes and hillbilly bands.

A few jazz greats were hanging on, buried in show bands or playing in remote spots. The great clarinetist Irving Fazola was in the pit band at the My-

O-My, a West End club that featured female impersonators. George Lewis, after a brief taste of fame on the road with the resurrected Bunk Johnson band, was again doing weekends at an out-of-the-way club called Manny's Tavern. Most of New Orleans' best traditional jazzmen, however, were either unemployed or out of town.

It is hard to believe that the musical ghost town of the '40s could have evolved into the varied, bristling, growing music scene of New Orleans today. The city is at the threshold of a new Golden Age of jazz. Once again New Orleans is a major city in music; it shows promise of becoming the music capital not only of the South, but of the country.

The first break was a modest revival of interest in New Orleans jazz around 1948. Spurred by a determined WDSU disk jockey, Roger Wolfe, and a small nucleus of jazz fans, the revival led to the Famous Door and Steve Valenti's Paddock Lounge.

The Famous Door featured Sharkey's Kings of Dixieland, a smooth, tightly knit group thought by many to be one of the best. At the Paddock, "Papa" Celestin led a hardy group of oldtimers, including clarinetist Alphonse Picou.

A number of young imitators began second-lining behind the older musicians. The Junior Dixieland Band, a spirited teen-aged group led by Frank and Fred Assunto, won first place on the Horace Heidt talent show. The juniors turned professional, become local celebrities when they proudly opened at the Famous Door under their new name—the Dukes of Dixieland. (Few realize that the Dukes' name was a frank tribute to Sharkey's Kings of Dixieland, the band that inspired them.)

The Dukes were the first in a series of New Orleans musicians who refined their talents in local clubs and recording studios, then broke into the money circuit through careful management and first-rate showmanship.

The Junior Dixielanders had a clarinetist named Pete Fountain who left the group after the Heidt contest to finish high school. But he was soon persuaded by drummer-promoter Phil Zito to join his new band, a fiery group that included the late George Girard on trumpet. Zito won a Columbia recording contract for the band, but after the first album the bandsmen struck out on their own as a cooperative, hiring drummer Charlie Duke and redubbing the group the Basin Street Six. With the Dukes on the road, the Six became the undisputed leaders in the Dixie revival.

But the revival soon waned. Rhythm and blues began to dominate the New Orleans music scene, with artists such as Fats Domino, Sam Butera, and Lloyd Price overshadowing the Dixielanders by 1952. Also, modern jazz was claiming the attention of a large number of young musicians impressed by the clean, contemporary sound of Al Belletto's sextet in nearby Biloxi, or the adventurous improvisations of neo-boppers like altoist "Mouse" Bonati and drummer Ed Blackwell in the French Quarter.

Yet the rhythm and blues artists, like the Assuntos, made Orleanians music-conscious and made the nation New Orleans–conscious when they leaped to major night clubs and recording companies. Slowly the image of New Orleans as a breeding place for top talent in the entertainment world was reestablished.

Pete Fountain and Al Hirt completed that image. Their success stories follow remarkably similar lines. Both were out of work in the early 50s, and both took jobs with a New Orleans pesticide company, playing music on weekends. Both were "discovered" almost by chance—Fountain by Lawrence Welk, Jr., who heard the clarinetist on some old Basin Street sides and recommended him to his father for a spot on his national TV show; and Hirt by agent Gerard Purcell, who heard him at Dan's Pier 600 (now the Al Hirt Club) and was amazed by his technical fluency and showmanship.

Fountain and Hirt kept the Crescent City as their home base after gaining national fame. Unlike the Dukes, who settled in Las Vegas, Fountain and Hirt returned to New Orleans to open their own clubs on Bourbon Street. Soon more and more tourists passed up the strip clubs, embarking instead on do-it-yourself jazz festivals—with Fountain's and Hirt's clubs first on the list.

Mayor Victor H. Schiro proclaimed Pete Fountain Day when the clarinetist returned to New Orleans, and the Chamber of Commerce gave Hirt and Fountain awards as the city's outstanding goodwill ambassadors in 1963 and 1964.

In 1961 traditional jazz aficionados led by Grayson Mills, Sandra and Alan Jaffe, and Barbara Reid borrowed a French Quarter art gallery from a friend, Larry Borenstein, and soon such musicians as Punch Miller, Kid Howard, Jim Robinson, and Billie and De De Pierce were appearing at the hall, which was named Preservation Hall.

After a few publicity breaks—coverage on *David Brinkley's Journal*, an Associated Press story, articles in major magazines—the hall became a mecca not only for jazz fans but for laymen, who found its relaxed atmosphere a welcome change. Today the hall retains its informality (customers sit on old sofas, straight-back chairs, or on the floor). There are no drink sales, and a nominal contribution admits you.

Ironically, a crackdown on vice in the French Quarter in 1963 resulted in an important boost for music. The main target was the strip clubs, a number of which had a long history of liquor-cutting, prostitution, and robbery.

Club owners began looking to musical acts—folk music, blues, and rock and roll—as a more secure means of keeping in business and out of jail. Even the owners who stayed with strip shows began to use live music instead of a blaring stereo set, another trend which had stymied musical activity. Club owners along Bourbon Street seem convinced that the days of the strip show are over, and that most clubs will survive only if they can find music that is competitive with the established jazz clubs.

The official breakdown of racial barriers has practically doubled the potential audience for any given performance, and the possibilities for exchange among Negro and white musicians are boundless. Several major clubs—Al Hirt's and Pete Fountain's, to name two—have integrated audiences as a matter of course, and at the Playboy Club the house band led by pianist Dave West has been integrated for over a year. More recently, trombonist Paul Crawford and cornetist George Finola have been leading integrated bands at the jazz revival halls.

Finally, New Orleans is becoming a "money town" with a "money circuit" all its own. Riding a wave of unprecedented prosperity, the city is becoming increasingly cosmopolitan, and riper for the big push into its new Golden Age. There is a larger, more sophisticated audience for music in New Orleans today, and the extent and variety of the musical fare on Bourbon Street reflects urbanity. Virtually every phase of jazz and popular music is represented on the exciting stretch that runs from Iberville to St. Ann Streets.

Well over a hundred musicians are employed in that small area alone. Strict traditional jazz is centered at Preservation Hall and its imitator, Dixieland Hall, where different bands nightly play in the original New Orleans style. The Court of Two Sisters is currently featuring Smilin' Joe, the Quarter's only itinerant blues singer, although Snooks Eaglin and Babe Stovall are seen frequently at various French Quarter clubs.

A slicker brand of jazz is offered by several Dixieland groups besides those of Hirt and Fountain. Most popular of the neo-Dixie groups are Santo Pecora's Tailgaters and Bill Kelsey's Quartet at the Famous Door. Pecora is a veteran trombonist whose well-oiled group alternates with clarinetist Kelsey's volatile new combo. Another new group, Ernest Holland's All-Stars, is currently at the Paddock, which has retained its jazz policy continuously since the revival began. Still in residence is the Paddock's perennial intermission pianist Snookum Russell, a musician who has deep roots in jazz—he once led a big band with J. J. Johnson, Ray Brown, Fats Navarro, and others who were to become pioneers of modern jazz.

Modern jazz is found most consistently at the Playboy Club, where Al Belletto and the Dave West trio play in the Penthouse, while Phil Reudy's trio is heard in the Living Room. Belletto has brought in such artists as trombonist Carl Fontana and pianists Fred Crane, Jimmy Drew, Ellis Marsalis, and Buddy Prima.

The Quarter's newest modern jazz room is Joe Burton's on Toulouse Street. Burton, a Chicagoan, is a widely experienced modern pianist with off-beat showmanship and an unfailing taste in choosing talented sidemen like bassist Bill Huntington and drummer Jimmy Zitano.

Al Hirt's club is the only one in the French Quarter booking major jazz groups. Dizzy Gillespie, Ramsey Lewis, Lionel Hampton, and Gene Krupa have appeared, and lesser known jazz artists (Don Goldie, Don Jacoby) are frequently imported. Hirt's club also produced a new local favorite, pianist Ronnie Kole. Kole played at Hirt's in 1964 with a traveling combo called the Heavyweights, then stayed on to lead the house band at the club. For several months now he has been playing at his own club, Kole's Corner, in a wing of the Absinthe House. Kole is a fluent and knowledgeable pianist in a Peter Nero vein, but his best break came early this year when he jokingly cut a record of the now-famous *Batman* theme. Since then the bearded pianist has been courted by several recording companies, and his club has become a gathering place for tourists and show people.

On the periphery of jazz, Bourbon Street offers the popular blues singer and pianist Clarence (Frog Man) Henry at the 544 Club. Despite the misleading photographs outside that show the Frog Man perched incongruously among the Beatles, Henry is a competent, bona fide rhythm and blues artist—certainly comparable to Fats Domino, Lloyd Price, and others who have had wider exposure. A younger exponent of rhythm and blues, pianist-singer-vibist Ronnie Barron, built a remarkable following at the El Morocco for several months before striking out for Las Vegas and a recording contract.

Headquarters for folk music on Bourbon Street is the Bayou Room, where the Village Singers appear nightly. While New Orleans has produced many genuine folk artists, the Bayou Room aims at a popular audience, most commonly booking such non-esoteric folk groups as the Benedicts and the New Horizon Quintet. Another club with the emphasis on "pop" is the Bikini-a-GoGo, where well known rock and roll groups like Bill Black's combo are brought in regularly.

Finally, jazz-tinged groups can be heard at the Red Garter and Your Father's Moustache, two clubs that recreate a Gay 90s atmosphere. A young entrepreneur named Joel Shiavone started the banjomania with a Father's Moustache in Boston; he opened a branch in New Orleans, hoping that the bouncy razzmatazz would be a natural for Bourbon Street. The banjo groups are intentionally corny, but they often include musicians with a jazz background—for example, tuba player Harold Johnson, a former Turk Murphy sideman at the Red Garter. The clubs also delve into straight traditional jazz on Sunday afternoons when clarinetist George Lewis plays at the Red Garter Annex and clarinetist Jim Liscombe appears at the Moustache.

The music scene in New Orleans is a dynamic one, alive with experiment and expectation, constantly shifting. New Orleans is ready for its New Golden Age.

THE NEW ORLEANS JAZZ SCENE TODAY
JAZZFEST PROGRAM, MAY 1968

Jazzfest '68 is New Orleans' invitation for jazz musicians and fans to join the permanent jazz festival that has been going on, in one form or another, for over half a century. As in other major cities, the jazz scene in New Orleans has had its high points and its low points; but the city has constantly produced a mainstream of jazz artists who testify to the enduring vitality of its musical culture.

Since the Dixieland Jazz revival in New Orleans in the late 1940's, jazz has become increasingly popular in the city that nurtured it. The local revival was followed in the 1950's by national acclaim for New Orleans jazz, blues, and pop artists like the Dukes of Dixieland, Pete Fountain, Al Hirt, Louis Prima, Fats Domino, and Al Belletto. When state segregation laws that had limited both artists and audiences in New Orleans for years were struck down in the early 1960's, the stage was set for the city to reclaim its historical position as a leading jazz and entertainment center.

Any attempt at a complete catalogue of the jazz activity in New Orleans during a particular week will meet with frustration, since policies and bookings at many local clubs are as fragile as a stripper's G-string. But the artists and clubs named below should provide a reasonably accurate map of the territory, and with a little legwork the complete jazz buff should be able to program an after-hours jazz festival that recapitulates the history of jazz itself.

Traditional jazz is heard nightly at the two French Quarter kitty halls, Preservation Hall and Dixieland Hall. The atmosphere is informal, with customers sitting on straight-back chairs or on the floor. Veteran musicians like George Lewis, Punch Miller, Billie and De De Pierce, and Paul Barbarin play a brand of jazz that is often instrumentally ragged, but always disarmingly honest. Admission is by a door fee. The no-booze policy means that the whole family can join in the foot-tapping and hand-clapping.

The city's long tradition of blues artists is represented by pianist-singer Smilin' Joe at the Court of Two Sisters. Just down the street at the Flame Lounge is pianist Dave Williams, best known for his work here and in Chicago with blues vocalist Blanche Thomas. More in a contemporary vein are the blues-pop stylings of pianist-vocalist Clarence "Frog Man" Henry at the 544 Club and singer Ernie K-Doe at the Dream Room. Snookum Russell, who once led a pre-bop big band that included Fats Navarro, Ray Brown, and J. J. Johnson, holds forth with blues-and-boogie intermission piano at the Paddock Lounge.

Armand Hug, internationally admired as a ragtime specialist, plays a single at the intimate Touché Lounge at the Royal Orleans Hotel. However, the "ragtime" label obscures the fact that Hug is essentially an eclectic who draws from Earl Hines and Art Tatum as well as Jelly Roll Morton and Scott Joplin. The Touché also offers lagniappe in the form of some striking jazz paintings by artist Noel Rockmore.

The city's most popular Dixieland artist is clarinetist Pete Fountain, who plays nightly at the French Quarter Inn. Last year Fountain brought New Orleans–born tenor saxophonist Eddie Miller back from California to join his group, and he recently lured drummer Nick Fatool from the West Coast. Fountain has also opened a new club called Storyville on Royal and Elysian Fields. Warren Luening, a fleet modern trumpeter who followed Fountain as a jazz soloist on *The Lawrence Welk Show*, is leading a combo at the club.

Al Hirt is seldom at Al Hirt's club, but the bearded trumpeter has been importing top jazz acts from Bobby Hackett to Dizzy Gillespie. The Dukes of Dixieland are currently at Hirt's, combining a hometown visit with a two weeks' engagement.

The Famous Door and the Paddock were the sites of the jazz revival of the late '40's, when Sharkey Bonano and Papa Celestin reawakened Orleanians' interest in their native music. Today both clubs feature the kind of slick, updated Dixieland combo that is generally rejected by purists but applauded by tourists. The Door spotlights two bands—one led by one-time New Orleans Rhythm Kings trombonist Santo Pecora, the other by trumpeter Roy Liberto, whose playing recalls the style of the late George Girard. The Paddock, reportedly in the midst of a policy change, has been vacillating between a Dixieland group led by swing-based trumpeter Thomas Jefferson and Ernest Holland's amorphous Dixie-blues-rock combo.

After functioning for years as an underground art in private jam sessions and out-of-the-way bars, modern jazz gained popular acceptance in New Orleans' leading club during the 1960's. Al Belletto has led modern groups at the Playboy since 1961, and today the club features Biloxi pianist Carrol Cunningham and a rock group called the Dead End Kids in addition to the Belletto quartet. Pianist Ronnie Dupont's quartet and vocalist Betty Farmer have succeeded with a jazz-for-dancing policy at an unlikely location, the Bistro Lounge on Tulane Avenue. Showmanly Ronnie Kole at Kole's Corner on Bourbon Street is bidding for national attention as a modern pianist in a Peter Nero vein. The Fairmont Room of the Roosevelt Hotel features Dr. Charles (Chuck) Berlin, who balances his week as a teacher at LSU Medical School with jazz and popular piano stylings during cocktail hours.

Jazz in the Parker-Gillespie tradition is heard at the Sho'Bar, where a pit band led by alto saxophonist Don Suhor manages to play shows flawlessly while soaring through charts and standards of the bop era. Home base for the city's leading avant garde combo, Willie Tee and the Souls, is the Ivanhoe on Bourbon Street. The group was discovered by Cannonball Adderley during one of his engagements at Al Hirt's club. Cannonball was so excited by the Souls that he personally sponsored the group in a recording session this year.

Many bands resist categorization in terms of a particular style of jazz. For example, the Crawford-Ferguson Night Owls, who play Saturday nights on the Steamer *President*, are usually classified as a revivalist band. But few revivalist groups, from Turk Murphy to the Village Stompers, can match the versatility of the Owls in moving from materials like Sam Morgan's rarely heard *Bogalusa Strut* to Duke Ellington's *Shiny Stocking*. Similarly, it would be easy to dismiss guitarist Paul Guma's combo at the Top of the Mart or Tony Mitchell's group at the Fontainbleau as "commercial"—except for the fact that Guma and Mitchell are both instrumentalists with deep roots in jazz, and perceptive listeners invariably tune in on the jazz dimension in each set.

In the long run, classifications and categories in jazz are irrelevant. The variety of jazz styles in New Orleans today and the many schools of jazz represented on the *Jazzfest '68* program should not be thought of as illustrating sharp divisions within the jazz community. Musicians and jazz fans alike are coming to reject arguments about what school of jazz is "purest" or which jazz styles are "dated." The internecine critical battles that raged in the '40's seem senseless, even ludicrous, today.

The late Charlie Parker said that there are no boundaries to art. Pee Wee Russell believes that any good musician, concert or jazz, possesses an instinct for swinging that will find expression in his art. Pianist Armand Hug has stated tersely, "If you're a piano player, you play piano; if you're a musician, you play music." The New Orleans jazz scene, like *Jazzfest '68*, is not a field for the exercise of narrow musicological classifications but a microcosm of the wide world of jazz.

THE UNIQUE, SYNCOPATED NON-JET SET RHYTHM OF NEW ORLEANS
GENTLEMEN'S QUARTERLY, APRIL 1970

The first thing to remember when you get to New Orleans is to forget everything you've ever heard about the city. If you believe what Billy Graham said—that New Orleans is "the sin-stained city of booze and bourbon"—you're liable to end your first night out with an empty wallet and not enough genuine, delectable vice to make an interesting entry on a bathroom wall.

If you believe that this is the city where jazz was born, you're fair game for every razzmatazz joint advertising that jazz was born here, on this spot, sixty years ago or is preserved here in its primitive essence by Joe Noblow, who, it turns out, was born in Manhattan.

If you're a history buff, beware of tour guides that begin, "Legend has it that. . . ." Such legends hang like moss on the sturdy oak of the city's history. Although they are charming parasites, they are parasites nonetheless.

As for New Orleans' continuing notoriety as a center of international intrigue, forget it. District Attorney Jim Garrison has stretched the definition of politics as the art of the possible past the snapping point, into the art of the improbable and the art of the fantastic. His cloak-and-dagger games are great theater, but they have nothing to do with political revolution.

New Orleans is a place of profound cultural evolution, not a revolutionary stronghold for the New Left or the Old Right. It has its own way of being contemporary, and if you want to enjoy the city as it is, you'll just have to slow down to its unique, syncopated, non-jet set rhythm. Any native will tell you that you don't rush through a dinner at Antoine's or worry about what time it is at an all-night jam session. Orleanians will not be skyscrapered, monorailed or rocketed into the twenty-first century while there's still some good living left in the twentieth.

Orleanians also say the French Quarter is the most convenient place to hang your hat before letting your hair down in New Orleans. You can walk through the Quarter with the aid of a street map from a gas station, and 10 cents will get you anywhere else you want to go (within reason) on the city's well-linked transit system. The weekly *Vieux Carre Courier*, available at swanky shops, corner groceries and laundromats for a nickel, gives straight, dependable information on what's happening as well as providing insight into local issues that are commonly absent from (or, more likely, avoided in) the city's two bland dailies, the *Times-Picayune* and *States-Item*.

Royal Street's antique shops and art galleries are the most alluring spots in the daytime Quarter. But only the connoisseur or intuitive buyer should venture beyond a box of pecan pralines or a pastel portrait by a sidewalk artist. The night Quarter is attempting vainly to keep up the old Sin City image, with lots of exotic dancers and sniggering, panting emcees. The night Quarter also provides numerous jazz, near-jazz and non-jazz clubs and halls, and no small number of barkers, hot dog vendors, hippies, and plainclothes detectives mixing it up with the tourists.

Although it's often difficult to separate the real from the synthetic in art, antiques, and jazz, the whole Naughty New Orleans bit is so patently phony that in the Seventies there would be more logic in presenting it as historical pageant rather than enticing visual pornography, which it seldom is. A top-less waitress in a California restaurant exposes more to a customer, and at a closer range, than a Bourbon Street stripper does. An underground movie is more likely to capture the rhythm of sensuality, and at a much lower price, than Baby Doll, the 280-pound stripper at the Guys and Dolls Club.

The fact of the matter is that vice is on the run in New Orleans. Its career in the city has been highly erratic every since Storyville, the officially approved Red Light District, was closed in 1917 by order of the United States Government. During the late Forties and early Fifties, reform Mayor De-Lesseps "Chep" Morrison tried to contain the vice and crime that was concentrated in the downtown area, where minors could purchase liquor freely and people of all ages and sexes were openly accosted by panderers.

In 1963 D.A. Jim Garrison padlocked the French Quarter clubs that had repeatedly violated laws against B-drinking, prostitution, and liquor-cutting. In one classic raid some plainclothesmen outwitted a watchful barker by boarding a bus at the head of Bourbon Street. Ordering the driver to stop in front of the club, they rushed in, arresting a performer who was drinking with a customer.

Many club owners switched from girlie shows to music during Garrison's rampage, and much of the city's vice operations reportedly went underground or moved to the various bars and motels on the highways in nearby Jefferson Parish. What happens every night on the stages of the little Bourbon Street clubs is mainly symbolism: recalling a lusty, wicked past, much as shoot-outs are staged in mock-Western saloons from Biloxi to Walla Walla. Practically nobody leaves New Orleans without seeing a strip show, but you'll put the whole thing into a better perspective if you put the strip-and-clip joints on your list of museums.

The jazz picture in New Orleans is so rich that a jazz lover can set up his own do-it-yourself jazz festival, catching everything from blues to *avant-garde*, tracing the entire history of jazz as he makes the rounds. The "rounds" include more than a stroll down Bourbon Street; not all of the best jazz is found in the French Quarter.

The Quarter does boast the famous traditional jazz mecca, Preservation Hall, and its imitator, Dixieland Hall. Preservation Hall began in 1961 as one of those mad evangelical schemes fostered by traditional jazz fans. The Hall, located at 726 St. Peter Street, is a converted art gallery featuring mainly musicians who were playing in New Orleans around the turn of the century. Despite faltering technique and short-windedness, the traditionalists at the hall play an expressive brand of jazz that isn't reproduced by musicians of later eras.

The club's format is probably part of the reason for its popularity. No drinks are sold, so customers aren't hustled for refills. A nominal admission fee ($2) entitles a customer to sit on a couch, a straight-back chair, or on the floor while listening to music that's untainted by the commercialism of most jazz clubs. (A sign on the wall reads, "Requests: Traditional—$1; Other—$2; 'Saints'—$5.")

Dixieland Jazz—which is basically the white musician's contribution to the early evolution of jazz music—is well represented on Bourbon Street by Frank Assunto and the Dukes of Dixieland at the Royal Sonesta (where the Jazz Museum is also housed).

Modern jazz can be heard at three clubs in the Quarter: the Playboy, the Sho'Bar, and the Jazz Workshop. The Playboy isn't selling jazz but atmosphere, so alto saxophonist Al Belletto's quartet is reduced to playing background music for bunny-oglers. The Sho'Bar is a strip club, but reed man Don Suhor's relentless combo manages to play some excellent bop as the girls bump and grind onstage.

And the Jazz Workshop ranks as one of the most exciting jazz spots in town. Its setting is one of the more interesting developments in the Quarter. It is part of the Decatur Street Phenomenon: artists from various fields who, weary of commercialism in the Royal and Bourbon Street areas, gravitated toward the dingy section of Decatur Street just below Jackson Square. Along Decatur, once a haven for winos, are the Bank, the city's only hard rock club; the Listening Eye, a photographic arts gallery contiguous with the Jazz Workshop; and the Sphinx, a coffeehouse.

The Decatur Street artists are generally zealots and idealists who won't accept artistic compromise. Consequently, their performances tend to be enthusiastic. Regrettably, they are in dire financial trouble. Natives still tend to think of Decatur Street as Skid Row, and too few visitors know that it exists. Already a very promising art school, the New Orleans Studio School of Fine Art, has been forced to move from Decatur to a more genteel part of town because of the image problem. The other artists are hanging on, but without more support (i.e., customers) the Decatur Street group will pass into the honorable limbo of disbanded art groups.

A seasoned traveler—a status apart from a tourist—knows that watching what the natives do is one of the best ways of discovering what's worth doing in a city. However, this is a puzzling game in New Orleans, because so often the natives seem to be doing nothing at all, or at least some very unswingerlike things. For instance, they will top off an evening with coffee and doughnuts at the French Market, and the powdered sugar that drops from the hole-less doughnuts will leave their clothes dappled with white dust. Not much fun, until you've tried it once and find yourself going for a third order of doughnuts after you swore you'd stop after the second. Or they might get on the St. Charles streetcar at some point above Lee Circle and let the clumsy, careening machine take them on a round trip through the Garden District and the University section. Pretty dull stuff, if you don't enjoy the elegant homes and trees that line one of the most gracious avenues in America. Or they might board the free ferryboat to Algiers—with full knowledge that a perfectly good bridge has been built for the purpose of getting across the Mississippi—and stare at the ripples that the boat cuts into the brown water.

Aside from being the backbone of the city's economy, the river is a perpetual source of mystery for Orleanians in moments of play and meditation. There is, for example, the Steamer *President*, the world's largest floating dance hall, where the working class has two-stepped to Dixieland music on weekend river tours for decades. And there's the Top-of-the-Mart, the businessman's refuge, a revolving lounge atop the International Trade Mart building that sticks out like an anachronism on Canal Street, but is redeemed by a breathtaking view of the river.

Then there's everybody's river, flowing by the observation deck in the rear of the Audubon Park Zoo, where students study, lovers love, and families watch whatever happens to be going up or downstream every day during the city's eight or nine months of mild and hot weather. And there are the miles and miles of levees that curve around and beyond the Crescent City, where the *nouveau riche* ride horseback, children of varying hues and backgrounds romp together, and nomads mingle with resident eccentrics in tar paper shacks.

Although you would look conspicuous scanning the levees with camera in hand in search of local color, the French Quarter is good for people-watching. At the Seven Seas cafe on Bourbon Street, for instance, you can run into Pinky (the Gate-Crasher) Ginsberg and his cronies, along with numerous musicians and barkers—not to mention hard-faced men rumored to be lieutenants of the local *mafiosi*. If you board the bus named Desire—the streetcar was removed long ago—on Royal or Bourbon you can hear some real New Orleans talk, which means black and white Ninth Ward dialects that sound like Afro-Bostonian spoken with a Brooklyn accent.

There is, after all, no Grand Tour of New Orleans. You have to be ready to improvise, to follow a marching band down a side street to a jam session that wasn't on your agenda, to watch candle flames draw slowly on their wicks as you enjoy good food, good fellowship, and coffee that was made for leisure and dalliance, not for breaks at 10:15 and 2:30.

Having a good time in New Orleans, as distinguished from being had in New Orleans, might be described as a series of instant Mardi Gras, prolonged meals, and rambling conversations. If that strikes you as too vague to be of much help in setting up a timetable, you have the right idea. Pull up a chair, *mon ami,* and we can talk about it for a while.

Appendix 2

Early Modern Jazz Musicians
in New Orleans, 1945–1960

In developing the following list, I threw a fairly wide net. I did not, however, include players from places like Baton Rouge, Hammond, and Biloxi unless they were also present on the New Orleans scene. The comments in the overview to section III and in the symposium on early modern jazz (chapter 26) account for many of the marvelous young artists at LSU, Southern University, and Southeastern, as well as on the Gulf Coast.

The cutoff date of 1960 might seem arbitrary, but there are three reasons for the time frame. First, it is safe to say that young players coming on the scene after 1960 were beneficiaries of the groundwork laid by their predecessors in the earlier postwar years. The latter were inventing with fewer musical models, fewer recordings, and fewer venues. They worked with less definition of the new genres, less codification of underlying musical theory, less scored material, and less instruction in modern jazz performance in institutional settings.

It is not difficult to call numerous post-1960 players brilliant artists. The Turbinton brothers (Earl, alto sax and Willie Tee, keyboard/vocal), and drummer Jimmy Zitano come to mind. Many have advanced the jazz art as avant garde players or have developed unique syntheses. But it is difficult to say that they were pioneers in New Orleans when modern jazz as was newly emerging.

Second, the New Orleans modernists of 1945–1960 are by and large the least known and most underresearched musicians. More data are available in from the 1960s on. As noted in chapter 1, my *Down Beat* "Ad Libs" columns and "Where and When" listings from 1961–1969 systematically covered local leaders, sidemen, and clubs. Also, the articles and reviews in section III and the four cross section articles in appendix 1, all written in the 1960s, report on artists and activities of that decade. Sources like Battiste, Broven, and Berry, et al., discuss aspects of the 1960s (e.g., the AFO [All for One] musicians' cooperative).

Third, at the practical level, going beyond 1960 would make for an unmanageably cluttered list. The number of modernists increased greatly as the music became part of our culture. And if one takes the list to 1970, then why not to 1980, 1990, and to the present? Hopefully, future researchers will take on the task of expanding the list to include later decades.

Given the built-in risks of error and disagreement in developing such a list, I expect that no one will fully concur with the results. Certain questions are sure to be raised (fill in the blanks): *Why isn't _____ on the list? What is _____ doing there? Wasn't _____ active before 1960? And who the hell is _____?* I hope that the concept, criteria, and contents of the list will be critiqued so that our understanding and appreciation of the early modern jazz artists will continue to grow.

Names of the early players were derived from numerous sources—extensive interviews, the symposium participants, my own memory of the times, and rare print resources like Harold Battiste's *New Orleans Heritage*. Almost all of the names were cited without reservation by two or more credible sources who were on the scene in the postwar years. Few of the early New Orleans modernists made recordings; but, as noted in the overview to section III, I agree with Brian Priestley and Jed Rasula's view that histories relying too heavily on recordings are in fact unreliable. A rich and representative picture must include, among other things, the testimony of artists and listeners who were present during the period under study.

I tried to exercise rigor in my own choices for inclusion. I did not shrink from the idea that many players simply did not and/or could not cross the line to modern jazz. For example, I enjoyed working with tenor saxist/ pianist John McGhee and pianist/vocalist Mickey Seivers, but the former was a solid swing player and the latter a tasteful combo pianist who at most dabbled in modern jazz.

In no way does this denigrate their talents as performers in other styles. I agree with Harold Battiste's statement in the symposium about respect for all kinds of music and for performers who excel in music other than modern jazz. On the other hand, I do not take such statements of principle to mean that there are no discernible differences between a polka and a symphony, Dixieland and swing, or rhythm and blues and modern jazz. Nor do I believe that breadth of musical acceptance implies that all competent performers in a style play equally well.

In postwar New Orleans some musicians were deeply involved with modern jazz, though they played in other settings; some listened to the new music a lot and played a little; most were playing other kinds of music, from TNOJ and Dixieland to swing to rhythm and blues. (This point is discussed at some length in the section III segment on swing and R&B in relation to early modern jazz.)

It is clear that the exploratory musicians of the time acknowledged that some of their collaborators were more probing and inventive than others. Pianist Frank Strazerri and reedman Don Suhor recall alto saxophonist Mouse Bonati as a musical pacesetter among the French Quarter jazzmen. Harold Battiste states in the 1994 liner notes to Ed Blackwell's *Boogie Live* CD that "among the young cats starting to play music in New Orleans in the 40's . . . Ed Blackwell was a musician's musician, a drummer's drummer. . . . He cast the mold, set the example, and led the way into Modern Jazz for us."

So I am trafficking in subjective judgments here. The entire list, in fact, is an aggregate of judgment calls by numerous firsthand observers. But without judgments (albeit tentative judgments) about the shape of events and the people who lived them, there is no chance for dialogue and nothing, even, to deconstruct. There are at least two dead ends to investigation—universal praise and universal skepticism. The inclination to praise springs from a loving desire to speak ill of no one by speaking well of all—a tendency among New Orleans musicians, as Battiste points out in *New Orleans Heritage*. The skeptical mind-set is represented in recent years by postmodernism, which neutralizes value altogether, resulting in what philosopher Ken Wilber calls "aperspectival madness."

Finally, I should note that many of the surviving, still active musicians on the list are playing little jazz these days, much less excelling as modern jazz players. In the absence of recorded evidence, I trust that the testimony of their contemporaries will be credible. As for myself, I still play, but I am at best the ruins of a good drummer, grateful that Bill Huntington remembers me in Riley and Vidacovich's *New Orleans Jazz and Second Line Drumming* as "the most focused one of our little clique. He is one of the few people I know who loves jazz, regardless of race, style, or era. He was influenced of course by Blackwell and had a dark sound, deep groove, good sense of form. Charlie was one of the best modern drummers of the fifties."

An anecdote from trumpeter Gerry St. Amand, a brilliant modernist in the mid-1950s, makes the point about faded excellence with elegant self-irony. A few years after he had stopped playing jazz regularly, Gerry told about subbing for the regular trumpeter one night at a Bourbon Street strip club. After a freewheeling backup tune, a sideman who knew Jerry's earlier work confided, "Man, you don't have to hold back on your choruses. This is a cool gig." Gerry smiled gently and said, "Thanks, but this is as good as it gets nowadays."

The list is organized by instrument and the musicians are sequenced alphabetically.

Trumpet: Sam Alcorn, Bruce Ahrens, John Brunious, Benny Clement, Rupert Copponex, Wallace Davenport, Johnny Fernandez, Herman Gagne, Rusty Gilder, Al Hirt, Black Mike Lala, Melvin Lastie, Charlie Miller, Tony Moret, Buddy Prima, Ted Riley, Gerry St. Amand, Umar Sharif (Big Emery Thompson), Herb Tassin, Bob Teeters, Vinnie Trauth, Billy White, Jack Willis

Alto Sax: Warren Bell, Al Belletto, Joseph (Mouse) Bonati, Ornette Coleman, Oscar Davis, Joe Fairbanks, Clarence Ford, Phil Hermann, Eddie Hubbard, Don Lasday, Don Suhor

Tenor Sax: Cy (Deedles) Arnold, Harold Battiste, Jerry Boquet, Sam Butera, Bob Cedar, Mike Costa, Charlie Fairley, Bill Fisher, Don Guidry, Edward (Kidd) Jordan, Bill Kelsey, Pete Kowchak, Bruce Lippincott, Joe

(Cheeks) Mandry, Charlie May, Brew Moore, John Patterson, Nat Perrilliat, Chick Power, Alvin Tyler, Hank Walde, Jimmy Wilson

Baritone Sax: Oscar Davis

Clarinet: Alvin Batiste, Clarence Ford, Tony Mitchell, Don Suhor

Trombone: Jack Delaney, Al Hermann, Larry Muhoberac, Joe Prejean

Piano: John (Pickett) Brunious, Joe Burton, F. A. Cassanova, Fred Crane, Tony D'Amore, Ronnie Dupont, Johnny Elgin, Ed Fenasci, Ed Frank, Red Fredd, Jack Hebert, Ellis Marsalis, Rusty Mayne, Pete Monteleone, Triggs Morgan, Larry Muhoberac, Freddie Nesbitt, Thelonious Pernell, John Probst, Buddy Prima, Don Reitan, Snookum Russell, Cedar Walton, Bunkie Withee, Dave West

Guitar: George Davis, Herman Pfeffer, Bill Huntington, Linc Ludington, Ernest McLean, Sam Mooney, Roy Montrell, Joe Pass, Curtis Trevigne

Vibes: Joe Morton, Joe Tarantino

Bass: Gerry Adams, Placide Adams, Bobby Alexis, Richard Alexis, Chuck Badie, Al Bernard, Milton Bourgeois, Otis Deverney, Oliver (Stick) Felix, Rusty Gilder, Joe Hebert, Herbie Hollman, Bill Huntington, Jimmy Johnson, Lou Jordan, Richard Payne, Walter Payton, William Swanson

Drums: Tony Bazley, James Black, Ed Blackwell, Charlie Blancq, John Boudreaux, Bob DeSio, Al Fielder, Vernel Fournier, June Gardner, Wilbur Hogan, Dick Johnson, Lee Johnson, Joe (Smokey) Johnson, Joe Morton, Harry Nance, Earl Palmer, Bill Patey, Joe Prejean, Charles Suhor, Lou Timken, Reed Vaughan, Charles (Hungry) Williams

Vocals: Germane Bazzle, Lee Burton, Benny Curtis, Bob Douglas (Henry Holzenthal), Theresa Kelly, Tami Lynn, Buddy Prima, Laverne Smith, Blanche Thomas, Earl Williams

Promoters/Supporters: Harold Battiste, Al Belletto, Bill Bise, Joe Burton, Dooky Chase, Melvin Lastie, Dick Martin, Frank Painia, Clinton Scott, Tex Stephens

Bibliography

Aiges, Scott, and J. McCusker. "Jazzmen: The End of the Beginning." *Times-Picayune*, October 12, 1993.

Allen, Richard. Personal communication.

Arlt, Helen. Personal communication.

"Armstrong's Birthplace Center of Confusion." *Down Beat*, July 16, 1964.

Balliet, Whitney. "Mecca, La." In *The Jazz People of New Orleans*. By Lee Friedlander. New York: Pantheon, 1992.

Bartlett, Larry. "Thomas and French: Jazz Immortals Reminisce." *Times-Picayune Dixie Roto Magazine,* August 29, 1971.

Basin Street: Newsletter of the National Jazz Foundation, New Orleans, La., 1945–1946.

Batiste, Alvin. Personal communication.

Battiste, Harold. "I Remember Boogie." Liner notes for *Boogie Live . . . 1958*. AFO CD 92-1228-2, 1994.

———. *New Orleans Heritage–Jazz: 1956–1966*. Los Angeles: Opus 43, 1976.

———. Personal communication.

Bazzle, Germaine. Personal communication.

Bell, Warren. Personal communication.

Belletto, Al. Personal communication

Berndt, Louis. Personal communication.

Berry, Jason, Jonathan Foose, and Tad Jones. *Up from the Cradle of Jazz: New Orleans Music since World War II*. Athens: University of Georgia Press, 1986.

Bethell, Tom. *George Lewis: A Jazzman from New Orleans*. Berkeley: University of California Press, 1977.

Blackstone, Orin. *Index to Jazz: Jazz Recordings, 1917–1944*. Westport, Conn.: Greenwood, 1978.

Boquet, Jerry. Personal communication.

Borneman, Ernest. "'Bop Will Kill Business Unless It Kills Itself First'—Louis Armstrong." *Down Beat*, April 7, 1948. Reprinted in *Down Beat: Sixty Years of Jazz*. Edited by Frank Alkyer. Milwaukee: Hal Leonard, 1995.

Braud, Bert. Personal communication.

Broven, John. *Rhythm and Blues in New Orleans*. Gretna, La.: Pelican, 1978.

Bruyninckx, Walter. *Sixty Years of Recorded Jazz, 1917–1977*. Belgium: W. Bruyninckx, 1979.

Bryan, Bill. "Jazz Fest Wrap Up." *Vieux Carre Courier*, May 1, 1970.

Burke, Kenneth. *Language as Symbolic Action*. Berkeley: University of California Press, 1968.

Burt, Eluard. Personal communication.

Butera, Sam. Personal communication.

Carstater, L. S. Letter to Charles Suhor, August 8, 1969.

Carter, William. *Preservation Hall: Music from the Heart*. New York: Norton, 1991.

Charlton, Lee. Personal communication.

Charters, Samuel. *New Orleans, 1886–1963: An Index to the Negro Musicians of New Orleans*. Rev. ed. New York: Oak, 1963.

Chase, Dooky. Personal communication.

Chilton, John. *Stomp Off, Let's Go: The Story of Bob Crosby's Bobcats & Big Band*. London: Jazz Book Service, 1983.

——. *Who's Who of Jazz: Storyville to Swing Street*. Philadelphia: Chilton, 1970.

Chomsky, Noam. *Language and Problems of Knowledge*. Cambridge: MIT Press, 1998.

Collins, Ralph. *New Orleans Jazz: A Revised History*. New York: Vantage, 1996.

"Congressional Act Helps Launch a Southern Jazz Festival." *Down Beat*, February 11, 1965.

Clay, Michael. Letter to the editor. *Utne Reader,* July–August, 1998.

Clements, Ed Lewis. Personal communication.

Corey, Shirley Trusty. Personal communication.

Cuthbert, David. "From Bourbon Street to Lenny Bruce." *Times-Picayune*, January 16, 2000.

Crosby, Richard ["Bing"]. Personal communication.

Dance, Stanley. *Jazz Era: The Forties*. London: Macgibbon & Kee, 1961.

Darois, Phil. Personal communication.

Davenport, Wallace. Personal communication.

Davis, Quint. Personal communication.

"Deadline Passes: Armstrong Birthplace Torn Down." *Down Beat,* July 30, 1964.

Deffaa, Chip. *Traditionalists and Revivalists*. Metuchen, N.J.: Scarecrow, 1993.

Delaney, Joe. Personal communication.

Dix, Dorothy. Cited in *Dear Dorothy Dix*. By Harnett Kane. Garden City, N.Y.: Doubleday, 1952.

"Dixie Battle." *Playback,* May 1949.

Dr. Daddy-O [Vernon Winslow]. "Boogie-Beat" column. *Louisiana Weekly*, August 10, 1950.

Driggs, Frank, and Harris Lewine. *Black Beauty, White Heat: A Pictorial History of Classic Jazz, 1920–1950*. New York: Da Capo, 1995.

Dunner, Sherwin. Liner notes for *Jazz the World Forgot*. Vol. 2. Yazoo CD 2025, 1996.

Erskine, Gilbert M. Personal communication.

——. "Six Interpretations in Jazz." *IAJRC Journal* [International Association of Jazz Record Collectors], Fall 1995.

Feather, Leonard. *New Encyclopedia of Jazz*. New York: Bonanza, 1960.

Felix, Oliver [Stick]. Personal communication.

Formento, Dennis. Personal communication.

Gagliano, Nick. Personal communication.

Gendron, Bernard. "Moldy Figs and Modernists: Jazz at War." In *Jazz among the Discourses*. Edited by Krin Gabbard. Durham, N.C.: Duke University Press, 1995.

Gleason, Ralph. "Bunk Johnson: An American Original." Liner notes for *New Orleans Jazz: Bunk Johnson*. Victor Hot Jazz 7. New Orleans Jazz Series, 1946.

Griffin, Tommy. "Lagniappe" column. New Orleans *Item*, August 19, 1950.

Hadlock, Richard. Untitled liner notes for *Sharkey Bonano, 1928–1937* CD. Timeless CBC 1- 001 Jazz, n.d.

Handy, D. Antoinette. *Jazz Man's Journey: A Biography of Ellis Louis Marsalis, Jr.* Lanham, Md.: Scarecrow, 1999.

Hermann, Al. Personal communication.

Hermann, Phil. Personal communication.

Hillman, Christopher. *Bunk Johnson: His Life and Times*. New York: Universe, 1988.

Hulsizer, Ken. "New Orleans in Wartime." In *Jazz Review*. Edited by Max Jones and Albert McCarthy. London: Jazz Music Books, 1945.

Huntington, Bill. Personal communication.

Ikegami, Teizo. *New Orleans Renaissance on Record*. Tokyo: Alligator Jazz Club, 1980.

"Jass and Jassism." *Times-Picayune*. June 20, 1918.

"Jazz Has Made It." *Times-Picayune*, November 11, 1961.

Jazzfest '68. Printed program. May 1968.

Jenkins, Willard. "Wynton Marsalis on What's Right and Wrong with Jazz Education." In *JazzTimes 1998–1989 Education Guide*. Silver Spring, Md.: JazzTimes, 1998.

Jepsen, Jorgen G. *Jazz Records, 1942–1962*. Denmark: Taastrup Reklametryk, 1965.

Johnson, Monifa. Personal communication.

Jones, Connie. Personal communication.

Jones, "Scoop." "NJF's Epic Program Rates Raves." *Louisiana Weekly*, June 12, 1948.

Jordan, Edward [Kidd]. Personal communication.

Kernfeld, Barry, ed. *Blackwell Guide to Recorded Jazz*. Oxford: Blackwell, 1991.

———. *New Grove Dictionary of Jazz*. London: Macmillan, 1988.

Kolb, Judy. "N.O. to Host Jazz Festival." *Vieux Carre Courier*, February 1970.

Kole, Ronnie. Personal communication.

Kmen, Henry. *Music in New Orleans*. Baton Rouge: LSU Press, 1956.

Lane, Chet. "Mays Is Amazin'" *Metronome*, April 1947.

Leer, Norman. "Bunk." *JazzBeat*, August 1992.

Leonard, Neil. *Jazz: Myth and Religion*. New York: Oxford University Press, 1987.

Lichtenstein, Grace, and L. Danker. *Musical Gumbo: The Music of New Orleans*. New York: Norton, 1993.

Lord [Loyacano], Steve. Personal communication.

Lord, Tom. *The Jazz Discography*. W. Vancouver: Lord Music Reference, 1992.

Lowe, Mundell. Personal communication.

Mann, Frankie [Frank Mannino]. Personal communication.

Marinello, Nick. "Red Hot and Cool." *Tulanian,* Winter 1999.

Marsalis, Ellis. Personal communication.

Marquis, Donald. *In Search of Buddy Bolden: First Man of Jazz*. Baton Rouge: LSU Press, 1978.

Masciere, Christina. "Do the Russell." *New Orleans,* April 1988.

Mengis, Peggy. "The Battle against Bebop." *Times-Picayune New Orleans States Magazine,* April 10, 1949.

Miller, Charlie. Personal communication.

Miller, Marc H. "Louis Armstrong: A Portrait Record." In *Louis Armstrong: A Cultural Legacy*. Edited by Marc H. Miller. Seattle: University of Washington Press, 1994.

Mitchell, Tony. Personal communication.

Morgenstern, Dan. *Jazz People*. Englewood Cliffs, N.J.: Prentice-Hall, 1976.

National Jazz Foundation. "You Own Part of a New New Orleans Gold Mine." Undated brochure, circa 1945.

Nelson, Don. "Bill Evans." *Down Beat*, September 1, 1960. Reprinted in *Down Beat: Sixty Years of Jazz*. Edited by Frank Alkyer. Milwaukee: Hal Leonard, 1995.

Nethercutt, Ron. Personal communication.

"New Orleans Hails Conquering Hero Pops." *Down Beat*, December 16, 1965.

New Orleans Jazz and Food Festival, 1969. Printed program. June 1969.

New Orleans' Jazz and Heritage Festival. Printed program. April 1970.

"New Orleans Jazz Festival 'Postponed' Till Further Notice." *Down Beat*, February 25, 1965.

Nolan, James. Personal communication.

Palmer, Earl. Personal communication.

Palmer, Earl, and Herman Ernest. *New Orleans Drumming: From R&B to Funk*. Video. Miami: CPP/Belwin, 1993.

"Papa." *Time*, July 6, 1953.

"Papa Celestin Comes Back." *Jazzfinder*, April 1948.

"Papa's on Hand for Return of Dixieland Jazz." Chicago *Sunday Tribune*, July 31, 1949.

Payne, Richard. Personal communication.

Percy, Walker. "New Orleans, Mon Amour." *Harper's,* September 1968.

Perry, Don. Personal communication.

Pettinger, Peter. *Bill Evans: How My Heart Sings*. New Haven: Yale University Press, 1998.

Porter, Roy. Interview on videocassette *Celebrating Bird*. Kultur VHS 1293, 1987.

Pottle, Ralph, Jr. Personal communication.

Priestley, Brian. *Jazz on Record: A History*. New York: Billboard, 1991.

Provenzano, John A. "New Orleans: Yesterday and Today." *Jazz Journal,* May 1950.

Pult, Jon R. "Pete Fountain Reminisces." *Jazz Beat,* Spring 1994.

Ramsey, Doug. Personal communication.

Ramsey, Frederic, and Charles E. Smith. *Jazzmen*. New York: Harcourt Brace, 1939.

Raeburn, Bruce Boyd. "New Orleans Style: The Awakening of American Jazz Scholarship and Its Cultural Implications." Ph.D. diss., Tulane University, 1991.

Rasula, Jed. "The Media of Memory: The Seductive Menace of Records in Jazz History." In *Jazz among the Discourses*. Edited by Krin Gabbard. Durham, N.C.: Duke University Press, 1995.

Riley, Herlin, and Johnny Vidacovich. *New Orleans Jazz and Second Line Drumming*. New York: Manhattan Music, 1995.

Roddy, Joseph. "Dixieland Jazz Is 'Hot' Again." *Look,* June 6, 1950.

Rose, Al. *I Remember Jazz: Six Decades among Great Jazzmen*. Baton Rouge: LSU Press, 1986.

———. *Storyville, New Orleans*. Tuscaloosa: University of Alabama Press, 1974.

Rose, Al, and E. Souchon. *New Orleans Jazz: A Family Album*. 3d ed., rev. and enl. Baton Rouge: LSU Press, 1984.

Rose, Diane. "Al Rose, William Russell: Guardians of the Gates at Dawn." Voice of Jazz Special, *Village Voice*, June 21, 1986.

Rossiter, Paul. "The Revivalists." In *Jazzbook 1955*. Edited by Albert McCarthy. London: Cassell, 1995.

Rust, Brian. *Jazz Records, 1897–1942*. 5th rev. and enlarged ed. Essex, U.K.: Storyville, 1982.

St. Amand, Gerry. Personal communication.

Salaam, Kalamu Ya. Liner notes for *The Classic Ellis Marsalis,* AFO CD 91-0428-2, 1991.

Sancton, Thomas, Jr. "Horns of Plenty." *Time*, October 22, 1990.

———. "Portrait of a Jazzman." *Down Beat,* February 9, 1967.

"Satchmo Statue Fund-Raising Drive Is On." *Down Beat,* January 8, 1970.

Scherman, Tony. *Backbeat: Earl Palmer's Story.* Washington, D.C.: Smithsonian Institution Press, 1999.

Schuller, Gunther. *Early Jazz: Its Roots and Musical Development.* New York: Oxford University Press, 1968.

Scott, Clinton. Personal communication.

Scully, Art. Personal communication.

Second Line. Journal of the New Orleans Jazz Club, New Orleans, La., 1950–1970.

Serpas, Mike. Personal communication.

Shafer, William J. *Brass Bands of New Orleans.* Baton Rouge: LSU Press, 1977.

Shapiro, Nat, and Nat Hentoff. *Hear Me Talkin' to Ya.* New York: Rinehart, 1955.

Sidran, Ben. *Black Talk.* New York: Da Capo, 1998.

Smith, Michael P. *New Orleans Jazzfest.* Gretna, La.: Pelican, 1991.

Spedale, Rhodes. *A Guide to Jazz in New Orleans.* New York: Holt, 1984.

———. Personal communication.

Spriggins, E. Belfield. "Excavating Jazz." *Louisiana Weekly*, April 22, 29, 1933.

Stagg, Tom. "The Basin Street Six." Liner notes for *The Basin Street Six: The Complete Circle Recordings* CD. George H. Buck BCD 103, 1994.

Stagg, Tom, and Charlie Crump. *New Orleans, The Revival: A Tape and Discography of Negro Traditional Jazz Recorded in New Orleans or by New Orleans Bands, 1937–1972.* Dublin: Bashall Caves, 1973.

Statiris, Gus. Personal communication.

Stearns, Marshall. *The Story of Jazz.* New York: Mentor, 1958.

Stephens, Tex. Personal communication.

Strazerri, Frank. Personal communication.

Sudhalter, Richard M. *Lost Chords: White Musicians and Their Contributions to Jazz, 1915–1945.* New York: Oxford University Press, 1999.

Sudnow, David. *Ways of the Hand: The Organization of Improvised Conduct.* Cambridge: Harvard University Press, 1978.

Suhor, Charles. "Jazz Improvisation and Language Performance: Parallel Competencies." *Et Cetera (ETC.),* Summer 1986.

———. Letter to the editor, *Vieux Carre Courier,* May 19, 1972.

———. Letter to the editor, New Orleans *States-Item*, September 3, 1966.

———. Letter to Ralph J. Gleason. Charles Suhor Collection, Tulane University Jazz Archive, August 14, 1961.

———. "Straight Talk from Al Hirt." *Down Beat*, September 4, 1969.

Suhor, Charles, with Royal Hartigan, C. K. Ladzekpo, and Ellis Marsalis. "Jazz and Language." Lecture/performance at Inter-Regional Conference, National Council of Teachers of English, New Orleans, La., March 3–4, 1995.

Suhor, Don. Personal communication.

Thompson, Woody. "The Rhythm and Blues Drummers of New Orleans." *Percussive Notes,* August 1996.

Timken, Louis. Personal communication.

Ulanov, Barry. Personal communication.

Ulmar Uthman Sharif. *Times-Picayune,* October 18, 1998.

Vaughan, Reed. Personal communication.

Wein, George. Personal communication.

"Why Grunewald's?" Advertisement in *Louisiana Weekly,* August 6, 1949.

Williams, Martin. *Jazz Masters of New Orleans.* New York: Macmillan, 1967.

Williams, B. Michael. "John Cage: Professor, Maestro, Percussionist, Composer." *Percussive Notes*, August 1998.

Williams, Luther. "*New York Times* Coverage of an Emerging Art Form (1921–1929)." Unpublished paper, Department of Journalism, University of Georgia, 1987.

Wilson, John S. *Jazz: The Transition Years, 1940–1960.* New York: Appleton-Century-Crofts, 1966.

Winston, Donald E. "News Reporting of Jazz Music from 1890 to 1927." M.A. thesis, University of Oklahoma, 1996.

Wood, Brian. *The Song for Me: A Glossary of New Orleans Musicians (and Others of That Ilk).* Kent, U.K.: Brian Wood, 1999.

Index

About the Author

Charles Suhor, Ph.D., is a freelance consultant, writer, speaker, and musician. He is Field Representative for the National Council of Teachers of English (NCTE), working with teachers who face censorship problems. Born and raised in New Orleans, Suhor attended public schools and received degrees in English and education from Loyola University, Catholic University, and Florida State University.

Suhor became enamored of jazz at a young age and played drums over the years with Tom Brown, Pete Fountain, Al Hirt, Buddy Prima, Bill Huntington, Chris Waterman, the New Orleans Pops Orchestra, Vaughn Monroe, and others. After an Army stint in 1958 he married Jessie Miller of Fort Smith, Arkansas, and had eleven children. He taught drums privately in the 1960s. Among his students was outstanding jazz artist Johnny Vidacovich. During that decade Suhor became New Orleans correspondent for *Down Beat* and contributing editor for *New Orleans*. His writings on jazz and education have continued with over 200 articles, numerous poems, and several textbooks, including the groundbreaking *Scholastic Composition* series.

From 1957–66 Suhor taught English in New Orleans Public Schools. Poet James Nolan and Journalist Tom Sancton Jr. were among his students. In 1967 he was appointed English Supervisor for the New Orleans district. His curricular innovations included contemporary literature, black literature, interdisciplinary programs, and performance testing in writing. In 1977 he joined the staff of the National Council of Teachers of English in Urbana, Illinois, as deputy executive director. His emphasis was on publications, secondary education, sociopolitical issues, and integrated curriculum. In 1997 he moved to Montgomery, Alabama, where Dr. Deborah Little, his wife since 1980, teaches in the graduate education program at Alabama State University.

Suhor's recent activities have been interdisciplinary. He founded the Jazz and Poetry Connection, a performance group of poets and musicians. Suhor and poet E-K Daufin of Alabama State University have performed as a duo and with jazz artists in the Southeast. His jazz and language lectures have been presented in collaboration with Tony Garcia, Royal Hartigan, C. K. Ladzekpo, John Mahoney, Rick Margitza, Ellis Marsalis, and the NOCCA jazz ensemble. He teaches a continuing education course on jazz history at Auburn University/Montgomery.